DEWLISH ROMAN VILLA, DORSET

Bill Putman's Excavations 1969–1979

by

Iain Hewitt, Maureen Putman, Jonathan Milward and Jonathan Monteith

with contributions from

Denise Allen, Grace Clark, Stephen Cosh, Gabrielle Delbarre, James Gerrard,

Lisa Gray, Kevin Hayward, Mark Maltby, Jo Mills, Graham Morgan, Richard Reece,

Anna Rohnbogner, Rachel Seager Smith and Holger Schutkowski

illustrations by
Jonathan Milward, Tilla Cammegh and David Watt

photographs by
Bill Putnam and John Boyden

Dorset Natural History and Archaeological Society Monograph Series No. 25
2021

© Contributors and Dorset Natural History and Archaeological Society 2021

Dr Clare Randall, Editor, Dorset Natural History and Archaeological Society
Dorset Museum, High West Street, Dorchester, Dorset, DT1 1XA

ISBN 978-0-900341-62-5

Design and typeset by Frabjous Books ~ www.frabjousbooks.com

Printed by Short Run Press, Exeter, UK

Front cover: Room 25 mosaic panel. Photograph: R3300

Back Cover: Partial reconstruction of Room 25 mosaic Panel B by S.R. Cosh

Bill Putnam

This volume is dedicated to the memory of Bill Putnam,
archaeologist, academic and teacher (1930–2008).

Dewlish: a journey completed, an ambition fulfilled.

It was the same old tantalising challenge to puzzles that had faced him since he was a boy. It was the knowledge that something had happened in the past – happened in an ordered, logical, very specific way. And the challenge had been, and still was, to gather the disparate elements of the puzzle together and to try to reconstruct that 'very specific way'.

Colin Dexter, 1999 *The Remorseful Day*. Basingstoke and Oxford. MacMillan.

In respectful memory of
Holger Schutkowski

(1956–2020)

Professor, contributor, colleague and mentor:

A guiding light and a friendly smile.

FOREWORD

The appearance of this report on Bill Putman's excavations at the Dewlish Roman villa is an occasion for celebration and its complier, Iain Hewitt, and his team at Bournemouth University are to be congratulated on the successful completion of what has turned out to be a gargantuan task. The story of Dewlish, told in this volume, is really two narratives skilfully combined. The first is an insight into the anatomy of an excavation and its aftermath, reflecting on the development of British archaeology over the last 50 years; the second explores the rise and subsequent demise of one of Britain's most opulent Roman villas presented in the context of the contemporary Dorset landscape.

How, at the outset, Bill Putnam conceived that the excavation would develop when he set out the first modest trial trench in 1969 is unrecorded but his immediate intent was to provide training opportunities for his students studying at Weymouth Collage of Education. The next year proceeded in much the same way with a second trial trench but thereafter, from 1971–9, he moved to a more ambitious area excavation based on the box grid system, a method popularised by Sir Mortimer Wheeler in the 1930s. The last four years of the excavations were undertaken when Bill Putnam was heavily involved in other work and the site records were less detailed, making subsequent interpretation of what was found far more difficult. There was then a twenty year gap before work began on the first post excavation programme. After Bill's death in 2008 a second post excavation programme was initiated by Bournemouth University, in 2010, and the present monograph is the result of that valiant effort. The limitations of the original field records, the frequent rehousing of the archive and collection and the thirty year delay, following the

end of the excavation have made the compilation of this report difficult. That said it is a significant achievement and provides a carefully argued record of lasting value.

The second story told is that of the villa itself, from the first modest masonry farm building, of the second or early third century, to the well appointed villa of the fourth century with its ostentatious mosaic-floored reception room designed more to impress the visitor than for comfort. The evidence for the complex history of the building is presented in meticulous detail but as the author points out, the site record allows for alternative interpretations. The most obvious area of complication lies in sorting out the sequence of Buildings 1–3 in the south-west range where it might seem more logical if the "truncated" aisled structure (Building 2A) was interpreted as an aisled hall of conventional type, later replaced by the long barn-like structure (Building 2). Future targeted research excavations, as outlined in Iain Hewett's final paragraphs, would help solve this and other outstanding questions. It is a reminder that there is a lot still to be done before the nuance of the Dewlish story becomes clear.

The Dewlish report now takes its place alongside the other Roman villa monographs published by the Society, Halstock (1993), Tarrant Hinton (2006) and Bucknowle (2009). It is an impressive record, a tribute not only to the individual authors but to the persistence and patience of the Society's successive editors. There is a pleasing post-script to this first phase of the Dewlish story. As this volume was going to press we heard that the Society had raised a not inconsiderable sum of money to buy part of a mosaic from Dewlish that was in imminent danger of being sold abroad. The vivid scene of a leopard savaging a Dorcas gazelle that had once graced the villa's great reception room will soon be displayed in the Dorset Museum for all to enjoy, only a few kilometres from where it was created sixteen hundred years ago.

Barry Cunliffe

CONTENTS

LIST OF FIGURES

LIST OF TABLES

ABBREVIATIONS AND CONTRACTIONS

aOD	above Ordnance Datum
BAR	British Archaeological Reports
BCE	Before Current Era
BM	Bench Mark
BNG	British National Grid (map co-ordinates)
BU	Bournemouth University
CE	Current Era
CBM	Ceramic Building Material
CP	Civil Parish
CPA	Certificate in Practical Archaeology
DC	Dorset Council
DM	Dorset Museum
DEW	Dewlish (parish)
DH	Dewlish Roman villa site code (i.e. Dewlish House)
DHC	Dorset History Centre
DIHE	Dorset Institute of Higher Education
DNHAS	Dorset Natural History and Archaeological Society
Fig.	Figure
GPS	Global Positioning System
HER	Historic Environment Record
HMSO	Her Majesty's Stationery Office
IA	Iron Age
MN	Magnetic North
MSL	Mean Sea Level (Newlyn) UK
NMR	National Monuments Record
OS	Ordnance Survey
PET	Post-Excavation Trench
PRIA	Pre-Roman Iron Age
R-B (RB)	Romano-British
RCHME	Royal Commission on Historical Monuments (England)
SEDOWW	South East Dorset Orange Wiped Ware
SFN	Small Finds Number
PEP1	Post-Excavation Project 1
PEP2	Post-Excavation Project 2
TBM	Temporary Bench Mark
TT	Trial Trench
WA	Wessex Archaeology
WCE	Weymouth College of Education
WGS84	World Geodetic System 1984
WF	Wall Fragment

ABSTRACT

The Roman villa at Dewlish, Dorset, was first identified in the late eighteenth century when unspecified areas of the site were excavated. Details of features and finds that were revealed by these excavations are limited and largely unhelpful. In 1969, Bill Putnam, then teaching at Weymouth College, rediscovered the site of the villa following a small-scale dig that was to lead to eleven successive seasons of archaeological investigations. A series of interim reports was published and it was Bill's intention to author a full report in due course. Circumstances conspired against Bill's good intentions and a definitive interpretation of the Dewlish villa site remained an aspiration only at the time of his death in 2008.

In 2010, Bournemouth University resurrected the Dewlish post-excavation project. Re-appraisal of the available evidence revealed that further specialist reports were required whilst others were in need of updating. These new and revised contributions have prompted a need to reassess Bill's interim interpretations with intriguing results. It is now possible to place Dewlish within the wider context of Roman Britain and Europe. This report identifies points of convergence and difference between Bill's interpretation of the Dewlish evidence and new directions of thought that have been suggested since 2010 by the renewed post-excavation project.

It is important to bear in mind that it is fifty years since the beginning of Bill Putnam's Dewlish fieldwork and the fact that the evidence has had to wait that long for full publication is far from ideal. In some cases, evidence has been lost, disseminated or, in some cases, corrupted. Vital first-hand experience of the excavation fieldwork is now limited. However, the principal core of data is available and the authors believe that this report has academic integrity. Where areas of uncertainty remain, these are made clear and suggestions for further research are proposed.

Iain Hewitt

RESUMEN

La villa romana situada en Dewlish, Dorset, fue identificada por primera vez a finales del siglo dieciocho cuando se excavaron varias zonas indeterminadas del yacimiento. La información conservada acerca de las estructuras y piezas localizadas en esas primeras excavaciones es muy limitada y, en gran parte, inútil. En 1969, Bill Putnam, quien entonces enseñaba en Weymouth College, redescubrió este yacimiento a partir de una excavación a pequeña escala que fue el primer paso de once campañas sucesivas de investigaciones arqueológicas. Se publicaron una serie de informes provisionales y era la intención de Bill publicar un informe completo a su debido tiempo. Debido a circunstancias fuera de su control, la publicación de dicho informe así como la interpretación definitiva de la villa de Dewlish permaneció como una aspiración hasta la fecha de su muerte, en el año 2008.

La Universidad de Bournemouth recuperó el proyecto post-excavación de Dewlish en el 2010. La reevaluación de la información disponible hasta entonces desveló que sería necesario actualizar algunos de los informes ya disponibles y que, igualmente, habría que producir una serie de nuevos informes realizados por especialistas. El análisis de estas nuevas contribuciones ha provocado que sea necesario reconsiderar las interpretaciones provisionales de Bill, lo que ha dado lugar a resultados intrigantes. Ahora es posible situar Dewlish dentro del contexto de la Britania romana, así como en la Europa de la época. Este informe identifica puntos de convergencia y diferencias entre las interpretaciones realizadas por Bill sobre las evidencias halladas en Dewlish así como nuevas interpretaciones que han surgido durante esta nueva etapa del estudio de la villa, a partir de 2010.

Es importante tener en cuenta que han pasado cincuenta años desde el comienzo del trabajo de campo de Bill Putnam en Dewlish. El hecho de que la información haya tenido que esperar tantos años para ser publicada no es una situación ideal. En algunos casos se ha perdido parte de la evidencia, ha sido diseminada o, en algunos casos, corrompida. La experiencia de primera mano en la excavación, considerada vital, es ahora muy limitada. Sin embargo, el cuerpo principal de la información se ha conservado y los autores de este estudio consideran que este informe mantiene su integridad académica. Siempre que han surgido áreas en las que la información se consideraba dudosa se ha señalado y se han hecho sugerencias acerca de los pasos a seguir en futuros estudios.

Anna Gonzalez Ruiz

RESUMÉ

La villa romaine de Dewlish, Dorset, fut identifiée pour la première fois à la fin du dix-huitième siècle, lors de fouilles effectuées dans divers endroits du site dont les emplacements exacts ne furent pas précisés. Les informations relatives aux structures et découvertes sont donc limitées et ne contiennent que peu de détails. En 1969, Bill Putnam, qui enseignait alors au Collège de Weymouth, a redécouvert le site de cette villa. Commencée sur une petite échelle, cette fouille durera pendant onze campagnes successives. Une série de comptes-rendus intérimaires a été publiée mais Bill avait l'intention de rédiger un rapport complet en temps voulu sur l'interprétation. Les circonstances ont voulu que le dessein de Bill demeure à l'état de projet jusqu'à son décès en 2008.

En 2010, l'université de Bournemouth a relancé le projet d'étude de la villa de Dewlish. Une réévaluation des documents disponibles a révélé que certains nécessitaient une mise à jour tandis que d'autres disciplines seraient mises à contribution. Ces travaux ont permis de réviser les interprétations provisoires de Bill et ont abouti à de nouveaux résultats intéressants. Il est maintenant possible de situer Dewlish dans le contexte plus large de la Grande-Bretagne et de l'Europe à l'époque romaine. Ce rapport, mis à jour, identifie les points de convergence et de divergence entre l'interprétation donnée par Bill et celle apportée par les nouvelles directions de recherche qui font suite à la reprise des fouilles en 2010.

Il est important de garder à l'esprit que cinquante ans se sont écoulés depuis que Bill Putnam a commencé le travail de terrain sur le site de Dewlish. Le fait d'avoir dû attendre aussi longtemps pour une publication complète est loin d'être idéal. Dans certains cas, des preuves ont été perdues, dans d'autres, elles furent éparpillées voire corrompues. Les informations indispensables, celles de première main sur les fouilles effectuées sur le terrain, sont maintenant limitées. Cependant, les données principales étant disponibles, les auteurs estiment que ce rapport est d'une rigueur académique intègre. Là où des zones d'incertitude subsistent, celles-ci sont précisées et des propositions pour de futures recherches sont suggérées.

Gabrielle Delbarre

ZUSAMMENFASSUNG

Ende des 18. Jahrhunderts wurde die Römische Villa bei Dewlish (Dorset) im Süden Englands erstmals zufällig bei Ausgrabungen entdeckt. Diese Arbeiten sind leider unzulänglich dokumentiert, so dass wenig Details über die Funde und Gebäudegrundzüge bekannt sind. Erst 1969 wurde die Villa von Bill Putnam wiederentdeckt, der zu dieser Zeit am College Weymouth Archäologie unterrichtete. Auf eine kleinere Ausgrabung folgten elf fortlaufende, archäologische Untersuchungen. Unter Putnams Leitung wurden eine Reihe von Zwischenberichten veröffentlicht. Seine Absicht, einen vollständigen Bericht zu publizieren, wurde durch seinen Tod im Jahre 2008 vereitelt und sein Werk blieb unvollendet.

Die Analyse der Funde und Ausgrabungen der Villa wurde 2010 durch die Universität Bournemouth wieder aufgenommen. Nach der Auswertung der vorhandenen Dokumentation waren sowohl Revisionen als auch das Abfassen neuer, fachlicher Berichte notwendig. Diese neuen und überarbeiteten Beiträge förderten faszinierende Ergebnisse aus den von Bill Putnam verfassten Zwischenberichten zutage. Es ist nun möglich, Dewlish in einem erweiterten Kontext mit Europa und Britannien im Römischen Reich zu interpretieren. Dieser Band dient in erster Linie der Auslegung und Diskussion der Dewlish Funde, insbesondere der Differenzen und Konvergenzen zwischen Bill Putnams erstmaligen Ausführungen und unseren heutigen Erkenntnissen seit der Wiederaufnahme des Projektes in 2010.

Fast 50 Jahre sind seit Bill Putnams ersten Feldforschungen bei Dewlish und dem vollständigen Bericht vergangen, was die Bedingungen dieser Publikation entsprechend erschwert hat.

In einigen Fällen sind archäologische Beweismittel verloren gegangen, zerstreut oder gar beschädigt und unbrauchbar geworden.

Wichtige Erfahrungsberichte aus erster Hand sind nur bedingt erhalten.

Über spezifische Bereiche der Villa besteht gewisse Unsicherheit, jedoch werden diese im Text individuell und als Gegenstand weiterer Forschungsarbeiten angesprochen. Das Herzstück der archäologischen Daten ist jedoch erhalten, und als Autoren sind wir überzeugt, dass diese Publikation standfest ist und akademischen Wert besitzt.

Anna Rohnbogner

PREFACE

The authors are conscious that this report is very late in appearing. The post-excavation work generated by eleven years' digging (was) enormous and require(d) space and time and personnel, and for many years this was not available. By modern standards the present report will be regarded as inadequate, but it should be remembered that the (field) work was done 40 years ago, and knowledge and facilities that we now take for granted were not available (then) (Bill Putnam *c.* 2007; BU100DEW0354).

The above quotation is from the 'Introduction and Summary' to Bill Putnam's unwritten report on the Dewlish Roman villa excavations. It is now over fifty years since excavations began at Dewlish. The first digging season was of short duration, just four days, but it ignited a slow fuse that was to burn erratically for five decades throughout which time the extended project has involved incalculable numbers of participants including students, volunteers, academic colleagues, archaeological professionals, and a plethora of interested folk who attended Bill's entertaining talks and lectures and who read his accessible and enjoyable publications.

Bill had always intended that he would bring his Dewlish mission to a worthy conclusion with a scholarly publication. That this did not happen has been a source of dismay and consternation to many. Nonetheless, the delay has had its compensations, more so because with the passing of the years it has become clear that the Dewlish story is a complex and multi-faceted account that has three principle strands which, in synoptic form are: the archaeology of the site, archaeology and education, and the development of the archaeological profession. The three-strands of the Dewlish project interact in a variety of subtle ways. In this monograph, the principle emphasis will be upon the archaeological

evidence and its interpretation with the specific aim to allow Dewlish to be placed securely within the context of other villas in Roman Britain and Europe. Therefore, this is an enabling report that seeks to provide a body of evidence that future scholars will be able to carry forward into a wider field of investigation. In pursuit of this aim, we refer to the two other strands of the Dewlish saga where appropriate and we believe that it is not possible to understand the nature of the excavated evidence without an appreciation of the vicissitudes of fortune experienced by Bill Putnam and his colleagues as the Dewlish project progressed and developed.

This is the second post-excavation and publication project and it has had to face its own obstacles and impediments. Not least of the challenges has been that Bill Putnam has not been available to advise and to clarify uncertainties, but Maureen Putnam has been a major contributor to the post-excavation team. Maureen was present on site at Dewlish throughout the eleven seasons of the dig and she was actively involved in the first post-ex project (PEP1) which spanned from 1999 to 2008. Maureen's overall contribution has been immense, and the archaeological community owes her a debt of thanks.

Finally, the authors are conscious that excavation archive is vulnerable and that of the Dewlish Roman villa has suffered losses during the 50 years since the field project commenced. There have been many occasions when trying to piece together the evidence has required the patience and tenacity of an accomplished cruciverbalist, but we are conscious that the answers that we have offered will be questioned by some and that projecting into the future, there will be a new generation of students and researchers who will wish to check and challenge our findings. This is healthy debate that we would wish to encourage and to facilitate this process, we have devised a document reference code system that will pinpoint individual documents within the Dewlish Roman villa paper archive for future scrutiny. This coding system is used throughout the text of this report. It is further explained in Chapter 3.

Iain Hewitt, on behalf of the project team.

ACKNOWLEDGEMENTS

THE DEWLISH EXCAVATIONS AND POST-EXCAVATION PROJECT 1969–1979 AND 1999 TO 2008

Bill Putnam would have wished to acknowledge the help and support that he received during the eleven seasons of field schools at Dewlish and in the subsequent post-excavation project (PEP1). Considerable assistance was given by the Boyden family of Dewlish House, notably the late Anthony Boyden and his wife Val, the latter being an enthusiastic supporter of the project. John Boyden of Chebbard's Farm, Cheselbourne provided invaluable assistance in respect of site access, and with accommodation for students and volunteers during the digging seasons. John provided air photographs, notably during the drought year of 1976. Undoubtedly Bill would have wanted to thank his colleagues, students and the volunteers who contributed time to the excavation programme but individual names were not routinely recorded and so these acknowledgements are a general gesture of appreciation on Bill's behalf.

PEP 2, THE SECOND POST-EXCAVATION PROJECT, 2010 TO PRESENT

The current post-excavation and publication project (PEP2) also has been a team effort and in a break with the usual procedure, the lead authors wish to thank all contributors by name in the hope that nobody has been excluded inadvertently. Every attempt has been made to keep up to date with name changes, and those who have been involved are listed alphabetically without regard to status or role. Thank you then to all whose names follow:

Rodney Alcock, Denise Allen, Natalie Andrade, Zoe Barrass, Matthew Bennett, Leo Biek, Bournemouth Archaeology, John Beavis, John Boyden, Grace Campbell, Tilia Cammegh, Paul Cheetham, Grace Clark, Stephen Cosh, Colin Daniels, Anita Diaz, Gabrielle Delbarre, Mark Dover, Jessica Fangmann, Hannah Foulger, James Gerrard, Mark Gillings, Abigail Golding, Lisa Gray, Kevin Hayward, Irene Hewitt, Kristina Berg Holmberg, Laurence Keen, John Jack, Kerri Jones, Philip Leahy-Harland, Mark Maltby, Astrid Mick, Jo Mills, Tracy Minall, Graham Morgan, Jon Murden, Joleen Periam, Claire Pinder, Michelle Putten, Jane Putnam, Clare Randall (Editor, Dorset Natural History and Archaeological Society monograph series), Richard Reece, Emily Rhodes, Lowri Roberts, Dawn Robinson, Anna Rohnbogner, Ana Gonzalez Ruiz, Miles Russell, Rachel Seager Smith, Holger Schutkowski, Hannah Simpson, Rachel Stacey, Bryn Walters, Mark Watson, David Watt, Kate Welham, Alan Whitaker, Rebecca White, and the anonymous reviewer whose guidance was invaluable.

Thanks go to the various individuals and bodies which have supported this project both financially and in kind over the years, including the Dorset Archaeological Committee. The series editor would like to thank Sue Vaughn for indexing the volume, and Val Lamb and Julie Blackmore of Frabjous Books for making this volume a reality.

INSTITUTIONAL AFFILIATIONS:

Bournemouth University: Denise Allen, Grace Clark, Gabrielle Delbarre, Iain Hewitt, Mark Maltby, Jonathan Milward, Jonathan Monteith and Holger Schutkowski

Newcastle University: James Gerrard

University of Reading: Kevin Hayward, Anna Rohnbogner

University of Leicester: Graham Morgan

Wessex Archaeology: Rachel Seager Smith

ORGANISATION OF THIS REPORT

Over five decades have elapsed since the inception of the Dewlish Roman villa field excavation programme, and the results of these investigations need to be placed in the public domain, which is the aim of this report. Nonetheless, the gulf in time between excavation and publication has altered the terms of reference because Dewlish is more than an archaeological project, it has a history that embraces the education and training of teachers and the formative steps in the development of archaeology as a professional discipline. All of these factors ultimately affected the course of the field programme, its strategy and the available human resource, and these factors need to be understood in making interpretations of the evidence and when formulating proposals for future research.

The authors are mindful that monographs are rarely read from cover to cover and that most scholars will wish to 'dip in' to those parts of the text that are relevant to their own interests. For guidance, what follows is a brief outline of the twenty-one component chapters of this volume followed by a suggested list of key words.

Chapter 1 provides the location details of the site and its wider archaeological context including the surviving but sketchy details of two excavations that took place on the villa site during the eighteenth century.

Chapter 2 describes the origin of the 1969–79 field project, the techniques employed and those that were available but not used. The chapter demonstrates that the excavation programme fell into three distinct periods of development: field evaluation (1969 and 1971); optimum resource research project (1971–1975); diminishing resource research project (1976–1979).

Chapter 3 documents the course and outcomes of the two Dewlish post-excavation projects, PEP1 1999–2008 (Putnam) and PEP2 2010–2020 (Bournemouth University, Faculty of Science and Technology). Phased plans for the site are introduced and illustrated.

Chapter 4 gives details of the evidence for Pre-Roman Iron Age settlement at Dewlish.

Chapters 5 to 9 inclusive detail the excavation of each of the seven excavated component buildings of the villa complex and relate these to the colour-coded phased plans that are contained within the portfolio of figures included in Chapter 3.

Chapters 10 to 20 inclusive are the specialist reports.

Chapter 21 is the discussion and synthesis of issues and ideas that have emerged from the preceding 20 chapters. The chapter also sets out suggestions for future work both at Dewlish and other Roman villas in the region of South West Britain.

Photographs reproduced in this monograph are derived from the Dewlish Roman villa archive and were taken by the excavator, Bill Putnam unless otherwise stated.

Plans and section drawings have been re-worked from the original site drawings, cross referenced to the site photographic archive, the site diaries of Bill Putnam and the individual grid trench notebooks-cum-context records.

Occasionally, features were excavated of which official site drawings were absent (presumed lost), although measured drawings have survived in grid-trench notebooks and/or student authored site reports unsupported by photographs. Plans and sections that fall into this category have been reproduced, with minimum refinement and appropriate annotation, if they are an important indicator of otherwise unrecorded or lost evidence.

Suggested key words, terms and names:
Boyden, Dewlish, Hutchins, Iron Age, kilns, long-house, mosaics, pit-shaft, Putnam, Romano-British, shrine, sub-Roman.

1

THE SITE AND ITS CONTEXT

LOCATION, TOPOGRAPHY AND LAND USE

Bill Putnam has suggested that Dewlish was one of a group of villas that was were clustered around the Dorset county town of Dorchester, formerly Roman *Durnovaria* (2007, 95–6). This group would also include the more recently discovered villa at Druce Farm (see below). The Dewlish villa is situated within a designed landscape appurtenant to Dewlish House which lies some 365m distant to the east within Dewlish Park, land described as pasture in the tithe apportionment of 1844 (DHC T/DEW). Immediately beyond the villa site the ground drops away to the valleys of the Devil's Brook (east) and the Chesel Bourne (west) with the confluence of these streams to the south. Excavation demonstrated that the villa was orientated towards the south-east and this setting would have provided the Romano-British occupants of its buildings with fine landscape views, almost certainly surpassing the vista from the present Dewlish House. Effectively, the villa's buildings were constructed upon a spur of land that might have defined part of the estate boundary (Figs. 1.1, 1.2 and 1.3).

In his first interim report on the excavations at the Dewlish villa, Bill Putnam gave the map reference for the site as SY 768972 (BNG 376834, 097222) (Putnam 1970, 187) and this is broadly accurate. However, as part of a recent geophysical survey carried out by Bournemouth University, GPS was used to provide three specific location references at key points within the complex of buildings that comprise the villa (Cheetham forthcoming). These reference points are shown in Table 1.1 with conversions to longitude and latitude. Other locational data, including height above Ordnance Datum (aOD), can be found in Table 1.2.

Table 1.1   Showing BNG map references for the Dewlish Roman villa, Dorset as derived from GPS survey with longitude and latitude equivalents.

DRV site feature	BNG Easting	BNG Northing	Longitude	Latitude	Longitude Dec.Min.Sec.	Latitude Dec.Min.Sec.
Room 30 NW corner	376753	097175	-2.331053	50.773686	-219'51.79"	5046'25.27"
Room 1 NE corner	376797	097234	-2.330433	50.774218	-219'40.56"	5046'27.19"
Building 2 NW quoin	376773	097163	-2.330769	50.773579	-219'50.77"	5046'24.88"

Table 1.2   Dewlish Roman villa essential site data by category

Category	Date Description	Detail
Codes and numbers	Site codes	DH (artifacts) DRV (drawings)
	Bournemouth University Archive no.	BU100DEW
	NRHE monument no.	454480
	National Monument Record (NMR) no.	SY 79 NE 5
	Dorset County Council HER no.	1 040 011-MDO 985
Location	National Grid Reference (NGR)	SY768972
	British National Grid (BNG) co-ordinates	376034 097222
	World Geodetic System (WGS) co-ordinates	50'26.3"N 0219'49.6"W
Altitude	Shailes Farm OS benchmark at BNG 376972 097506	82.87m AOD
	DH site TBM 'A'	78.90m AOD
	DH site TBM 'S'	77.31m AOD

GEOLOGY AND SOILS

The underlying geology of the villa site is Tarrant Chalk overlain by a superficial deposit of Clay-with-Flints (Geological Map Data, BGS 2018). Alluvial deposits lie within the valley of the eponymous Devil's Brook and its tributary, the Chesel Bourne. Dennet's Bottom, a third valley, is dry (RCHME 1970b, 84).

PLACE NAME

As explained by A.D. Mills of the English Place-name Society the Dewlish parish and settlement name is derived from the Devil's Brook, which means 'black stream' (1998, 66). The name is pre-Roman in origin and cannot be associated with the former presence of the villa. However, on the 1844 tithe award map for Dewlish the field in which the Roman villa is situated is shown as plot 65, and on the accompanying apportionment named as Manor House, Water Meadow and Chinchester (DHC Ref. T/DEW). At 55 acres, 3 rods and 11 perches (22.6 hectares) this was a relatively large field, probably the conflation of at least three land parcels that date from the inclosure of the medieval West Field of Dewlish (DC HER 1 040 009A-MOD981). This amalgamation of plots probably occurred in 1702, or soon afterwards, with the

construction of Dewlish House and the emparkment of its grounds.

According to Mills, the field name *Chinchester* (locally pronounced 'Chinister') has as its second element a possible example of OE *ceaster* 'an old (especially Roman) fortification'. Mills goes on to say that the first element of the name is more difficult but could mean *cinu* 'fissure, ravine, chine', or less likely, OE *cinn* 'chin' used in some transferred sense of a hill of a certain shape. The explanation of the name *Chinchester* would be something like 'the fortification in or near the chine' (A.D. Mills 1969, *pers. comm. to* A. Rainey, BU100DEW0238). The two alternative interpretations of *cinn* as offered by Mills are both a good fit for the topography of the villa site: it is situated upon a spur of land ('chin') that separates the Devil's Brook and the Chesel Bourne, and the valleys of these waterways might suggest the fissure, ravine or chine explanation. Evidence for extensive and repeated medieval and post-medieval cultivation of the villa site over many years was apparent throughout the course of the Putnam excavations at Dewlish (Putnam 1975, 54) and it is inconceivable that the remains of the villa were not encountered during episodes of past seasonal ploughing, thus giving rise to the *chester* element of the field name. The field name encapsulates a folk memory of the location of an ancient building.

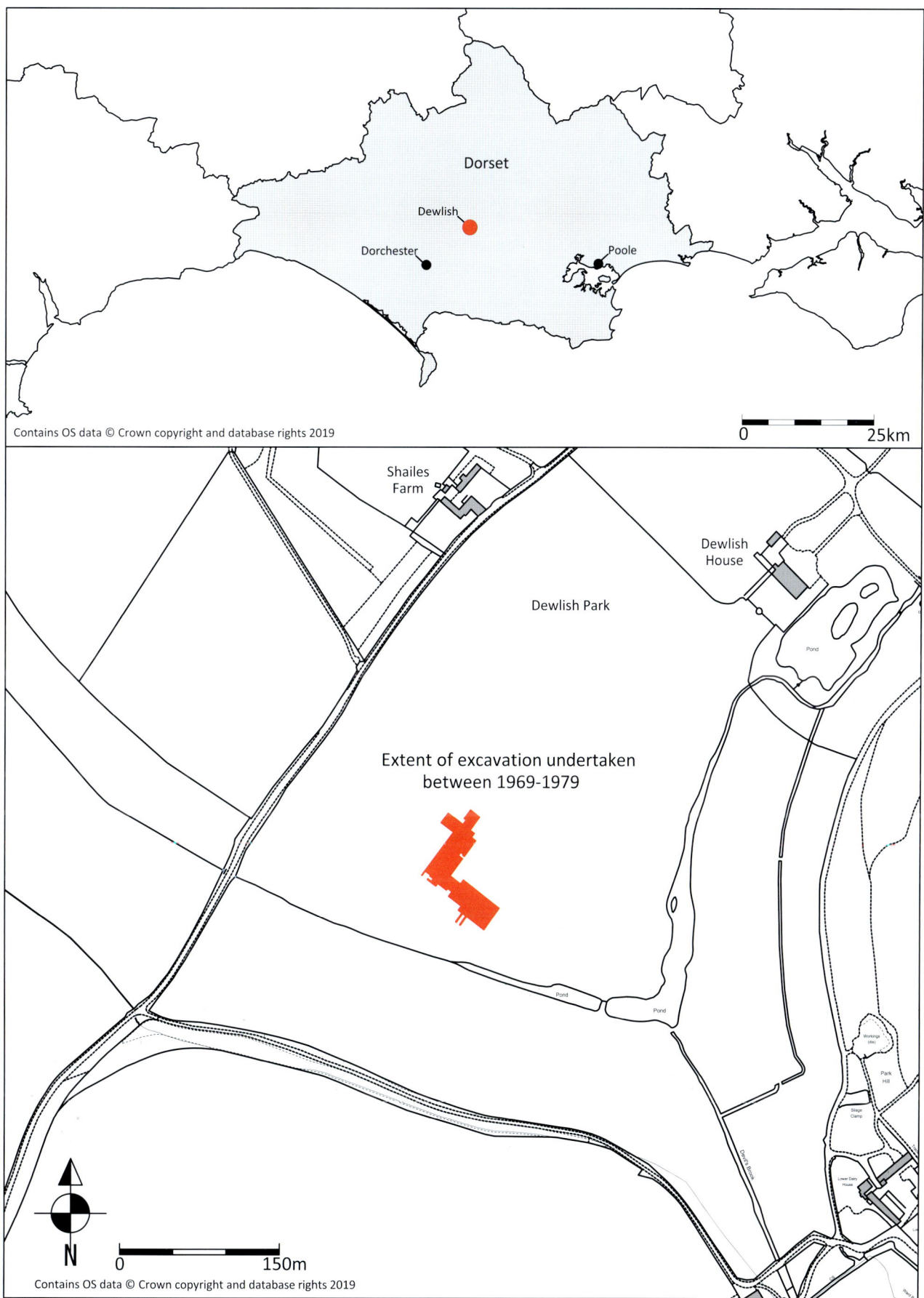

Figure 1.1   Dewlish Roman villa location maps in relation to the county of Dorset and Dewlish House. Jonathan Milward.

Figure 1.2   Air photograph (1976) looking west showing Dewlish House with ornamental lake (bottom left) and the emparked field of Chinchester. The site of the villa is represented by the chalk patches (top centre). Photograph: John Boyden (Bournemouth University archive BU100DEW).

HISTORY OF THE SITE UP TO 1969

Dewlish is mentioned in the Domesday Book of 1086 (Morris 1983, 25,1) but there is no evidence that the Dewlish Roman villa can be associated with the medieval manor within the parish. The core of medieval settlement at Dewlish is represented by earthworks at Court Close adjacent to, but east and south of, the parish church of All Saints, 1140m north-east of the villa site (RCHME 1970b, 87–8; DC HER no. 1040 007A-MOD997). According to RCHME (1970b, 88), little is known of the medieval open fields of the parish but what remained of the former West Field in 1819 was situated in Dewlish Park, which is also the site of the Roman villa (DC HER no. 1 040 009A MOD981). Medieval manuring of the West Field probably explains the occasional finds of pottery fragments and other artefacts of this period during the 1969–79 excavations.

Eighteenth century discovery and excavation of the site

Prior to the Putnam excavations, the first recorded reference to the Roman villa at Dewlish was made by the Dorset historian Reverend John Hutchins in his seminal publication *The History and Antiquities of the County of Dorset*. The information provided by Hutchins was influential in the interpretation of the archaeology of the Dewlish villa throughout Putnam's 1969–79 campaign, and Hutchins' words were regarded as being particularly relevant to the archaeology of the *domus* (Building 3) and Room 11 specifically. Consequently, it is imperative to consider critically the context and content of Hutchins' text.

Hutchins had commenced research into his 'History of Dorset' by the 1740s; it was a lengthy enterprise. The date of publication is usually given as 1773, also the year of the author's death, but in fact it was published posthumously as two volumes in 1774. Hutchins' career as rector of Holy Trinity, Wareham, and Swyre (near Bridport) enabled him to establish important connections within the circles of the aristocracy and gentry of Dorset (Legg 2002, 166). On the title page of the *History of Dorset* Hutchins states that his work was compiled from,

'The best and most ancient historians, inquisitions post mortem, and other valuable records and mss (manuscripts) in the public offices and libraries, and in private hands.'

This is an important insight into Hutchins' sources and in the case of Dewlish, contact with the incumbent family of Dewlish House and access to any relevant estate papers held therein are likely to have been the origin of the first of the two entries that appear in his great work. Copies of the first edition of Hutchins' work are rare and for this reason references to it are routinely derived from the third edition, revised and significantly augmented by William Shipp and James Hodson (Legg 2002, 166). The third edition was published in four volumes between 1861 and 1873 and it is this version that is cited here. It is also the edition that was available to Bill Putnam as he prepared to launch his investigations at the Dewlish villa site. There are two entries in Hutchins relating to the Dewlish Roman villa, both are on the same page (1873, 607) but they will be treated separately for the purpose of this discussion. In its entirety, the first entry reads as follows,

'In a meadow, a little south of the seat of the Michels, about 1740, on some trees being blown down, or rooted up, was discovered a very large Roman pavement, supposed to be 65 paces by about 15. The tesserae or cubes did not much exceed an inch square and were white and black. There was little of it opened, and that was soon covered up again. A copper medal of Faustina, and an iron spur were also found here.'

This short statement raises some important issues, not least of which is the number of uncertainties exemplified by phrases such as 'about 1740', 'supposed to be' and 'did not much exceed'. These conditional phrases reveal that Hutchins was aware of the limitations of the sources that he was using. Primarily, the text refers to the discovery of a Roman mosaic and provides an interesting indication of its dimensions measured in paces. By convention, a 'pace' is reckoned at 30 inches or 0.75m and based upon the information provided by Hutchins, the Dewlish mosaic in question would have measured about 49m by 11m, dimensions that might approximate to the length of Room 12, the corridor of the *domus*. However, Hutchins' details of the pavement's size and composition are followed by

Figure 1.3   A section of a 'gutter' similar to the 'brick clay' examples described by Hutchins in his description of the eighteenth century excavations at Dewlish. Such tiles were found only in association with Building 4, the bath house. Photograph: Tilia Cammegh.

a contradiction: 'there was little of it (the pavement) opened, and that was soon covered up again' which suggests that the given length in paces cannot be regarded as reliable, an indication of the second hand nature of the sources that were used.

An additional problem in relation to this first Dewlish entry in Hutchins' text is that it uses the name 'Michel's' in relation to the ownership of Dewlish House. If the initial discovery of the villa did occur 'about 1740', as stated, then it was not the Michel family that owned the house at that time, but Thomas Skinner, whose father had commissioned the building of the house in 1702. The property was not sold until after Skinner's death in 1756, the purchaser being David Michel (Legg 2002, 50). This inconsistency in Hutchins' details suggests that he either sourced this information after 1756; that the mention of the Michel ownership of the property was a later editorial insertion; or that the date of the discovery of the villa is inaccurate. Whilst this uncertainty might appear to be a minor debating point, it does reinforce the notion that Hutchins' information was not based upon recently sourced first-hand material which in turn indicates that whilst the details of the mid-eighteenth century

excavations are interesting, they do need to be treated with caution.

There are concerns too regarding the second Dewlish entry in Hutchins' *History of Dorset*. The text runs as follows,

> 'About the year 1790" (says Mr Knight) "I obtained leave to open the ground to view the Roman pavement, and on its being cleared on the lower side (for it is on the slope of a rising) a gutter in complete order was found, composed of tiles laid one within another, and running round the outside of the pavement to the lowermost side, where it went off down the slope. They were of a beautiful red, not hard burnt, and were evidently of our finest brick clay. Some of them were taken out quite perfect, and were deposited with Mr Michel. They were about 10 inches long (c. 0.25m), and about 7 or 8 broad (c. 0.20m), crooked, and laid one within another'.

Here the problem is transparent: the second opening-up of the villa site is said to have taken place 'about the year 1790'. Hutchins died in 1773 and so this second part of the early Dewlish story is not by Hutchins but more probably the work of a subsequent editorial hand, perhaps William Shipp, a hundred years later. Curiously, the stated aim of the '1790' excavation was to examine the Roman pavement first seen during the 1740s, but given this priority, there are no specific details regarding its colour, shape or size in this second description of the villa site. However, the excavator did encounter an associated drain consisting of conjoining red tiles, and the description of these is compatible with a section of a drain that was recovered from the *apodyterium* of the bath suite during the Putnam excavations of the 1970s but nowhere else on the site (Fig. 1.3).

In summary, both entries in Hutchins that describe aspects of the Dewlish villa represent information that was supplied much later than the events that they describe. The entries read as fragments of history that provide an intriguing insight into how the site was discovered and explored but their fragility in terms of accuracy needs always to be considered when interpreting the findings of the Putnam excavations two hundred years later. These are issues that will be examined in more detail in the following chapters of this volume.

DEWLISH ROMAN VILLA POST 1800

Field systems

Following the two episodes of investigation recorded by Hutchins and his editors, the Dewlish Roman villa effectively faded from academic and public awareness and in the years leading up to the 1969–79 excavations, new information was of a contextual nature only. Principal amongst the landscape features within which the Dewlish villa is situated are the 'Celtic' (prehistoric) field systems. Field systems of this type are recorded as 'Groups' and the Dewlish villa lies within the eastern margins of Group 45, also known as the Dole's Hill field system as recorded by RCHME (1970b, 331–2, including the end-map and Plate 87; DC HER no. 1 031 046 – MOD885). Group 45 is an extensive field system that covers parts of five civil parishes, and the eponymous Dole's Hill is within the parish of Piddlehinton. Given the extensive topographical spread of Group 45, close dating of the entire network is not a precise science. Indicative archaeological assemblages have been recovered from within the Group 45 field system, notably in Civil Parish (CP) of Cheselbourne, adjacent and to the north of Dewlish CP, where Romano-British pottery and earthenware tile fragments have been found as field scatters (Farrah 1952, 88–9). Artefacts of similar type and date have been recorded at other locations within the same parish (DC HER 1 031 044 – MOD852; 1 031 044B – MOD853).

Enclosures

It has been noted that there is a coincidence of enclosures of irregular shape, with the Celtic fields in Dewlish and the adjacent environs. One example that is on the Dewlish boundary with Cheselbourne CP was the source of a 'large concentration' (*sic*) of Roman (*sic*) pottery. However, RCHME (1970b, 79), wherein a note on this site is published, advises caution in associating the date of the finds with that of the surrounding field system.

Another enclosure of this type was excavated as part of the Dewlish Roman villa project in the summer of 1972 (Beavis 1974, 88–9). The site was at Warren Hill, 850m west of the villa complex (BNG 376028, 97263). The excavator noted a roughly elliptical enclosure ditch with a long axis of *c*. 45m. The ditch achieved a maximum width of 2.15m and a maximum depth of 0.95m with a V-shaped profile. Finds included coarse pottery types, though no dates for these artefacts were offered. One abraded fragment of tegula came from the material of a possible destroyed internal bank.

After 1972, no further field work took place on the Warren Hill enclosure. The reasons for this were probably logistical but the cessation of the Warren Hill sub-project represents a missed opportunity to establish links between the Group 45 field system, enclosures of the Warren Hill type, and the economy of the villa landscape both at Dewlish and at the neighbouring villa at Druce Farm (Ladle and Morgan 2017, 146–8). Druce Farm lies *c*. 2830m south-west of the Dewlish villa and on the southern periphery of the Group 45 Celtic field system.

THE VILLA'S WATER SUPPLY: POTENTIAL SOURCES

During the early years of the Dewlish field programme, concerted efforts were made by the Weymouth College team to enhance understanding of the archaeology of the wider archaeological landscape of the Roman villa. This initiative is exemplified by the content of a typescript in the Bournemouth University archive that is a transcript of a discussion with the owner or tenant of Brook Farm, probably Mr G. Parsons (BU100DEW0319).

Brook Farm is situated 620m north-north-east of Dewlish parish church at BNG 377911, 98676. With the farm as a central reference point, Mr Parsons described four locations within his fields that were difficult to plough and thought to be the sites of buildings. No information was provided regarding associated finds consequently no indicative dates for these hypothetical structures can be inferred. Of considerable interest though, was Mr Parsons' description of a curvilinear earthwork close to the Devil's Brook at BNG 377898, 99604 and elsewhere along the banks of the brook. Mr Parsons believed that this earthwork represented the remains of an aqueduct, an interesting thought given the need for a water supply to the Dewlish villa's baths and to ensure its viability as a centre of settlement in general. However, any villa-related aqueduct in this area would have needed to have followed the contours of the landscape, and the levels aOD of the Devil's Brook do not inspire confidence that it would have worked as the principal source of water supply to the villa buildings. A more promising candidate for an aqueduct source for the villa would have been the Chesel Bourne within the settlement of the same name, a little to the north-north-west of Waterside Farm and close to the 100m contour at BNG 376482, 99362, which is the site of a spring or well. From here, a contour aqueduct could have delivered water to the north-west side of the villa (see Chapter 8).

DEWLISH AS A MILITARY BASE

In 1944 Dewlish House and its surrounding park land, became a Marshalling Area during the preparations for the D-Day landings. Chinchester, the field within which the Roman villa is situated, became a temporary camp for United States troops with a capacity for 1,800 personnel and 260 vehicles (J. Mills 2018, *pers. comm.* to M. Putnam). The camp probably functioned for no more than six months and was never intended to be permanent. However, the number of individuals present during this short period of time, with the implied infrastructure needed to support them, has to be taken into account when considering phenomena such as parch marks that were recorded within the vicinity of the villa buildings and the associated field system. In 1976, a 0.45m square 'trial pit' in grid square Q96 revealed whitewashed bricks and mortar of 'recent' origin and these were thought to represent traces of the Word War II activity on the site (BU100DEW0007, 8).

OVERVIEW

This section of the report has provided locational information and an archaeological summary of the context of the villa at Dewlish. These are details that will assume greater significance when assessing and interpreting the evidence of the archaeology of the villa itself. In particular, the impact of Hutchins' account, the question of water supply and that of the relationship of the villa to the Iron Age features within its immediate landscape setting all emerge as important themes in the Dewlish narrative.

2

THE WEYMOUTH COLLEGE/DIHE EXCAVATIONS, 1969–1979

The genesis of the Dewlish Roman villa excavation project was the product of the convergence of a career path with the development of an institution. Indeed, it was sometimes the case that tensions arose between the demands of teaching and the requirements of satisfying the aim and objectives of a research project design. These conflicts of interest will be discussed in the paragraphs below and in Chapter 3. Ultimately, it was the interaction of the competing responsibilities of teaching and project management that was to determine the quality of the evidence derived from the site and significantly influence its interpretation.

The institution in question was Weymouth College of Education (WCE), Dorset. In the 1960s, Weymouth was a teacher training college. It was an important time in the development of the teaching profession that was to have a significant impact in the re-shaping of Weymouth College as it moved towards the final years of that decade and into the 1970s. Principal amongst the new initiatives was the development of degree courses for teachers in response to the deliberations of Lord Robbins' Committee on Higher Education (1963, 107–109). By 1968, a number of teacher training colleges were in the advanced stages of preparation for offering the new Bachelor of Education degree. This was the case at Weymouth and it was no doubt in preparation for the new degree that in 1967 the History Department advertised for an archaeologist with a teaching background to join

their team with a view to developing a practical dimension to its curriculum, albeit with academic underpinning (Soffe 2009, 14).

The successful applicant for the post was Bill Putnam. Bill was a Classics graduate of University College London. During his time as a student, Bill had participated in several excavations in London and elsewhere, having been impressed by some of the principal characters in British archaeology of the time including Wheeler, Grimes, and Richmond. Upon completion of his degree, Putnam secured a Post Graduate Certificate in Education which provided the essential foundations for a teaching career. His first post at a high school in Montgomeryshire (now Powys) allowed Bill to continue his interest in archaeology, developing experience of project design, excavation and report writing (Beavis and Hunt 1999, 1–5; Soffe 2009, 13–14). Bill was the perfect match for the post of teacher-cum-archaeologist that was required at Weymouth College of Education, and he was appointed.

ARCHAEOLOGY AT WEYMOUTH COLLEGE OF EDUCATION

Having secured the post, Bill Putnam was now required to supplement the existing history syllabus with the teaching of archaeological theory and practice. At an early stage it must have been decided that practical field schools were an important part of the teaching of archaeology. Field school projects required appropriate contacts with local societies, committees and clubs, permissions from landowners and a raft of logistical considerations that included equipment, time and goodwill. Putting all of this in place must have been a major component of Bill Putnam's first academic year at Weymouth College. The first field school took place in 1968 on a section of Roman road at Thorncombe Wood, near Dorchester (Putnam 1971, 147–8; fig. 13; see Chapter 21 for details). A participating student and, later, colleague of Bill Putnam was to recall that there was little access to technology to assist with the fieldwork (Beavis and Hunt 1999, 5) and this situation would have prevailed in 1969, the inaugural year of the Dewlish Roman villa project. Given this relative paucity of equipment and resources, the following paragraphs describe the strategy and techniques that were employed at Dewlish and the constraints that these imposed upon the progress of the excavation and the integrity of the archive.

EXCAVATION STRATEGY AND METHOD

In 1969, at the request of the landowners Mr and Mrs J.A. Boyden, Bill Putnam carried out a trial excavation in the parkland west of Dewlish House. This inaugural Dewlish field school took place over a period of four days in late July and it involved students from Weymouth College of Education and local volunteers, a total workforce of eleven. Effectively, this was an archaeological evaluation that required manual digging skills, the drawing of plans and sections, the collection of artefacts, and the recording of levels.

No geophysical equipment was available during the initial years of the Dewlish project (see below), therefore Putnam adopted the simplest and most effective evaluation strategy that was available to him: trial trenching. Val Boyden had noted scatters of Roman pottery 'on ground ploughed for the first time since the 18th century at least' within Dewlish Park. By inference it was in this area of the Park that a single linear trench was set out across a slight eminence (Putnam 1970, 186–7). The trench measured 25m long and 1m wide and

it was subdivided into ten trial trenches or linear test pits, each separated by a baulk (Fig. 2.1). This method had the advantage of providing individual spaces within which all of the student and volunteer participants could engage with the practical aspects of archaeology providing each with the opportunity to experience and develop a range of archaeological skills that were eminently transferable to the professional aspirations of trainee teachers.

RECORDING TECHNIQUES AT DEWLISH, 1969

The individual trial trenches (I to X) were not sequentially numbered and those labelled X, I, IX, VI, and VIII were eventually conjoined to form a single trench (Fig. 2.2). Section drawings and plans were kept to a single sheet of A2 graph paper which, in this pre-decimal era, was calibrated in inches, the only occasion that this was to happen during the eleven seasons of the Dewlish project. The drawings were supplemented by descriptions of contexts and their depths and these were kept in the director's site 'diary' or notebook. Effectively, each of the ten trial trenches had its own series of context numbers, in most cases numbered 1 to 3. Trench IV originally had four contexts, though numbers 2 and 3 were subsequently combined. No attempt was made to amalgamate the contexts of the individual trial trenches in cases where they continued through a baulk. Context record *pro formae* were not used. Unfortunately, it proved to be difficult to equate any of the 1969 and the subsequent 1970 trial trench contexts with any of the contexts that were later identified in the box grid trenches of the 1971–1979 seasons. Consequently all of the 1969 and 1970 trial trench contexts were later regarded as unstratified by the excavator. There were no feature numbers, a policy that was maintained in the succeeding years of the Dewlish field research programme. 'Small', or recorded finds numbers (SFNs) were used.

LEVELLING AND LEVELS

No electronic distance measuring devices were available to the excavator and, in these formative years of archaeology at WCE, there was no site

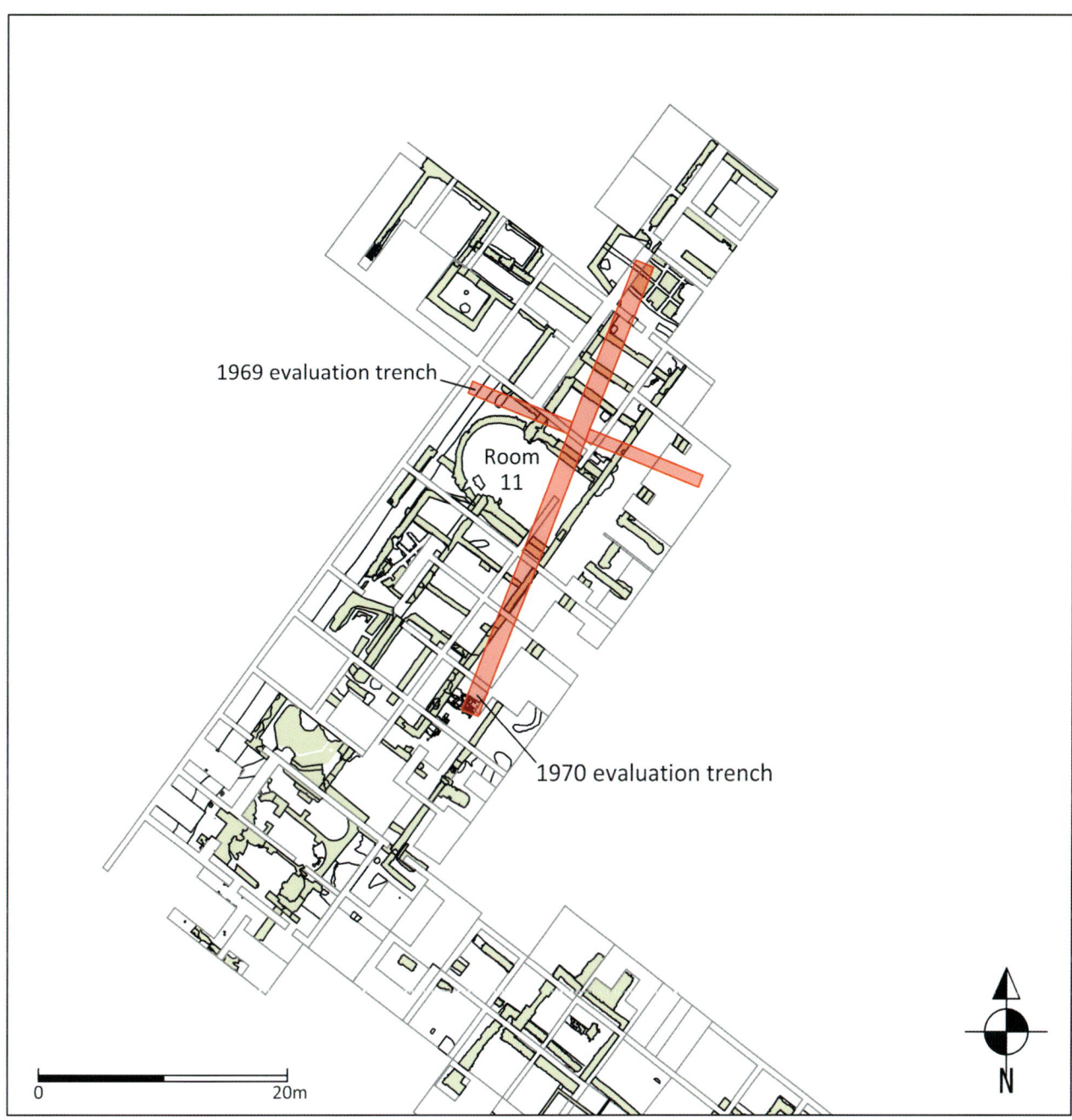

1969 evaluation trench

Room 11

1970 evaluation trench

0　　　　　　　　　　20m

N

Figure 2.1　Location of the 1969 and 1970 evaluation trenches in relation to the plans of Building 3 (the *domus*) and Building 4 (the bath house). Jonathan Milward.

theodolite either. From the outset, a dumpy level was used, a device with inherent limitations in accuracy over distances above *c.* 20m, a tendency that was ultimately to result in a significant error in the layout of the site grid in later seasons. Probably, the error had been cumulative since the first year of the site grid in 1971. A further complication was the need to establish a temporary bench mark (TBM) on the villa site with reference to an Ordnance Survey bench mark (BM) at Shailes Farm, 320m distant

(Table 1.2), an exercise that would have required a number of fore sights, back sights and the methodical movement and repositioning of the instrument. No field book for levels was kept and this continued to be the case throughout the duration of the Dewlish project. Instead, each season, levels were recorded on a single sheet of paper that seems to have been the responsibility of one designated individual for that year. Fore sights and back sights were generally recorded but not in a standard format. The altitude

Figure 2.2   The 1969 evaluation trench sub-divided by baulks in order to accommodate individual and paired excavation experience for students and volunteers (see Fig. 2.1). Photograph: R1555.

of the BM at Shailes Farm was never ascertained and therefore the height of the site's TBMs was never given as a true value, or reduced level, relative to the OS bench mark. This approach to levelling proved to be challenging when the reduced levels of individual site features needed to be established during the current post-excavation project.

DEVELOPMENTS IN 1970

The 1969 trial excavations cut through the entire length of what became known as Room 8, which was tessellated, and across the width of the corridor

(Room 12) which had a mosaic pavement with a key pattern (Fig. 2.1). Initially, this sample gave reason to believe that the villa remains were in a relatively undisturbed state. As a result, the excavator felt sufficiently confident as to conclude his first Dewlish interim report by declaring that (in the next season) it was hoped to cut a similar trial trench, oriented north–south 'before commencing larger scale operations' (Putnam 1970, 187).

In 1970, the test trench strategy resumed, and a new linear trench intersected the 1969 cut at ninety degrees to its mid-point (Fig. 2.1). This trench was more ambitious than its predecessor measuring 35m in length by 1.5m wide and comprising 12 component trial trenches divided by baulks. As in the previous year, the individual trenches were not numbered in linear sequence. The recording system was much the same as it had been in 1969. However, plans and section drawings were made using metric scales in accord with the calibrations printed upon the sheets of A2 graph paper as supplied by WCE: teaching was going metric and the Dewlish project had to follow.

The 1970 trial trench cut through a number of the villa's rooms starting to the east-north-east with Room 4, then successively Rooms 5, 6, 7, 8, 11, 17, 18, 19, and finally Room 12 to the west-south-west. This demonstrated that the villa floors had sustained more damage in the past than had been supposed previously (Putnam 1971, 146). Nonetheless, on the strength of the evidence recovered thus far, the decision had been made by WCE to commence 'long term research' at Dewlish in future years (Putnam 1970, 187). To inform this proposed research excavation, it was necessary to determine the size, layout, and extent of the villa buildings. In the absence of geophysical equipment, it was decided that a series of 1m square 'test holes' (or trial pits) would be excavated. The position of these test pits is recorded in the site notebook for 1969–70 (BU100DEW0008, 35); they were plotted from the site TBM at the north end of the 1970 trial trench and extended from it in a wide arc ranging from the south-west, through to south and then to east of the peg (Fig. 2.1, Peg A). The sketch in the director's notebook suggests that there were six pits in all, and these were identified using letters from the Greek alphabet (α, β, δ, θ, η, γ), whilst the site plan (BU100DEW Sheet 627) has no trench labelled α, but does have one designated ε. No individual pit plans were drawn but the features within each pit were recorded on colour slides and these survive within the Putnam archive.

The digging of the 1970 trial pits was a pivotal moment in the design of the research plan for the villa site. There was an element of calculated randomness to the distribution of the pits which placed only 'theta' (θ) in a position that was likely to reveal any evidence of the north-east range of the villa. At the time, the features that were observed within trial pit theta were not regarded as being indicative of the presence of a building and from this point onwards it was assumed that the villa consisted of north-west and south-west ranges only, a misconception that has adversely affected understanding of the site hitherto.

In the absence of geophysical surveys, trial trenching was a favoured Putnam strategy throughout the Dewlish excavation campaign. This method of archaeological prospecting was employed during the summers of 1973–4, 1976, and 1978 sometimes with important results although the precise position of some of these later trenches was not recorded with precision, a problem that impacted upon the subsequent post-excavation projects. The 1976 and 1978 Trial trenches and their significance are the subject of Chapter 4.

THE SITE GRID

With effect from the 1971 season Dewlish Roman villa was the subject of a research excavation and this required a more sophisticated strategy for the excavation and recording of features, artefacts, ecofacts and geofacts. Bill Putnam was well-acquainted with the box grid system of excavation during his university days, and this is the technique that he adopted for this project. The initial site grid was set out around the projected maximum extent of the north-west range or *domus* of the villa and the grid lines were laid out in conformity with the lines of the walls of the buildings as determined by the evaluation trenches of 1969 and 1970.

The site grid comprised 5m squares with the x-axis (rows) labelled numerically from 1 to 8, and the y-axis (columns) designated alphabetically, initially from A to R (Fig. 2.3). Later, column S was added to the y-axis as knowledge of the extent of the site developed. Rows 4 and 5 were separated by a 1m wide band upon which ran the site datum line. At a central point within this datum band and at both the 'A' and 'S' column extremes, there was a TBM and these were used for all levelling exercises until the end of the excavation project in 1979. However, no contour survey was carried out. The site grid was set out every excavation season thereafter. After 1975, when work on the south-west range of the villa began, it became necessary to extend the grid

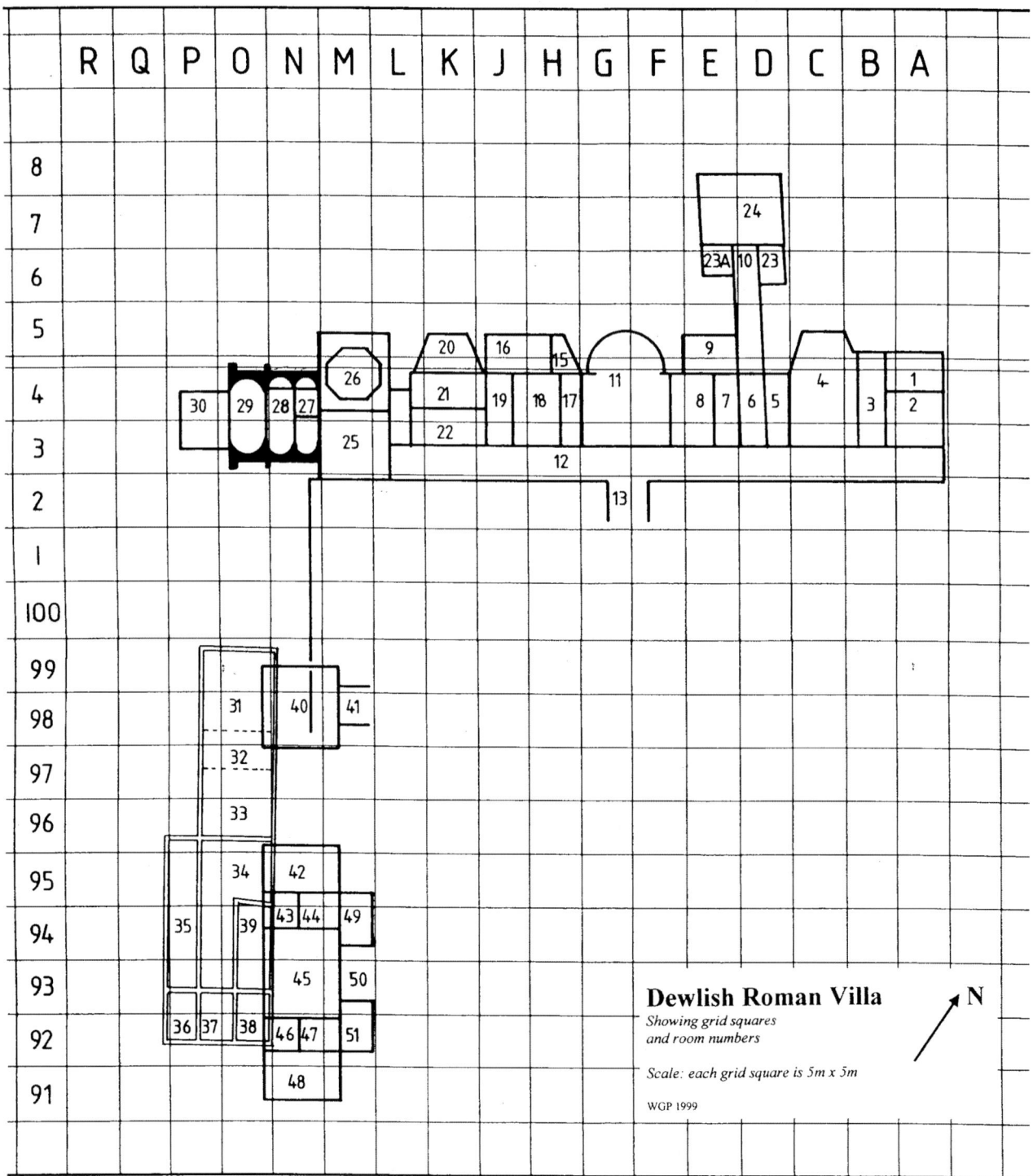

Figure 2.3   Bill Putnam's alpha-numeric site grid, committed to paper for the first time at the start of the first Dewlish post-excavation project (PEP1) in 1999.

which required the addition of further rows below row 1 and these were numbered from 100 to 91 in descending order (Fig. 2.3).

In each excavation season, a predetermined number of grid squares was excavated, each square acting as a discrete 'trench' (Fig. 2.4). Individual grid trenches were separated by a 0.5m baulk, the width of which was derived from the area of the grid square itself and/or that of a neighbouring square. Thus, some grid trenches measured a full 5m × 5m, whilst others were 5m × 4.5m, and some measured

Figure 2.4   Grid trenches under excavation on the site of Building 4 in 1975. Photograph: R3389.

only 4m × 4m. As the excavations of individual grid trenches progressed, some adjacent squares were amalgamated in order to record common features such as continuing walls or trenches.

RECORDING PROCEDURES: CONTEXTS

The 1971–1979 research excavations borrowed heavily upon the techniques and procedures used in 1969 and 1970 but with some important refinements. The director's site diary was supplemented by grid trench excavation books. Each grid trench was allocated a yellow exercise book which was used to record the progress of the excavation of that component square of the site grid. These books were maintained by designated student-excavators who were expected to record within them lists and descriptions of contexts, a catalogue of finds and occasional plans and sections. In 1974 a set of printed guidelines for completing these yellow books was made available (BU100DEW0358; Appendix 1) but standards and techniques of completion varied considerably, and this was especially the case regarding context descriptions. Each grid trench had its own series of context numbers, always starting with context 1 for topsoil. Although the grid notebook system was not without its limitations, it did represent the beginnings of a

systematic recording method that has proved to be an invaluable aid to post-excavation interpretation.

RECORDING PROCEDURES: FINDS

Finds were recorded in list form in the relevant grid trench excavation books, grouped under their appropriate context numbers. The books were

Figure 2.5   Outdoor finds processing in 1971. Photograph: R2399.

Figure 2.6　Proton magnetometer survey, 1972. Photograph: R2509.

inspected daily by the site director who annotated the finds lists and initialled authorised 'disposals'. Basic finds processing took place on site and this included washing and initial packaging, activities that generally took place alfresco with limited clerical facilities (Fig. 2.5).

RECORDING PROCEDURES: SITE DRAWINGS

Plans and sections were drawn at appropriate scales throughout the excavation programme. They were created as pencil drawings on sheets of A2 graph paper; drafting film was not normally used at Dewlish and the drawings do not routinely include levels. A 'sheet number' system was used to record individual plans and sections.

SITE PHOTOGRAPHS

There is an extensive archive of site photographs, both monochrome negatives and colour slides in 35mm format. Only final photographs were taken, the interim stages of each grid trench excavation were not recorded. All photographs were taken by

Bill Putnam and the standard is high although in the penultimate year of the field work, 1978, shutter failure caused the site camera's film chamber to leak light and this had an adverse impact upon the quality of the photographic archive for that year. Appropriate scales are always in evidence. The colour slides are card-index catalogued within their own record system that stands alone from the Dewlish archive. Monochrome images were taken in much smaller numbers but they provide a useful cross-reference to the colour slides and the site drawings.

GEOPHYSICAL SURVEY

Geophysical survey of the site was attempted after the initial years of the excavation programme but the data in electronic form has not survived. The director's diary records that in 1972, during the fourth season of work at Dewlish, Dr John Wood, an assessor for the Underwater Weapons Establishment at Portland, Dorset, visited the site in response to an application by Martin Aitken of Oxford University, to use a proton precession magnetometer to detect and map demolished walls and ditches. The equipment used was effectively home made using a coil, batteries, amplifiers and counters (Fig. 2.6). This experimental geophysical exercise produced limited evidence of the villa plan because the chosen survey area was almost devoid of buried archaeology, a fact that became apparent during the dry summer of 1976 when parch marks were absent from the surveyed part of the site. However, the geophysics did show the villa's south-western boundary ditch and indicated that burnt material was associated with Building 4, the bath house, and its hypocaust (Putnam, BU100DEW0006, 32–3).

In response to a similar survey in 1973, a trial trench, numbered 9, is recorded as having been dug during the 1974 season (Putnam, BU100DEW0095, 42–3). The location of this trench was grid square Q4. It measured 0.5m by 2m and contained fragments of pottery and broken tile but no definite building remains other than loose flints. During the first Dewlish post-excavation project (PEP1), Bill Putnam noted that 'the magnetometer surveys over several years produced no useful information and are now lost,' although some unhelpful binary print-outs have survived along with some perplexing sketch plans (BU100DEW0156). It is assumed that no geophysical survey took place within the area of the unsuspected north-east range of the villa.

PROGRESS AND CONSTRAINTS

This chapter began by explaining how developments in provision for teacher training brought about the beginnings of archaeological fieldwork and research at Weymouth College of Education. Those developments affected the quality of excavations at Dewlish in positive ways: healthy student numbers including aspirants to the new B.Ed. degree made for sound progress on site and a standard of recording that was generally high. By the end of the 1975 season the whole of the north-west range of the villa had been excavated including Building 3, the *domus*, and Building 4, the bath house. Annual interim reports had been published in the *Proceedings of the Dorset Natural History and Archaeological Society* (PDNHAS), on three occasions with Ann Rainey who, as co-author, provided useful descriptions of the villa's mosaics (Putnam and

Rainey 1973, 81–6; 1975, 59–62; 1976, 54–7). Selected site plans had been redrafted in pen and ink in Bill Putnam's own hand, some of which have been published in the interim reports and in subsequent books and papers by other authors (e.g. Witts 2016, 166). In fact, preparations for the eventual excavation report were quite well advanced and this included a typescript that postulated and explained the three perceived phases of the north-west range of the villa (Building 3). However, these positive circumstances were about to change in ways that would have a detrimental impact upon the Dewlish research project, and an adverse effect upon the integrity of the site record.

By 1974, the expansion in Initial Teacher Training courses was drawing to a close (Beavis and Hunt 1999, 6). In the same year, the Houghton Committee on Teachers' pay presented its findings and in the following year, salaries were significantly enhanced for serving teachers; money was being redirected from training to the retention of qualified teachers. This policy change had a significant impact upon colleges such as Weymouth that specialised in teacher training. Student numbers fell, and this meant that the human resource was significantly diminished for projects like Dewlish. By implication, college staff redundancies were in the air unless alternative courses could be devised that would make good the shortfall in students and income. Bill Putnam's response, as Head of Department since 1973 (Beavis and Hunt 1999, 6) was to throw his energy into launching the Certificate in Practical Archaeology (CPA), a move that was to prove successful in the longer term but which struggled for numbers initially. Consequently, it became necessary for Weymouth College of Education to merge with the Dorset Institute of Higher Education (DIHE) in 1976. This was also the year that Bill Putnam became editor of the PDNHAS and there were changes in personal circumstances in the background too. The pressures were being ramped up.

For the first few years of the CPA the course was still based on the premises of Weymouth College but resource rationalisations including office availability and storage locations for excavation finds assemblages and the paper archive ultimately added to the complication of reduced numbers of students on site at Dewlish from 1976 onwards. Coincidentally, the summer of 1976 was hot and dry, and these conditions were to play their part in the closing episodes in the story of the Dewlish project (see Chapter 4).

On the positive side, the drought conditions of 1976 revealed a series of parch marks that to some extent compensated for the unsuccessful geophysical surveys of previous seasons although it seems that they did not disclose the presence of the villa's north-east wing which remained undetected. However, it seems certain that some of these parch marks represented the boundaries of the Group 45 Dole's Hill Celtic field system and associated features such as enclosures and pits. In response to the opportunity thus presented, local farmer John Boyden, archaeologist, pilot and polymath, took a series of air photographs that he presented to Bill Putnam's growing Dewlish site archive. Accordingly, the small excavation team dug a series of 'trial trenches' across a small number of the newly revealed features. Simultaneously, excavation had commenced upon the south-west range of the villa, specifically Building 2, which was then known as the 'aisled barn'.

The thin spread of the available human resource combined with the demands upon the site director's time and the logistical consequences of the institutional merger probably explain a series of negative impacts upon the site archive, specifically:

1   Grid trench plans for the 1976 excavations of Building 2 have been lost (though presumed drawn) a problem that was initially noted in April 2000 during the first Dewlish post-excavation project (PEP1)

(BU100DEW0350, 17). The likely cause of this loss is the reorganization of archive storage that took place following the WCE merger with the DIHE from 1976 and afterwards.

2   The 1976 Trial Trenches explored a selection of parch marks visible both on the ground and on air photographs taken the same year. These trial trenches were situated in two groups, broadly to the north and south of the villa's *domus* (Building 3). This placed a considerable strain on a small excavation team and it is significant that no useful record was kept of the precise locations of these 'Trial Trenches' or the exact number of them. A further series of trial trenches was excavated during the 1978 season none of which can be located with any useful accuracy (BU100DEW0004). By contrast, all trial trenches that were excavated before 1976 were tied into the site grid.

3   The series of annual interim reports declined in both size and detail. In 1980 (for 1977) the interim report was a meagre four lines long. The final offering (for 1978) stated that, 'It now seems likely that the 1979 season...will be the last..., (therefore) publication of the final plans and... summary will be (in) the next... Proceedings' (Keen 1980b, 114).

In fact, the publication of the final plans and statement did not happen, and in general what is understood of the excavated evidence from the south-west range of Dewlish villa has challenged the many scholars who have used the annual interim reports to place the site in the broader context of villa development in the Roman world. The slender nature of the site record from 1976 to 1979 has also perplexed two post-excavation projects in ways that must have exasperated Bill Putnam too as he grappled with the dissemination of the Dewlish story in the three decades following the end of the project (e.g. Putnam 1987, 97–116). It is the two post-excavation projects and their results that are described in the next chapter.

3

THE POST-EXCAVATION PROJECTS

BACKGROUND

Preparations for the post-excavation research and report publication were an integral part of the Dewlish project from 1971 onwards. This had as much to do with the need to teach and assess the student participants as it did with the requirements of sound archaeological practice. Dewlish was a field school and as such the students involved had to pass, but archaeological field projects are an expensive undertaking and the financial resource was finite, especially for a relatively small college of education such as Weymouth. Funding for a summer field school was one demand on the college exchequer, bank rolling a post-excavation project was quite another. Somehow, the joint demands of a post-excavation project and the need to assess students had to be fulfilled to mutual advantage. The mechanism for achieving this balancing act was to extend student assessment into a post-excavation assignment and in many instances, this amounted to using the field school experience to set up individual dissertations based upon specific themes or archive groups that had emerged from the previous summer's dig. Both paper and material archive from Dewlish were stored at Weymouth College and so in practical terms, it was available as a resource for student research and dissertation preparation. It was envisaged that completed dissertations would be added to the Dewlish archive where they would form the basis for the eventual post-excavation project and inform the eventual publication of a monograph.

This student-centred approach to post-excavation input was positive in that it developed an enhanced sense of ownership of the annual field project, but ultimately it was to prove to be a flawed strategy. However good the intentions, and however great the level of support, by definition, students were not specialists in their field and the burgeoning Dewlish dissertation archive could never be a substitute for expert analysis. Furthermore, it would have proved impossible to effectively oversee the necessary and regular handling of archive over the years, and thus it is virtually certain that this unique resource deteriorated to an unquantifiable extent.

At the end of the Dewlish field project, an additional transformative event was about to occur. Weymouth College of Education had been part of the Dorset Institute for Higher Education since 1976, but it had remained on its home campus for the time being. Bill Putnam, Head of Department since 1973, faced the additional challenge of moving it to the Wallisdown (Poole) campus in 1985 (Beavis and Hunt 1999, 6, 9). This entailed moving all archaeological archives across the County of Dorset as part of the process. The timing of this essential move was inopportune in the history of the Dewlish Roman villa project. The consolidation of higher education in the county inevitably led to increased commitments for the academic staff including the planning and delivery of new courses, adjustments to roles and travel arrangements. Nonetheless, after Dewlish, summer archaeological fieldwork projects had to continue albeit on new sites, and these ventures created demands of their own. As a result, the Dewlish post-excavation programme was postponed and it effectively went into cold storage. Furthermore, Bill Putnam needed to lead other excavation field schools notably at South Eggardon Farm (Askerswell), Compton Valance, and the Dorchester Roman Aqueduct (all in Dorset) leaving him with no opportunity to commit to the writing up of Dewlish.

POST-EXCAVATION PROJECT 1 (PEP1)

By 1995 the DIHE had metamorphosed into Bournemouth University and it was in this year that Bill Putnam retired from his post as Senior Lecturer, but he continued to work with the University during the summer months with the aim of completing his field investigation into the course of the Dorchester Roman Aqueduct, a target that was achieved in 1998. The moment for Dewlish had arrived, and in 1999 a post-excavation project proposal was put together and submitted to the Leverhulme Trust which granted Bill a two-year Emeritus Fellowship underpinned by funding. This facilitated the appointment of a research assistant and the establishment of an *ad hoc* post-excavation team which included Maureen Putnam.

This first Dewlish post-excavation project (PEP1) was beleaguered by the problems of its past. Principal amongst the obstacles was the size and location of the archive which was in storage on the Bournemouth University campus within which it had been moved on at least three occasions, and during which time it had been re-boxed and partially re-catalogued. Eventually, the archive was found a place of storage at an industrial unit on the outskirts of Bournemouth. Bill Putnam had no operational base at Bournemouth University after 1995 which meant that PEP1 had to be a home-based initiative. Consequently, permission had to be sought from the University's Collections Management Committee to move the Dewlish archive from the University stores to the Putnam home and, in the case of the building materials, to borrowed space in an agricultural barn (BU100DEW0236).

PEP1 PROGRESS AND OUTCOMES

The Plaster sub-project

A self-determined priority of the PEP1 research team was to assess and report upon the corpus of wall-plaster from the Dewlish villa site. In all, this amounted to 184 museum archive standard boxes the contents of which required space and a large flat surface for meaningful inspection to take place. The borrowed temporary storage space at Cheselbourne barn was the only suitable available option. A working group of five volunteers was assembled and directed by the project's research assistant, Astrid Mick. The aim of the project was to attempt to reconstruct patterns, motifs and images from fragments of painted wall and ceiling plaster that had been recovered from the various rooms of the villa's buildings. It was the ultimate jig-saw puzzle (Fig. 3.1). Over a seven-week period every fragment of plaster was examined and photographed, and a written record was kept (BU100DEW0180).

The plaster sub-project was an interesting exercise but one that produced limited results. The project required an infinitely greater financial input to extend the depth and scope of scientific investigation and analysis. Nevertheless, progress was made towards understanding this important corpus of material, but the written output did not progress beyond draft format and further resource is required to bring this important assemblage to publication. The plaster sub-project is an example of the considerable obstacles that confronted the PEP1 team at a time when other circumstances were driving the eventual outcome.

Specialist reports and other outputs

The Leverhulme Fellowship grant was not sufficient to pay for a raft of specialist reports although expertise was forthcoming for the mosaics (Stephen Cosh) and the identification of coins (Richard Reece), the former contributing a written report (since revised, Chapter 12), the latter providing a dated coin list (Gerrard with Reece, Chapter 13). A scientific analysis of a limited number of painted plaster samples was carried out by Graham Morgan (see below and Chapter 11). Otherwise

Figure 3.1   The PEP1 plaster project in action: fragments of painted wall-plaster were pieced together in the search for a meaningful image. Photograph: Bill Putnam, not coded.

the post-excavation team relied heavily upon the assemblage of student dissertations that had been written during the Dewlish excavation seasons and subsequently. These dissertations varied in quality, but none was of sufficient substance to be included in an academic report. It was also the case that some of the dissertations were written at an early stage in the fieldwork project and these were based on sources of information that were obsolete by 1999. Much work was left to be done on a finite budget and with a small post-excavation team. In addition, Bill Putnam's health was in decline at the start of PEP1 and this dogged his efforts to work towards the publication of the Dewlish excavations.

Other PEP1 outputs were limited in number. An account of progress written for the Leverhulme Trust in October 1999 asserted that reports had been written on the building materials, artefacts of iron, bronze and glass, 'pottery fragments', and coins. The document also indicated that a report had been written on the villa excavation itself (Putnam October 1999, BU100DEW0236). Much of this written material was in draft form only and in need of much reworking. An 'Introduction and Summary' for inclusion in the intended publication provides a good example of the additional work that needed to be done (Putnam, undated, BU100DEW0354). After

the conclusion of excavations in 1979, few updated sections of analytical text were forthcoming either in digital format or on paper apart from occasional contributions to popular local periodicals (e.g. Putnam 2002, 20–29). PEP1 had been under-resourced financially and there was no routine access to Bournemouth University facilities such as laboratory, layout and storage spaces that were desperately needed. Regular contact with academic colleagues and their expertise also was limited. Consequently, PEP1 had produced just three new publishable independently authored specialist reports. There were no new site drawings of the standard of those that had been produced in the first five years after the inception of the field excavation programme. In sum, the project had struggled to move on from the early interpretations of the villa that are reflected in the published interim statements of the 1970s.

The post-excavation team met on a regular basis with set agendas on each occasion the details of which were recorded in Bill Putnam's notebook entitled 'Research Questions 1999' (BU100DEW0350). At a meeting in May 2007, a publication date for Dewlish was set for December 2008. However, Bill Putnam's failing health was to rob him of achieving this self-imposed deadline: he died on 14th October 2008. The post-excavation project remained incomplete and the site unpublished except for a short chapter that was dedicated to Dewlish in the second edition of his book, *Roman Dorset* (Putnam 2007, 97–116).

POST-EXCAVATION REPORT 2 (PEP2)

In 2009 the School of Applied Sciences at Bournemouth University (now the Faculty of Science and Technology) took the decision to work towards the systematic publication of its early field school excavations. Dewlish was identified as the highest priority site for two reasons:

1   By virtue of inheritance, Dewlish was the University's founding archaeology field school and publication was long overdue.
2   The site archive was at risk as a result of its dispersal during the course of PEP1.

Consequently, in 2010 a second Dewlish villa post-excavation project was devised that would:

1   Assess the extent of completion of the first post-excavation project.
2   Evaluate the content of any specialist contributions and student dissertations to date and to cost any further work that might be needed.
3   To work towards publication of an academic report in order that the results of the Dewlish excavations could be made available in the public domain within a ten-year time frame.
4   Formulate research questions and guidance for PEP2 and for future investigations at the Dewlish villa site and its immediate environs.

The site archives

There was a pragmatic demand in the wake of PEP1. The Dewlish site archive remained dispersed between six locations: Dewlish House (one mosaic), Chebbard Farm (plaster, pottery and building materials), the Dorset Museum (selected exhibits deposited on loan during the early 1970s), Bournemouth University (faunal and human remains) and the Putnam home (excavation grey literature, pottery and certain small finds). The first imperative of the second Dewlish post-excavation project was, wherever possible, to gather up the material, paper and digital archive and to redeposit this in the University stores. The Dorset Museum exhibits remained *in situ* but were

made available for study. The building materials and wall-plaster that were in store in an agricultural barn had fared less well. The boxes had become extremely soiled and damp since 1999 and with few exceptions the materials were not recoverable. However, access was possible for specialist inspection (see Hayward, Chapter 10) and a sharp-eyed student did spot a box of environmental samples that was retrieved and subsequently analysed (Gray, Chapter 20).

Once recovered, the archive needed to be assessed for condition and content. This was a supervised process during which certain refinements were made:

1   Repackaging and labelling as appropriate.
2   The addition of box content lists to all material archive. During this process it was noted that there are two site codes that have been used in relation to the Dewlish archive. DH, an abbreviation of Dewlish House, is the original code. DRV (Dewlish Roman Villa) was a by-product of the arrival at Bournemouth University of a new storage system for plans and sections during the 1990s. The code supplemented the original sheet numbering system. Both site codes have been retained and are used for reference purposes in this publication as appropriate.
3   Rationalisation of the paper archive has been supplemented by a digital equivalent wherever practicable. For the convenience of future scholars, an archive code has been devised for key documents. The code consists of three elements:

~   BU – Bournemouth University
~   100 – collection number for BU historic excavation sites
~   DEW – Dewlish (parish code)
~   Unique four-digit document(s) number (e.g. 1234).

Examples of this code are used as citations in this report and appear as per this example: BU100DEW1234. In the case of multiple page documents such as site notebooks, the relevant pages are indicated after a final comma.

Specialist reports

At an early stage in PEP2 it became obvious that several additional specialist reports were urgently needed. Specifically, expertise was required regarding the ceramic assemblages, window glass and glass wares, coins, archaeo-botanical samples, building materials, human remains, and faunal remains. The problems in accessing the plaster archive and its sheer size suggested that a separate publication will be required for this category of material. Publishable drawings of finds, plans and sections were also identified as urgent requirements.

Phased plans

PEP2 inherited no useful phased plan of the villa complex. Bill Putnam had produced a phasing document for the *domus* and bath house (Buildings 3 and 4) in 1975 and this was amended to include the south-west range, probably during the 1999–2008 post-excavation project (PEP1). These documents do not reflect the developmental complexity of the site and therefore the decision was made to take advantage of AutoCAD software to produce a site plan that shows information at-a-glance. This was a challenging task because no composite plan existed for the whole of the south-west range of the villa and as a preliminary exercise it was necessary to construct a working site plan, drawn to scale on drafting film based upon a plethora of preliminary site drawings cross-checked against written observations, recording proformae and site photographs. Phase colours were added to this working plan using coloured pencils (Fig. 3.2). Using this manually constructed draft site plan as the prototype, the team at Bournemouth Archaeology began the process of producing a publishable site plan. AutoCAD version of the site plan went through a number of stages, a preliminary version being that depicted in Figure 3.3.

As the result of critical discussion, it was decided that two versions of the site plan would be produced for publication: one would feature buildings and room numbers (Fig. 3.4) whilst the second version would place emphasis upon the site grid and the alpha-numeric grid codes (Fig. 3.5). Both versions of the phased site plan underpin the unfolding story of the development of the Dewlish villa throughout *c.* three centuries. AutoCAD software has been used to produce publishable versions of section drawings and individual buildings plans which enhance explanation of the archaeology of the site in chapters 5 to 9 inclusive.

The original site archive including the Director's 'diaries', trench notebooks, context records, scale drawings (plans and sections), photographs and interim reports have been used to inform this, the second post-excavation project. The addition of the specialist reports as listed above, provided insights into aspects of the previously accepted chronology and development of the Dewlish Roman villa and as a result, a revised phasing of the site has been central to the revisions that have been made to the interpretations that were aired in the 1969–1979 interim reports and subsequent *ad hoc* publications.

Building numbers

Bill Putnam followed the convention of numbering the individual rooms of the villa and his numbering sequence remains unchanged. However, buildings were not numbered but described by their perceived purpose for example, the 'Priest's House,' or the 'temple', or the 'barn'. Some of these interpretations are questionable and so this second post-excavation project has opted to assign Arabic numbers to each of the recognised component buildings of the site. Table 3.1 below, is a concordance of the newly introduced buildings numbers with the Putnam buildings' names as they appear in his interim reports and elsewhere. The newly introduced Dewlish building numbers system was first used in print in 2014 (Hewitt 2014, 203–4) and again by Hewitt and Cammegh the following year (2015, 3–5). Since that time, the buildings number range has been adjusted in order to accommodate an additional structure that has been detected as the result of close scrutiny of the excavation drawings and Bill Putnam's site diary observations (Fig. 3.4).

Table 3.1 Concordance of Dewlish Roman Villa Post-excavation Project 2 (PEP2) building numbers and Putnam building names

PEP2 buildings numbers	Putnam building names
Building 1	The Priest's House (part of)
Building 2	The aisled barn (or long house)
Building 3 (the *domus*)	The main villa (sometimes including the bath house)
Building 4	The bath house
Building 5	Un-named
Building 6	The temple (or sometimes shrine)
Building 7	The Priest's House (part of)

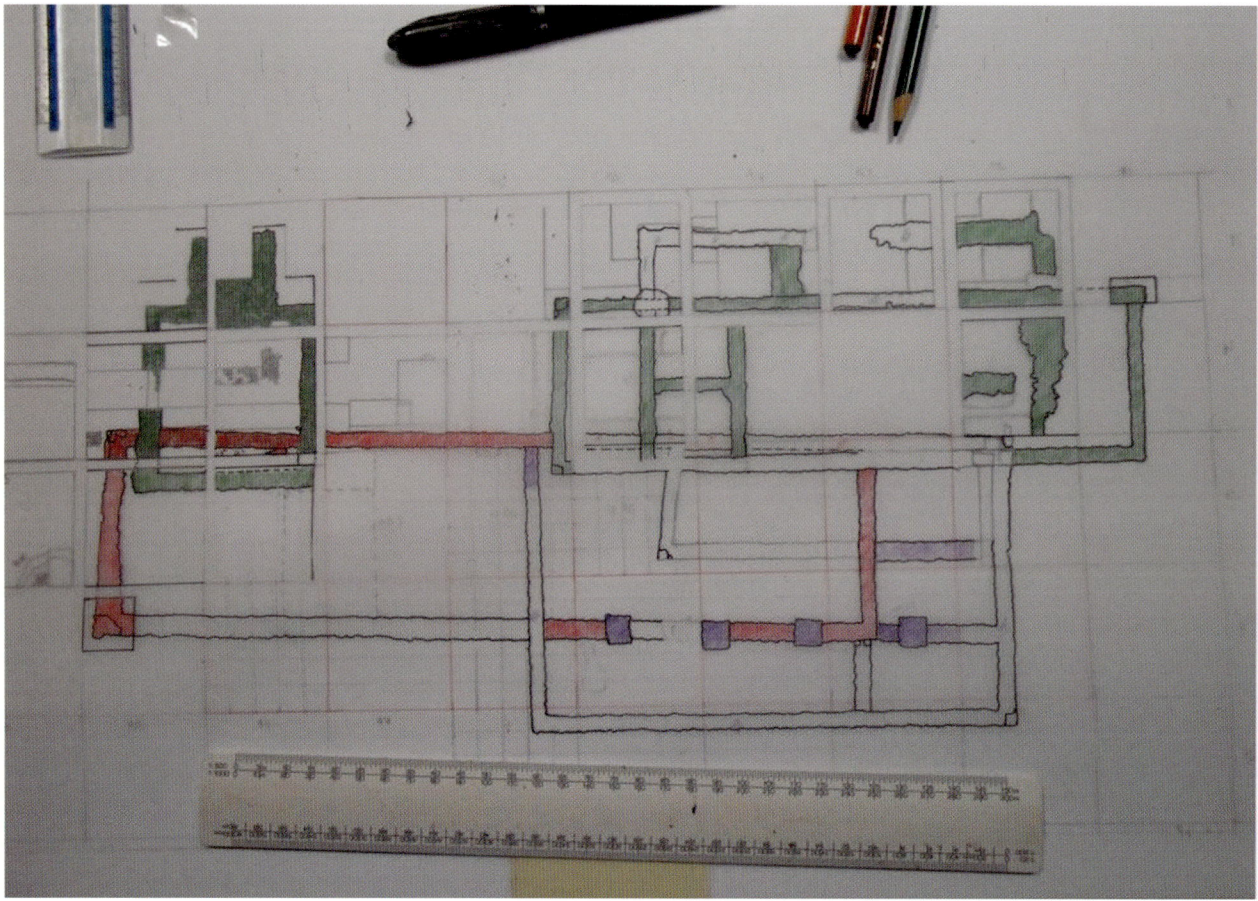

Figure 3.2 The initial step in the construction of a phased site plan for the Dewlish Roman villa: pencil tracings on drafting film. Photograph: Iain Hewitt for Bournemouth University.

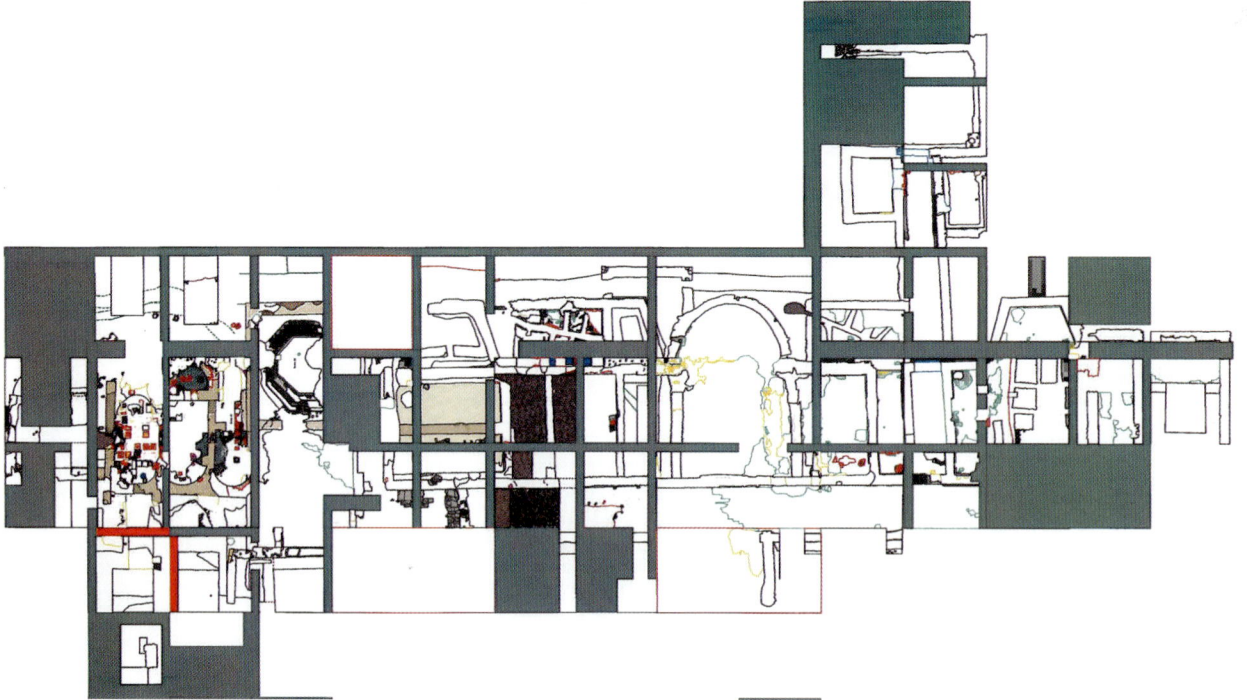

Figure 3.3 Dewlish phased plan construction: an AutoCAD draft version featuring Building 3.

Figure 3.4 Dewlish Roman villa phased plan final version showing building and room numbers. Jonathan Milward.

Figure 3.5   Dewlish Roman villa phased plan final version showing the site grid in outline and grid trench codes. Jonathan Milward.

Funding

This second post-excavation and publication project has required financial support exceeding the sum that was available to the Putnam post-excavation project of 1999–2008. Grants were obtained from the following sources:

~ The Association for Roman Archaeology

~ Bournemouth University (former School of Applied Sciences and the Faculty of Science and Technology)
~ The Dorset Archaeological Committee (twice)
~ The Friends of Bucknowle Roman Villa

This financial input has enabled understanding of the archaeology of the Dewlish Roman villa to be enhanced, and the results of this work are explained in the chapters that follow.

4

PRE-ROMAN SETTLEMENT EVIDENCE

PRE-IRON AGE ACTIVITY

Evidence of prehistoric activity was recovered from the excavation trenches at Dewlish in the form of 2910 worked flints. Within the 103 box grid trenches that were all or partially excavated, worked flints were recovered from 79. In some cases, the flints were retrieved from topsoil contexts or those just immediately below, but others were located close to natural, possibly within residual ancient soil horizons. The worked flints are regarded as being of mesolithic date based upon limited macroscopic observations (Pulman 2002, 6) but the assemblage is more diverse than this because it includes burnt flints with no particular morphological characteristics, and these might be of Iron Age date in some cases. Unfortunately, no other contextual artefacts were recovered that could be associated with the lithics in this assemblage and it is not possible to say if they came from working floors or from temporary settlement sites.

PRE-ROMAN IRON AGE

It has been suggested that the Dewlish Roman villa occupies a site of Late Iron Age settlement (Lucas 1993, 129, 130). This statement requires qualification. The excavation of the villa's buildings provided no substantive evidence of Iron Age settlement remains immediately beneath its floors although earlier features were observed that could not be positively dated and which are better explained as traces of an earlier phase of Romano-British occupation. No convincing case can be made for the superimposition of villa buildings upon a pre-existing Iron Age settlement site such as occurred at Bucknowle and at Tarrant Hinton, both Dorset (Light and Peters 2009; Graham 2006 respectively).

In fact, the discovery of Iron Age settlement evidence at Dewlish was a serendipitous episode in the Dewlish field excavation project. During the very dry summer of 1976 a series of parch marks appeared in the field within which the villa is situated. This prompted an aerial reconnaissance exercise by John Boyden whose excellent monochrome photographs were donated to the site archive. The features represented by the parch marks were visible on the sloping ground to the south and east of the villa field, just above the Devilish Brook, where a thin clay overlies the chalk of the downland (Putnam 1978, 54), and on the higher ground to the north of the villa (Fig. 4.1). In response to this ephemeral phenomenon, a series of trial trenches (TTs) was excavated in each of the two principal parch mark areas, both groups being allotted Arabic numbers from 1 upwards. For the sake of clarity, the trenches are described here as TT(S) numbers 1 to 4 and TT(N) numbers 1 to 5.

Figure 4.1 The excavation site looking north-west. The 1976 (North) Trial Trenches 1 to 5 were excavated to explore the features of a 'double' linear feature (the 'Roman lane') in relation to an Iron Age enclosure that was cut by a modern road. The approximate locations of the 1978 Trial trenches (Roman numerals) lie within the network of ancient field boundaries to the south-east. John Boyden (Bournemouth University archive BU100DEW).

Trial Trenches (South), 1976 and 1978

In a working document that was written for the first post-excavation project (BU100DEW0004) Bill Putnam described the southern group of 1976 trial trenches thus:

TT(S)1 revealed a 'working hollow' (Fig. 4.2, R3834),
TT(S)2 exposed what was initially thought to be a 'tree pit'

(or tree-throw) but which was later interpreted as a Late Iron Age grain store (Fig. 4.3, R3802),
TT(S)3 uncovered the junction of a square sided field and a wandering boundary (Fig. 4.4, R3803), and finally
TT(S)4 'in the south corner of the field' exposed another boundary mark (Fig. 4.5, R3814).

Although site photographs were taken of each of the southern group of Trial Trenches, descriptions

Figure 4.2   TT(S)1 A 'working hollow'. Photograph: R3834.

Figure 4.3   TT(S)2 Iron Age grain storage pit. Photograph: R3808.

of the stratigraphy of TT(S)1–3 are lost however, excavation records of TT(S)4 are in the site record book for grid trench Q94 (BU100DEW0091). A plan of the 1976 parch marks (BU100 Sheet 048) shows the approximate location of TT(S)4, and a second plan (BU100 046) includes the relative location of TT(S) 1–3, but this latter plan was unfinished. Therefore it is not possible to locate any of southern group of 1976 trial trenches with certainty and for

this reason they are not marked on Figure 4.1. The best that can be said is that the 1976 TT(S) group of trenches was in the same general location as the 1978 Trial Trenches that will be described below. As a general observation, the director's site diary records that in TT(S)1 and TT(S)2 the deeply sealed layers are Iron Age but goes on to note that Romano-British building 'rubble' was evident higher in the stratigraphy (Putnam BU100DEW0007,

Figure 4.4   TT(S)3 Field boundary intersection. Photograph: R3803.

Figure 4.5   TT(S)4 Field boundary junction. Photograph: R3814.

29). This comment has interesting implications for the interpretation of the villa's Building 1 (see Chapter 5).

Trial Trenches (North), 1976

Paradoxically, the site diary is devoid of comment on another series of trial trenches that were excavated in 1976 to the north of the villa complex. These were set out to explore other parch marks on the north-western side of the villa field approximately 70m north of the *domus* and outside the area covered by the site grid (BU100DEW0092). The positions of the individual trenches were triangulated in relation to standing trees rather than the site's TBM pegs. Parch marks demonstrated that here, there were 'traces of an irregular pattern of enclosures' associated with circular pits (Putnam 1978, 55).

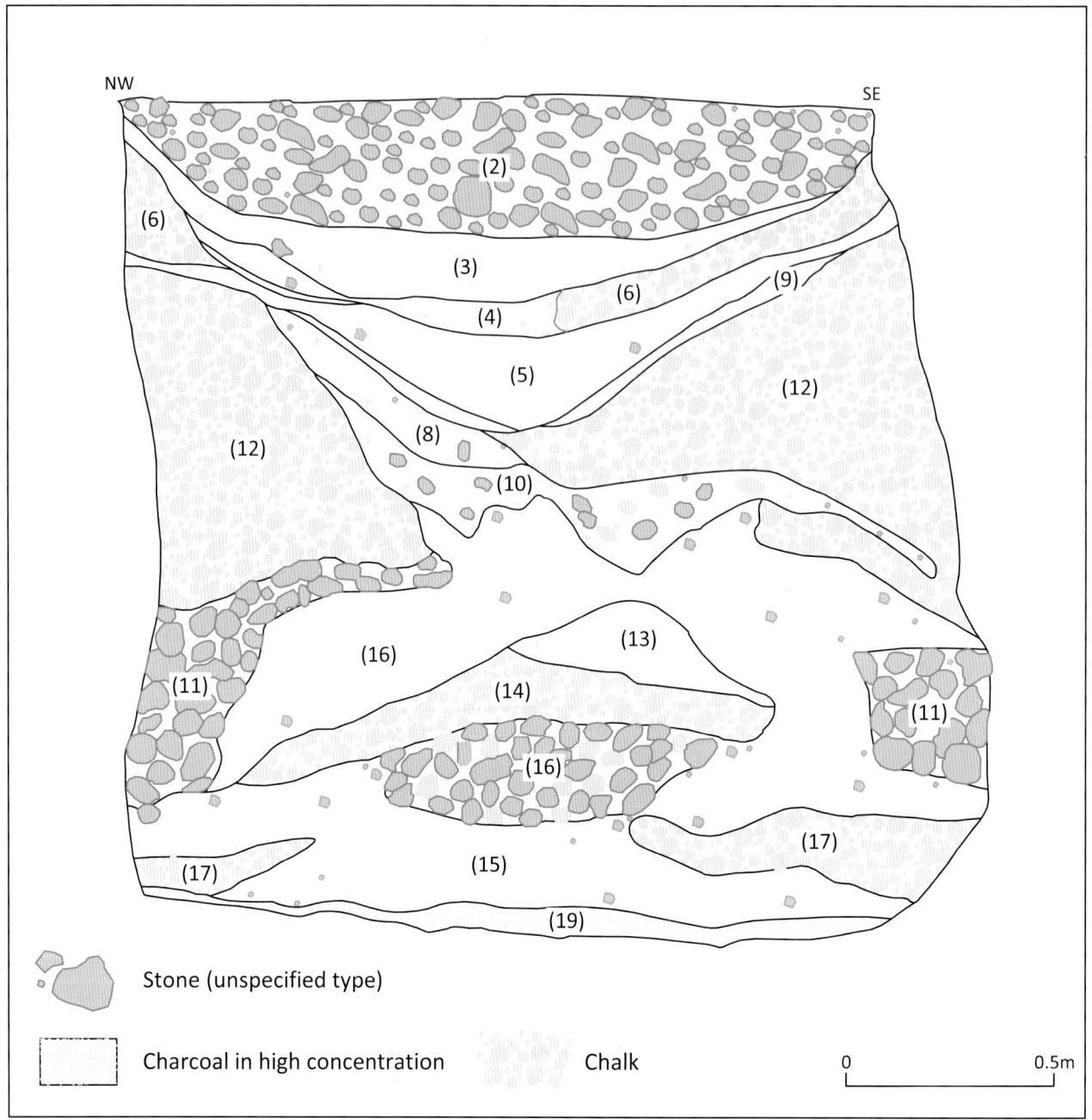

Figure 4.6 Section through a grain storage pit excavated in, or close to, the Iron Age enclosure to the north-west of the villa buildings in 1976. Recorded details of the contexts have not survived.

There are no detailed records of the archaeology of the northern group of 1976 trial trenches, but a sketch plan in a grid notebook (probably derived from the Boyden air photograph) shows the approximate locations of the five trenches that are described as being where the:

TT(N)1 ...Iron Age enclosure crosses the Roman lane (*sic* – probably *vice versa*) (Fig. 4.1),
TT(N)2 ...Roman lane crosses the ditch (to) the south (Fig. 4.1),

TT(N)3 ...ditch crosses the Iron Age enclosure boundary,
TT(N)4 ...Roman lane crosses (the) ditch (to the) north,
TT(N)5 ...square field line crosses the lynchet.

In addition, a section drawing through an Iron Age storage pit has survived (Fig.4.6, DH Sheet no. 577). The pit was described as being 5.07m above (broadly north-west of) site TBM S1 within or close to an enclosure, a feature that is clearly visible in Figure 4.1. This might be a description of TT(N)1 as listed above, but certainty is elusive.

Table 4.1   Dewlish Roman villa Iron Age enclosure/settlement location details

Grid ref NGR	SY 76664 97261
BNG	37664 97261
WGS.84	50° 46 '28" N 02° 19' 56.3" W
aOD	80–85m

The above locational descriptions do not pinpoint the individual positions of the members of the northern group of trial trenches, but collectively their close association with the enclosure boundary and the Roman 'lane' indicates that they were grouped close to those two features. The Boyden air photograph shows a cluster of features within an elliptical enclosure cut by a modern road at BNG 376664, 97261 within the 80m–85m contour band and therefore above and to the north of the site of the villa itself (Fig. 4.1 and Table 4.1). Conceivably, this modern road follows, or is laid upon, the course of an ancient ridgeway that was associated with the enclosure. Bill Putnam noted that the drought conditions had revealed several pits in this area. Associated features within the enclosure showed as being irregular in form (although straight lines are present too) and excavation indicated that they were earlier in date than the larger rectangular fields to the south of the villa buildings as demonstrated by the evidence from the southern group of 1976 trial trenches. The air photograph, Figure 4.1, also reveals that a double linear feature approaches the Iron Age enclosure from the south but upon reaching it, turns sharply to the east thus respecting the enclosure's presumed perimeter bank and ditch. This is the feature that the fragmentary trial trench record describes as a Roman lane but there is no firm evidence to support this interpretation. The 'lane', appearing as a double ditch, respects the enclosure but also provides a partial curtilage boundary for the villa itself. The real purpose of the 'lane' might have been one of demarcation between the enclosure and the villa, perhaps a subtle indication that the two settlements were occupied contemporaneously but functioned as distinctly separate entities.

Taking the above evidence into account, it can be argued that the enclosure to the north-west of the site represents the Iron Age settlement at Dewlish, a point that did not escape the attention of the excavator (Putnam 1978, 55).

No finds from the northern group of 1976 trial trenches have survived; perhaps none were retained. However, the pottery from the southern trial trenches was available for specialist analysis. The pottery report summary indicates that the Iron Age material from the southern trial trenches dated from around the first century BCE into the early decades of the first century CE (Seager Smith, Chapter 15). The report author goes on to suggest that this might argue for a hiatus between Late Iron Age and early Roman activity on the site. This does not take account of the evidence of the samian ware finds which are the subject of a separate report (Mills, Chapter 16) and it must be emphasised that the evidence from the 1976 trial trenches constitutes a very small and random sample. Effectively, the trial trenches explored a fraction of the past activity within the Dole's Hill ancient field system in the vicinity of the villa.

1978 Trial Trenches

In 1978, a further series of trial trenches was excavated in the area of the 1976 Trial Trenches (South). This was not in response to a renewed manifestation of parch marks but in order to further examine unspecified features that had been observed on the 1976 air photographs that had been interpreted as evidence for the existence of an early Roman building. The 1978 Trial Trenches were coded TTI to TTVIII and a written record of these is extant (BU100DEW0094). As there were no parch marks for guidance, the position of the trenches was based upon approximations to features that were visible in the APs as shown on Figure 4.1. As a result, the evidence derived from the 1976 Trial Trenches was not enhanced and the site of the conjectural early Roman building remained elusive. This is a matter that will be further discussed in Chapter 5 in relation to Building 1.

OVERVIEW

Having completed the excavation of the villa's *domus* and bath house in the years before 1976, and having produced a considered sequence for the buildings explored thus far (BU100DEW0005), Bill Putnam acknowledged that the investigation of the parch marks had opened up the 'whole sequence problem in a most interesting way' (BU100DEW0007, 34). These limited trial trench excavations provide a fascinating insight into the pre-Roman origin of the villa at Dewlish that would repay a future field investigation project informed by appropriate geophysical techniques.

5

BUILDINGS 1 AND 7 (THE PRIEST'S HOUSE)

ESSENTIAL GLOSSARY

- *opus signinum:* a waterproof cement made with crushed brick or pottery (Taylor 2003, 277).
- Priest's House: the combined footprint of Building 1 and Building 7.

CONTEXT

The remains of Buildings 1 and 7 were excavated jointly during a single summer season in 1977 and they were component parts of the south-west range of the villa (Fig. 3.4). Initially, the combined buildings were interpreted as a 'small residential building', sometimes referred to as a 'small villa' that cut, and therefore post-dated, the aisled 'barn' (Building 2 with 2A) that had been partially revealed the previous year (Keen 1980a, 120). With the discovery of what was believed to be a shrine or temple (Building 6) just to the north-west in 1978 (see Chapters 6 and 7), the small residential building became known as the Priest's House, or temple offices, on the basis of the shared alignment of the north-east elevations of the two buildings (Keen 1980b, 114). This association of house and temple has persisted since then (e.g. Putnam 2007, 99, fig. 35).

During the current post-excavation and publication project, the various strands of excavated evidence that are pertinent to the 'Priest's House' have been revisited, re-assessed and re-analysed, a process that has prompted a re-classification of this building as two separate overlapping sets of structural remains. The process of reappraisal has not been undertaken lightly and probably it would not have happened at all but for the written observations of Bill Putnam as recorded in his site diary for 1977 (BU100DEW0007, 41–67), a document that provides the substance for the re-interpretation. It is this source that is cited throughout this chapter unless otherwise stated.

THE 'SMALL VILLA' (OR 'PRIEST'S HOUSE'): LOCATION AND CHARACTERISTICS

The remains of the 'small villa' are contained within a rectangle of the site grid as defined by the columns M, N and O, and the rows 91 to 96 inclusive incorporating rooms 42 to 51 on the Putnam grid plan (Fig. 2.3). The house is situated at the south end of the villa's south-west range (Figs. 3.4 and 5.1). Further to the west and beyond this position, the land drops sharply away into the valley of the Chesel Bourne. This area was part of the medieval West Field of Dewlish, and its position on the crest of a west-facing slope implies that the 'small villa' was situated upon a field lynchet that had been intensively ploughed in accordance with seasonal demands. The site diary for 1977 notes that plough damage in this area was considerable and particularly so in grid squares N92 and N93. Walls had been reduced almost to base levels and were nowhere surviving to more than 0.3m in height.

Consequently, no floors remained and there were no loose tesserae to indicate the former presence of mosaics: only 'undefined foundation layers' were encountered. Convincing evidence for doorways, both internal and external, was absent. During the initial stages of clearance, the excavators were removing what was referred to as sub-floor rubble, but as a pattern of walls emerged, it was observed that the whole building seemed to have been levelled and covered by a courtyard. The archaeology of the building was in a poor state of preservation, and accurate interpretation was challenging.

The excavated remains were thought to represent a single structural entity with flint walls bonded by yellow sandy mortar throughout. The discovery in grid trench N92 of samian ware sherds and the rim of a Black Burnished ware flat-rimmed bowl, triggered associations with similar finds from the southern group of 1976 trial trenches which had given rise to the notion that there was an earlier phase of the villa to be found on the site (Chapter 4). Based upon the evidence of the early date of some of the finds, Bill Putnam's initial interpretation was that the elusive early villa had been found but this working hypothesis was soon abandoned and the evidence of the early ceramic finds was set aside, although there were sound reasons to support this revised judgement.

THE CASE FOR THE SINGLE BUILDING: 'SMALL VILLA' OR 'PRIEST'S HOUSE'

The primary objective of the 1977 field school was to test the relationship between the emerging (presumed early) small villa and the walls of Building 2 that had been excavated during the previous year. For this purpose, a section was excavated between site grid squares M94 and N94 (see Figure 5.1 upon which the section is marked X-Y). Here, the wall foundations of Building 2 are shown in red and the western most wall of the small villa (A, D) is marked in dark green. Excavation in grid trench N96 (see Fig. 3.5) confirmed that the foundation trench of the 'house' wall A, B, cut the foundation of the Building 2 wall close to point A, thus demonstrating that the 'small villa' post-dated Building 2. In an unpublished text on the phasing of the site, Bill Putnam assigned

Building 2 to the third century which, in turn, indicated a probable fourth century date for the 'small villa' (BU100DEW0002, 2). It was this re-phasing of the 'small villa' remains that prompted its association with the temple-like structure (Building 6) that was excavated in 1978 and the 'small villa' became the 'Priest's House'. In this scenario, with reference to Figure 5.1, the Priest's House must be envisaged as comprising a combination of the dark green walls and the light green walls (i.e. A, B, C, D + E, F, G, H).

THE CASE FOR TWO BUILDINGS: BUILDING 1 AND BUILDING 7

The review of the evidence from the 'small villa' site during the course of the present post-excavation project (PEP2), has revealed that the single building hypothesis is circumstantial. The single building interpretation does not take account of the recovery of samian ware sherds (Mills, Chapter 16) and other early finds, some of which were from sealed contexts. There were other interesting and significant features too which are itemised in the following sequence.

1   The foundations of walls F, G (light green) were stated as being 'very wide'. This contrasted with walls shaded as dark green in grid trenches M95 and N96 which were noted to have 'deep vertical foundations' (Fig. 3.5). At the time of the excavation, it was suggested that this might be because the walls in grid trench M94 (light green on Figs. 5.1 and 5.2) represented an extension to the original building but another explanation is possible as articulated in items 2, 3 and 4 below.

2   Within the combined walls of the small villa, traces of floors were scare, but in grid trench N94 and just beneath context 1, there was extensive building rubble which included wall-plaster, *opus signinum* flooring and stone roof tiles of Purbeck limestone. In M94, overlapping limestone tiles were also found and it was suggested that these represented a fallen roof. Actually, clay roof tiles were also recovered but evidence for these being derived from the section drawing (Fig. 5.2), the grid trench notebook for M94 (BU100DEW0052 and photograph R3852 reproduced as Fig. 5.3). Sometimes, clay tiles were found within the deeper contexts, but invariably they were recorded as 'discarded' by the project director. At Dewlish, clay roof tiles are overwhelmingly associated with third century or earlier contexts whereas limestone roofing

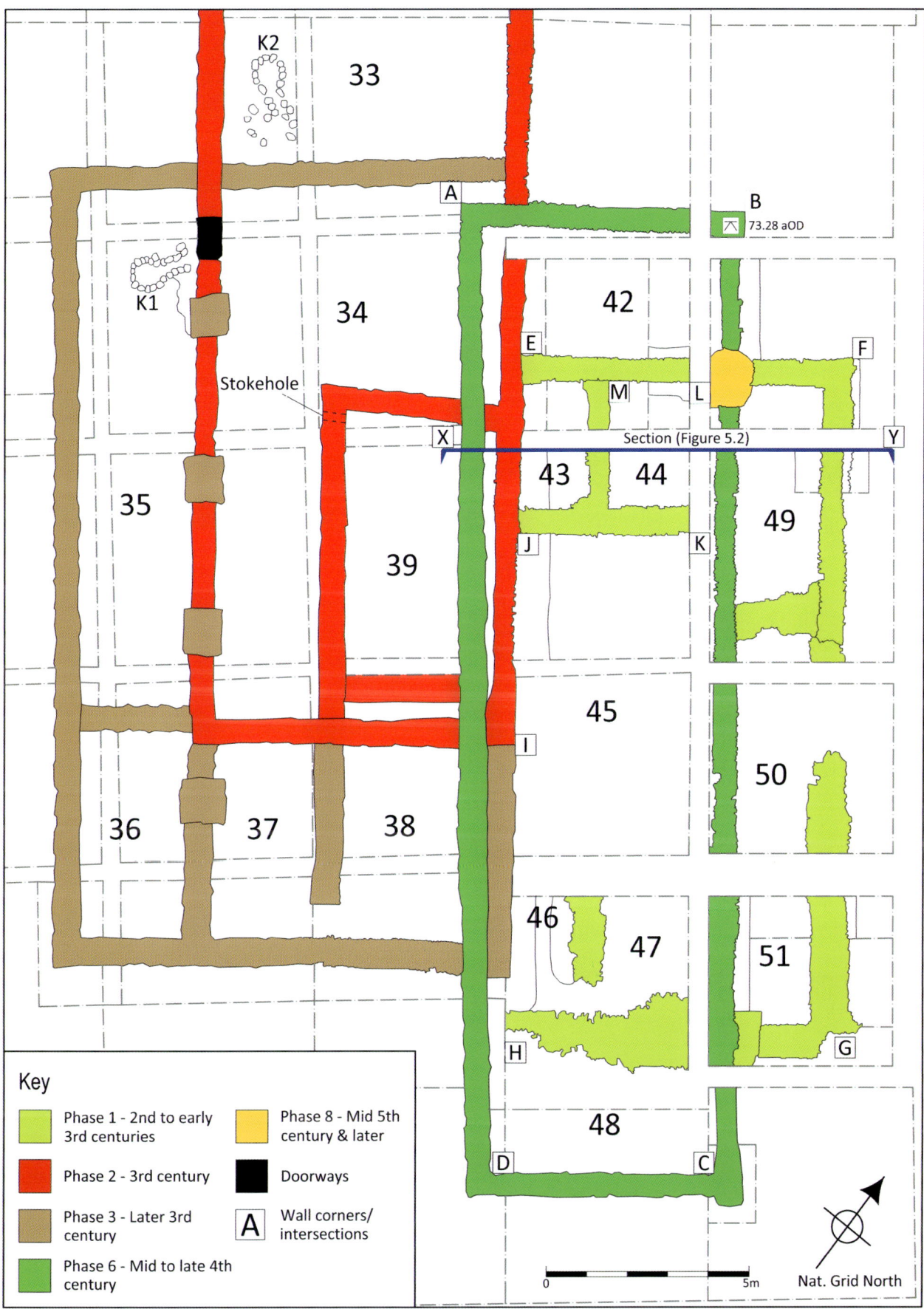

Figure 5.1   Detail from the phased plan of Buildings 1 (Phase 1), 7 (Phase 6), 2 (Phase 2) and 2A (Phase 3). Jonathan Milward.

tends to be found in the fourth century phases of the site (see also Hayward, Chapter 10 this volume).

3   The quoins of the rectangle of walls A, B, C, D were represented by a limestone example of 'enormous dimensions' at corner B (which was also the site TBM for 1977). This is in contrast to the wall F, G which had once been punctuated by a central entrance to the building in grid trenches M93 and M94. This entrance was flanked by quoins of Chilmark stone from Wiltshire. This variation in the materials used in different walls of the small villa has to be considered when assessing the evidence for the structure and development of the component buildings.

4   In grid trench M95, the surfaces external to the building walls comprised courtyard materials that included fragments of broken clay tiles. Indicatively, these tile pieces represent the roof of an earlier building that had been broken up and repurposed as hard core.

Overall, the variation in wall foundation, the presence of both limestone and clay tiles, the alternative sourcing of building materials such as quoin stones and the re-use of building materials, together indicate that there is a case for proposing a two-building interpretation of the small villa site. The evidence would indicate an earlier structure was represented by the wall rectangle E, F, G, H (light green; Building 1) measuring 11.5m south-west to north-east by 13.1m north-west to south-east, an area of 150.66 square meters, together with a later building that comprised walls A, B, C, D (dark green; Building 7) with dimensions 9.5m south-west to north-east by 19.5m north-west to south-east (185.5 square meters). The building numbers used reflect their relative place in the developmental history of the Dewlish villa as a whole (Figs 3.4, 3.5 and 5.1).

The objection to this two buildings model is the apparent absence of a south-west wall for Building 1 (E, F, G, H) which should exist between the points H and E on Figure 5.1. Comments made in the director's site diary prove that the missing wall did exist. Referring to the sectioning of the Building 2 wall foundations (red) in N94, it is recorded that two mortar colours were involved in its construction. A 'creamy' mortar had been used in the very bottom courses of the wall and a yellow sandier mortar in the remaining courses above this. At the junction

of the two colours of mortar, one layer of flints had both of these mortar colours. These important details are confirmed in the section drawing X-Y (Fig. 5.2) where the Building 1 south-west wall is shown as being sealed by the later Building 2 north-east wall. The two walls are also shown as being offset, which confirms the separate identities of the two walls. Furthermore, it is significant that the internal walls J, K and E, L abut the north-east wall of Building 2 rather than the south-west wall (A, D) of Building 7. This is a point that was noted in the site diary with some consternation but it is a matter that is easily explained if it is accepted that originally, these two south-west/north-east walls (Fig. 5.1, light green) had adjoined the former south-west wall of Building 1 prior to being cut by the north-east wall of the later Building 2 (red). The north-east wall of the third century Building 2 (Fig. 5.1 E, J, I) had re-used the base foundations of its predecessor, Building 1, thus obscuring its integrity as a discrete structure. The evidence of the drawn section Figure 5.3 confirms the case for the two building interpretation of the small villa or Priest's House.

IMPLICATIONS

The two building model proposed here argues in favour of Building 1 dating to c. second century as supported by the evidence early Roman glass (Allen, Chapter 14) and samian ware finds. Building 7 (A, B, C, D) cuts Building 2 which was dated to the third century, thus suggesting that Building 7 probably dates to the fourth century. Building 1 would fit Bill Putnam's initial interpretation as being a small villa (a 'cottage villa') with internal walls, and it is quite possible that it was this building that was associated with the fields of regular shape to the south of the villa that were also indicatively dated by samian ware finds (Chapter 4). Building 7 had no internal walls and appears to consist of a single internal open space. If this is correct, then Building 7 may be regarded as a storage facility for produce from the adjacent field network. Building 7 probably served as a fourth century replacement for Building 2 when it was demolished at the end of the third century (Chapter 6). No evidence could be found of heating systems but in the case of Building 1 braziers or fire places could have been used for this purpose.

Figure 5.2 South-east facing section drawing across grid trenches M94 and N94 (marked X-Y on Fig. 5.1). Jonathan Milward.

Figure 5.3   Grid trench M94 showing the south-east facing section (X-Y) at the top of the photograph with the common baulk with N94 to the left. Clay roof tile fragments are from Building 1, and the limestone roof tiles are from Building 7. Photograph: R3854.

Figure 5.4   Grid trench N93 looking south-west. The sub-ovoid feature bridged by the ranging rod probably pre-dates Building 1 but its purpose is unknown. Photograph: R3887.

Fragments of wall-plaster were recovered and these imply a residential function, probably for Building 1. Neither building could be regarded as a Priest's House: Building 1 is too early to be associated with the temple/shrine (Building 6) and arguably Building 7 was not a house.

The PEP1 diagrammatic Dewlish site plan of 1999 (Fig. 2.3) illustrated ten numbered rooms for Buildings 1 and 7, jointly known as the Priest's House. The re-interpretation of this one house as two buildings has prompted abandonment of the room numbering system for these buildings only.

EVIDENCE FOR EARLIER OCCUPATION

There are a number of entries in the Putnam site diaries for 1977 that refer to features that might be 'pre-building' or 'pre-house' layers. These comments probably refer to Building 7 because it substantially overlies Building 1. Nonetheless, it is also possible that some of the sub-floor features pre-date Building 1 too. For example, in grid trench N93 a linear 'shelf' was found to run *c.* north-south close to the east section of this grid trench and at an angle to the lines of the walls of both buildings. Traces of this shelf were found to continue through the baulks into N92 and N94. In N93, almost adjacent to the shelf and west of it, was a post hole, west-south-west of which was another, larger example. This latter post hole was sectioned and found to be full of rubble of an unspecified nature. Associated with these features was an ovoid hollow that was joined from the north by two 'gulleys' that originated in grid trench N94 (Fig. 5.4). The site diary suggests that the hollow functioned as a soakaway but without an obvious purpose.

CONCLUDING REMARKS

Buildings 1 and 7 occupied an archaeologically complex part of the Dewlish villa site. Buildings 1, 2, 2A and 7 all occupied a zone of 30m × 30m square meters, and between them representing five phases in the building history of the complex (Fig. 5.1). The excavation of this palimpsest of buildings happened at the time when the Dewlish field project was in decline (see Chapter 2) and for this reason, it was not fully understood. The above paragraphs have made the case for a two building interpretation of the small villa or Priest's House with Building 1 representing the earliest known component structure of this Romano-British villa. Evidence for even earlier Romano-British settlement underlying the site of Building 1 has to be kept open pending a future field investigation programme.

Building 2 and its relationship to Buildings 1 and 7 is the subject of further scrutiny in Chapter 6.

6

BUILDING 2 WITH BUILDING 2A,
A MULTI-PURPOSE STRUCTURE

INTRODUCTION

The location of Building 2 with Building 2A was identified by of a series of trial trenches that were excavated in 1973 and 1974 but detailed excavation took place in 1976 and 1978. In common with Buildings 1 and 7, Building 2/2A was situated within the south-west range of the villa (Grid trenches O92 to 96, P92–96 and Q92–96); Building 2A represented a distinct development phase of Building 2 and together they occupied an area that was on the brow of the heavily ploughed western slope of the site (Figs. 3.4 and 3.5). During excavation, walls were visible at a point just above foundation trench level though in most cases at least three courses of wall flints testified to the plan of the buildings in this area. Retrospective interpretation of the evidence from Building 2/2A has been constrained by the absence of plan and section drawings for grid trenches N91–95, O93–96, O98, P92–3, P95–6, and P98. There was also a disastrous loss of quality in the photographic archive for 1978 when the site camera developed a shutter fault. In the same year, the size of the Dewlish workforce reached its nadir, probably seven student participants in all, and this limited the scope of the work that could be achieved. Consequently, interpretation relies heavily upon the Director's site diaries for 1976 and 1978 (BU100DEW0007, 2–38 and 69–98 respectively), and the individual grid trench record books which include draft plans and sections of variable quality drawn to a scale of 1:50.

Buildings 2 and 2A received scant comment in the published interim reports and interpretations changed little during the two-year period 1976–8 and beyond (Putnam 1978, 54–5; Keen 1980b, 113–14). In fact, the extended chronology of the excavation of Building 2 influenced the interpretation of its function; at various times it has been described as a 'long strip building', a 'barn', an 'aisled barn' and a 'long house'. Overwhelmingly the 'barn' designation has found favour but essentially Building 2/2A was a more complex structure than an agricultural store as explained in the following paragraphs which are grouped under three principal sub-sections, one for each of the two principal building phases, 2 and 2A, followed by an analysis of the post-demolition use of the footprint of the site.

BUILDING 2 COMPRISING ROOMS 31 TO 34 AND 39 (PHASE 2)

Building 2 was constructed upon a terrace, the evidence for which could be seen in grid trench O99 as context 11 (Fig. 6.1). The terrace was cut into a slope with an aspect to the south-west where a V-shaped ditch with bank formed a linear boundary. In its original form, Building 2 extended c. 32.5m in length (north-east to south-west) by c. 7.5m wide (Fig. 6.1, A, B, C, D) with internal walls and stud partitions that demarcate agricultural and domestic

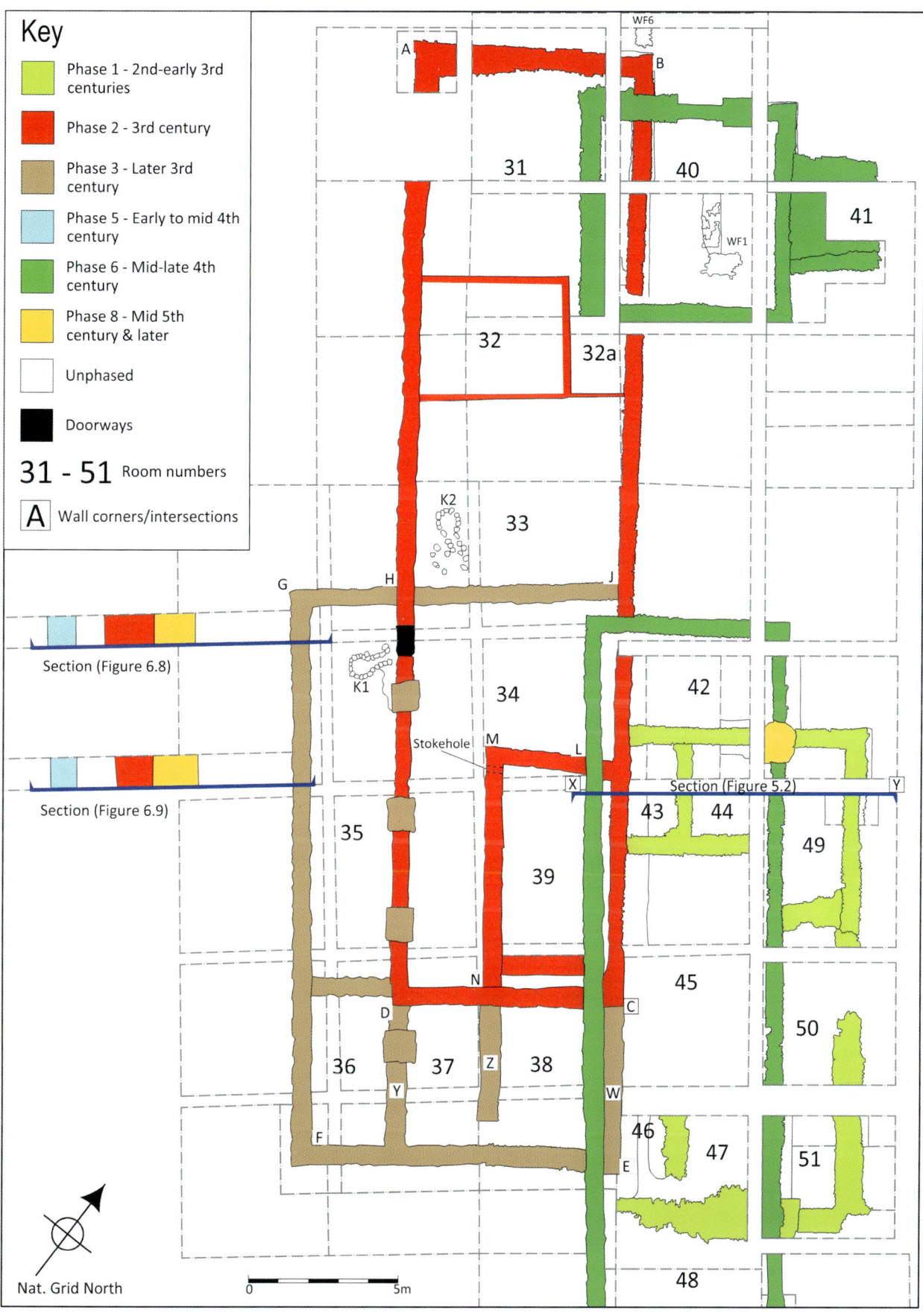

Figure 6.1 Detail from phased plan of Buildings 2 (Phase 2) and 2A (Phase 3) in relation to Buildings 6 and 7 (Phase 6). WF1 = Wall Fragment 1. Jonathan Milward.

Figure 6.2 Building 2, north-east corner quoins in 'stepped' arrangement. The pointed end of the 2m ranging rod lies across the north-west wall of Building 6 which cuts the south-east wall of Building 2. Photograph: R3928.

zones of activity thus categorising it as a variant of a row building (McCarthy 2013, 50–53) or, according to Putnam, a long house (March 2002, 22). The foundations of the building were described by a 0.5m wide wall of flint bonded by a white mortar matrix and set within a construction trench. It was noted that there were occasional inclusions of limestone roof tiles within the walls (typically a fourth century feature at Dewlish) but none of these is convincingly apparent in the site photographs for this phase. Scattered throughout the remains of Building 2 and its periphery were clusters of clay roof tiles, both imbrex and tegula types, which indicated that the roof had consisted of this material during this initial phase. The corners of the building were constructed of dressed limestone quoins (Fig. 6.2) and the abundant scatter of large building flints suggests that this was the predominant building fabric for the outer walls. External doorways could not be identified with confidence, but a gap was observed in the south-west outer wall (A, D) that spanned the area of the baulk between P95 and P96, possibly the position of a doorway at the midpoint of the building (Fig. 6.1). Perhaps by way of confirmation, a heavy-duty latch-lift door bolt was recovered in the adjacent grid trench, P96 (Fig. 6.3). Alternatively, this break in the wall line might be associated with the stoke hole of a later kiln or oven that was situated

Figure 6.3 Heavy duty iron latch-lift/door bolt from grid trench P96. See also Fig. 17.7. Photograph: R3757.

Figure 6.4 Buildings 2 and 2A: the agricultural zone looking south-east. The possible malting facility (Room 39) is situated above the horizontal ranging rod (centre left). A banjo-shaped oven or kiln (centre right; grid trench P95) lies within the south-west aisle close to the flint rubble base of a pier. Photograph: R3829.

nearby. A second possible doorway that had been blocked with dry flints was noted in grid trench P94 but no photograph or surviving drawing records this feature.

The agricultural zone of Building 2 was at the south-east end, but its boundary with the residential zone to the north-west is not proven. A dividing wall (H, J) between walls A, D and B, C across grid trenches O96 and P96 separates Rooms 33 and 34, and it is tempting to regard this as the line of demarcation (Figs. 6.4 and 6.5). However, the date of wall H, J is not certain: it abuts the north-east and south-west outer walls of Building 2 (Fig. 6.1 A, D and B, C) at foundation level and contained fragments of clay roof tile that probably became available following the re-roofing of the building with limestone tiles at the time of the construction of the later extensions that comprise Building 2A (see below).

The key feature of the agricultural zone of Building 2 was Room 39, which lies substantially within grid trench O94. The north-east and south-west walls of the room were measured as 55cm in width, built of flint and bonded by mortar. Limestone quoins were used at the point of intersection (M) with a butt joint with wall C, D at N (Fig. 6.1). The point of conjunction

with wall B, C was not recorded in detail during the excavation. Site photographs indicate that the walls of Room 39 did not include re-used materials such as clay tile fragments suggesting that these walls were contemporary with the original Phase 2 construction of Building 2.

The excavation of Room 39 involved a series of four 'trial trenches' cut within the area of grid trench O94 (BU100DEW0088). The combined evidence within these trial trenches revealed that a stoke hole was situated in the south-west wall of Room 39 where it aligns exactly with an area of intense burning on the internal north-east wall of Building 2 (B, C), as observed during the excavation of Buildings 1 and 7 in 1977 (Fig. 6.1). In describing this phenomenon, Bill Putnam noted that the fire had had the effect of 'shattering flints and roasting mortar' within the fabric of wall B, C (see Chapter 7). No explanation was attempted, but the probable function of Room 39 is that it was a cereal drying facility rather than a room and that the interior walls of this feature (L, M, N) supported the oven floor. The Room 39 stokehole would have been the source of the heat that caused the damage to the internal face of wall B, C. A length of wall across the width of Room 39 was visible in grid trench O93

Figure 6.5   Comparative walls of Buildings 2 and 2A looking north. The south-west wall of Building 2 runs diagonally from bottom right to top left (typically 0.5m wide). The north-west wall of the Building 2A aisle runs bottom left to top right and achieved a typical width of 0.65m. The foundations of the oven/kiln in grid trench P96 are bisected by the ranging rod (top centre). Photograph: R3774.

and this probably represents an additional support platform for the oven floor.

Examples of indoor cereal drying ovens have been found at other villa sites including that of Clear Cupboard, Farmington, Gloucestershire (Gascoigne 1969, 47–9). Experiments in the construction and firing of Romano-British 'corn driers' were reported in detail by Reynolds and Langley (1979, 27–42). This paper records the details of the construction of a roofed drier based upon an excavated example. In synoptic form the authors' findings revealed that:

1   Cereal drying would need to have taken place within a roofed but vented facility.
2   The heated floor was constructed of nailed planks sealed by a slurry of chalk and clay about 30mm thick that was laid over the whole of the upper surface of the floor. Test firings at high temperatures using this structure inflicted no damage upon the wooden components of the drying floor.
3   Repeated firings proved unsuccessful in reducing the moisture content of grain samples to the required levels and that in any case, drying cereals in this way was probably unnecessary.
4   An alternative hypothesis for the purpose of corn driers was that they functioned as malting floors (see also Corney 2003, 11–12).

At Dewlish, no recorded samples were collected from within Room 39 and so verification of the corn drier/ malting floor hypothesis is not possible. However, evidence derived from a later phase of the use of Buildings 2 and 2A confirm that cereal processing was an important part of the economy of the villa estate, thus exploiting its strategic location within the Dole's Hill ancient field network (see Chapter 1).

The domestic zone lay at the north-east end of Building 2, beyond wall H, J, where the interior space was subdivided into three rooms by stud walls with a base layer of flints.

Within this zone, the purpose of Room 33 is not clear and little survived of the floor of this room apart from a small concentration of cobbles that indicated the need for a hard-wearing surface in this area. Otherwise there were no features of note in Room 33 apart from a deposit that included a New Forest thumb pot and a group of small animal bones with a fragment of cattle rib.

In the north corner of Room 33, Room 32a with an *opus signinum* floor, served as a connecting passage to Rooms 31 and 32. The floor of Room

Figure 6.6   Fragment of painted wall-plaster from Room 32. Photograph: Bill Putnam (not coded).

Figure 6.7   Reverse side of Fig. 6.6 (Room 32). Note the impression of coppiced hazel wall material to which the plaster was applied. Photograph: Bill Putnam (not coded).

32 consisted of rammed chalk within which was a deposit of infant remains, one of three such deposits recovered from beneath room floors at Dewlish (see Rohnbogner, Chapter 19). The surviving partition walls were defined by a single row of flint cobbles with at least two surfaces of residual painted plaster work surviving up to 0.15m in height. Adjacent to the surviving partition walls there was a large concentration of plaster fragments painted in cream with red and blue splashes representing fallen material from both the walls and ceilings of the room. The reverse side of these plaster fragments revealed that when wet the material had been smeared on to panels of wattle or lath (Figs. 6.6 and 6.7).

Room 31 was also distinguished by the presence of painted plaster pieces from ceiling and wall surfaces. Tight against the north-east wall of the room and within grid trench N99 the remains of a limestone flag floor were found, indicative of the overall composition of the entire floor space within this room at the time of its construction and active service.

The few details that were gleaned from the excavation of Rooms 31, 32a and 32 are indicative of an accommodation suite of more than ordinary status. Taking into account factors such as size and proportion, it might be inferred that Room 31 fulfilled a multi-purpose role as a family room which would probably have been heated for food preparation and for general comfort. A hollow filled with burnt material against the north-west wall was the probable location of the household hearth, the content of which had been spread across the floor of Room 31 over a period of time (grid trench P99).

BUILDING 2A COMPRISING ROOMS 35 TO 38 (PHASE 3)

Rooms 37 and 38

The original row house building was extended to the south-west by at least one additional unit (Room 37) which comprised north-east and south-west walls abutted against wall C, D of Building 2. The south-west wall of this added unit (i.e. between Rooms 36 and 37) was described as being 'late and superficial' with just one course of flints remaining (BU100DEW0007, 21, 31). It was noted that ground level in this room was at least *c.* 0.5m below the floor level of the Building 2. In fact, it is not certain that Room 37 was a room at all; it might have served as an attached lean-to outhouse or a storage bay. Room 38 was potentially contemporary with Room 37 but probably not, because its south-west and north-east walls were well founded rather than superficial (Fig. 6.1). There was a ledge above ground level on the north-east wall of Room 38 and on the strength of this evidence a case was made for the former existence of a suspended wooden floor. The case for the wooden floor was strengthened by a blackening of the ground surface beneath what was thought to represent decayed floorboards but no samples of this material were available for analysis. The purpose of Rooms 37 and 38 is conjectural. Prior to the construction of wall E, F access to Rooms 37 and 38 could have been via external south-east facing doors through an earlier wall, but this is speculation

and not supported by the excavated archaeology of Building 2A.

The south-west aisle

Building 2 was enlarged by what has been described as an aisled extension (Putnam 1978, 55). The construction of the new aisle entailed the demolition of almost half of the length of the original wall of Building 2 from points H to D. A new wall E, F, G, H, was constructed that added *c.* 3.5m to the width the building (Fig. 6.2). This enlargement enhanced the footprint of Building 2 by approximately 50 per cent, a possible indicator of increased cereal production from the nearby fields.

The aisle walls of Building 2A were significantly different to those of the adjoining Building 2. They comprised mortared flint nodules as before, but with inclusions of clay roof tile, almost certainly demolition debris from the roof of the dismantled original south-west Phase 2 elevation of Building 2. In addition, the new walls were constructed to a width of *c.* 0.65m with a base foundation course 0.15 wider using a hard, white bonding mortar as opposed to the 0.5m width and yellow/cream mortar of Building 2. The corners of the new aisle (E, F, G) were strengthened by limestone quoins. These characteristics were generally consistent throughout the structure of the new build and proved to be an essential aid to interpretation and phasing. The construction of the aisle demanded an extension of the roof towards the south-west, implying a change in roofline that probably involved an adjusted angle of slope. The original south-west wall of Building 2, within grid squares P96 to P92, was reduced down to ground level and the surviving foundation courses were used to provide the base for four pillars, each of which stood upon a rectangular platform of flints (grid squares P93, P94 and P95; Fig. 6.1). The function of the pillars was to support the extended roof of Building 2/2A.

The demolition of the common wall and its replacement by a pillar meant that Rooms 36 and 37 must have been united into a single unit but Room 38 might have survived as a separate entity. At some point, the construction of the aisle included the creation of a shallow founded wall in P93 / Q93 between wall A,

D and wall G, F that ran south-westwards from point D on Fig. 6.1. This wall was interpreted as a room divider and therefore the south corner of Building 2/2A was designated Room 36. However, there is no evidence to suggest that this wall was a full height structure and its true function remains uncertain.

Building 2A external features

Excavation did not reveal any evidence of doorways in the new aisle but that cannot argue in favour of their absence. However, it was noted that the area immediately outside and the aisle (south-west) had been surfaced with 'gravel', a feature that was explored by extending the excavation into grid squares Q95 and R95 and subsequently into S95 and T95 (Figs. 3.5 and 6.1). The essential details of this initiative are shown in the section drawing across grid trenches Q95-R95 that is reproduced as Figure 6.8.

The gravelled surface sealed three ditches that were coded 'A', 'B' and 'C'. Of these, ditch A was V-shaped and achieved a depth of 1.2m. There was a primary chalk fill (context 12) but above this, ditch A was replete with building rubble from the demolition of the original south-west wall of Building 2. Therefore ditch A was contemporary with Building 2 but pre-dated the Building 2A modifications. Ditches B and C were c. 2.5m apart and were relatively shallow compared with ditch A. Ditch B cut ditch A and had been subject to a re-cut for the burial of a horse (context 9). A coin of the House of Constantine (345–58 CE) was sealed within context 6 which offers an approximate date range for the horse burial but not for the cutting of the original ditch. The evidence of the Q95-R95 section was confirmed by a second trial trench across grid squares Q96 and R 96 c. 5m to the north-west (Figs. 6.1 and 6.9).

The relationship of all three ditches was checked further to the south-east by a trial trench that was opened in grid trenches R91 and S91. Here it was observed that ditch B cut ditch A confirming that the former is later in date. It was further reasoned that ditch A was a boundary ditch on the south-west side of the villa complex that was open but partly silted when the south-west wall of Building 2 was demolished to make way for the aisle extension. The R91 / S91 excavation confirmed that Ditch A was then filled with demolition material, an event that would have occurred during the third century. The trial trench evidence confirmed that ditches B and C were parallel and were thus interpreted as the drainage features of a Roman lane (see Chapter 4).

REDUNDANCY, DEMOLITION AND RE-USE

From the available evidence Building 2 served as a grain store for the villa estate with cereal drying or malting being essential parts of its function. The north-east end of the building was set aside for a suite of rooms that might have served as accommodation for the family of a farm steward or manager. Coin and pottery finds indicate that the building was in operation during the third century and possibly into the early fourth century.

During the excavations, attention was given to an examination of the foundations of the exterior walls of Building 2, and specifically to the east and west corners where two characteristics were noted:

1 The base layer of the foundations was wider than that of the surviving courses above (Fig. 6.2).
2 The colour of the plaster in the lower courses of foundations was different to that of the courses immediately above.

From these observations, it was deduced that the surviving outer walls of Building 2 were of two identifiable phases, i.e. the first walls had been demolished and replaced on the same footings (see Chapter 5). However, increments in wall width are a stabilising technique in a foundation structure and this technique has been observed elsewhere, for example in the aisled building at Ingleby Barwick (Willis and Carne 2013, 35 figs. 3.8 and 3.9). Lime mortar colour is also an unreliable guide to wall phasing because as a bonding agent lime mortar needs to dry slowly which delays the building process thus leading to variations in batch mix and colour.

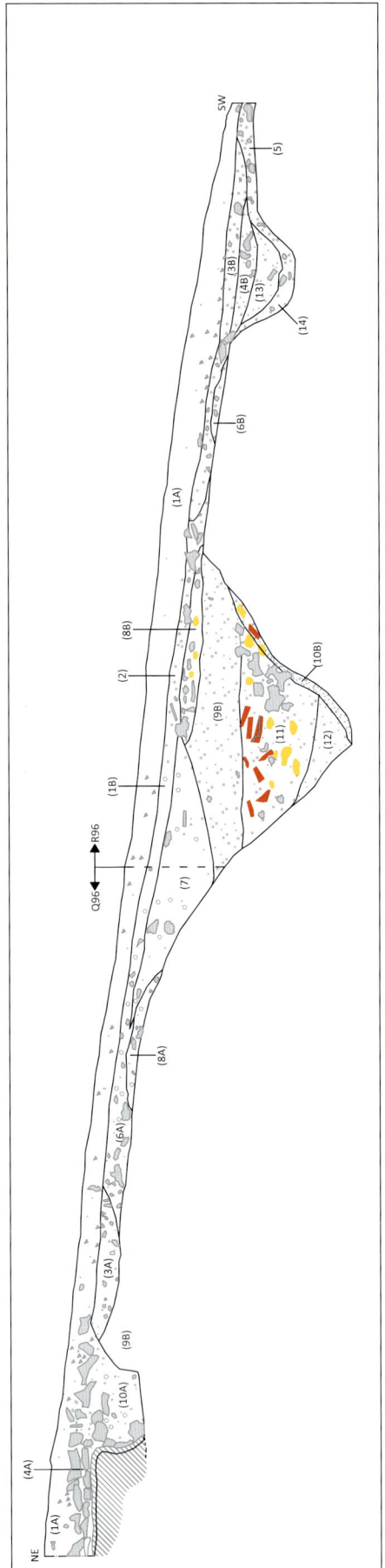

Figure 6.8   North-west facing section across grid trenches Q95 and R95. Jonathan Milward.

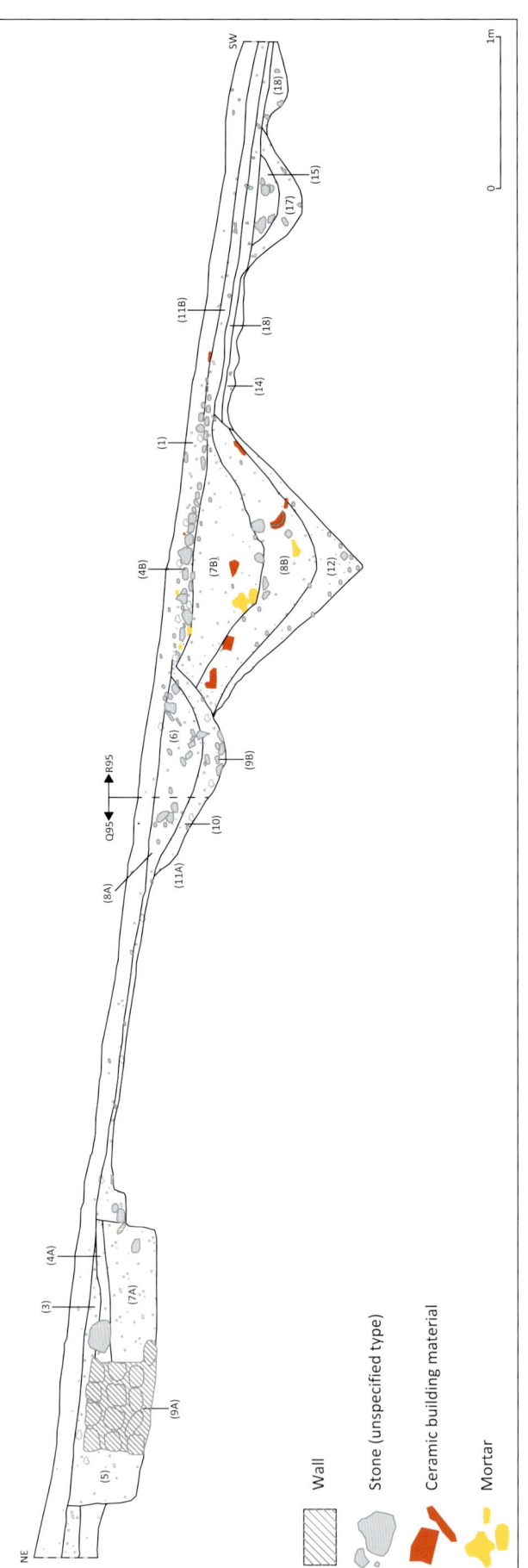

Figure 6.9   North-west facing section across grid trenches Q96 and R96. Jonathan Milward.

Wall

Stone (unspecified type)

Ceramic building material

Mortar

1m

0

Building with lime mortar tends to be a seasonal occupation (Schofield 2011, 11).

The end of the working life of Building 2/2A was signalled by its replacement by Building 7 which was shown to cut its south-east wall and those of Room 39, the oven or malting floor (Fig. 6.1). Evidence of demolition was recorded as a section of collapsed wall that had fallen into Room 38 (093) and a 'mortar mass' that probably originated from the former south-east wall. A third section of demolished wall consisting of 22 courses had tumbled into Room 31 sealing an horizon of burnt material associated with its hearth in the process (098 context 7; 099 contexts 3 and 4). This fallen section of wall must have derived from Building 2 because it had been cut by the south-west wall of the later Building 6 (Fig. 6.1). A 5kg sample of the burnt material, including a tight mass of charred grain, was recovered from the spread of burnt material from Room 31 but this has not survived for analysis. This burnt material did not extend beyond Room 31 and so it is not an indicator of a widespread catastrophic fire, but it probably demonstrates that the function of the accommodation suite had changed and that material from the hearth or brazier was not cleared on a regular basis.

The abandonment of Buildings 2 and 2A was represented by a spread of demolition rubble some of which undoubtedly originated from the combined buildings themselves. However, this material also included box flue pieces, *pilae* and tesserae all of which are indicative of heated floors which were not a feature of Buildings 2/2A. Significantly, a Kimmeridge shale tile was recovered from context 5 in grid trench O98 (Room 31) amongst a spread of flints and plaster. Tiles of this type were a feature of the Building 4 Room 26 cold plunge bath only which suggests that much of this demolition material was derived from the Buildings 4 and 5 bath house structures which are known to have had a number of phases (see Chapter 8).

Buildings 2 and 2A were replaced by Buildings 6 and 7 by the mid-fourth century. Building 7, an elongated rectangular structure possibly replaced the grain storage function formerly fulfilled by its demolished predecessor. However, Building 7 did not have any provision for grain drying or malting and these vital agricultural functions had to take place elsewhere. Evidence for alternative provision was revealed in grid trenches P95 and P96 where two drying ovens were discovered (Figs. 6.4 and 6.5 respectively; see also Chapter 9). Fragments of quern stone were found in close association as were sherds of fourth century pottery thought to have been broken *in situ*. It is difficult to phase these two ovens with certainty. Figure 6.1 shows that the oven in grid trench P95 was so close to the south-west wall and door of Building 2 that they are unlikely to have co-existed without considerable inconvenience and fire hazard, making it likely that this oven post-dates the demolition of that section of the wall that facilitated the construction of the Building 2A aisle. In this scenario the efficiency of one or both ovens might have been enhanced by being enclosed within the combined Building 2/2A. Equally feasible is that both ovens were constructed after the demolition of Building 2/2A in which case no evidence was found or recorded to suggest that either oven was enclosed by a purpose built structure. Carbonised grain was recovered from both ovens and this was sent for analysis (Gray, Chapter 20). However, grain included within these samples might have been used as fire tinder rather than providing a reliable indicator of the ovens' precise purpose.

POSTSCRIPT

In spite of the demise of Building 2/2A and the consequent loss of its grain drying/malting facilities, it will be argued in Chapter 9 that those same processes continued to play an important part in the villa estate's economy into the fourth century.

BUILDING 6 (ROOMS 40 AND 41), PIT-SHAFT O100 AND THE WESTERN INTERSPACE

INTRODUCTION

Building 6 was located in the south-west range of the villa, specifically within six grid squares: N, M, and O 98–99 that were excavated during the 1978 season of fieldwork (Figs. 3.4 and 3.5). In the absence of detailed comment in the terse final Dewlish interim statement (Keen 1980b, 113–4) the best sources for understanding the archaeology of Building 6 are the Director's site diary for 1978 (BU100DEW0007, 69–97) and the four relevant grid notebooks (BU100DEW0053, 0054, 0055 and 0057). A further complication in reaching an understanding of the site is that the foundations of Building 6 cut those of the demolished Building 2 meaning that excavation of both buildings was simultaneous. Entries in the site diary regularly alternate between the archaeology of each of these buildings but greater emphasis was afforded to the evidence from Building 2. The regular switching of attention from Building 2 to Building 6 was a potential source of chaos but it was also symptomatic of the pressures and uncertainties that confronted the Dewlish project team after 1975 (see Chapter 2) which in turn was doubtless the cause of a significant misinterpretation of the Building 6 site (see below).

In common with other buildings on the south-west side of the villa's courtyard historic ploughing had removed the fabric of the remains to 'well below floor level' (Keen 1980b, 113). The foundations of the building were relatively shallow and in plan the

walls of the principal room (40) described a near square the external measurements of which were 7.2m (north-west to south-east) by 7.4m (south-west to north-east). Set central to the north-east wall were the foundations for a 'grand' porch or stepped entrance visible principally as foundation rubble that formed a rectangle (designated Room 41) of *c.* 3.8m north-west to south-east by 2.8m north-east to south-west (Putnam 2007, 103; Fig. 7.1). The height of the surviving walls of Building 6 was not recorded but a site photograph indicates that they did not exceed *c.* 0.4m (Fig. 7.2) and they were set within shallow foundation trenches of an average width of 0.6m. Wall fabric was predominantly flint and lime mortar although the remains of a levelling course of limestone tiles was observed within the north-west wall (Fig. 7.1 A, B). The walls of Building 6 described an internal space of *c.* 6.0m × 6.0m (i.e. Room 40) and the corners of the building were strengthened by quoins, also of limestone.

The excavation of Room 40 revealed a confused picture and the descriptions of the contexts within the two relevant grid trenches, N98 and N99, lack coherence. Beneath the topsoil was a layer of limestone tiles which was thought to have represented the collapsed roof of the building. This horizon of tiles sealed a mixed deposit of wall-plaster fragments, pottery sherds, Ham stone quoins, and tesserae. The whole of this mixed deposit sank into a hollow in the east corner of the building (BU100DEW

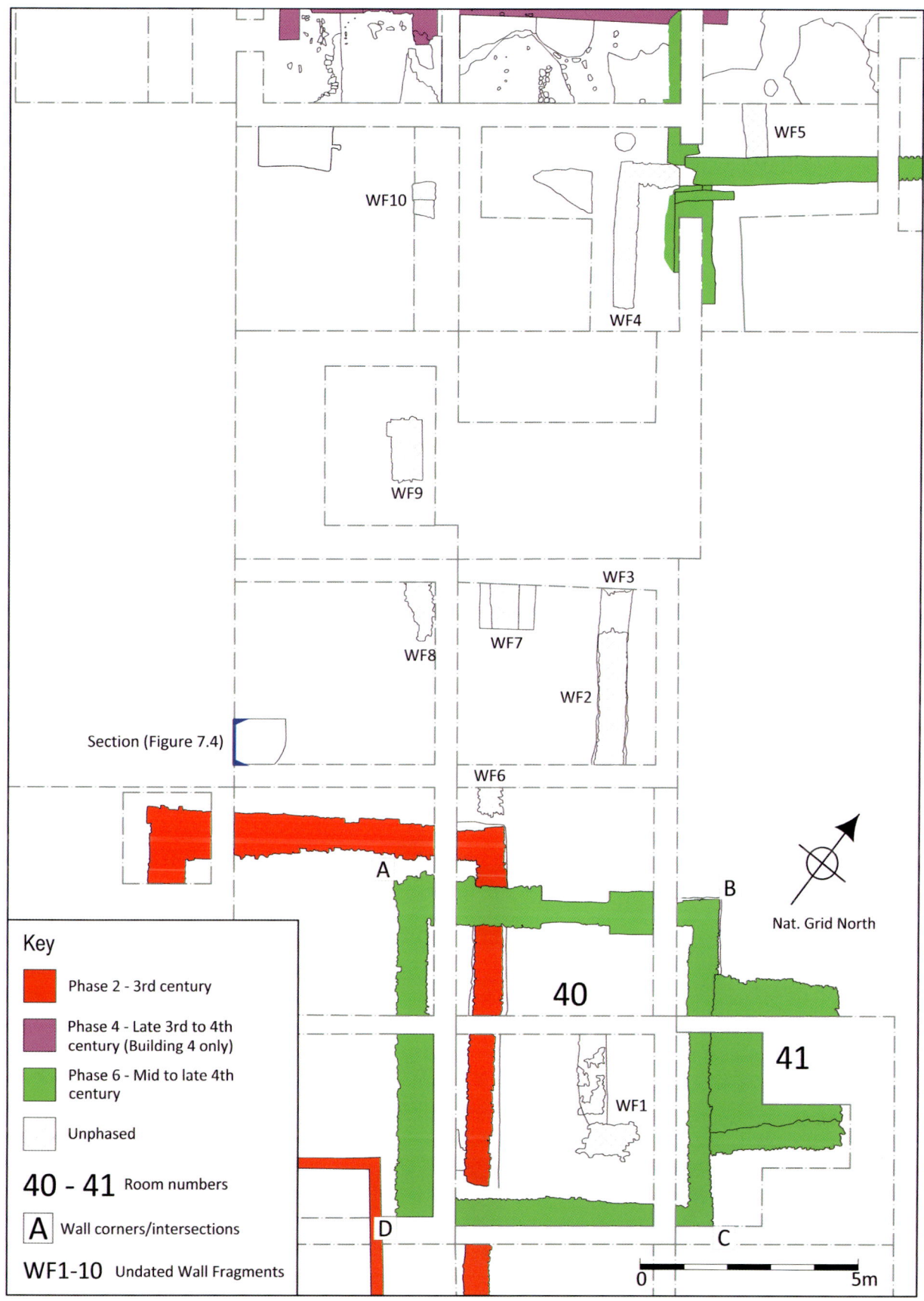

Figure 7.1   Detail of Building 6 (Rooms 40 and 41) in relation to the north-west end of Building 2 (Rooms 31 and 32). The group of wall fragments (WF 1 to 10) probably relate to Building 5 which remains unphased but pre-dates Building 6 (Phase 6) and possibly Building 2 (Phase 2). Grid trench O100 was the site of a pit-shaft. Jonathan Milward.

Figure 7.2   The foundations of Buildings 2 and 6 facing north-west. The near-square footprint of Building 6 cuts the north-east wall of Building 2. Photograph: R3953.

0007, 76). Three coins were found (SFNs 774, 775 and 799) dating from the late third century to early fourth centuries (Gerrard with Reece, this volume) but they were all from unsealed contexts although they are likely to be associated with the miscellany of debris listed above. The provenance of this hard core material is open to speculation but on balance, Bill Putnam believed that it was derived from a previously demolished structure. A possible source is the combined Buildings 2/2A which flourished in the third century, but which had been demolished by the early fourth century when the foundations of its north-east wall were cut by the construction of Building 6 (Fig. 7.1). However, there is no evidence that Ham stone blocks were used in the structure of Buildings 2 or 2A. Alternatively, the hard core could have been sourced from Building 1, dated to the second to early third centuries, which did include two quoins of Chilmark Stone, but Ham stone is not known to have been included in its fabric.

Bill Putnam also suggested that collectively, the mixed rubble materials from Room 40 provided the foundation hard core for a destroyed mosaic floor as suggested by the number of tesserae recovered from this part of the site. Surviving wall fragments of Room 40 were plastered internally almost down to natural which would suggest that if a mosaic pavement had been a feature of Room 40 then it was laid after the internal walls had been plastered.

In reality the case for a mosaic floor in Building 6 is not strong and the issue remains open.

With reference to the walls of Building 6, the site diary records that the plaster had been applied to both internal and external surfaces (BU100DEW0007, 71).

Room 41, the north-east facing porch, survived as a foundation layer only; all quoins and any other dressed facing stones had been robbed out during antiquity or later. As a structure the porch probably included a flight of steps that provided access to a raised floor within Room 40 (BU100DEW0007, 94). These steps might have been flanked by two dwarf limestone columns, an example of which was a surface find close to the site of the excavation. Another column was found sealed within the burnt hearth material in Room 31, Building 2. In this conjectural model, these columns could have supported the porch roof, but they cannot be associated with Building 6 with confidence.

THE FUNCTION OF BUILDING 6

Based upon the ground plan alone, the excavator surmised that Building 6 was a temple or shrine (e.g. Keen 1980b, 114, citing Putnam) and this interpretation has become part of the Dewlish story since 1979. In order to achieve a balanced judgement, it is important to consider at least one alternative hypothesis. The Roman villa at Brading, Isle of Wight, has a mosaic pavement that includes two images of buildings, one of which has a footprint that bears a remarkable resemblance to Building 6: it is square in plan with a ladder or steps that provide access to the interior floor (Henig 2013, 256 and fig. 13.4). In his discussion of the panel in question, Henig suggests that the Brading image could represent a *mansio* (or inn) but this provides an unconvincing explanation of the function of Building 6 at Dewlish. In reality, there are too many uncertainties regarding Building 6 for any confident interpretation to be made. Based upon stratigraphic evidence a fourth century date for the building is certain but greater precision is not possible.

Building 6 might have functioned as a temple or shrine, but the excavation record is very confused, and in at least one instance, the archaeology of the building has been misrepresented in print. In a chapter dedicated to Dewlish, Bill Putnam made a number of statements about the 'temple' which include its destruction by 'a fire of an intensity that cracked even the stones in the foundations', and a possible scenario for this episode of destruction was offered (Putnam 2007, 103). However, there is no evidence to support the occurrence of a catastrophic conflagration in the excavations records for Building 6. The site diary and the grid trench notebooks are silent regarding the case for the fire, the context records include no entries for burnt materials and cracked stones. Conceivably some of the Ham stone blocks that were recovered from the building were made conspicuous by a natural ferruginous content (K. Hayward *pers. comm.*, BU100DEW0361) that might have been mistaken for fire-scorching (Fig. 7.3). The presence of 'mainly red' Ham stone blocks within the internal rubble of Building 6 was recorded without further comment in the grid trench notebook for N99 (BU100DEW0053, 19). To reiterate, there is no evidence for the destruction of the temple by fire, a confusion that requires explanation. The answer is to be found in the records of Building 2 the north-west end of which (Rooms 31, 32 and 32a) was being excavated simultaneously with Building 6. The exposed Rooms of Building 2 were characterised by a spread of charred material probably derived

Figure 7.3 A slab of ferruginous Ham Stone. The red colouration is natural, but it was interpreted as fire-reddening by the excavation team in the 1970s. Photograph: R3397.

from associated hearths, kilns and ovens. Building 2 also supplied the evidence for fire-cracked flint foundation material from a possible malting floor in Room 39 (Chapter 6). Some of the archaeological characteristics of Building 2 appear to have been transposed to Building 6, no doubt in a genuine attempt by Bill Putnam to do justice to the Dewlish project by bringing it to publication whilst his health was in terminal decline.

PIT-SHAFT O100

Situated north-west of Building 6 in grid square O100 but overlapping into adjacent squares, was a pit-shaft approximately 4m deep that had been cut into the natural chalk within 10m of Building 2. In plan, the mouth of the pit was *c.* 2.2m in diameter

SE   NW

(a)

(b)

3(c)

(c)

(e)

(d)

(g)

F1

F2

Stone (unspecified type)

Mortar

Plaster

0   1m

Figure 7.4   East-facing section through the pit-shaft in grid trench O100. Jonathan Milward.

(BU100DEW0081, 4). Initially this feature was thought to be a well, but when it became clear that this was not the case, it was re-classified as a cold store, an unproven purpose. By reason of its notable depth, this feature is referred to here as a pit-shaft. Given the provision of grain drying facilities in Building 2 (Chapter 6), it seems possible that the pit was associated with the storage of agricultural produce such as grain although other interpretations may be considered. It was thought that the feature might have been wood lined but this suggestion remained unconfirmed (see Chapter 21).

Excavation of Pit-shaft O100 took place over two seasons, 1978 and 1979, and the boundary between these two episodes of investigation is apparent on Figure 7.4 upon which only the position of the upper three contexts was recorded. For this reason only a general description of the order and composition of the fills can be given.

The primary fill was a mass of chalky silts which were sectioned but not bottomed-out. Above the primary fill there were at least five major episodes of tipping from the direction of Building 2 (south-east). Much of this fill consisted of building rubble which included limestone and clay roof tiles, *pilae* (tile stacks) and flue fragments, Ham stone pieces and a significant bulk of painted wall/ceiling plaster that was estimated to total 1,750 pieces. In between the deposit of building material, domestic refuse including pottery and food waste represented by oyster and other seashells, was tipped into the pit in smaller quantities from the north-west, presumably from the kitchens of the *domus* (main house), Building 3. There was also limited, but intriguing

evidence of small-scale industrial activity in the form of a fragment of a crucible with a trace of bronze adhering to it, and a tuyere. Seager Smith (Chapter 15) has drawn attention to the amount of South East Dorset Orange Wiped Ware from pit-shaft O100 which argues in favour of it being open for tipping well into the fourth century, possibly as late as the early fifth century. Animal bones were also recovered (see Maltby and Clark, Chapter 18). Effectively, pit-shaft O100 was the equivalent of a Roman landfill site. No known samples were taken for analysis.

WALL FRAGMENTS OF THE WESTERN INTERSPACE

Between Building 2 and Building 4 (the bath house) 10 fragments of wall were identified. The most north-easterly group of four wall fragments (WF1 to 4 inclusive; Fig. 7.1) were described as being solidly built but robbed to foundation level. These four wall sections aligned to form a logical continuation of the corridor wall from grid square M2. The south-easterly end of this wall continued beneath Building 6 where, apparently, it terminated in a return towards the north-east in grid trench N98 as WF1.

Wall Fragment 6 was first thought to be a poorly built extension to Building 2 but this was not confirmed by excavation and it is probable that it represents part of an earlier structure along with WF7, 8, 9 and 10. Indeed, this group of fragments might be pertinent to reaching an understanding of Building 5 which will be described in relation to the bath house, Building 4, in Chapter 8 and further discussed in Chapter 21.

BUILDING 4 (THE BATH HOUSE, ROOMS 25–30), BUILDING 5 AND PIT-SHAFT P4

INTRODUCTION AND CONTEXT

Building 4, the bath house suite, stood at the at the south-west end of the north-west range of the villa complex (Figs. 3.4, 3.5 and 8.1). To date, the most thorough account of this building is contained in the sixth interim report of the Dewlish excavations which includes a well drafted plan and two photographs (Putnam 1975, 59–62). The introductory paragraphs of the report make it clear that the 'whole area of the baths had attracted stone robbing to a much greater degree than the rest of the villa [meaning the *domus*, Building 3] and consequently there was an absence of substantial pieces of stonework and other building materials'. It was also suggested that the site of the bath house had been 'cleared' during the 18th century excavations as recorded by Hutchins whose topographical description is a good fit with this part of the villa site (Putnam 1975, 59; see Chapter 1). The 1970s excavations revealed that the heated rooms of Building 4 had been destroyed down to their sub-floors.

Given these conditions, Bill Putnam found it difficult to be certain about the phasing of Building 4, asserting that from the available evidence, 'there were at least three and probably several more phases' to the baths (1975, 59). Critically, it seemed to be impossible to relate any of the perceived bath suite phases to the 'main' villa building, Rooms 1 to 24. However, the 1975 interim report pre-dates the final season of excavation of Building 4, which took place in 1979,

when previously undetected features were revealed that contradicted the original interpretation and phasing of the baths. Nonetheless, no revisions to the 1975 interim report were published.

REVISED CONSTRUCTION SEQUENCE OF THE BATH HOUSE SUITE

With reference to the updated evidence from the director's site diaries and other excavation records for 1979, it has been possible to present a revised construction sequence for Building 4 as a series of sub-phases of Phase 4 (late third to fourth centuries CE; Figs. 3.4 and 3.5). Critical to understanding the sub-phases of the bath house is the archaeology of a pit-shaft that was situated within grid trench P4. This feature requires discussion as an essential precursor to an analysis of the evidence from the bath house itself.

Pit-shaft P4

This was similar to the feature that was situated just to the north-west of Building 2 in grid trench O100 (Chapter 7, Fig. 7.4). In plan the pit measured *c.* 2m × 3m and reached 4.8m in depth (Putnam and Rainey 1976, 54). Unlike Pit-shaft O100, the P4 feature was not fully excavated but sectioned, only the eastern half having been removed. This needs to be considered when comparing the volume and nature of the finds that were recovered from each of the two pits.

The original purpose of Pit-shaft P4 remains undetermined but possibly it was a storage pit, although the excavation site diaries use the term 'cold store'. Upon conclusion of its primary purpose, the P4 pit-shaft became a repository for building rubble and other rubbish including a crucible (SFN 342, Biek, Chapter 17), a blow hole fragment (SFN 344; 343) and deposits of ash. The pattern of tipping episodes can be detected with reference to the section drawing, Figure 8.2. Principally, deposits into the pit-shaft were made from the south-east with ash layers being detected at depths lower than 2.0m (contexts 22, 23 and 24). The ash deposits probably originated from the hypocaust stoke holes of Building 4, but the recovery of a crucible from within the pit argues that the furnaces of small scale metallurgical activity offer an alternative source for this material. A number of animal bones were also recovered from these contexts have been examined by Maltby and Clark (Chapter 18). A sample of goose bone was submitted for radiocarbon dating (in 2019) from pit-shaft context P4 (23). This produced an approximate date range from the mid-third century to the first quarter of the fourth century CE (See Chapter 18 and Appendix 2).

Pottery from Pit-shaft P4 included fourth century forms such as South East Dorset Orange Wiped Ware (Seager Smith, Chapter 15) demonstrating that the pit was active as a tip at this time. This would not have been possible if the north-west wall of Room 30 had been continuous because it would have been built across the upper fills of Pit-shaft P4 thus sealing it from further deposits. However, the site plan, Figure 8.1, reveals that the wall in question was not excavated along its entire length and that there is no evidence that it was ever a continuous structure. Therefore, it is possible that Pit-shaft P4 remained accessible for the deposition of rubbish into the late fourth and early fifth centuries.

SUB-PHASES OF BUILDING 4

Based upon the available evidence, four sub-phases of the villa's bath house are suggested.

Sub-phase (i)

Figures 8.1 and 8.3 show two further pits arranged along the south-west wall of Building 4. The most southerly of these pits measured *c.* 2.8m in diameter and extended to 0.8m in depth. This pit was filled with layers of ashy and charcoal rich materials, but it was partially sealed by the south-east wall of Room 30 and also by the south-west wall of the bath house (contexts 4, 7, 8b,10b, 11b and 12b). It is therefore certain that this ash pit pre-dates all of the known components of Building 4 and therefore it must belong to an earlier arrangement of buildings in the immediate vicinity which might have included the remains of Building 5, the features of which were observed in grid trenches O2 and N2. These remains comprised a floor of *opus signinum* set upon a foundation of heavy rubble that included fragments of a tile arch. It was suggested that this surface might have provided the base for a (destroyed) mosaic pavement (BU100DEW0006, 122). These features were potentially associated with a section of wall that was observed in grid trench N2 coded as WF10 (Fig. 7.1). Interpretation of these spatially associated remains is fraught with uncertainties but arguably there is sufficient evidence to reinforce the case for the presence of Building 5 to the south-east of Building 4 with, perhaps, the former being an earlier version of the latter.

Sub-phase (ii)

This comprised a rectilinear structure c. 10.00m long × 7.3m wide that included rooms 27, 28 and 29 which together formed a suite of baths. In its original form this building was not attached to either the south-west or north-west ranges of the villa. The presence of Pit-shaft P4 and an unexplored pit that was discovered beneath the floors of Room 25 (grid trench M3) potentially determined the parameters within which Building 4 could be constructed, for the encroachment of load-bearing walls upon these pit fills would have precipitated subsidence (Fig. 8.1). The excavator stated that the P4 pit-shaft had been filled prior to the construction of the bath house (Putnam 1976, 54) but the presence of late pottery within the upper fills argues to the contrary.

In this sub-phase Building 4 had wall strengthening buttresses added to the north-west and south-east

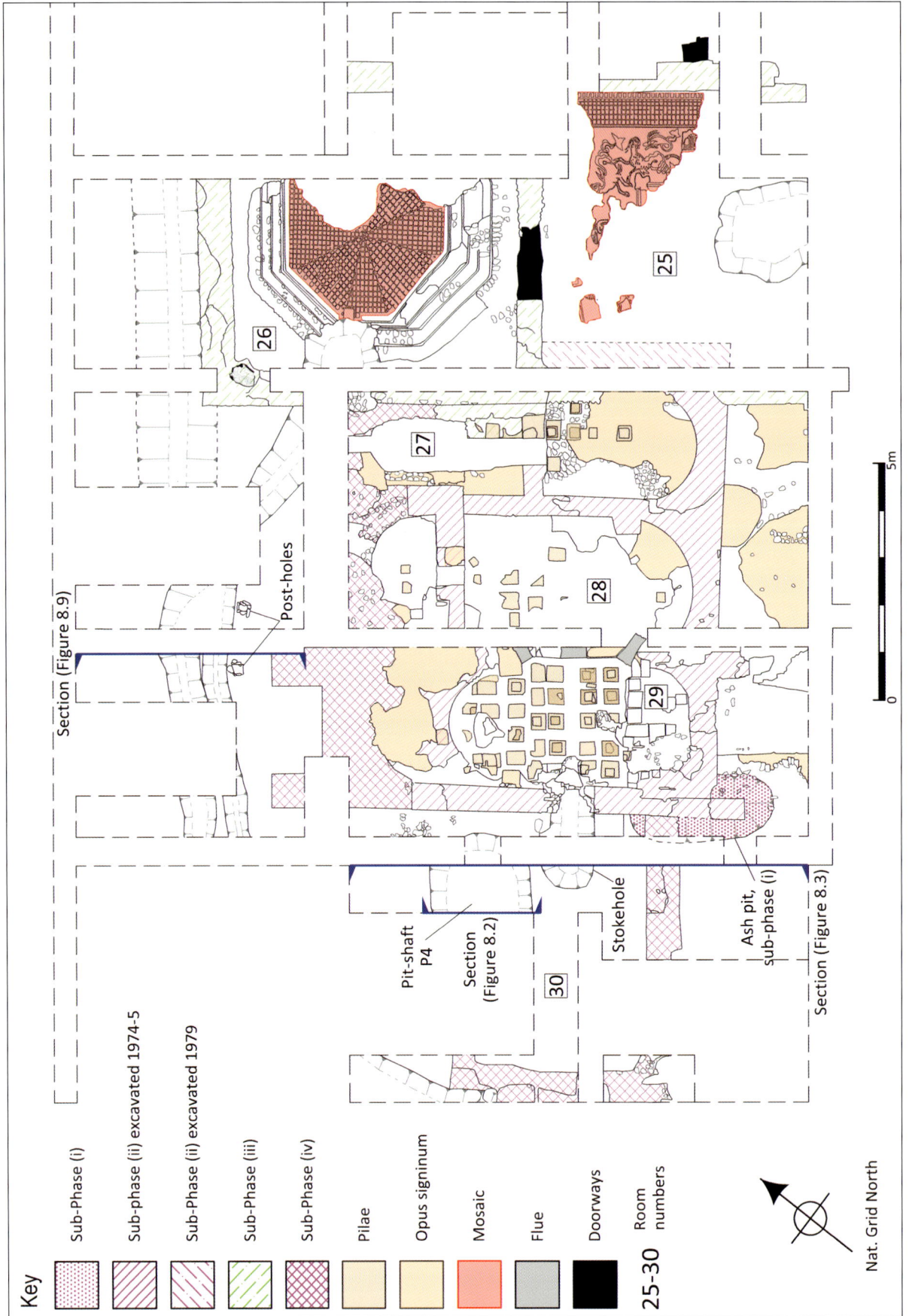

Figure 8.1   Phased plan of Building 4, the bath house.

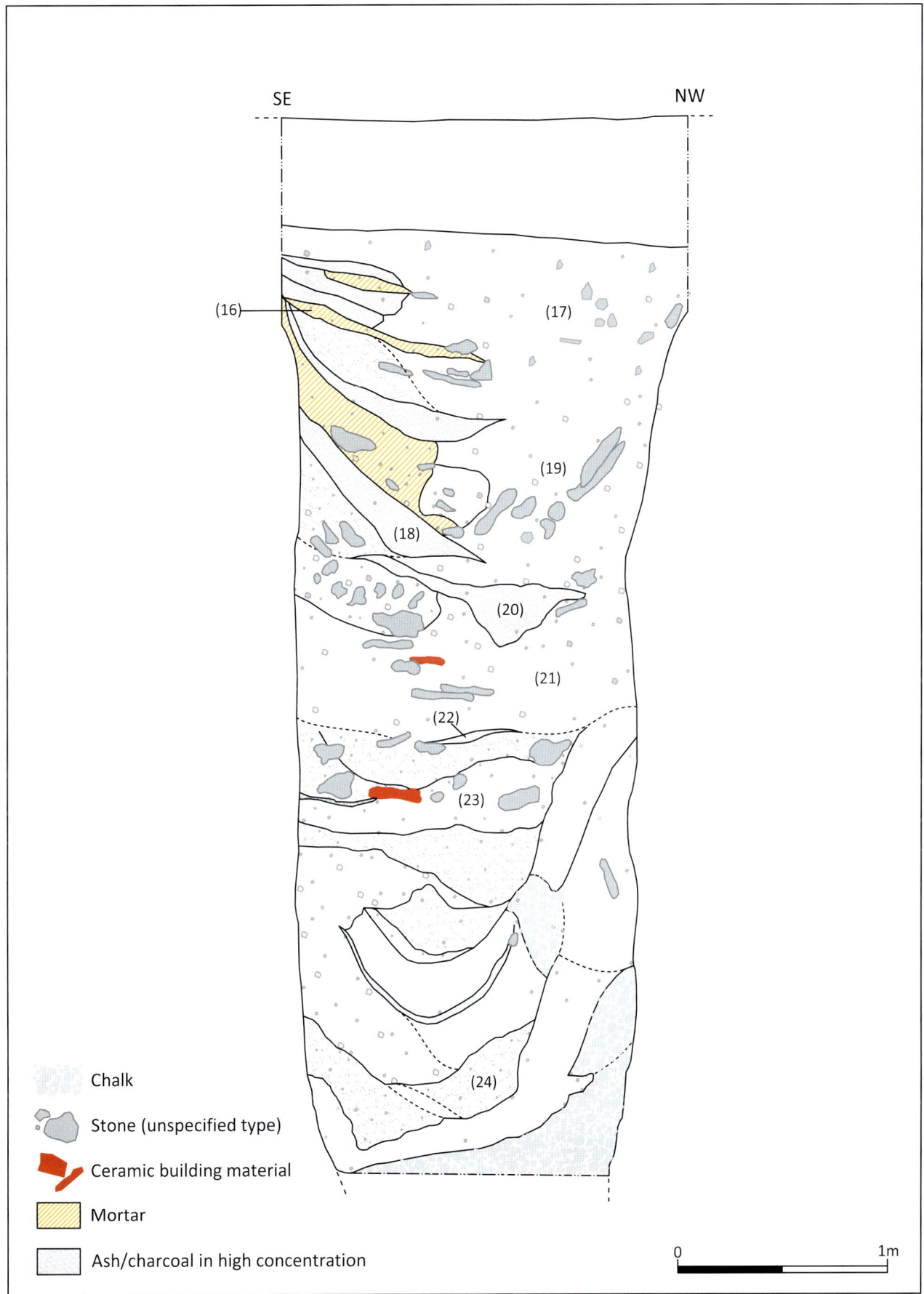

SE

NW

(16)

(17)

(19)

(18)

(20)

(21)

(22)

(23)

(24)

Chalk

Stone (unspecified type)

Ceramic building material

Mortar

Ash/charcoal in high concentration

0   1m

Figure 8.2   North-east facing section through the P4 pit-shaft.

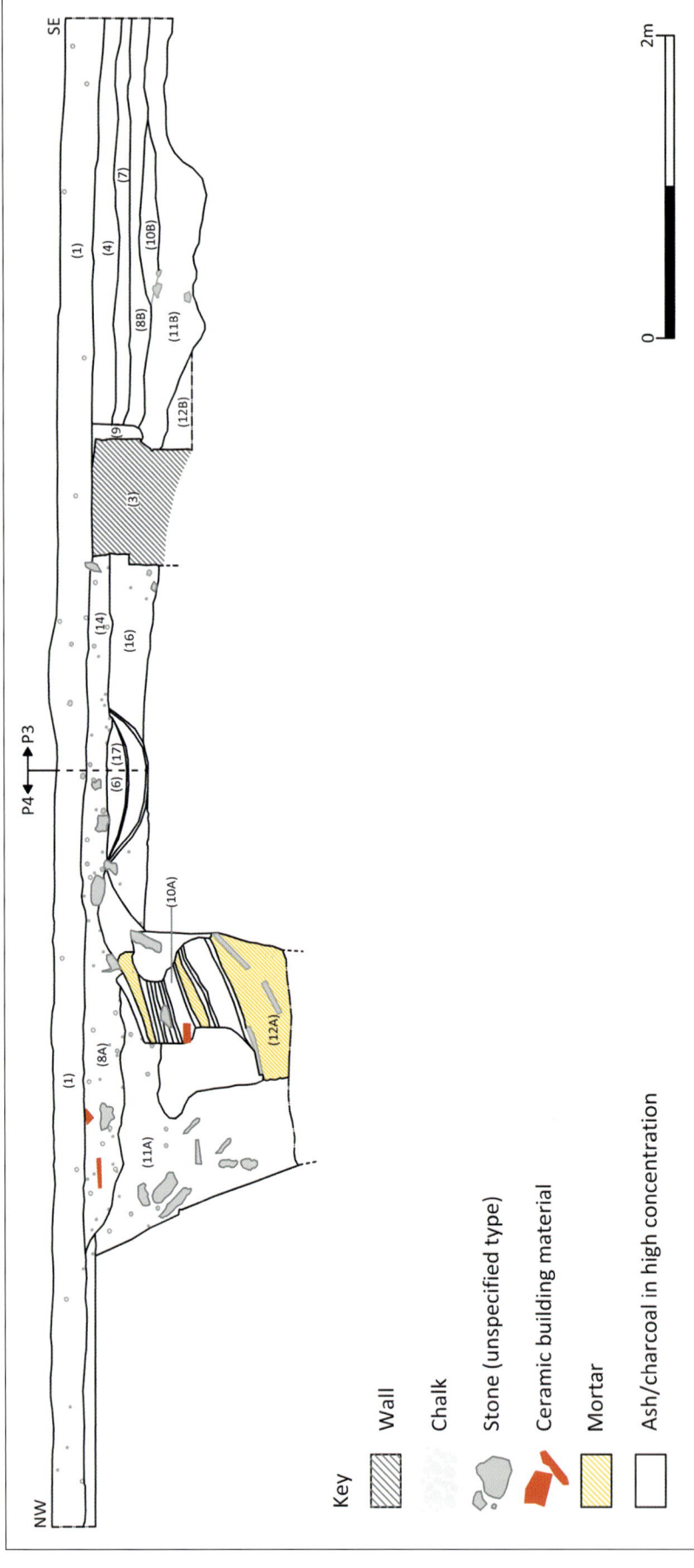

Figure 8.3 South-west facing section through Room 30 and its associated features.

Key

Wall

Chalk

Stone (unspecified type)

Ceramic building material

Mortar

Ash/charcoal in high concentration

Figure 8.4   A clay voussoir from Room 28. Photograph R3337.

Figure 8.5   The arrangement of *pilae* stacks set upon large clay tiles in Room 29. Photograph: R3342.

elevations suggesting that it was provided with a vaulted roof made rigid by hollow voussoirs of clay, examples of which were recovered from the site (e.g. Fig. 8.4). The ovoid Room 29 had a hypocaust that was supplied with hot air direct from the stokehole that was located centrally in the south-west wall of the building (Fig. 8.1). This room must have been the *caldarium* (hot bath), the floor of which was carried upon *pilae* (tile stacks) set upon a tegula base tile

cast within a matrix of flint and mortar (Fig. 8.5). The north-eastern foundation wall of Room 29 was pierced by three ducts through which the hot air passed to the under-floor space of Room 28. This floor was supported by pillars of similar type to those of Room 29 but lacked the tegula tile at the bottom of the stack. The fact that this room was not heated directly from a stokehole suggests that it was the *tepidarium* (warm bath). For reasons that are not

Figure 8.6   Impressions of Romano-British hobnail boots set in *opus signinum* in Room 28. Photograph: R3336.

clear, Room 28 was provided with an apse at the south-east end only, the opposite end being square in plan. The apse might represent the location of a plunge bath (Fig. 8.1).

There was no facility for the supply of heated air to Room 27 in this sub-phase and so it seems likely that this room was the *frigidarium* (cold bath). Stone-robbing and ploughing removed much of the useful structural evidence for Rooms 28–9 and whilst it is possible that the *frigidarium* included a cold-plunge bath, the only clue that this might have been the case was the discovery of a section of clay drain which cut a buttress that projected into the west corner of grid square M2 (BU100DEW0006, 117; Fig 1.4). Building 5 to the south-east of Room 27 might have acted as the *apodyterium* (changing room) during this sub-phase.

Water supply to the baths was indicated by the presence of two 0.15m square-sectioned post-holes set *c.* 1.1m apart and parallel to the north-west wall of Building 4 (Fig. 8.1). These post-holes probably mark the position of a raised conduit that delivered water to the baths via a sluice-operated spur from

an aqueduct that approached from the north-west (see Chapter 1).

Sub-phase (iii)

During this sub-phase the bath house block was extended to the north providing new apsidal ends to Rooms 27 and 28 with an additional semi-circular space at the north-west end of Room 29. It was probably at this time that the decision was made to heat Room 27, perhaps as a *laconicum* (dry sweating room) as suggested by Putnam (1975, 59). Thus, a stokehole was constructed through the north-west wall with a flue that passed through the newly erected apse and continued beneath the earlier antechamber south-eastwards to Room 27 which was now provided with a pillared hypocaust of a different build to those provided for Rooms 28 and 29 (Putnam 1975, 59).

The north-west apse that was added to Room 28 was heated; the remains of two pillars of its hypocaust survived and a vent was cut through the earlier north-west wall to provide an indirect source of warm air from the hypocaust chamber of Room 28 via a vent that was let into the original north-west wall of sub-phase (ii) (Fig. 8.1). The re-arranging of the sub-floor and *pilae* of Room 28 required the application of fresh mortar during which process the impressions of a Euro size 43 (UK 9) hobnail boot had been used to compact the mix (Fig. 8.6). The apsidal extension to the *caldarium*, Room 29, seems also to have been heated. In its original form, Room 29 was the only bath house chamber with a double apse. The new north-western extension required that the arc of the original apse was demolished and replaced by a similar structure approximately 2m further distant, and new hypocaust pillars were set up within the enlarged space thus created.

It is possible that Room 30 was added to the south-west wall of Building 4 during this sub-phase although it might have been a feature of sub-phase (ii). In reality, it was not a room but a demarcated service area for the *praefurnium* (stoke hole) which probably included ash disposal (Pit-shaft P4) and fuel storage facilities. The walls of Room 30 also provided a screen for the furnace chamber against the prevailing south-westerly winds.

Sub-phase (iv)

This sub-phase represents a major remodelling of the bath house. An *apodyterium* (Room 25) and a cold plunge bath (Room 26) were constructed at the north-east end of Building 4, a development programme that required the demolition of the north-east wall of the pre-existing phase of Building 4, the evidence for which was derived from the final and unpublished season of excavations in 1979. These facilities were constructed over the line of the demolished north-east wall, the foundations of which were concealed by a mosaic floor (see Cosh, Chapter 12). The north-west wall of the new *apodyterium* contained an opening, probably arched by a series of clay voussoirs that led into the chamber that contained a cold plunge bath or *frigidarium*. This north-eastward extension to the bath house left just a passage ('room' 12a) between it and the north-west wall of the *domus*, Building 3 (the common wall of Rooms 21 and 22). Effectively, but not in fact, this integrated Building 4 with the *domus* for the first time and adjustments were made to the north-west end

of the corridor (Room 12) that would have included a flight of steps and a doorway that provided access to Room 25, the *apodyterium* (Fig. 3.4).

The Room 26 cold plunge bath was octagonal in shape, the north-eastern third of which was later destroyed as a consequence of stone robbing, antiquarian excavation or possibly tree root damage. The bath achieved 1.1m in depth and *c.* 4.0m in width with a white, tessellated floor. Set into the floor, on the north-west side was a single clay tile that marked the position of a drainage pipe. The course of this outlet pipe was delineated by a curvilinear robber trench that ran west through to south passing the north-west end of the bath house and, on its course southwards, clipping the west corner of *praefurnium* building, Room 30 (Fig. 8.1). A cluster of lead fragments associated with this feature suggests that this was the constituent material of the outlet pipe itself (see Chapter 17). The plunge bath was not sheer-sided but made up of three or four steps with treads and risers of Kimmeridge shale (Fig. 8.7). The bath was not placed centrally within Room 26 and in fact it was not a regular octagon. To the north-west, the gap between the bath's perimeter and the room wall was just 0.6m. To the south-east, adjacent to the opening to Room 25, the floor space was larger but there was evidence that this area had been expanded over a period of time by at least two re-linings of the tank that reduced its volume on each occasion, thus causing the asymmetrical floor plan (Fig. 8.8). These developments would have required that the floor and wall of the plunge bath were replaced on each occasion. Around the perimeter of the bath no mosaic pavement survived except in the west corner, where a fragment of decoration survived within a niche that was probably intended to house a statuette (Fig. 8.1).

The *apodyterium*, Room 25, was found to have a sequence of at least two floors and a sub-floor. The sub-floor consisted of building rubble or hard core that served to fill a pit of unknown purpose that was situated at the south-east end of grid trench M3. Site photographs show that the stratigraphy of the M3 trench reached *c.* 0.75m in depth and that the inter-relationship of features and finds was complex. The rubble fill of M3 was overlain by a layer of mortar that provided the foundation for a

Figure 8.7 The Room 26 octagonal cold plunge bath facing south-west. The floor of the bath has been damaged on the north-east side, possibly by tree roots and/or eighteenth-century excavation of this part of the site. Photograph: R3305.

mosaic. This first Room 25 mosaic was dated to after 353 CE on the basis of its similarity with the mosaic in Room 11 of the *domus*, Building 3 (Cosh, Chapter 12). However, the rubble-filled under-floor was not stable, and subsidence caused the mosaic to sink, perhaps within 5–10 years after it had been laid. In order to rectify this problem, the depressions in the mosaic were made good and a second mosaic was laid immediately above the first. Putnam and Rainey ascribed a tentative date for the second mosaic as 370–80 CE (1975, 57) which would not be at odds with the dates for the late pottery from the P4 pit-shaft in the *praefurnium* service area, Room 30.

BUILDING 4 CONSTRUCTION PHASES: DISCUSSION

The overall chronological sequence for the four identifiable construction episodes of Building 4 are difficult to define with precision because sub-phase (i) received scant attention during the 1969–79 excavations, consequently it has been little understood. Pottery is useful for dating the P4 pit-shaft but elsewhere on the bath house site ceramic recovery was limited. The dates of fragments of window glass confirm the testament of the pottery

Figure 8.8 The Room 26 octagonal cold plunge bath showing a succession of linings. Photograph: R3313.

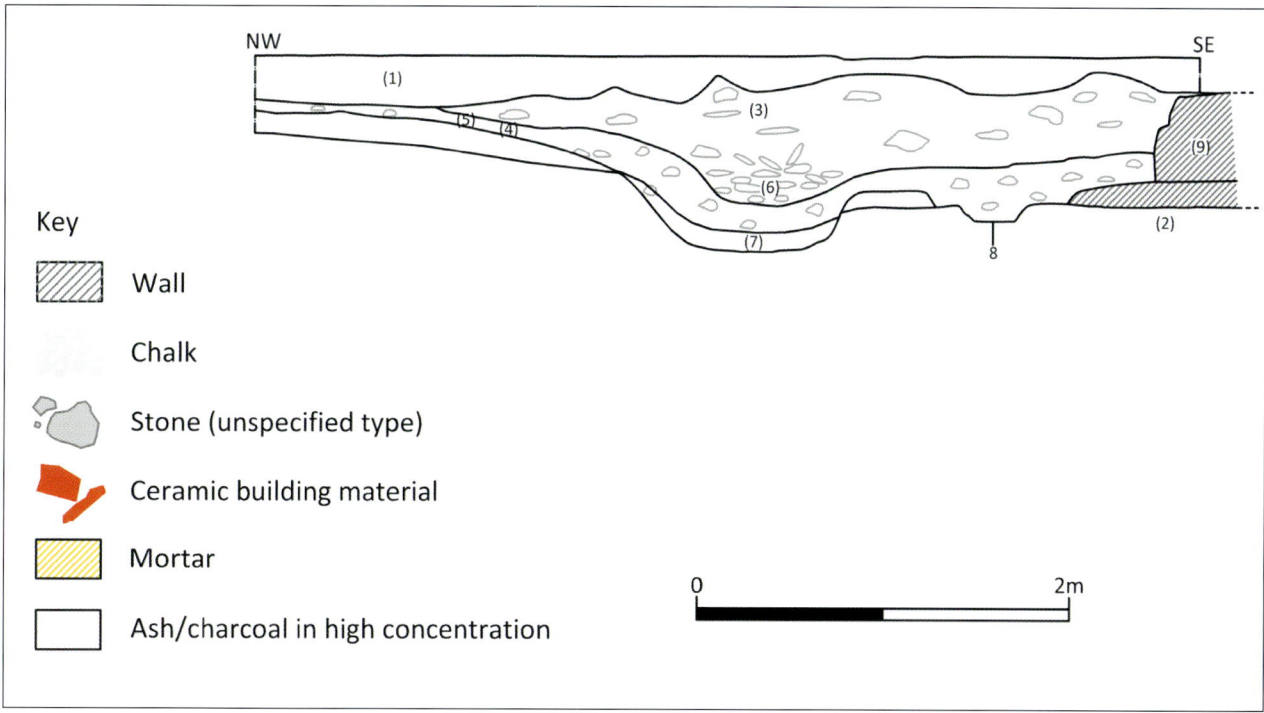

Figure 8.9   South-west facing section through grid trench O5 (Trial Trench I) showing the course of the waste water pipe trench from the Room 26 cold plunge bath (fills 6 and 7) and one of two post-holes (context 8) that probably served as part of the water delivery sub-structure (BU100DEW0075, 14). Jonathan Milward.

(Allen, Chapter 14). Eight coins were recovered but none of these was from a sealed context; for guidance, as a group they date from the late third to the late fourth centuries which is an indicative date range for the development of Building 4 throughout its sub-phases. This is a relatively tight time frame, but it is probable that there was overlap between some of the constructional elements of these sub-phases. The existing evidence from the site is insufficient to make an unequivocal distinction between sub-phases (iii) and (iv).

Resolution of some of the uncertainties between the phases of Building 4 might have been achieved if more time had been devoted to the excavation of the foul water outlet pipe from the cold plunge bath, Room 26. Three trial trenches through this pipe trench were cut in grid trench O5 but of these just one useful section was drawn, and this is shown as a blue line on Figure 8.1 and reproduced as Figure 8.9. The original record is contained within the grid notebook coded as

BU100DEW0075. The section drawing shows that the pipe trench was open when a number of limestone roof tiles were displaced from the bath house roof. This probably happened when the trench had been re-opened in search of lead for re-processing when the bath house suite had ceased to function: after sub-phase (iv). It is a snapshot of the information that was potentially retrievable from this feature, but it is also indicative that evidence of construction phases of the bath house was sealed within the pipe trench at the time of installation of the plumbing for Room 26.

The final addition to the bath house was a supplementary buttress that was built to reinforce the east corner of Room 25 (the *apodyterium*) possibly because it continued to suffer from the episodes of subsidence noted in sub-phase (iv). It is suggested that this episode of construction occurred in Phase 7 of the villa's development. Discussion of the interface between Building 4 and Building 3 may be found in chapters 9 and 21.

9

THE NORTH-WEST RANGE: BUILDING 3 (ROOMS 1 TO 24)

INTRODUCTION AND CONTEXT

The principal component of the north-west range of the villa was the *domus* or main house (Building 3). Within this construct, Bill Putnam identified 31 rooms (numbers 1–30, including 23 and 23a) that represented two principal phases of development. This vision of the *domus* included the bath house, Building 4, as an integral feature (Putnam 2007, 97). The current Dewlish research project (PEP2) has included a reassessment of the evidence from the site with the result that five broad construction phases have been identified within Building 3. What has emerged from this reassessment is a recognition of a more complex pattern of building development that includes a foundation building (Phase 2), an early appendage (Phase 3), the later addition of peripheral heated rooms with other aggrandising modifications (Phase 5), and two later but chronologically distinct extensions (Phases 6 and 7). In the revised interpretation, the bath house has been identified as a separate structure: Building 4 (see Chapter 8 below, and Figs. 3.4, 3.5 and 9.1).

The key to understanding the development of Building 3 is an awareness of its topography. The builders needed to cope with a slope from north-east to south-west with a second uphill gradient to the north-west. Two recorded levels illustrate the nature of the problem: the mosaic pavement in Room 1 was calculated as being 78.24m aOD whilst the upper mosaic floor in Room 25, the apodyterium of Building 4, was recorded as being 75.86m aOD. Between these two points, a distance of c. 30.0m, the difference in level from north-east to south-west was 2.38m. The builders' response to this dilemma was to construct a level building platform that included demolition debris, (probably from the demolished Building 1, Phase 1), upon which to sink the wall foundations of the domus, the greater depth of platform material being at the downhill south-west end. These ground works and re-used materials were the cause of considerable consternation throughout the course of the excavation of Building 3.

For Phases 2 and 3, this chapter will describe the origin and development of Building 3 room by room from north-east to south-west in accord with the progress of the excavation programme, although it is recognised that the Putnam room numbering sequence applies more strictly to the final phases of the building from the mid-fourth century onwards. Where inconsistences occur, these will be highlighted at the appropriate point in the text.

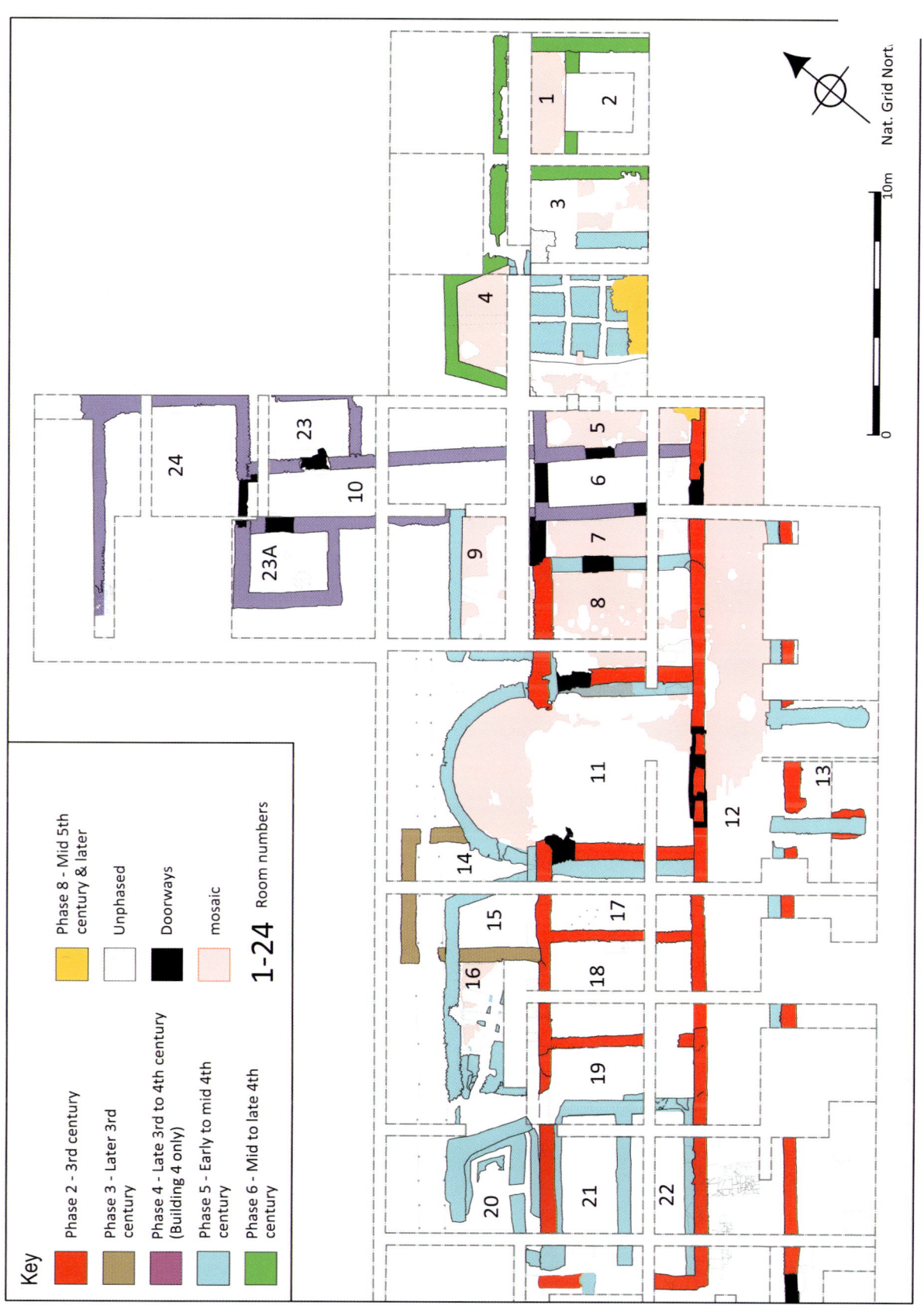

Figure 9.1 Detail of phased plan: Building 3. Jonathan Milward.

Key

Phase 2 - 3rd century

Phase 3 - Later 3rd century

Phase 4 - Late 3rd to 4th century (Building 4 only)

Phase 5 - Early to mid 4th century

Phase 6 - Mid to late 4th century

Phase 8 - Mid 5th century & later

Unphased

Doorways

mosaic

1-24 Room numbers

Nat. Grid Nort.

0   10m

PHASE 2, THE THIRD CENTURY

In common with Building 2, Building 3 began as a row house measuring *c.* 28.5m north-east to south-west by 7.0m north-west to south-east, with a number of internal partition walls that demarcated its component rooms. The underlying building platform was of sufficient width to include the corridor (Room 12). One terminal end of Building 3 was represented by the north-east wall of Room 5 in grid trench C4 where it was obscured by a baulk between grid columns C and D. This baulk was only sampled, thus revealing few useful details as to the wall's construction although it almost certainly consisted of flints and lime mortar as elsewhere in this phase. The location of the south-west terminal end of Building 3 was recorded in detail: it was situated in grid trenches L3 and L4, limestone quoins having reinforced the west corner (BU100DEW0042, 49).

Room 5

This had a pit in the west corner of its final floor which contained a disturbed infant burial and signs of an earlier floor that was broken up at the time of the interment (Rohnbogner, Chapter 19).

Room 6

This had no evidence of a sub-floor but it was noted that its common wall with rooms 5 and 7 had straight line rather than bonded joints with the north-west perimeter wall of Building 3 at ground level. This observation led to the conclusion that these internal walls were not original features.

Rooms 7 and 8

These were described as having a flimsy partition wall between them. At the south-east end of grid trench E4 removal of the final floor of Room 7 uncovered a thick burnt layer with a hearth of heat-cracked clay roof tiles against the south-east wall. Room 8 had four pits and other surface blemishes cut into its floor on the south-east and south-west sides. Through these pits an earlier floor of white mortar could be seen. In response, Room 8 was sectioned on its north-east and north-west sides and this strategy revealed the stratigraphy of the earlier floors which included two ovens in burnt (sooty) areas below which a third floor was noted that lay on natural soil (possibly beneath the material of the building platform). The earlier floor of Room 8 included a pit in the south corner within which was another deposit of infant remains (Rohnbogner, Chapter 19). It was also noted that the original south-west wall, common with Room 11, had been demolished and replaced by a new wall adjacent to, and south-west of, the remains of the earlier wall which was sealed by the latest floor in the sequence along with three coins:

(i)	SF 115	Magnentius	350–3 CE
(ii)	SF 119	Constantius II	353–6 CE
(iii)	SF 121	Barbarous Radiate	270–90 CE

Overall, it seems probable that in Phase 2, Rooms 7, 8 and possibly Rooms 5 and 6, were part of a single unit of domestic occupation. Given the presence of hearths and the abundance of burnt material, it is likely that this group of rooms constituted, at least in part, a food preparation zone in the third century villa. No samples have survived for analysis.

Room 11

This was the axial room of Building 3 through all of its phases. During Phase 2, the north-west wall of the room was a straight east-west line, there was no apse, making the dimensions of the room 7.35m (north-east / south-west) by 6.1m (north-west / south-east). There was no earlier floor but a flint filled drain beneath the fourth century mosaic was observed although not recorded in detail. It might be represented by a scatter of flints that is visible in site photograph R 2528 (Fig. 9.2). This drain feature is the subject of further discussion in Chapter 21. The excavators formed the impression that the room was set out upon made ground, an observation that would be consistent with the presence of the building platform upon which Building 3 had been constructed (BU100DEW0006, 66).

Rooms 17 and 18

The floors of both Rooms 17 and 18 had been ploughed away, the only fragment of mosaic remaining being in the west corner of Room17.

Figure 9.2   Room 11 in Phase 5 looking north-east showing the apse mosaic and the earth and rubble bed upon which the panelled room mosaic was laid. This mosaic had been substantially destroyed prior to the 1969–79 excavations. Photograph: R2528.

However, earlier floors of trampled soil had survived in both rooms. The dividing wall between the two rooms had horizontal courses of flints-in-mortar over the earth fill of this area and it had deeper foundations at its south-east end where it descended into a depression (BU100DEW0006, 63). It was recorded that beneath the early floors was made ground (the building platform), similar in nature to that observed in Room 11.

Room 18 had a rectangular hearth against the approximate mid-point of its north-east wall (common with Room 17). The hearth comprised a stone slab, set into the floor and topped by clay tiles. Charred material and soot was spread over a wide area. Three pots were found to be set into the chalky mortar of the floor of the two rooms but the details are confused. All three pots are recorded as being from Room 17 but the site diary suggests that one of them might have been set into the floor

of Room 18 (BU100DEW0006, 65–6). These pots are considered to date from the third to fourth centuries (Seager Smith, Chapter 15), but probably to the third century in this instance. Room 17 was provided with a clay-tiled hearth in its south corner.

Two sections were dug to test the relative depths of the combined rooms. The foundation trench of the dividing wall between Rooms 15 and 17 was found to be deeper than expected, but this is unsurprising because it was an outside wall in Phase 2 and therefore load-bearing. Of greater significance, was a deep section through the south-east wall of Room 18 and into the corridor, Room 12. Here it was found that the wall foundations extended to 1.8m below floor level and that some 1.2m of rubble, including painted wall-plaster, had been added to raise the floors to the level of those of the rest of Building 3, a clear indicator of building platform construction.

Room 19

This room occupied the space that was described as an unquantified 'step down in level' between grid columns J and K as the excavation programme proceeded south-westwards. However, this was not the south-west terminal end of the building platform and another explanation for this feature must be sought. Unlike Rooms 17 and 18, Room 19 displayed no sign of an early floor, just shallow layers of 'rubble' followed by 'natural', although the usual phenomenon of made ground was encountered. Whilst removing the fill of the Room 19 floor space it was realised that the foundation courses of the common wall with Room 18 leaned towards the north-east by 20° off vertical, and also that it was tied into the north-west and south-east load bearing walls of the *domus*, thus suggesting that this wall was an original feature (BU100DEW0036, 10–11, context 6). The wall's foundations did not cut into the natural chalk and so it relied upon the rubble of the building platform for its stability: thus the integrity of wall 18/19 was seriously compromised causing it to lean. This provides the basis for understanding the development of the south-western end of Building 3 which in Phase 4 was occupied by a group of three rooms (20, 21 and 22) that hitherto have remained unexplained and these will be discussed within the context of Phase 4 below.

Room 12

This was the corridor that ran along the south-east side of Building 3. As a feature it could be traced as far south-west as Room 19, although it might have extended beyond that point during Phase 2 as suggested in Figure 9.1. Convincing evidence for this earlier phase of the corridor is circumstantial and relates to the excavation of the associated porch (Room 13) in 1979. Beneath the upper floor level of the porch was a smooth mortar surface that included flat stones. This surface passed beneath the fourth century mosaic floor of the corridor indicating that the porch was of at least two phases. The corridor also had the remains of two parallel south-east walls, the outer wall being the earlier of the two and this has been assigned to Phase 2 (Fig. 9.1).

Phase 2 summary

Phase 2 of Building 3 was represented by occupation floors throughout except Rooms 11, 19, 21 and 22, all of which received significant modification during the fourth century which accounts for the absence of evidence for their Phase 2 function. Most of the excavated rooms provided confirmation of the presence of the building platform upon which the *domus* had been constructed. Pottery and coin finds were consistent with a third century date for this phase.

PHASE 3, THE LATE THIRD CENTURY

Perrin (2002, 210) has observed that frequently recorded villa improvements were the addition of a corridor, the improvement (or provision) of an end reception room, the construction of baths, and the insertion of mosaics and hypocausts. A re-examination of the excavated evidence indicates that this is exactly what happened in the case of Building 3 at Dewlish which had a more complex construction history than previously thought. Enlargement and enhancement took place in a series of discrete building projects, presumably conditioned by the *ad hoc* availability of surplus funds for investment in the villa estate's building stock (see Chapter 21).

Room 14 (including Room 15)

The only identifiable development to Building 3 in Phase 3 was the addition of Room 14 on the north-west side (grid trenches G5 and H5). This new unit was almost square in plan measuring 5.1m (north-west to south-east) by 5.5m. Its walls were well founded, of sturdy lime mortar and flint construction, 0.5m wide on a base layer of 0.6m width. The Room 14 walls had been built against the original north-west wall of Building 3, therefore verifying that this room was an addition rather than an original feature. Plaster had been applied to the interior walls but the purpose of this room is not known. There was no hypocaust and the room's footprint and floor space were almost extirpated by the features of subsequent building projects. For this reason, there were no datable finds within sealed contexts and so assigning a date for Room 14 is challenging but it certainly pre-dates the Phase 5 Room 11 apse (see below) and therefore it is probable that it was a late third century development. After demolition, the foundations and floor of Room 14 were cut, at the north-west end, by a drainage trench that imposed a north-west limit on building extensions during Phase 5 and thereafter (Fig. 3.4).

Phase 3 summary

In this phase, Room 14 represented the sole addition to Building 3. The walls of the room betrayed no evidence of doors but it is likely that access to the room was gained from the corridor, Room 12, via Room 17. Room 14 was destroyed by, or during, Phase 5.

PHASE 5, EARLY TO MID-FOURTH CENTURY

For Building 3, Phase 5 represents various additions, modifications and refinements to the original layout of the *domus*. In describing these developments, the room numbering system has greater relevance but, where appropriate, the rooms have been grouped under common sub-headings if they share important characteristics and/or functions. The excavated evidence does not consistently demonstrate the precise sequence of construction but in cases where a possible order can be postulated a rationale is provided.

The hypocausts: Rooms 4, 9, 16 and 20

During the earlier years of the fourth century, four rooms were added to the periphery of Building 3, each with what was thought to be a hypocaust.

Room 20 with associated rooms 19, 21 and 22

These rooms comprised a spatial group that was encountered prior to the discovery of the bath house block (Building 4) in 1974. Rooms 21 and 22 had depth below ground level (they cut into the upper surface of the building platform), indicatively 2.54m below site TBM, the walls and floors being lined with a

screed of *opus signinum*. Thus, both rooms possessed tank-like properties and were first interpreted as being plunge-baths (Putnam, 1974, 89–90, fig. 8). In plan, Room 20 was a straight-sided apse that appeared to include a channelled hypocaust that was linked to Rooms 21 and 22 by a duct that was thought to be the means of heating the water within the putative baths (Figure 9.1). Problematically, the *opus signinum* surface rendering of Rooms 21 and 22 was not of sufficient thickness for baths, and there was no means by which water could be drained from the tanks for cleaning and maintenance. When the true bath house block was identified in the following year, 1975, the original interpretation of this group of rooms as baths was dropped but not revised.

An alternative hypothesis is that collectively, Rooms 20, 21 and 22 were central to the economic plan that underpinned the viability of the Dewlish villa estate. It has been argued in Chapter 6 that Room 39 (Building 2) was a malting kiln. By the end of the third century, or the beginning of the fourth century, Building 2 had been demolished which suggests that in the interest of economic viability, the malting facility needed to be replaced. Here it is proposed that the solution was to insert a new malting kiln at the south-western end of Building 3, where the building platform was at its deepest and an adequate depth could be achieved for the insertion of a malting floor and the circulation of warm air within the lined chambers of 'rooms' 21 and 22. The space known as Room 19 had no occupation floor of any phase because it functioned as the space from which the kiln building team was able to operate when the construction process was underway. Therefore, in Phase 5, Room 19 was not a room but merely an access portal through which excavated waste and rubble could be removed including any evidence of earlier floors. This process of digging and construction disturbance in Room 19 was probably responsible for the north-eastwards lean of the common wall with Room 18 (see Room 19, Phase 2 above).

It is likely that the construction of the Building 3 malting kiln was planned ahead of the destruction of the original malting facility in Building 2 and it probably continued to function throughout the fourth century and possibly later, after which time the warm air chambers were filled with demolition rubble from an unspecified area of the villa site. This rubble fill sealed a coin of Theodosius I, 388–95 CE (SFN 349) that rested on the surface of the *opus signinum* floor of 'room' 22. Allowing for continued circulation after the minting of the coin, it is possible that the kiln continued in operation into the early fifth century.

One unresolved problem regarding this group of rooms concerns the furnace for the kiln which should be associated with Room 20. The likely position of the stokehole was on the north-west side of the apse in grid trench L5, but this area had been destroyed by stone robbing, or ploughing, or antiquarian activity and no features could be recovered. To the north-east, a fragment of wall was recorded as lying between the apse and the west corner of Room 16 which possibly represented a portion of *praefurnium* wall, but the evidence is not conclusive, and the problem remains unresolved (Fig. 9.1).

Room 4

This was built against the north-east wall of the Phase 2 row building where it conformed to the line of the corridor (Room 12) which was probably extended north-eastwards to facilitate access to the new extension, but this could not be verified because the presence of a mature ash tree on the site of grid squares B3 and C3 prevented exploratory excavation in this area. North-westwards, Room 4 terminated as a straight-sided apse with walls of unequal length which suggests that it was a later addition (Fig. 9.3). Room 4 was an end reception room with mosaic pavements in the apse and in the principal chamber where only a fragment of the floor survived (Figs. 11.3 and 11.4 Cosh, Chapter 12) beneath which was a hypocaust. The position and nature of the south-east wall of the room was not determined because of the presence of the ash tree in the relevant grid squares.

A hypocaust occupied the whole of the sub-floor space of the principal chamber of Room 4 to a depth of 0.86m. It comprised six 'pillars' of flint and limestone rubble. Between the pillars were channels that had been blocked by flint and mortar debris that represented the collapsed vaulting which supported the base of the mosaic floor above. Vaulting of this type was also a feature of the hot air duct of the *praefurnium* that ran beneath the apse of Room 4. The interim report for 1971 asserted that the Room 4 hypocaust was a later addition to the room because the foundations of the walls lacked sufficient depth for it to be an original feature (Putnam 1972, 160). If this was the case then retro-fitting the hypocaust channels would have been a precarious task that probably precipitated a significant wall collapse at the south end of the north-west wall of Room 4. The collapsed wall section was made good with a replacement foundation of limestone roof tiles in herringbone order (Fig. 9.4).

Two hypocaust stoke holes were discovered. Principally, the excavation of Room 4 took place during the summer of 1971 and at this time a stoke hole and flue was observed to pass beneath the apse from the north-west. In 1972, a retrospective excavation of a 1m × 5m trial trench in grid square B5 was extended south-eastwards into the shared baulk with B4. This exercise attracted almost no comment in the site diary or in the context records, but a competent annotated sketch plan in the grid trench notebook (BU100DEW0357) records the presence of a second flue that provided access to the Room 4 hypocaust from a robbed area to the north-east. A photograph also records this feature and the interface between the north-facing wall of the Room 4 apse and the common north-west wall of Rooms 1 and 3 (Fig. 9.5). This evidence suggests that Rooms 3, 2, and 1 were added to the east side of Room 4 at a later date, at which point the original stokehole in grid squares B4/B5 became obstructed and a replacement was provided that ran beneath the floor of the straight-sided apse which was added to Room 4 at the same time (see below). Two coins (SFN 034 and 036; B14 context 17) that were sealed beneath the floor of Room 3 date this room and, by inference, the construction of the apse, to the middle years of the fourth century, effectively a Phase 6 addition to a Phase 5 room.

The mosaic floors aside, Room 4 was lavishly decorated as evidenced by the straight-sided apse where painted wall-plaster survived to a height of 0.38m above floor level (Figs. 9.6 and 9.7). Upon the

Figure 9.3   The chequer board floor of the Room 4 apse looking north. The tip of the ranging rod indicates the location of a pit. The internal base of the north-east wall retained residual painted plaster decoration. Photograph: R2418.

Figure 9.4   The Room 4 hypocaust looking east. The stretch of limestone tile wall in herringbone order forms one side of a channel that is bridged by a surviving fragment of mosaic floor. Photograph: R2412.

Figure 9.5   Trial trench showing a detail of the Room 4 apse and mosaic with the north-west wall of Room 3 attached. The Phase 5 (original) stokehole of the Room 4 hypocaust was revealed by the trench extension to the right (south-east). Photograph: R2511.

Room 4 has been regarded as a winter *triclinium* (dining room) because it was heated (Putnam 2007, 97–8), but the excavation diary states that there was little sign of soot-soiling or burning within the network of hypocaust channels (BU100DEW0006, 20–1). A similar observation was made regarding the stoke hole and duct that passed beneath the apse (Putnam 1971, 160). No detailed information is available regarding the frequency of use of the original hypocaust furnace situated to the north-east. On the strength of the available evidence, the Room 4 hypocaust system had been used sparingly.

Excavation of Room 4 did recover evidence of the 18th century excavations that were recorded by Hutchins (Chapter 1) in the form of clay tobacco pipe pieces. These are now lost and therefore not tightly dated but they are likely to be contemporary with the antiquarian activity of the 1740s and/or 1790s. In addition, Figure 9.8 shows two cuts (A and B) in the east-facing and south-facing excavation sections respectively. These cuts indicate the position of the 1970 evaluation trench that ran diagonally across Room 4. Figure 9.4 shows that the southern third of the hypocaust channel network had been dug away, and this might have been the result of medieval (or earlier) stone robbing. Alternatively, this feature is 18th century excavation disturbance for which Room 4 has convincing evidence.

floor of the apse, sealed by lumps of fallen wall-plaster, were fragments of window glass exclusively of fourth-century date (Allen, Chapter 14). The red and white chequer board mosaic floor of the apse was unheated, but the flue of the replacement hypocaust stoke hole, situated outside and to the north-west of the room, passed beneath its north-west/south-east axis and this is likely to have provided some incidental warmth to this area of the room. The apse floor was disturbed in the north-west corner by a square sectioned post pit which probably accommodated a timber roof prop towards the end of the villa's working life. The eventual collapse of the roof was attested by the presence of limestone pennant roof tiles and Ham stone ridge tiles that sealed all evidence of earlier activity within the apse.

Room 9 (with Room 7)

This was built against the north-west wall of the Phase 2 row house within the area defined by grid trenches E5 and E4. These two grid trenches were separated by the 1m wide site datum baulk the presence of which prevented excavation of the southern third of this room (Fig. 9.1).

Room 9 was a rectilinear room with a channelled hypocaust into which hot air was supplied from a stokehole at the west corner. In common with Room 4, and for similar reasons, this hypocaust was considered to be a secondary feature. The principal channel of the hypocaust ran diagonally across the room from the stoke hole flue to the east corner. There were at least four branch channels beneath a

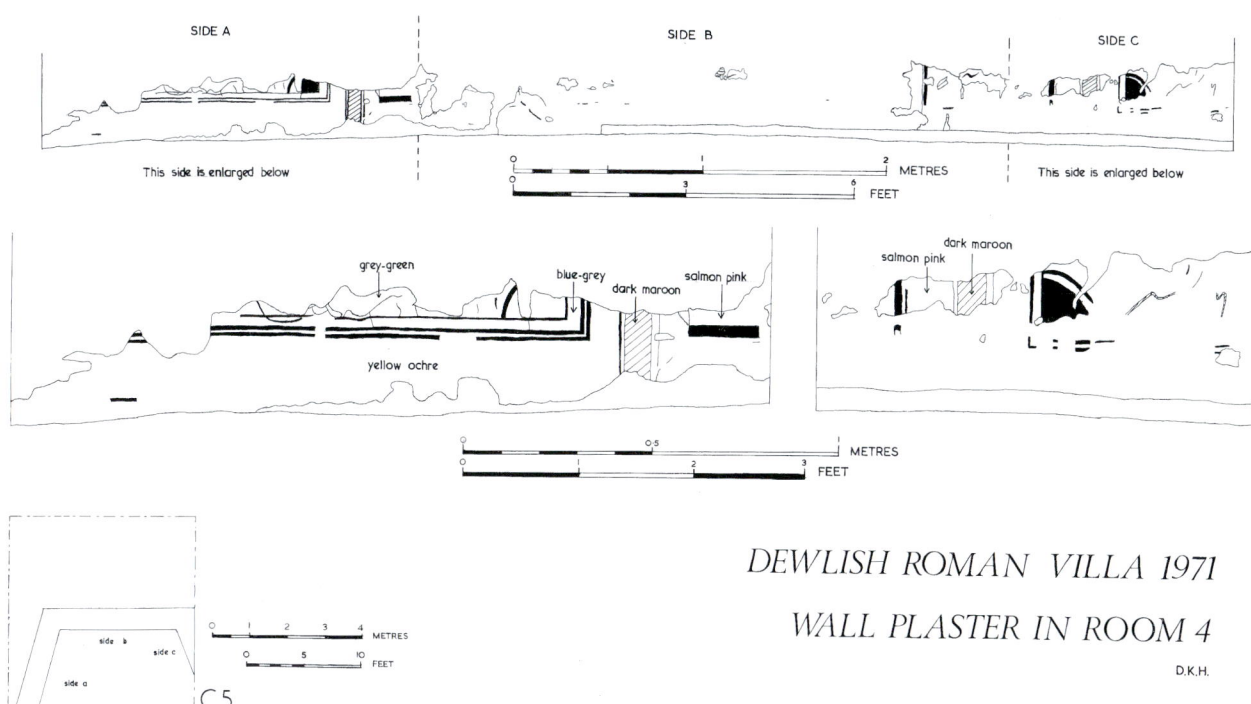

Figure 9.6   Scale drawing of the residual painted plaster in the Room 4 apse (Phase 6).

Figure 9.7   Painted wall-plaster from the north wall of the Room 4 apse. Photograph: R2427.

Figure 9.8   Room 4 hypocaust in grid trench C4 looking north-west. Two earlier excavation cuts (A and B) can be seen in section at the west corner and at the approximate mid-point of the north-west side of the trench. Photograph: R2413.

fragmentary mosaic floor of geometric design with a coarse red border. The channel bottoms, possibly lined with mortar (BU100DEW0018, 29), reached a depth of *c.* 0.95m, 0.15–0.2m deeper than the foundations of the room walls. In places (e.g. to the north), the channel walls had been reinforced by a herringbone arrangement of limestone roof tiles.

The fill of the hypocaust channels included painted plaster, presumably from the walls of the room (E5, context 14) above which a scatter of limestone roof tiles indicated the construction materials of the roof (E5 context 5). In contexts of deep rubble to the north-west of Room 9, and in the upper fills of the room itself, five coins were found (SFN 4, 7, 19, 20 and 28). None were recovered from secure contexts and their dates ranged from Constantinopolis 330–45 to Arcadius 388–402 CE (Gerrard, Chapter 13). Though unstratified, potentially, these coins indicate the time span within which Room 9 was used.

Access to Room 9 was gained via a connecting door to Room 7 and thereby to Rooms 6, 8, and the corridor, Room 12. Room 7 had a floor of coarse red tesserae with a broad white stripe 0.42m wide down the centre but missing from the north-west end of the room where the floor had been re-laid during the life of the villa (Fig. 12.6). As in the case of Room 40, Building 6, the walls had painted plaster surfaces that reached below floor level (BU100DEW006, 41), however Room 7 was probably functional rather than grand. Here and in Room 8, occupation layers were consistent with food preparation activity suggesting that Room 9 might have served as a *triclinium* as indicated by finds of fragments of stone table furniture within the confines of this space (Hayward, Chapter 10).

Rooms 16 and 15

In common with Room 9, Room 16 was built against

the north-west wall of the Phase 2 row house. It was sited adjacent to Rooms 18 and 19 and to the south-west of the Room 11 apse (Fig. 9.1). The wall foundations were of flint and mortar, the surviving quoins being of tufa (B100DEW0006, 49; grid trench H5, context 3) possibly derived from a demolished part of the bath house (Building 4). The room was heated by a channelled hypocaust which was considered to be a secondary feature as in the parallel cases of Rooms 4 and 9 (see above). Constructional features were similar too, including the use of limestone roof tiles set in herringbone fashion as a means of strengthening the hypocaust channel walls. The stoke hole was at the west outer corner of the room. The rubble fill of the hypocaust channels (grid H5, context 18) included fragments of red brick flue, Black Burnished ware sherds, ceiling moulding, lumps of painted plaster (maroon), animal bones and an unsealed coin of Constans, 345–8 CE (SFN 183). At 1.5m north-west of Room 16 was the course of a drainage trench that achieved 0.48m in depth and contained limestone tiles derived from roof collapse mixed with pieces of blue-green painted wall-plaster (grid trench J5, context 8).

To the north-west and north-east of the internal space were the remains of a mosaic floor with a coarse red tesserae border (Cosh, Chapter 12) which together with the painted wall-plaster suggest that Room 16 had been maintained in pleasing decorative order. No particular purpose can be assigned to the room and it might have been used as a general purpose space. Little evidence of doorways was preserved in Building 3 south-west of Room 11 but it is probable that access to Room 16 was by way of Room 17 via Room 15 which possibly acted as a vestibule although it had no surviving floor and it was not served by a continuation of the Room 16 hypocaust. The unusual feature of Room 15 is its north wall which is aligned c. 120° to the baseline of the site plan (Fig. 9.1). This suggests that it was initially intended to comprise part of a straight-sided apse in an earlier arrangement of this part of the villa, or that this unusual wall angle was a response to developments regarding the apse of Room 11 (see below).

ROOM 11, THE AXIAL HALL AND ASSOCIATED ROOMS 8, 7 AND 17 (WITH 12 AND 13)

Room 11

This was transformed during Phase 5. A semi-circular apse that measured 6.16m wide by 4.1m deep was added to the north-west elevation of Building 3. The wall of the apse was built upon deep foundations and its construction required the demolition of Room 14 of Phase 3 (Fig. 9.2). The apse was provided with a mosaic floor (Cosh, Chapter 12) and painted wall-plaster. Fragments of window glass were recovered but these were principally from the drainage ditch situated just to the north-west (Fig. 9.1), not from sealed contexts. Semi-circular apses do not accommodate large windows, but it is reasonable to infer from the presence of the window glass that fenestration was present, though perhaps in the form of lancet-type windows only, albeit of a romanesque style. A further clue to the presence of windows is suggested by the north wall of Rooms 15/16 (also Phase 5) which was constructed at an angle to the Room 11 apse, possibly to allow the final vestiges of daylight to fall upon the windows of this feature from the west.

Within the rectilinear main chamber of Room 11 other dramatic changes occurred. Significantly, the common walls with the adjoining Rooms 8 and 17 were replaced by new walls immediately to the south-west of the original structures (Fig. 9.1). These new walls were probably intended to provide a sound foundation for a roof lift, the original 'bungalow' height of Room 11 being elevated to provide a lofty hall-like room that would have created impact and enhanced the acoustics of the space, perhaps lighted by a clerestory. Usually regarded as the villa's summer *triclinium*, it is perhaps more likely that the impressive proportions of Room 11 identify it as being rebuilt as a grand reception room or audience chamber, designed to impress and to inspire awe. Such emotions would have been heightened by the quality and design of the mosaic floor of the main chamber that was installed at this time (Cosh, Chapter 12). The mosaic survived in a fragmentary state only but a single panel that depicts a leopard predating upon a Dorcas gazelle (Putnam and Rainey 1973, 86) illustrates the quality of the mosaicist's art in this room. There was no hypocaust but a fire-darkened area in the eastern segment of the apse mosaic hints at the occasional use of braziers. Putnam and Rainey (1973, 81) suggest that damage to the Room 11 mosaic was the consequence of tree root damage as implied by Hutchins in his 18th century account of the villa site (1873, 607). However, this is a speculative assertion for there is no visual evidence of tree root damage on the site photographs and plans (see, for example, Fig. 9.2). For further comment, see Chapter 21.

Access to and from Room 11 was carefully choreographed. The remains of connecting doorways to Rooms 17 and 8 could be traced in the north and west corners of the main chamber from where stone thresholds had been plundered. Room 17 was re-floored with what must have been an elegant wave patterned mosaic with a border of terracotta tesserae that would have befitted a waiting room for guests of status. This floor was probably installed when the new common wall with Room 11 was built. Room 17 could also have acted as a service area and access route from the corridor (Room 12) and possibly from Room 16 also.

Room 8

If Room 11 was used as a dining room as well a reception hall then the door to Room 8 would have been pivotal to its purpose. In this phase Room 8 was provided with a simple and functional clay tesserae floor that covered the stub of the earlier common wall with Room 11, thus demonstrating that the Room 8 floor is contemporary with the Phase 5 enhancements to its neighbour. Figure 12.8 reveals that the floor of Room 8 was discoloured by patches of burnt material, perhaps betraying the location of braziers or ovens in a kitchen. Pottery sherds were found on this floor and also that of Room 7 (Putnam 1972, 157, 160). When the Room 8 clay floor was lifted a coin of Constantius II (SFN 119) was found to be sealed beneath it. The date of this coin (353–6 CE) has been used to suggest a *terminus post quem* for the Room 8 floor and therefore for the mosaic floor in Room 11 with which it is stratigraphically

associated. However, Figure 12.8 also shows that the floor of Room 8 had been repaired on several occasions and that therefore the coin of Constantius II could have been intrusive. Two other coins were found in the same context (F4 context 5). One of these was a coin of Magnentius (350–3 CE; SFN 115), the other a barbarous radiate (270–90 CE; SFN 121). Taking into account the various permutations of the coin evidence, then a mid-fourth century date for the upgrade to Rooms 8 and 11 is reasonable. A similar date might be ascribed to Room 7 which had a floor like that of Room 8 but with a single white central band to provide contrast with the red-brown tesserae of the rest of the floor. The northern half of the floor had been taken up and re-laid at an unspecifiable date. Room 7 was linked to Room 8 by a door in their common wall and had access portals to Room 9, Room 6 and thereby to the corridor, Room 12 (Fig. 9.1).

The location of Room 11 as being axial to Building 3 raises the next discussion point. The status of the room required that it should impress from within and without. To this end its views south-east to the courtyard across the corridor and through the porch (Room 13) needed to inspire, whilst for those approaching the building from the south-east, messages of wealth and power would need to be conveyed. Consequently, the refurbishment of Room 11 included a rebuild of the porch which seems to have been enlarged, perhaps to widen the view, and a revamp of the corridor, the outer (south-eastern) wall of which was replaced by a new wall built just within the line of the original (Fig. 9.1). These refurbishments might have been essential maintenance projects, but they would have acted as enhanced status signals too. In keeping with this, the access portal from the corridor into Room 11 was upgraded and this new feature has been described as 'a timber-framed division of some complexity which may have included folding doors'. Apparently, the timber framework had been burnt and the ashes contained a number of nails and spikes up to 0.24m in length (Putnam and Rainey 1973, 81). The hint that folding doors might have been used is not substantiated by the available evidence; the site plan and the grid trench notebook are both incomplete and the single site photograph is unhelpful (Fig. 9.9). The impression given though is that the Room

Figure 9.9   Room 11 doorway threshold that opened onto the corridor (Room 12) with its key pattern mosaic. Photograph: R2538.

11 entrance feature was a tripartite doorway with flanking fenestration, hinged upon wooden jambs, with a wider central portal relative to the ones to the left and right.

The early fourth century aggrandisement of Room 11 was indicative of the developing wealth and status of its owners: it was a symbol of local power and prestige.

Room 12

The corridor, Room 12 was modified by the construction of a replacement south-east wall, a refinement that might have been associated with the addition of a colonnade (see Putnam, 2007) even though it was less substantial than the original wall. In connection with this, fallen masonry in grid trench K2 included the remains of a Romanesque arch c. 2.75m in diameter made from lime mortar with occasional tegula tiles and flints accompanied by pieces of moulded

plaster (BU100DEW0034, 14) which might represent a surviving feature from a colonnade (Fig. 9.10; Putnam and Rainey 1976, 54). Overall, one complete dwarf column and the fragments of six others were recovered from across the site and the pieces of three of these were found in close proximity to Room 12 (BU100DEW0358) although they could represent debris from the Building 6 'temple' porch (see for example, Fig. 9.11). Nonetheless, these finds suggest the former presence of a corridor colonnade and if this feature was added during this phase (5), then it would explain the need to replace the Phase 2 corridor wall which was found to have been leaning outwards and to the south-east. Alternatively, the K2 arch head might have capped the known access point to the corridor that was situated in grid trench L2 (Fig. 9.1).

At the end of Phase 5 with all adjustments taken into account, Room 12 measured 2.7m in width (Putnam 1972, 81) and with a maximum length of c. 55m (see Phase 6, Rooms 1, 2 and 3 below).

Figure 9.10   Fallen door or arcade arch excavated in grid trench K2 in 1975. Photograph: R3416.

Room 13

The porch, Room 13, was included in the Phase 5 enhancements, it being important to the impact created as the visitor approached Room 11, the principal reception chamber. The upgrade involved the destruction of the earlier porch floor which was replaced by a mortar surface, the top layer of which consisted of chippings derived from tesserae making, perhaps a preparation for a lost mosaic floor. Both of the side walls of the porch were plastered on the inside (BU100DEW0006, 40).

Phase 5 summary

The evidence from the 1969–79 excavations demonstrates that Phase 5 was a period of enlargement and refinement of Building 3 with hypocaust heating being retro-fitted to new building extensions. Each of these additional rooms required access either directly or indirectly from the corridor, Room 12, and this demanded the insertion of a number of access passages: Rooms 5, 7, 17 and the Room 15 vestibule. These access channels explain the somewhat cramped layout of rooms that is self-evident upon the plan of the final layout of Building 3. The balance of evidence indicates that Room 20 was not a hypocaust but part of a malting kiln that is likely to have been a planned replacement for a

similar feature that had been a cardinal component of the demolished Building 2 and which was vital to the economic sustainability of the villa estate.

PHASE 6, MID- TO LATE FOURTH CENTURY

Rooms 1, 2 and 3

These comprised a group of rooms that was built against the north-east wall of Room 4. In this position rooms 1 to 3 were not situated upon the earth and rubble building platform of the Phase 3 *domus*, and the Romano-British construction team needed to cope with natural uphill slopes of the land towards the north-west and the north-east. Although not stated in the site records, it appears that preparatory groundworks for the building of these rooms included the cutting of a terrace into the natural chalk in order to achieve floor levels that were consistent with the rest of Building 3. This strategy was confirmed by the excavation of the north-west wall of Room 1 that had deep foundations, with the natural ground outside being higher than the floor level inside the building.

The footprint of the extension was pushed beyond the north-west wall of the adjacent Room 4, thus

Figure 9.11   A reworked section of a dwarf column re-purposed as a quoin from a straight-sided apse, probably from the west corner of Room 20. The fragment was not found in a sealed context. Photograph: Bill Putnam (not coded).

blocking and sealing a hypocaust stokehole in grid square B5 in the process. A replacement stokehole was provided to the north of Room 4, the flue of which was surmounted by a straight-sided apse that was constructed simultaneously (see above and Fig. 9.1). The site of grid trenches A2, A3, B2, B3, C2 and C3 were occupied by a mature ash tree that prevented excavation in this area. Consequently, it was not possible to determine the location of the south-east wall of Room 2 which might have conformed to the line of the corridor, Room 12. If such was the case, then the corridor would have been extended north-eastwards to provide access to the new suite of rooms. This is the most convincing interpretation because it would explain the purpose of Room 3 as an access passage. Alternatively, Rooms 2 and 3 extended south-eastwards beyond the line of the corridor and in this eventuality the roof ridge might have been aligned north-west/south-east with gabled elevations at each of these bearings. In this model, the south-east elevation could have constituted an interface with the unexcavated and previously unsuspected north-east range of the villa (see Chapter 21).

The internal features of Rooms 1, 2 and 3 had been severely damaged by stone robbing activities. In particular, the partition wall between Rooms 1 and 2 had been much reduced and Room 2 had no surviving trace of a floor. Room 1 retained a fragmentary mosaic set upon a deep bed of yellow sand that alternated with layers of crushed brick (BU100DEW0006, 20). No plaster remained on the stub walls of Rooms 1 and 2, but lumps of plaster that had been affixed to a reed / hazel under-surface and painted in yellow and white stripes lay directly on the mosaic floor of Room 1. Neither room was heated by a hypocaust.

Room 3 had a mosaic pavement that was set upon a base of puddled chalk topped by a thin layer of mortar (BU100DEW0006, 20) that sealed coins of Helena (337–41 CE) and another of the House of Constantine (345–8 CE). These coins provide a *terminus post quem* for the floor and, by implication, the whole of the north-eastern extension comprising Rooms 1, 2 and 3, plus the contemporary north-west apse of Room 4. The mosaic design featured a central decorative band 0.48m wide set between margins that might have been reserved for furniture. If so, then the consequent narrowing of the thoroughfare was probably responsible for wear and tear to the decorated panel that had been frugally repaired by the application of puddled chalk.

Pieces of painted wall-plaster were recovered from the interior of Room 3 and these, together with the mosaic floor, suggest that it was a space of more than functional status, but probably not a bedroom (*cubiculum*) as first suggested (Putnam 2007, 98). It is more likely that Room 3 was an access passage for Rooms 1 and 2 although how this arrangement would have worked is unclear because the position of interconnecting doorways was not identified.

Phase 6 summary

This phase continued the development of Building 3 but it was limited to the north-east wing extension and some adjustments that were made to the south-west end of the corridor (Room 12) which continued as far as Room 19 before the mosaic floor gave way to a shallow flight of steps that provided access down to the *apodyterium* of the bath house (Room 26) via a paved passage (Room 12a). The north-east end of the corridor was probably modified too but this area remained unexcavated during the 1969–1979 field project.

PHASE 7, LATE FOURTH CENTURY – EARLY FIFTH CENTURY

Room 6 and the Annexe (collectively Rooms 10, 23, 23A and 24)

In Phase 2 it was suggested that Rooms 5, 6, 7 and 8 were originally combined as a one room unit. By, and during, Phase 7 this single unit space had been partitioned to form four separate rooms. To recap, the internal walls between rooms 5 to 8 were not tied into the north-west and south-east walls of Building 3 but abutted against them, a strong indicator that they were later features (see Phase 2 above).

Room 6 was a creation of Phase 7 and its purpose was to provide a hub for movement around the north-east end of Building 3 and beyond. Room 6 was the only room at the north-east end of the building that is known to have had a door that opened onto the Room 12 corridor, whilst the internal west wall of Room 6 gave access to Rooms 7 and 8 which had functioned as a kitchen space in earlier phases and which probably retained a food preparation role in Phase 7. Room 6 represents an early example of a cross passage. The new east wall of Room 6 had an access door to Room 5, the north-east returns of which were finished in rounded plaster moulding, presumably to ease the passage of persons carrying wide serving trays or the wheeling of the equivalent of a trolley.

In recognition of its importance as a heavily used pathway, Room 6 was enhanced by a mosaic pavement of geometric design, and to facilitate movement between them, the surface of the new floor was set to the same level as that of the corridor, Room 12 (BU100DEW0006, 120). In contrast, the floors of Rooms 5, 7 and 8 were surfaced from coarse terracotta cubes and were not of uniform level. As a further indicator of its importance, the walls of Room 6 were finished with painted plaster.

The north-west end of Room 6 was occupied by a single doorway that measured a generous 1.6m in width and which probably originated as an access door to the north-west exterior of the Building 3 in Phase 2. This door gave entry into a passage, Room 10, which aligned towards site grid north, but *ca* 5° west of that bearing. The north-east and south-west walls of Room 6 shared this irregular characteristic, an unusual deviation for Dewlish villa (Fig. 9.1).

Room 10

This room had not been disturbed since the building had collapsed (Putnam 1972, 157). First in the order of the disintegration sequence was the limestone pennant tile roof, followed by the flints and mortar fabric of the walls together with pieces of the painted plaster finish. The nature of the floor of this passage was difficult to determine, but an area of puddled chalk was noted in the south corner, and elsewhere there were patches of mortar (BU100DEW0006, 18 and 59). Thick occupation layers were observed in the corners including soot, pottery and bones. The south-west wall of the room had been built against the north-east wall of Room 9 thus obscuring the limestone quoins of the latter. Consequently, Room 9 was considered to be earlier than Room 10.

Room 24

This room at the north-west end of Room 10, presented as a rhombus in plan rather than a rectangle, a characteristic that it shared with the associated Rooms 6 and 10. It was the largest of the component rooms of the Annexe with a door at the centre of the south-east wall. The surviving walls of Room 10 were not fully excavated but the visible lower courses comprised flint and lime mortar with quoins of limestone and clunch (BU100DEW0016). It was recorded that some of the visible lengths of the Room 24 walls had a levelling course of limestone roof tiles (BU100DEW0015) but site photographs suggest that some of its wall sections acted as sills for squared timbers, perhaps an indication that all or part of the building was timber framed (Fig. 9.12). Similar timber frame features have been observed at Brading, Isle of Wight (Cunliffe 2013, 91–3, 97 and figs. 5.13 and 5.14) and were also noted locally in Structure 5198 (Trench E) at Fordington Bottom, Dorchester (Barnes 1997, 219).

The internal walls of Room 24 had an unpainted plaster finish and there was an 'earth floor' (effectively chalk) that had been discoloured by numerous areas of burning (Putnam 1974, 89), possibly the location of ovens or braziers. Unfortunately, this floor had been severely damaged by ploughing (Putnam 2007, 99). Nonetheless, tight in the east corner of Room 24, a large rope-rimmed jar of SEDOWW fabric perforated with small holes, had survived (Putnam 2007, 89). The jar had been lying on its side with its opening towards the north-east wall, partially set in mortar and mounted upon stone slabs. The chalk around the pot had been heat reddened (BU100DEW0015, 9). The SEDOWW jar can be ascribed to the late fourth century or possibly the early fifth century (Seager Smith, Fig. 15.7, Chapter 15). Perforated pottery of this type was also recovered from Structure 5198 at Fordington Bottom (Morris 1997, 234 fig. 108) which suggests that it was broadly contemporary with Room 24 at Dewlish. Fallen limestone pennant roof tiles and Ham stone ridge tiles bore witness to the nature of the roof here and in other parts of the Annexe.

Rooms 23 and 23A

These flanked the Room 10 passage at its point of juncture with Room 24 (grid trenches D6 to 8 and E6 to 8). These two rooms were not of identical size or proportion and they might not have been contemporary structures although they both conformed to the rhomboid plan that was shared with the other units in this linked room group. Both rooms had been decorated with painted wall and ceiling plaster. The wall-plaster stopped short of soil level, an indication that the floors of both rooms were boarded, and they both had doors that opened from the access passage. In the case of the Room 23 door, the north-east side of the opening exhibited the curved plaster returns that were noted on the Rooms 6 and 5 portal (see above). The doorway into Room 23A was too damaged to reveal any trace of similar features (BU100DEW0014, 20; BU100DEW0015, 23).

Figure 9.12　The Annexe: Room 24. The north-east wall (right) is characterised by a rectilinear central depression along its entire length suggesting that the wall provided a sill for a timber-framed superstructure. Photograph: R2771.

Phase / summary

Phase 7 of the villa is represented by the rooms of the Annexe: 10, 23, 23A and 24 with the associated Room 6. This phase is characterised by the irregular ground plan of its component parts and the hint that some of the walls were sills that supported timber box frames. It is likely that Room 24 was a kitchen that replaced the original provision that was located in the space later taken up by Rooms 5, 6, 7 and 8. This could have been in response to concerns regarding fire risk: the new cooking / baking facility was isolated from the rest of the accommodation in Building 3. Estate kitchens required pantry and administrative space therefore it is probable that Rooms 23 and 23A were added for these purposes.

Table 9.1   Roman coins recovered from sealed contexts in the Building 3 Annexe

Small Find Number	Grid code & context number	Room number	Emperor/Imperial House	Date CE	Remarks
014	D6 (03)	10	House of Theodosius	388–402	Sealed by the rubble of collapsed roof
017	D6 (12)	23	Constantius II	353–5	Sealed by collapsed roof within a matrix of brown earth
156	D6 (14)	23	House of Theodosius	388–402	Sealed by rubble of collapsed roof within an occupation layer of dark soil
158	D6 (14)	23	House of Theodosius	388–402	Sealed by rubble of collapsed roof within an occupation layer of dark soil
167	D6 (14)	23	House of Theodosius	388–402	Sealed by rubble of collapsed roof within an occupation layer of dark soil
171	D6 (14)	23	House of Theodosius	388–402	Sealed by rubble of collapsed roof within an occupation layer of dark soil
174	D6 (16)	10	Arcadius	388–402	Sealed by rubble of collapsed roof within an occupation layer of dark soil
182	D6 (14)	23	Theodosius I	388–95	Sealed by rubble of collapsed roof within an occupation layer of dark soil
187	D6 (14)	23	House of Theodosius	388–402	Sealed by rubble of collapsed roof within an occupation layer of dark soil
189	D6 (14)	23	House of Theodosius	388–402	Sealed by rubble of collapsed roof within an occupation layer of dark soil
195	D7 (8)	24	House of Constantine	350–60	Sealed in occupation layer of dark sooty soil
201	D7 (8)	24	House of Constantine	350–60	Sealed in occupation layer of dark sooty soil
202	D7 (8)	24	House of Theodosius	388–402	Sealed in occupation layer of dark sooty soil

The dining areas of the villa were likely to have been in one or more of Rooms 4, 9, 11 and 16 and the distance from kitchen to *triclinium* was of sufficient distance for hot food to become cold. Consequently, Room 10 was probably constructed as a closed passage in response to this problem. In this role, Room 10 would have been subject to frequent and heavy use which no doubt explains why there was little evidence of a surviving floor.

The Annexe rooms produced some intriguing dating evidence. In addition to the SEDOWW rope-rimmed storage jar, 13 coins were found in sealed contexts within the Annexe rooms and these all date to the late fourth/early fifth centuries (Table 9.1). These finds indicate that the Annexe and Room 6 together constituted the last developmental phase of the excavated buildings of the Dewlish villa.

PHASE 8: SUB-ROMAN AND LATER

Beyond Phase 7, there are indications that at least some of the villa's constituent buildings and rooms continued to function but not necessarily in accord with their original purposes. The evidence for continued occupation at a time of decline will be discussed in Chapter 21.

THE WORKED STONE BUILDING MATERIALS AND FURNISHINGS

by Kevin Hayward

INTRODUCTION

The extant 210 examples (710kg) of worked stone retained from the 1969–79 excavations at Dewlish, necessitated a considered stylistic and functional review of the foundation rubblestone construction, architectural embellishment, paving and roofing in this multi-phase villa complex. As well as this, the sheer variety of stone types, and the quality of preservation prompted more detailed appraisal by form and geological type of its key individual structural components. A dearth of studies into the geological fabric of Roman villas is repeated throughout the province, compounded further by a near absence of surviving Roman quarries and epigraphy making a geo-material investigation all the more necessary.

This chapter begins to redress the balance by introducing a set of tried and tested geological techniques that will enhance understanding of the stone building materials that were used in the villa's construction. This will involve focusing upon what types of deposits the stones were extracted from and to identify, where possible, their geological source, since Dewlish Roman villa is in a region that had no pre-existing tradition of working these materials. Furthermore, the morphology and function of selected architectural components such as roofing and paving, have received little or no coverage in previous accounts of the villa complexes. Comment too will be made on the portable stone objects

associated with the crafts in the Dewlish villa complex, e.g. quern, whetstone and stone mortar. The hugely impressive mosaic pavements have already been published (Neal and Cosh 2004; Cosh, Chapter 12), but the sheer number of mosaic fragments and tesserae made an in-depth petrological study untenable given the time restraints imposed by this project and would be better served by an individual piece of research.

EXISTING STUDIES

The geological succession of Dorset is one of the most intensively studied and well-understood regions in the world (Reid 1899; Arkell 1947) and continues to attract considerable interest and research in the light of the coastal section having been elevated to World Heritage Status (Barton *et al* 2011). With the notable exception of Halstock (Bellamy, 1993, 107–111) which lies far to the west, very little is known about the geological character and source of the worked stone used to construct, roof, pave and embellish the large number of villas from this county. A review of the Roman quarrying industry (Putnam 2007) introduces us to some of the key rock types (Ham Hill; Portland stone; Chilmark stone) from Dorset villas but little else, whilst substantive texts on Dorset stone (Thomas 2008, 7–8) and Portland stone (Hackman 2014, 11–12) merely skim the surface with regard to Roman exploitation and use. The key reference by J.H Williams (1971b) on building materials and construction styles in the "South-West" region (Gloucestershire, Somerset, South Wales, Oxfordshire, and Avon), completely omits Dorset whilst existing sculptural catalogues for this region such as Wessex (Cunliffe and Fulford 1982) and the Cotswolds (Henig 1993) employ hand specimen terms such as *"oolitic limestone"*. This is a generic name to describe a whole range of similar looking Middle Jurassic freestones not only from Dorset and Somerset but from along their entire outcrop.

Recent provincial petrological studies have begun to redress the balance. Our understanding of whetstone (Allen 2014) and quern stone source materials (Shaffrey and Roe 2011; Green 2017) has improved immeasurably, whilst the source of the earliest examples of limestone sculpture in southern England including Bath and Fishbourne (Hayward 2009; 2015) is now much clearer. In each case, comparative hand and thin section analysis has begun to distinguish many different outcrop sites.

With individual villas, geological expertise has only recently focused on sites along the Solent including Brading (Gale 2013; Tasker *et al* 2011; Hayward 2013), Shapwick (Hayward 2010), Fishbourne (Allen and Fulford 2004; Hayward 2009), Chedworth in the Cotswolds (Hayward in prep.) and to the north of this present study region in Berkshire and Wiltshire (Hayward in prep.). Dorset lags behind here too. Dewlish will be the first of a succession of villas such as Dinnington and Shapwick (Hayward in prep.), where a more considered earth science approach will tackle the geological character and source of its construction materials.

LOCAL AND REGIONAL GEOLOGICAL SETTING

The underlying geology of Dewlish villa and its immediate environs is defined as Upper Chalk. Reid (1899, 13) described it as being '... *in the steep scarp east of the village ...in massive chalk* (with) *few flints, over which is chalk with grey flints.*' Progressively older outcrops of Middle Chalk, Lower Chalk, Upper Greensand and Gault lie 2–4km to the north of the village, whilst the Chalk outcrops themselves are in places capped by sandy Reading Beds and Pleistocene Gravels to the south and east of the village, where springs can be located at their juncture (Reid 1899, 47–48).

In terms of stone suitable for walling rubble, a ready supply of hard nodular flint is located in the immediate area, which is borne out the by their extensive use in the masonry walling foundations throughout Dewlish villa (Putnam 2007, 103–5), whilst locally quarried tufa, though not proven (Putnam, 2007, 106), probably comes from the springs nearby at the juncture with the Reading Beds.

Better quality freestone for ashlar, quoin and architectural embellishment is much harder to come by. The nearest suitable freestone are outcrops of Portland-Purbeck (Upwey limestone) which lie some 10km to the south-west, but these are often of an inferior standard compared to the more open textured even grained Portland Whit Bed from the Isle of Portland itself (20km distant).

Fortunately, Dewlish lies within easy reach of most of the other high quality limestone, roofing slates, paving stones and tesserae stone materials in the Dorset-Somerset area. This is because of its proximity to Dorchester (*Durnovaria*) not only the key population centre for this region but an important transport hub too, with roads radiating out north-west to Ilchester, west to Exeter, south to Portland and the Coast and east to Shapwick, the latter running just 3km to the south of the Dewlish villa. Not only does this permit access to the stone from the Cotswold escarpment, the Isle of Purbeck, Hamdon Hill, and Vale of Wardour, but further out to the Fosse Way and thence access to much harder Palaeozoic sandstones from South Wales and the Forest of Dean suitable for portable quern and whetstone manufacture.

METHODOLOGY

Hand Specimen Analysis

The macroscopic character of each of the 210 examples of worked stone from the villa site were

Table 10.1   List of worked stone samples (DEW1–10) from Dewlish Villa and outcrop material (DEW11) that underwent thin-section analysis

Thin Section	Context	Small Finds Number	Function
DEW1			Shaft unstratified oolitic limestone
DEW2	E4 (21)		Plain shaft open-textured oolitic limestone
DEW3	O99 (5)	800	Architectural element open-textured oolitic limestone
DEW4	O100 (6)	851	Stone mortar shelly limestone
DEW5			Plain shaft open-textured oolitic limestone
DEW6	D3 (3)	271	Sideboard element with star design oolitic limestone
DEW7	N6 (2)		Sideboard element flattened cornice element oolitic limestone
DEW8			Plinth greensand
DEW9			Trough – red shelly limestone
DEW10			Voussoir block Tufa
DEW11	Outcrop		Upper Portland stone Portesham Hill, Dorset

examined using a hand lens (Gowland ×10) and long arm stereo-microscope and their texture, colour (Munsell Color Group 1975) and inclusions were recorded. Treatment of dilute Hydrochloric acid determined whether or not the rock had a calcareous composition. With the roofing tile, consultation with Trev Haysom determined whether all the material was coming from the Isle of Purbeck or from additional source regions.

Thin Section Preparation and Analysis

Eleven sub-samples (Table 10.1) underwent thin-section preparation using the rock preparation facilities at the School of Geography, Archaeology and Environmental Sciences at the University of Reading. The application of a 1kg mason's hammer and sharp chisel to each building material sub-sample ensured that a small fresh fabric surface was exposed. A 20mm long × 15mm thick sample was large enough to undergo thin-section preparation and analysis. Although destructive, this method ensured that the maximum amount of information could be obtained from the smallest possible sample size thus fulfilling the museums and archives sampling policies.

The procedural implications and sample preparation can be referred to in Hayward (2009). However, each sample was additionally embedded in coloured araldite resin (CY1301) which was necessary for two reasons. First, the process of embedding with the addition of a hardener (HY951) strengthened particularly the soft mortar samples. Second, the

addition of a green colouring agent (BW1034) during this process highlighted the pore spaces in the sample enabling the overall porosity to be determined. Staining is a necessary process (Adams and Mackenzie 1998) during the production of the more lime rich thin sections. It picks out the variability in colour between ferroan and non-ferroan calcite as well as dolomite, with the addition of Alizarin Red C and Potassium Hexocynoferrate.

This high-resolution petrographic approach enabled, each 30-micron thick slice of stone to be viewed under the polarising microscope at magnifications greater than × 400 (Leica DMLP). Thin sections can help distinguish between different types of calcite grains, minerals, cements and microfossils. Finally, a series of photomicrographs of the worked stone types (Leica DFC 320 Digital Camera) were produced to illustrate the different materials being used.

PETROLOGICAL OVERVIEW AND RESULTS

Hand specimen and thin-section comparative petrological analysis of 183 items (666kg) of sculptural, decorative and plain architectural elements, ashlar, paving, and roofing from Dewlish villa has made it possible to identify nine rock types from some of which it has been possible to establish a geological source. The proportions of each rock type identified from the construction, flooring and roofing debris of the villa and associated structures including its drainage as well its architectural and

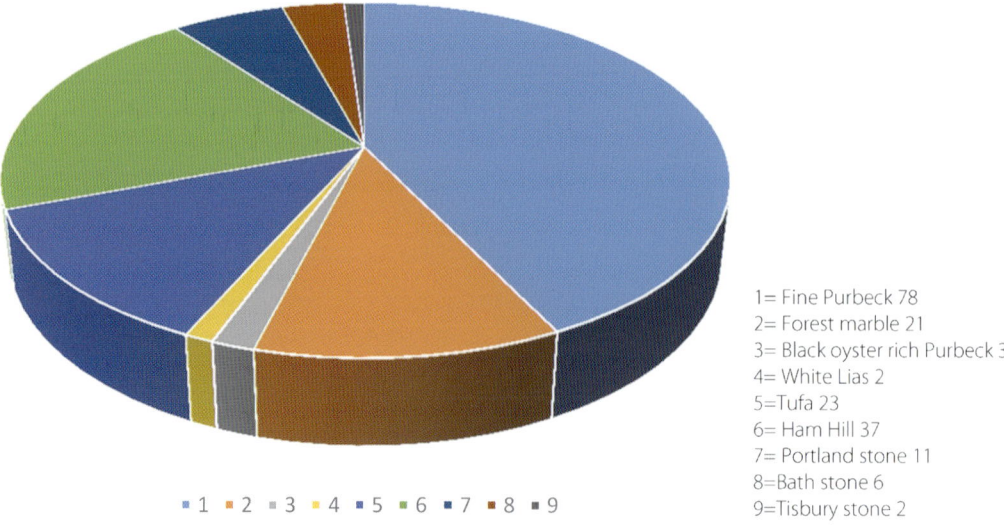

1= Fine Purbeck 78
2= Forest marble 21
3= Black oyster rich Purbeck 3
4= White Lias 2
5=Tufa 23
6= Harn Hill 37
7= Portland stone 11
8=Bath stone 6
9=Tisbury stone 2

■1 ■2 ■3 ■4 ■5 ■6 ■7 ■8 ■9

Figure 10.1   Proportions of each rock type used in construction and embellishment of Dewlish Roman villa (n=183).

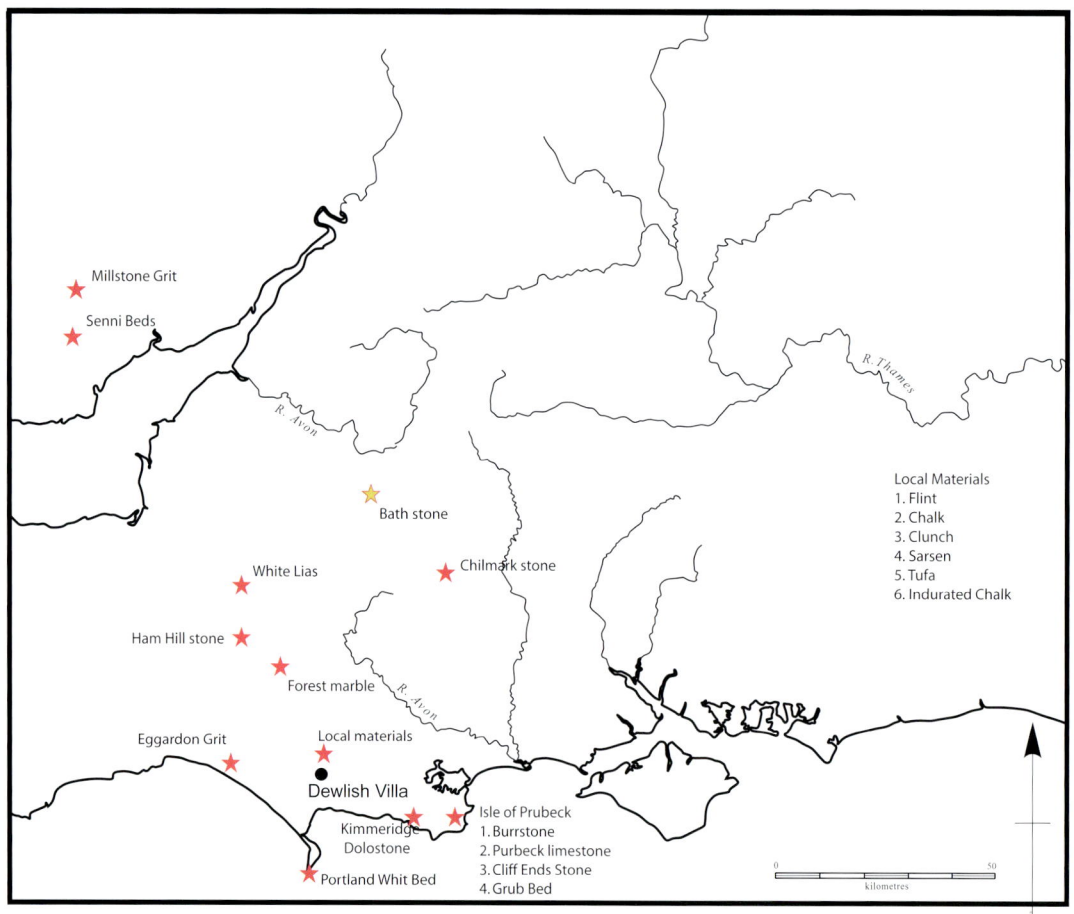

Figure 10.2   Map showing Dewlish Roman villa in relation to source rocks of worked stone.

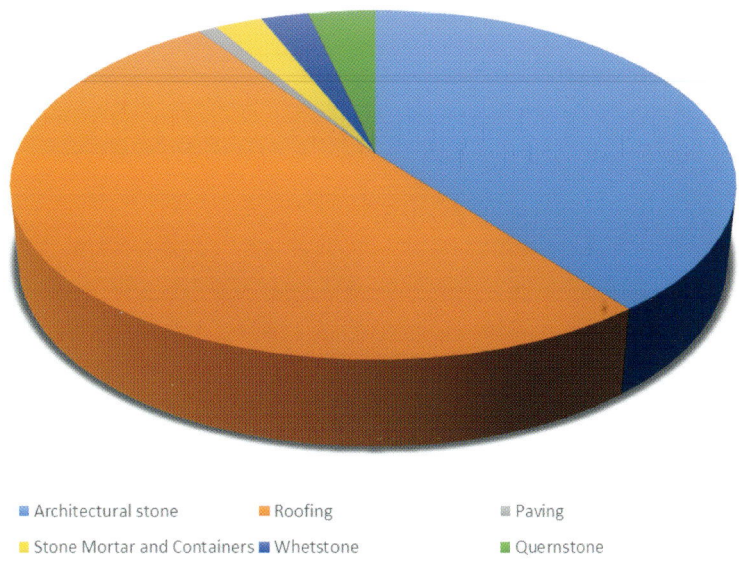

Figure 10.3   Proportion (number of examples) of worked stone by function, Dewlish Roman villa. n = 210.

sculptural embellishment are summarised in Figure 10.1.

In addition, there are 9 lithotypes identified in the smaller 27 items of the 44kg of portable utilitarian assemblage (quern, whetstone, spindle whorl, stone mortar/bowl). A distribution map (summary; Fig. 10.2) summarises the probable sources of these materials.

The Architectural Elements

A first objective of this chapter is to assess the petrological character and source of the architectural stone followed by the morphology and function of selected categories from Dewlish.

Petrological Types

ARCHITECTURAL ELEMENTS AND ASHLAR

Five material types are represented in the 221kg, 79 items (38% of the archived assemblage), that can be classed in the column shafts, finials, sideboards and the more rudimentary groupings of vaulting, roughly-dressed construction blocks and guttering (Fig. 10.3).

The material in question, freestone, a limestone with a soft open porous texture which enables the rock to be worked or carved in any direction to take inscriptions and yet withstand external weathering

(Leary 1989, Stainer 2000, Sutherland 2003) would have been acquired from the Jurassic geology of Somerset and Dorset. By frequency and weight (kg) the main lithotypes are described below.

Ham Hill Stone (Yellow Beds) (Hamdon Hill, Somerset) *Banded ferruginous skeletal grainstone* (Dunham 1962) – *Upper Lias (Toarcian).*

Ham Hill stone is by far the most common (29 examples, 101kg) and versatile (e.g. guttering, archway elements, decorative finials) freestone material type to be used in the villa at Dewlish. It is easily identifiable in hand specimens as hard banded shelly, orange-brown (10 YR 7/6) grainstone packed full of broken up molluscan debris, which when coupled with its limited geographical extent, permits easy and rapid geological characterisation. Many of the examples are reddened not due to burning but simply a reflection of a higher ferruginous content within the bedrock.

In thin section bioclasts (93.3%) are the dominant grain type. Two main fossil groups are represented, dissolved molluscan fragments (bivalves (55%) and gastropods (15%) and echinoderm plates (25%). Arrangement in bands occurred on a millimetre scale, with bivalves showing some preferred orientation (Fig.10.4, DEW9). Silt size quartz fragments (5%) and iron oxide are occasionally present and scattered randomly through the section. It also has distinctive

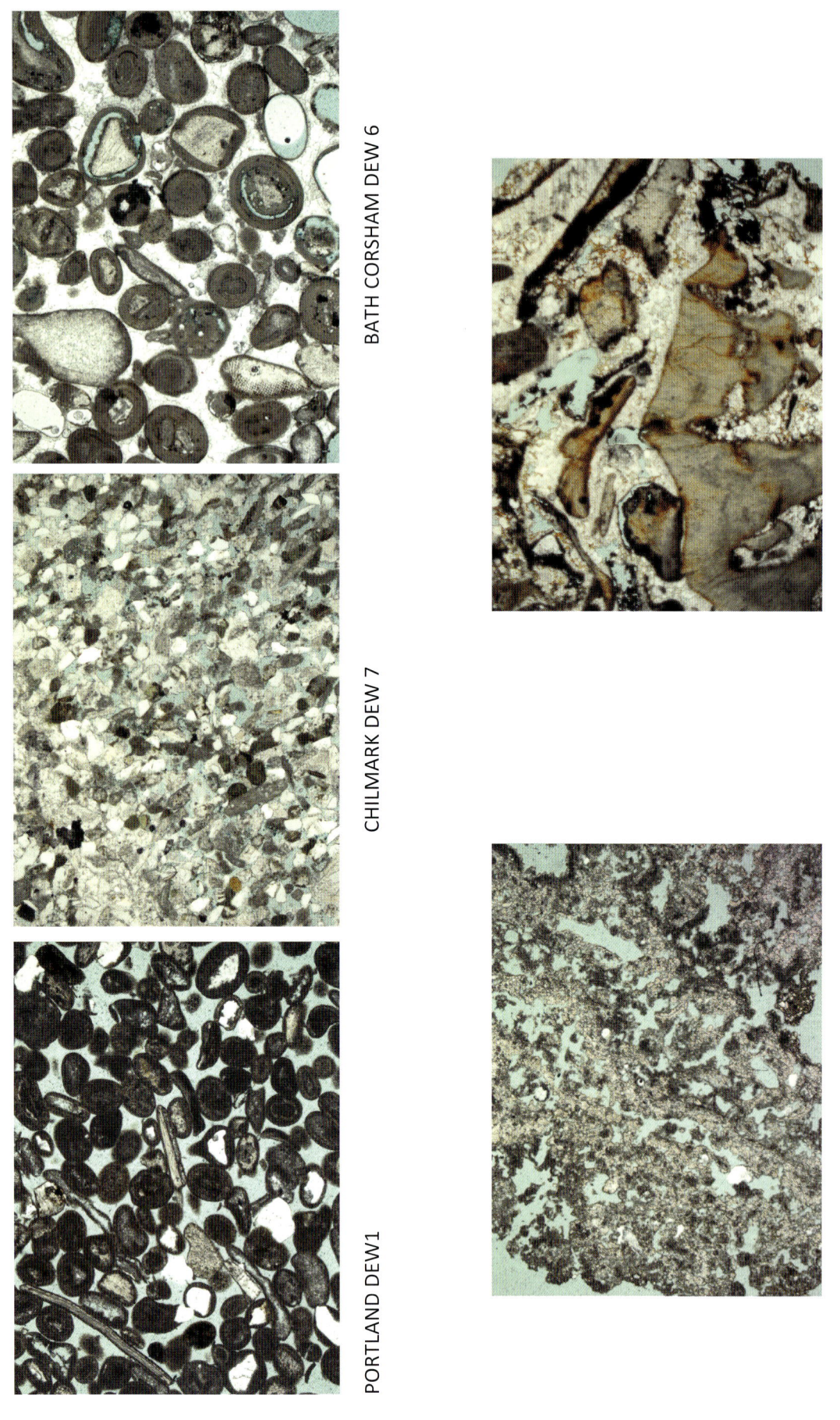

BATH CORSHAM DEW 6

CHILMARK DEW 7

PORTLAND DEW1

HAM RED DEW 9

TUFA DEW 10

Figure 10.4   Photo micrographs of the worked freestone types identified from Dewlish Roman villa. Field view of 4.8mm. Plane Polarised Light.

cement and underwent extensive compaction and breakage during burial, and a high overall porosity of 17.5% (Leary 1989) resulting in the rock having both a very hard compact texture but with regularly spaced jointing to allow the freestone to be easily worked and extracted.

The rock is thickest (27 metres) in the southern part of 120ft (36.6m) high Hamdon Hill at Deep Quarry (BNG 348106, 116404). This has excellent road links to the Fosse Way (1 km) and Ilchester (6 km) and lies about 25km from Dewlish. It is sometimes associated with the embellishment of important religious buildings elsewhere in the province such as in large plinth elements from the Temple of Claudius precinct in Colchester (Hull 1955; Hayward 2009; Hayward pers. obs.) or in London (Bradley and Butler 2008). However, its primary use is with late Roman sarcophagi (Farwell and Molleson, 1993) or large architectural elements from villas in Somerset (Hayward 2017) and Dorset (Hayward in prep.) where it can be used in enormous quantities.

Tufa – *pale cream-grey coloured, open-textured, cavernous chemically precipitated calcareous limestone* Local Holocene Spring Water Deposit (Fig. 10.4, DEW 10).

Small wedge and rectangular shaped durable blocks of pale cream-grey coloured, open-textured, cavernous calcareous Tufa or Travertine (Potter 2000) are present in 23 examples (29%), weighing 47kg at Dewlish mainly from unstratified deposits. In thin section, these blocks have the characteristic low density, nodular, highly porous spongy textured features of this chemically precipitated Holocene spring-water deposit. Identifying a precise local geological source for the tufa is not a straightforward process. It has been widely assumed but not proven (e.g. Putnam 2007, 106) that tufa was quarried locally at Dewlish. If so, then the most likely candidate is at the spring-line juncture of the chalk and nearby Reading Beds where the chalk bedrock is ideal for the precipitation of tufa.

Portland Whit Bed (Portland Freestone Member) (Isle of Portland, Dorset) *open textured oolitic grainstone with oyster fragments* (Dunham 1962) *Upper Jurassic (Portlandian)*

The use of Portland Whit Bed at Dewlish is restricted in the main to column shafts, with 12 examples present (13.9%) or 24.1.kg. This hard, light grey fine grained and durable material can be quarried into large blocks. Its highly porous texture of up to 23.1% (Leary, 1989) which gives the material a distinctive ring when hammered, and permits accurate and stylised carving. Column samples are identical in hand specimen and thin section to quarried samples of Portland Stone Whit Bed from the Watson Collection (Accession 388; e.g. Tote Quarry (BNG 368500, 72600). Both have very small sub-rounded ooids (0.3–0.4mm across) with quartz nuclei set in an open textured porous matrix with large highly ferroan (iron rich) oyster fragments. By contrast, thin-sectioned outcrop samples closer to hand to Dewlish on the mainland at Portesham (Fig.10.4, DEW1) and along the Purbeck-Portland coastline (Pond Freestone) lacked the high porosity and distinctive faunal content.

In terms of quantity, this collection of architectural stone made from Portland Whit Bed supersedes anything else that has been discovered so far in the province. Province-wide quarrying and supply of Portland stone from the Isle of Portland is however very rare with just one example from Harlowbury used in a column shaft (Hayward 2016) identified outside of the confines of Dorset. Even locally, its use in Roman Britain is rare with just one exquisitely carved example of an auxiliary tombstone depicting the Horsemen with Fallen Enemy Motif (Hayward in prep; Mackintosh 1986) and sarcophagi both from Poundbury, Dorchester (Farwell *et al,* 1993) and the Isle of Portland itself.

Source Undetermined – *Fine oolitic grainstone* (Dunham 1962) – *Middle Jurassic (Bathonian)* (Fig. 10.4, DEW6)

Another type of freestone is restricted in its use with a handful (6 examples 7.6%) 11.8kg of specialist "plain" and decorative sideboard elements. This homogeneous soft pale cream oolitic limestone, has plucked out ooids in hard specimen, a characteristic only of Middle Jurassic (Bathonian) limestones, especially from the south Cotswolds escarpment of the Bath-Corsham area (Hayward 2009). Two sub-types are distinguished a very fine oolitic limestone associated with plain table tops and a coarser shelly variety associated with the single decorative example. In thin section (Fig. 10.4, DEW 6) this oosparite (Folk 1959; 1962) has very small, perfectly formed spherical ooids each with a distinct quartz nucleus bound by a regular ferroan microcrystalline cement. This texture is conducive to crisp intricate and geometrical lathe-turned carving, as shown by the sideboard fragment with a star.

Furnishings

Further geological refinement was not possible, but what is clear is that this limestone been intricately carved, probably at source, and travelled some distance from the south Cotswolds to close to the East Dorset coast. Samples taken for thin-section analysis from other purpose-made sideboard components in large villas, e.g. Chedworth (Hayward in prep.) show these too to be made of similar high quality oolitic limestone material, indicating the selective quarrying of high-quality stone purely for the purpose of sideboard elements.

Chilmark stone (Wockley Micritic Member) Upper Jurassic (Portlandian) Fine glauconitic sandy packstone (Dunham 1962) Vale of Wardour, Wiltshire (Fig. 10.4, DEW 7).

Just two quoins (2.6%) 2.1kg from the area of Phase 1 (second to early third century) Building 1 consist of a distinctive pale green limestone with calcite veins or watermarks (Jope 1964) characteristic of Chilmark stone, Upper Jurassic (Portlandian) from the Vale of Wardour. In thin section, the regular silt size quartz fragments and small pelletal allochems set in an open porous texture of up to 23.1% (Leary 1989) are identical to outcrop examples from Tisbury Quarry (ST 976 313) and Chicksgrove Quarry (ST 962 296) (Hayward 2008). Elsewhere, provincial use of this freestone is restricted to later Roman use in ashlar in local villas at Tisbury (Hayward 2016), a sarcophagus and lid at Amesbury (Hayward 2008) and milestones (Sedgley 1975). Therefore, the use of Chilmark stone at Dewlish extends the supply of this stone much further out.

Architectural Form

Very few of the 84 elements recorded and catalogued have been published, other than the Ham stone finial, which because of its complete and elaborate form has received detailed scholarly attention (Blagg 2002; 149; fig. 41; Putnam 2007; 105; fig. 59). The Portland

stone column (Putnam 2007, 103; fig. 4.6) and tufa vaulting (Putnam 2007, 106) meanwhile command only passing comment. A dearth of architectural ornament from this site is borne out by Tom Blagg's British Archaeological Report (2002), with no decorated capitals and bases nor even Tuscan capitals and undecorated columns mentioned.

Guttering and the Roof Finial

The importance attached to stone elements associated with the channelling of water in the gently sloping south-west valley side of the villa can be shown by a small group of ridge or roof guttering elements (12%) all made of Ham Hill stone. Eight were from unstratified contexts, with the remaining two from the area of Rooms 4 and 6 of the domus (Building 3). Six separate stone gutters were identified (total weight 40kg), three of which had two or three conjoined sections creating flat based elements 810mm long × 220mm wide × 90mm deep. They were fashioned into open square cut channels, with a narrowing, deepening interior profile and crudely dressed inward facing chisel tool markings geared towards increasing the outflow or channelling of water.

At Chedworth (Hayward in prep.) and at Brislington (Blagg 2002) these channels were shown to be comparable in width to those emanating out of the underside of the Type B roof finials and it is clear that this was also the case with the triangular shaped outlet channels of the Dewlish finial found nearby in Building 3, Room 11. This highly decorative and complete (48cm high) example of a Type A Tower finial, Fig. 10.5), with four-way arches and a base hollowed out underneath to sit on the ridge of the roof (Blagg, 2002, 149, fig. 41; Putnam 2007; 105; fig. 59) merely functioned as guttering to channel water off the stone and tile roofing of the villa buildings. It has been shown that these Tower finials are often associated with Romano-Celtic temples in late third to late fourth century contexts in association with table tops with chip-carved decoration (Blagg 2002, 152).

Vaulting and Ashlar

Chamfered vaulting blocks in two material types (Tufa and Ham Hill stone) form the most common type of architectural element at Dewlish 26 examples, total

By contrast, a second much larger group of chamfered blocks (16 examples 85kg) of comparable dimension but made of a much denser more robust Ham Hill stone were found to specifically concentrate in the temple or shrine (Building 6, Room 40) or the large reception room (Room 11) of the *domus* (Building 3). These appear to have had a more structural function again as vaulting elements or as arches in two of the most important and opulent masonry rooms of the complex and were clearly meant to have supported high ceilings.

PLAIN AND DECORATED SIDEBOARDS OR TABLE TOPS
Dewlish has a small group (4) of succinctly (chip) carved sideboard or table top fragments. These are extremely common in villas and Romano-Celtic temples throughout the Wessex region with over thirty decorated examples catalogued in CSIR 1:2 (Blagg 1977. 56, fig. 4.2). Dewlish has a previously unpublished example of the common decorated rosette geometrical design from the corridor area near Rooms 5 and 6 of the *domus* (Building 3, D4 (3), SFN 272). Not only that but there are also three more less well researched plain table tops (Blagg 1977; Blagg 2002, 74) with angular facets from E5 (11); E5 (13) from Room 9, Building 3 (the *domus*). The origin and function of these edge-carved stone slabs remains unclear although the chamfering and location of decoration suggests these slabs or tops were fixed in a slightly raised position (Cunliffe and Fulford 1982, xiv) probably against a wall within a niche or apse as altars.

Like Chedworth (Hayward in prep.) the decorated examples are carved out of a slightly coarser shelly oolite (Fig. 10.4, DEW 6) with the plain table tops carved from finer oolitic limestone far more conducive to intricate geometric carving. This petrological distinction may have important ramifications on the locality of different schools of stone-masons in the Cotswolds producing specialised products using particular rock types. Blagg (1977, 56, fig. 4.2.), had already alluded to an off-kilter northern distribution for the plain table top form in the Cotswolds, so their similar petrology is another body of evidence to support a quite separate workshop activity.

Figure 10.5 Type A tower finial in Ham Hill stone. Photograph: R2568.

weight 85kg (39%). Although largely unstratified, the crisply cut smoothed chamfered blocks of Tufa, also used in ashlar and rubble are found to locate in the area of the third / fourth century bath house (Building 4). Each wedge-shaped element was regularly fashioned into 240mm × 240mm blocks that tapered in thickness from 80mm to 35mm. Traces of waterproof pink *opus signinum* mortar sealant, was sometimes present on their faces and edges which would suggest as elsewhere, e.g. Chedworth (Hayward in prep.), that many were adhered together to form an arch. These may have been for stoke holes or entranceways in the different rooms in the bath house complex or more probably as vaulted arches for the roofing of the bath house buildings, its high porosity and low density making it an ideal material for roof vaulting.

COLUMN SHAFTS

Just eleven plain shaft fragments (25kg) of varying diameters and one near complete simple Tuscan column (Putnam 2007, 103; fig. 57) provide the sum total of colonnaded architectural stone from Dewlish. All in Portland stone (see above), they are found to concentrate either in the area of the fourth century 'temple' (Building 6, Room 40; 099 (5) (SFN 800) including the aforementioned complete example or the fourth century Room 8 of the *domus* (Building 3). Their diameters are small (15–22.5cm), particularly in the area of the Building 3 frontage, which might suggest that they formed a small colonnade to support the corridor of the *domus* or in the case of Room 40, to support the 'temple' porch roof, in each case the White Portland contrasting nicely with the yellow and red Ham Hill stone vaulting.

The Tuscan column from the Building 6 'temple' area (Putnam 2007, 103, fig. 57) shows a mathematical precision to the profile typical of lathe-turning (Blagg 1976), a feature of many other column bases used in opulent fourth century residences in the south west including Great Witcombe, Gloucestershire (Blagg 2002; Plates IV and VI), and at Chedworth, Gloucestershire (Hayward in prep.).

Paving Materials

White Lias, Langport, Somerset. *A pale grey-cream laminated limestone or micrite* (Folk 1959; 1962) Upper Triassic (Langport Member- Penarth)
The two paving slabs from the villa excavations are made of this hard homogeneous fissile poorly fossiliferous limestone. With no outcrops of White Lias in Dorset, the closest exposures to Dewlish lie 30km to the north-west at Langport in Somerset (Prudden 2001) the source of much of the paving and rubblestone in villas from this district, e.g. Lufton (Hayward 2018). It is this homogeneity and even-bedding that allows the rocks to be easily split into large, linear, thick (35–40mm), level flooring slabs and steps, ideal for delineating a villa complex sited on a gently undulating natural topography. The use of White Lias at Dewlish, however, does not extend to roofing, unlike for example the villa at Halstock (Lucas 1993, 111) which lies closer to the outcrops. The widespread local availability of suitable alternative material types in the area,

e.g. Middle Jurassic and Lower Cretaceous fissile limestones, provides the most likely explanation. The largest block, some 510mm long and 200mm wide from N5 (7) from an area just to the north of the fourth-century bath house building (Building 4, Rooms 27 and 28) was almost certainly intended as a step perhaps leading to or set within a bath house floor.

Stone Roofing

Introduction

Stone roofing is a later Roman phenomenon (Boon 1974) even in Dorset and Wiltshire where there is a good local supply of tilestone. Villas at Dinnington, (Hayward in prep.), and Lufton (Hayward 2017; 2018), both in Somerset, show sizeable groupings, as do the villas from the south west of Wiltshire at Bridge Walk (Hayward 2016; 2017) and Teffont Evias, Wiltshire (Hayward 2017; 2018). However, over such a large area there is considerable variation in type of rock type used from villa to villa. It has been shown already (Fig.10.3) that quantities of stone tile from Dewlish are large (102 examples), amounting to 447kg (or 63% by weight) of all the recovered stone. As all these retained tilestones were complete examples so the true proportions of roofing tile may be much greater.

Complete stone roofing tile of all shapes and lithotypes was found to cluster in the area of the fourth century bath house (Building 4), specifically the *in situ* collapse Room 30, the *praefurinum,* and dumps immediately to the north of Rooms 26 to 29 (the *frigidarium,* anteroom, *tepidarium* and *caldarium*) presumably also here due to the result of *in-situ* collapse. A second area of complete roofing tile was grouped in Room 40 (Building 6). The use of stone roofing tile at Dewlish therefore appears to relate to the later fourth century enlargement of the baths and the construction of Building 6 in relation to the later buildings of the villa. As well as a review of the main stone types, this section will also categorise the form and dimensions of the tilestone in order to understand how the roof was assembled.

Petrology

Three material types, two of which probably came from the same outcrop, represent the stone roofing material or tilestone at Dewlish villa. The proportions of each lithotype are referred to in Figure 10.1.

T1 Purbeck limestone (Corbula Beds – Isle of Purbeck, Dorset). *Fissile pale-cream shelly limestone packed full of small white 3–4mm bivalves (Corbula atala)* (Arkell 1947, 131–132) *also known as (Downs Vein)* (T. Haysom pers.comm.; Thomas 2008, 63) *(Lower Cretaceous – Durlston Formation Purbeckian).* Easily the most common roofing lithotype (78 examples – 77%) from Dewlish villa examples of this highly fossiliferous limestone almost certainly derive from Durlston Bay on the Isle of Purbeck (Purbeck limestone) known locally as Downs Vein (T. Haysom. pers. comm.; Thomas 2008, 63). Although the stone is not particularly fissile, partings within this massive cream limestone still allows the tilestone to be shaped into all of the rudimentary designs, as well decorative and closure forms. Today, thinner slabs up to 2 centimetres thick have been used throughout the Isle of Purbeck and split easily and are firm enough to knock a peg hole into (Thomas 2008, 69). This material is comparable to the examples of the common lithotype 2 tilestone from Brading villa from the Isle of Wight (Hayward 2013, 140).

T2 Forest Marble (Long Burton fossil flag) (T. Haysom pers.comm.) Longburton, north west Dorset (Thomas 2008, 39–40). *Grey, poorly fossiliferous, hard crystalline sandy limestone Middle Jurassic (Bathonian)* One fifth (20.6%) of all the complete stone roofing tiles, consisted of a denser, poorly fossiliferous rusty-brown grey sandy limestone that is like a type of Forest Marble quarried from north-west Dorset, specifically from Lillington Hill to Longburton (Thomas 2008, 39–40), 12–15km north-west of Dewlish. Specifically, the presence of ripple marks on some of tiles unequivocally points to a type of Forest Marble described elsewhere as ... *thin sandy beds with ripple marks on the upper surface* that *have been used as roofing tiles over a large area of West Dorset* (Thomas 2008, 39–40). Examples of large worm trace fossils (*Chondrites*) and an ammonite were also identified. Not the easiest rock to cut, roofing tiles typically split at between 25 and 35mm, resulting in thick, poorly-shaped hexagonal designs and the occasional closure and chevron forms.

T3 Purbeck limestone (Grub Beds–Freestone Vein- Isle of Purbeck, Dorset). *Thick pale-cream shelly limestone packed full of large black oyster-like fragments Praexogyra 30–40mm across (Thomas 2008, 68) (Lower Cretaceous – Durlston Formation Purbeckian).*

Just three complete examples of roofing tile made from this rock type probably quarried from the same locality as lithotype T1 were identified. The flagstones each weighing 6kg each and measuring between 35–45mm in thickness were certainly not easy to split, compounded by the variably sized large black oyster fossils creating an uneven surface. Occasionally slabs from the Grub Bed have been thin enough for use as roofing tiles (Thomas 2008, 70). This material is comparable to the examples of the very common lithotype 1 tilestone from Brading villa from the Isle of Wight (Hayward 2013, 140).

Form

Examining the morphology of 102 complete and near-complete stone roof tiles held in the archive permitted their subdivision by form into a standard number of types.

OVERLAPPING ROOF TILE

It has been shown at Brading villa (Hayward 2013, 141), that a majority of the roof tiles overlapped with one another by a third lengthways and a half widthways producing a rhomb-shaped or fish-scale roofing surface. At Dewlish, two standard shapes of stone roofing tile each weighing 4–5kg could be distinguished and identified throughout the villa complex, probably as recurrent variations. Variations in size and shape are also commented upon.

Type 1 - Broadly conforming in shape with pentagonal Type A at Brading villa (Hayward 2013, fig. 8.2) are twelve complete tiles from Dewlish. All tiles have defined angular sides apart from the rounded end with a nail hole where an iron nail or wooden peg would have been affixed to the eaves. These are of one standard size, though smaller (385mm × 265 × 25mm) tiles than those at Brading (Fig. 10.6). A further three pentagonal forms of similar size but with all of the sides angular were also identified.

Figure 10.6   Arrangement of overlapping pentagonal roofing stone tiles made from Forest Marble (Type A) creating a rhomb fish scale pattern. Photograph: R2486.

All of these examples were made from one particular rock type, L2 the poorly fossiliferous rusty brown-grey sandy Forest Marble quarried specifically from north-west Dorset, between Lillington Hill and Longburton (Thomas 2008, 39–40), 12–15km north-west of Dewlish. Standardisation of roofing profile and rock type has been commented on elsewhere.

Type 2 – By far the most common profile (42 examples) was a small elongate angular hexagonal form, slightly longer and narrower than the Type B examples from Brading Villa (Hayward 2013, fig. 8.2) (410mm × 175mm × 25mm). The nail hole was again located on the upper right-hand edge of the tile.

Type 2a – Identical in shape, but almost twice the weight (9–11kg) were seven very large hexagonal tiles with lengths approaching 600mm, widths 380mm and 35mm thickness. The function of these much larger roofing tiles found widely dispersed throughout the site in Rooms 30, 40 and 23 is unclear. Tiles of comparable dimension and weight were identified from one area of Chedworth Roman villa in Dining Room 26 *"long roofing tiles"* (Hayward in prep.). Whether the examples from Dewlish or from Chedworth were constructed for a particular building or roof shape cannot be ascertained and with no other parallels from the archaeological literature, it is only possible to speculate, and suggest that perhaps they were used to roof the lower angled verandas of the main bath house building. Hexagonal roofing tile forms at Dewlish are associated with both the fine and coarse Purbeck limestone (grid trenches L1 and L3).

DECORATIVE TILES

A sizeable group of small (240mm across) purpose made rhomb, chevron and circular roofing tiles probably functioned to decorate the eaves of the bath house and 'temple' roofs. Excluding broken examples, half tiles cut lengthways or across the width to create straight edges at the roof limits are represented by a myriad of closure forms. They are made from both the Purbeck Limestone and Forest Marble lithotypes.

Portable stone objects

Whetstones

Brief comment only is necessary on the small group purpose-made bar-shaped whetstones (Allen 2014, 6) and stone refashioned into smooth stones or secondary whetstones (Shaffrey 2011) used specifically for sharpening tools, weapons and leather processing. These materials are spread diffusely in the area of the west-facing wing, particularly the earlier second and third century Buildings 1 and 2.

Senni Beds sandstone South Wales, Abergavenny westwards (Welch and Trotter 1960, 33–34). *Green fine micaceous sandstone (Litharenite) Lower Devonian (Emsian).*

All five examples are comparable in hand specimens with samples of Senni Beds sandstone, a geologically old, hard Palaeozoic green micaceous sandstone from the Devonian of South Wales. This stone material is ideally suited to the purpose for which it was intended, in that it has a very hard fine regular quartz rich surface which acts as an abrasive to re-sharpen metal objects and can be used time and time again. Two examples, one with a perforation M97 (2) (SFN 807) for attachment around the neck, the other bar-shaped O93 (7) (SFN 497), were clearly purpose made and brought in over some considerable distance. Other examples like the very smooth irregular object [5] appear to have been used initially as a tilestone or paver before being recycled into a larger smooth stone.

Quernstones

The need for hand querns and larger donkey, human and water driven millstones for grinding corn into coarse flour or in the production of malt for example was a necessary part of the villa economy. The materials need to have a coarse hard even grained surface and at Dewlish, three stone material types fulfil these criteria. Mainly unstratified the only example of a large millstone was located in the area of the building; the second to early third century Building 1.

Eggardon Grit, western end Eggardon Hill, West Dorset (Thomas 2008, 77) *well-cemented green-grey medium-grained shelly sandstone Upper Greensand (Cretaceous).*

Eggardon Grit is the most common rotary quern and mill stone material, but it is also of the poorest quality. This is a well-cemented green/grey medium-grained shelly glauconitic sandstone quarried from as far as Eggardon Hill, near Bridport which lies 18km to the west of Dewlish. In all, four quernstones (40–50mm thick) and one millstone (90mm thick) were recovered but all from unstratified contexts. Each rotary quern and millstone have an approximate diameter of between 450–500mm, with only lower or under stones present. The best-preserved example has a large 65mm spindle hole.

Sarsen Probably Local. *Fine light-grey cryptocrystalline quartz sandstone. Local Tertiary (Palaeogene-Eocene) source or contained within clay with flint deposits.*

A singular unstratified, deeply curved and smooth saddle quern (unstratified) was made of the local Tertiary sandstone. Although made of quartz it is not a particularly suitable rock for quern use as these grains are poorly cemented.

Millstone Grit South Wales or South Yorkshire. *Very hard grey sandstone made from large (grit sized) >2mm, regular angular quartz grains Namurian (Upper Carboniferous)*

The entire lower half of a 45mm thick, 450mm diameter millstone (Fig. 10.7) made of a hard gritstone was recovered from the grid trench N94 (4). The material in question was identical in hand specimen to examples of Millstone Grit. This, the most durable lithotype recovered from Dewlish had also travelled the farthest. The closest source

Figure 10.7   Lower half of a millstone made from Millstone Grit from grid trench N94 (4). Photograph: Bill Putnam (not coded).

at an estimated 110 km is South Wales, but it is also possible that the comparable material could have come from as far as South Yorkshire or Derbyshire.

Stone Mortars and Containers

The preparation of foodstuffs in a stone mortar container affixed with handles or lugs, requires a rock to have an easily worked flat, even-grained surface. Two rock types were identified from the five examples at Dewlish. These locate in an area between Building 2 and Building 4.

Burr stone or Burr Isle of Purbeck, Peveril Point.
Massive light creamy grey randomly orientated broken shell limestone cf "Featherstone" Lower Cretaceous (Durlston Formation).

Mortars made from this distinctive shell limestone are entirely supported by *Neomiodon* bivalve shells, leaving open pore spaces as seen in thin section (Fig.

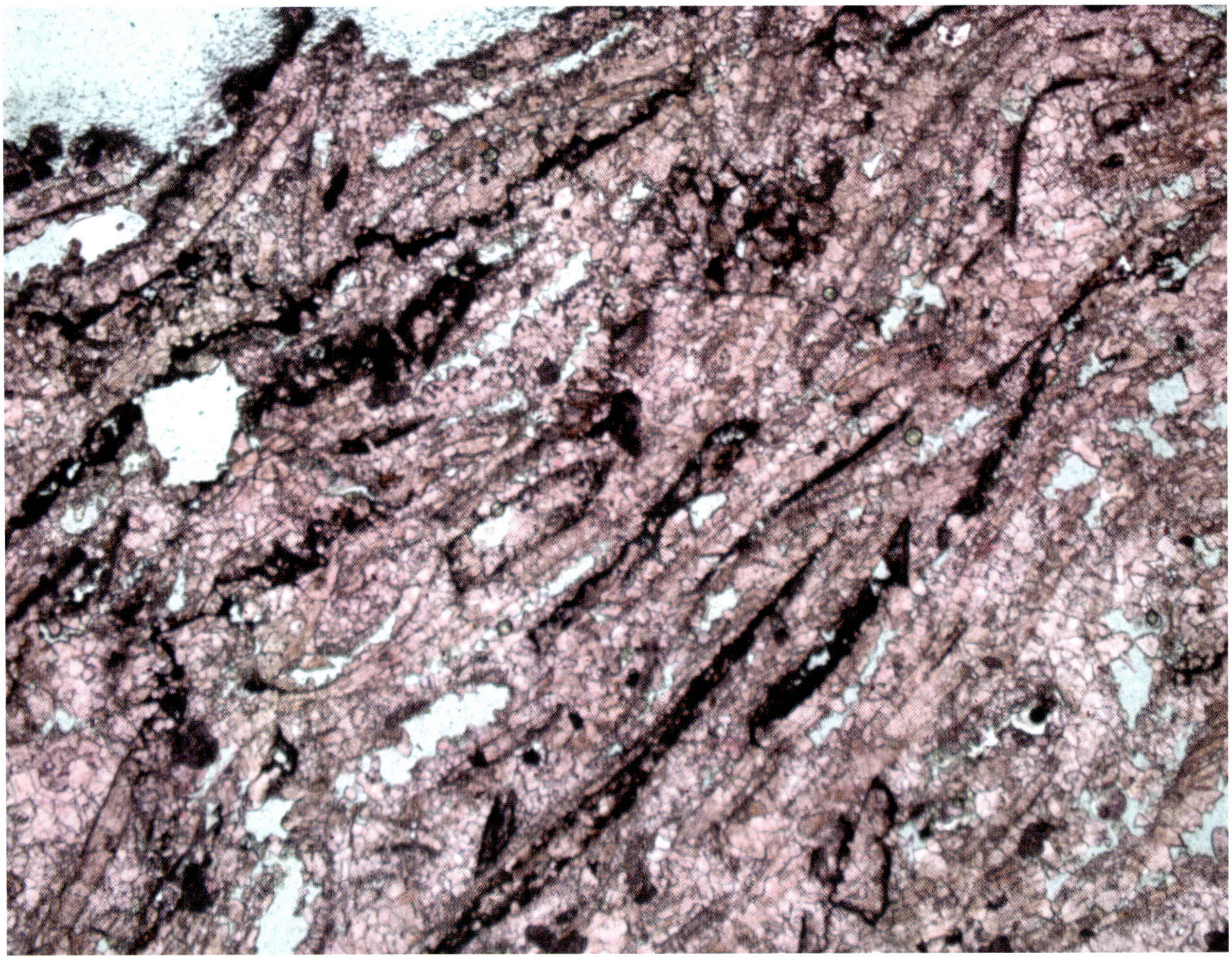

Figure 10.8   Photo micrograph of a Burr stone (shelly limestone) used in a stone mortar. Field view of 4.8mm. Plane Polarised Light.

10.8) that give the stone good porosity enabling it to dry out quickly (Thomas 2008, 63). Two examples O100 (6) (SFN 851) and E4/L2 (27) (Seager Smith, Chapter 15) and a lug L3 (33) are represented.

Purbeck-Portland Cliff Stone Isle of Purbeck, Dancing Ledge. *Dense pale grey sparsely oolitic packstone with occasional shell fragments infilled with calcite. Upper Jurassic (Upper Portlandian)*
Very few stone mortars have been identified (Lucas 1993, 95) made from this much denser fine-grained limestone. The stone quarried from the southern coastal edge of the Isle of Purbeck is variously termed Purbeck-Portland, (Barton *et al* 2011), or Under Freestone (Thomas 2008). This example with prominent lugs came from an unstratified layer at Dewlish.

DISCUSSION

Geological Source

A petrological review of the very large assemblage of stone construction materials, architectural elements, roofing, paving, quern stone, whetstone and mortar relating to Dewlish villa has been successful in identifying at least 18 different geological materials most of which have been assigned a geological outcrop (Fig. 10.2).

LOCAL (0–10KM)
The geological source of nearly all of the worked stone foundation rubble (flint, chalk, clunch) and all of the chamfered vaulting blocks (tufa) used in the fourth century bath house, Building 4, were acquired from the immediate environs of the villa itself. Indeed, the use of on-site Tufa is a feature of many villas throughout central southern England that were sited at carbonate rich spring water junctures on the Middle Jurassic limestone ridge (Hayward in prep.) and chalk deposits (Gale 2013). Use of local bulky construction materials does of course make economic and practical sense.

REGIONAL (10–100KM)
By contrast to the foundation materials all of the roofing slates, paving stone, table top, tower finial, colonnaded, vaulting and drainage materials were acquired from outcrops from greater distances, accessible by road mostly via the transport hub of Dorchester. Most of these rock types had particular attributes that set them apart from the locally acquired bulk materials and for this reason most were acquired for use at other villa sites in this part of the province, e.g. Shapwick (Hayward 2011), Dinnington (Hayward in prep.) and Lufton (Hayward 2016; 2018). The earliest quality stone materials appear to be the Chilmark stone quoins from the Upper Jurassic of the Avon Valley near Salisbury recovered from the second century entrance around Building 1 and supplied via boat down to Poole Harbour and thence probably by road from Shapwick.

It can be seen from Figure 10.2 that a large grouping was acquired from the Isle of Purbeck, specifically Purbeck limestone for 80% of the roofing tile, and Burr stone and Cliff End stone for stone mortars. This source supplied most of the roofing slate for Shapwick (Hayward 2011) and for Brading villa on the Isle of Wight (Hayward 2013). Stone mortars made from a plethora of rock types from the Lower Cretaceous Purbeck limestone turn up in villas throughout Dorset, e.g. Halstock (Lucas 1993, 95) and were made accessible via the Shapwick to the Dorchester Roman road, Margary's route section 4e (1973, 85 Map 3 and pages 108–110; Putnam 1971, 177–8 and fig. 13). A second grouping concentrates to the north-west of Dorchester along a line broadly consistent with the Dorchester to Ilchester road and beyond to the Fosse way. Roadside material types acquired include geological older south Cotswold material types including Forest Marble for roofing (90kg), Ham Hill stone for vaulting, drainage and Tower finials (123kg), White Lias for paving and steps (12kg) and fine Middle Jurassic bath stone from Frome/Corsham for table tops. (12kg).

The major petrological finding from this assemblage was the acquisition, supply and working of the hard white-grey freestone from the Upper Jurassic (Portlandian) of the Isle of Portland, specifically Portland Whit Bed for columns. So far, this is the largest assemblage of Portland stone to have turned up anywhere in Britannia and its use, like the Tufa for bath house vaulting, Ham Hill for finials, guttering and vaulting and Purbeck limestone and Forest Marble roofing is related specifically to the later fourth century construction of Building 6, and the rebuilding of the bath house and *domus*, Buildings 4 and 3 respectively. This very late Roman upsurge in high quality freestone and roofing slate quarrying, supply and working forms for these buildings represents just one small part of a much larger southern and south-west provincial acquisition of quality stone for villa and temple construction and embellishment.

PROVINCIAL (100–200KM)

All of these stone materials were portable utilitarian objects associated with buildings in the south-western range (quern, millstone and rubstone), acquired from outcrops of stone over distances over 100km (Fig. 10.2). The other feature they share in common is that they are all extremely hard, older, Palaeozoic fine (Senni Beds) and course (Millstone Grit) sandstones. As local and regional sources of stone are neither hard nor compressed enough for efficient use in sharpening tools, grinding grain or preparing malt it became economically viable to select these more exotic stones from much further afield in western and northern Britain.

CONCLUSION

Identifying the geological character and source of so many types of local, regional and provincial wide stone types from just one Dorset villa, using petrological techniques should provide the impetus for further scientific work to be undertaken. Only then can we begin to ascertain the wider regional picture of later Roman stone material acquistion and supply in central southern England, an area with the highest concentration of villas in the country.

11

THE PAINTED WALL-PLASTER

by G.C. Morgan

INTRODUCTION, BY IAIN HEWITT

The Dewlish plaster assemblage was removed from the stores at Bournemouth University in 1999 in order to facilitate Bill Putnam's post-excavation work (PEP1 1999–2008). Currently, the corpus of plaster is unavailable for further study. Consequently, this report is a review of the work that was carried out by the Putnam research team and it includes (below) a specialist report on seven samples that were examined by Graham Morgan of the University of Leicester in 2003.

The size of the painted plaster assemblage cannot be stated with confidence. According to records within the Dewlish archive 17,190 fragments were recovered from the site and of this total 10,710 pieces are presumed to have come from the walls of the villa and the rest from the ceilings. According to the archive records, most of the plaster fragments that were recovered from the villa site had one painted surface and 6,480 of these displayed markings on the reverse side that betrayed the nature of the material to which they had been applied. These under-surface markings fell into one of five categories:

1 Rough but generally flat under-surfaces, probably applied to solid (keyed?) masonry.
2 Curved under-surfaces as though applied to a wall comprising flint nodules.
3 An impression of reed bundles with each stem

Figure 11.1   Marsh Fern (Thelypteris palustris) foliage impression set within a fragment of painted plaster retrieved from K3 (7), SFN 363. Photograph: Bill Putnam (not coded).

c. 20–30mm thick many with plant leaves in evidence, perhaps indicative of plaster applied to ceilings (see, for example Fig. 11.1).
4 Woven hazel rods in bundles of four or five with each rod c. 15mm thick. The bundles were tied to rods fixed to the ceiling joists at c. 100mm intervals.
5 Woven laths with each component strand c. 25mm wide by 3mm thick.

Table 11.1 contains the essential details of the plaster samples that were submitted to Graham Morgan for analysis. They were derived from all but two of the buildings on the site, the exceptions

Table 11.1   Details of Dewlish Roman villa plaster samples submitted for scientific analysis at the University of Leicester in 2003 (*denotes sealed context; **bold** = probable grid trench and context origin of sample)

Report sample number	Grid trench and context number	Site specific location details	Description	Comment
1	P4 (19)*	Pit-shaft P4	Pigment sample	Within a pit-shaft sealed beneath Room 30
2	B4 (3)	Building 3, Room 3 or 4	Painted plaster	Context unsealed
3	N92 (12)*	Building 2A, Room 38	Painted plaster	From foundation trench of north-east wall (of Building 1?)
4	O1 (2) or **O98 (5)***	**Building 2, Room 31**	Painted plaster	**Sealed by collapsed wall of Building 2**
5	E5 (1) or **O99 (5)***	**Building 2, Room 31**	Painted plaster	**Sealed by collapsed wall of Building 2**
6	N99 (4)	Building 6, Room 40	Painted plaster	Context unsealed

being Buildings 1 and 7 although these were potentially the most interesting samples from the site for reasons that are explained in Chapter 5. It is perhaps surprising though that four of the submitted samples were not from sealed contexts and it is unclear what the rationale for selection was, given that there were over 17,000 fragments to choose from. A further problem is manifest in the fact that during the process of analysis it was noted that two of the samples were labelled ambiguously thus potentially undermining their value as evidence. With reference to Table 11.1, the labelling of these two enigmatic samples will be subject to further scrutiny with a view to providing clarification of their provenance.

Defining the problem

Table 11.1 (and Graham Morgan's report) show that two of the submitted samples had contradictory site codes. In both cases the sealed sample bag was labelled with a different site code to that written on the cardboard label that was sealed within the bag. In the case of Sample 4, the alternative labels are O1 (2) and O98 (5). Of these, the sample from grid trench O1 is in a zone of the site grid that lies equidistant between Buildings 2 and 4 (Fig. 7.1). The archaeology of this area was confused and the relevant context (2) is described as 'lower topsoil' which did contain some lumps of painted wall-plaster (BUDEW1000071, 3) but their position in the near surface location of the stratigraphy suggests that these painted plaster examples were of limited

value as evidence and it is unlikely that they would have been selected for analysis. In contrast, the alternative candidate, O98 (5), lay within Room 31 of Building 2 and fits within Phase 2 of the villa's development. In this location the plaster fragments were sealed beneath a collapsed wall, a context that can be dated to the third century with reasonable confidence (see Chapter 6). Furthermore, the grid trench notebook (BU100DEW0082, 5) confirms the existence of painted plaster in this context that was decorated in red, black and yellow, a colour scheme that is not entirely inconsistent with the description in Graham Morgan's report.

The second erroneous label appertains to Sample 5. In this instance the conflicting labels are E5 (1) and O99 (5). Grid trench E5 includes the north-west portion of Room 9 but context (1) was categorised as topsoil which was recorded as containing a 'small quantity of painted plaster' (BU100DEW0018, 29). However, the topsoil location devalues the worth of these fragments as evidence which suggests that they were unlikely to have been chosen for sampling in a constrained financial environment. Conversely, O99 (5) was derived from Room 31 (Building 2) and was sealed by the same collapsed wall that incarcerated O98 (5). Probably, these two samples are from the same context that transcended the boundary between adjacent grid squares. Sample 5 was described in the grid trench record as having hazel wattle impressions on the reverse surface whilst the obverse of one piece was adorned by 'a painted scene with yellow and red band', a description that

Table 11.2 showing the more significant values for the metals determined by ICPS, for the Egyptian blue lump arranged in order of magnitude

element	Cu	Ca	Al	Fe	K	Na	Ti	Mg	Ba	Zn	Sr
count	85,630	56,540	12,200	6,580	4,770	3,700	1,470	1,350	290	270	260

accords well with Morgan's recorded observation of the colours of this sample in his report.

For the reasons here stated it is overwhelmingly likely that Sample 4 should read O98 (5) and Sample 5 should be designated O99 (5), a combined area of the site that revealed much about the eventual decline and replacement of Buildings 2 and 2A. For this reason, these samples and their relevant details have been emboldened in Table 11.1 and in Morgan's report as follows.

PAINTED PLASTER ANALYSIS, BY G.C. MORGAN

The samples were examined microscopically and representative portions subject to chemical analysis. The relative amounts of aggregate and acid soluble material, approximating to the lime content, were measured. The residual aggregates were then graded by sieving and particle size distribution graphs produced. The pigments were identified using micro-chemical methods, followed by confirmation by x-ray diffraction analysis. Induction Coupled Plasma Spectroscopy was used for the Egyptian Blue sample.

Sample 1: pigment

P4 (19)

An irregular lump of Egyptian blue composed of light and dark blue grains of Egyptian blue and un-reacted white quartz grains. Egyptian blue was made by heating copper with sand and a calcium source, although Vitruvius's instructions say copper, sand and natron (Morgan 1961). It was usually made of small balls, ranging in diameter from about 5mm to 20mm. As they were fired together in a crucible they are often found stuck together in clusters. This example is unusual in being a fairly large amorphous lump weighing 55.82g. It was probably imported. The chemical analysis of a small sample by [ICPS]

showed that its constituents match those of copper calcium silicate, although silica is not measured by this method. Samples have been found where scrap copper alloys have been used, with elements; tin, lead and zinc being found, but this one is quite pure, with only a trace of zinc being detected. The analytical results are given in Table 11.2.

Sample 2: painted plaster

B4 (3)

A white line over the junction of pale mauve with Egyptian blue on white to pale cream *intonaco* traces <0.1 – 0.25mm, on cream sandy plaster, 10mm + 18mm, with straw impressions and linear key marks on the reverse. The pigments were: dark red ochre, white lime and Egyptian blue with white quartz grains.

Sample 3: painted plaster

N92 (12)

1   Burnished red <0.1mm, on pale brown to yellow traces, on white *intonaco*, 0.5mm on cream sandy plaster totalling 35mm, possibly layered. The burnished red is cinnabar, the brownish yellow layer may be caused by a reaction between the cinnabar and the lime.

2   Un-painted pale cream sandy plaster, 7mm, on coarser yellower sandy plaster, with lime lumps, to 40mm thick.

Sample 4: painted plaster

O1 (2) on bag but O98 (5) on label

Egyptian blue and white traces on burnished cinna-bar, <0.1, on white *intonaco*, 0,55mm, on cream sandy plaster, 8mm thick.

Sample 5: painted plaster

E5 (1) but O99 (5) on label

White and black on burnished red, <0.1mm, on pale yellow on white traces, up to 0.1mm, on pale cream

Table 11.3 Summary results for the analysis of the plaster samples from the Dewlish Roman villa. The aggregate values total 100% of the acid insolubles. The 'lime' value is the acid soluble component, which approximates to the lime content.

Context no.	>2mm	2–0.15mm	<).15mm	'lime' %	comments
E5 (1)	0	91	9	32	top layer
	3	78	19	52	lower layer
B4 (3)	1	83	16	38	lower layer
N92 (12)	2	81	17	35	top layer
	2	77	21	44	lower layer
N99 (4)	0	89	11	40	top layer
	1	86	13	40	lower layer

sandy plaster, 7mm, on chalk and sand plaster, 10mm to 65mm thick. The irregular section suggests a wall edge. The red is cinnabar.

Sample 6: painted plaster

N99 (4)

Three phases of painting:

3　　pink on white patches – cinnabar with lime –

2　　on white over-paint

1　　on a white line, 0.1mm, over the junction of burnished red, 0.1mm, and dark green, 0.1 mm, areas. Also, on the dark green are traces of yellow, white and pale blue, the whole being of off-white to pale buff *intonaco*, 0.5mm, on slightly vesicular cream sandy plaster, 16mm, on cream sandy plaster with grass or straw impressions down to split lath casts on the reverse, 35mm thick. The interlaced laths were about 30mm wide and 8mm thick. This is probably a ceiling plaster. A very similar example of ceiling plaster was found at the Colliton Park town house in Dorchester (Drew and Collingwood Selby 1937, 1938; Morgan 1992).

Comments

The values are all fairly similar, with perhaps rather a large 'lime' value. This may reflect on the geological nature of the aggregate, with some components dissolving with the lime. Small amounts of chalk or lime lumps were noticed in the samples. A more usual value for lime plasters is about 25% – 30% lime (Morgan 1992). The particle size distribution graphs show that most of the sand grades peak at about 25mm, but one sample, N99 (4) lower, peaks at 425mm, suggesting a different sand source. Apart from N99 (4) lower, two main

sand grades are shown, those with a step between 0.85mm and 0.425mm. This does suggest that the aggregates were dug from the sand deposit on two separate occasions if not from two similar sources. The major component of the aggregates is angular to sub-angular quartz sand, with smaller amounts of flint fragments, in the larger sizes, with traces of glauconitic sandstone and amorphous silica. The amorphous silica is almost certainly derived from the lime. The number of plaster layers present is typical from Roman Britain, with only *intonaco* and two layers, being far short of the Vitruvian ideal of six or seven.

Pigments

The pigments are of high quality, with significant amounts of imported cinnabar being used. To date, only about 27 other sites in Britain have been found to have cinnabar on painted plaster or on palettes. Cinnabar was mined at Sissapo, modern day Almaden in Spain, shipped to Rome to be refined and then sold as a very expensive pigment. Commonly occurring red ochre, yellow ochre and green earth (glauconite) were also used. White lime was used on its own and as a lightening agent. The blue was Egyptian blue, as described above. The intensity of the blue depends on its particles size and purity. As light is refracted through its crystalline structure, finely powdered blue reflects more white light than is refracted through it, resulting in a lighter appearance. The painting appears to have been carried out in the true or *buon fresco* technique, powdered pigment slurry being applied directly to the top layer of pure lime, the *intonaco*, whilst it was still wet.

12

THE MOSAIC FLOORS

by Stephen R. Cosh

INTRODUCTION

Apart from a vague eighteenth-century reference to a black and white mosaic found when a tree was uprooted (Hutchins 1863, 607), the mosaics at Dewlish were discovered during the excavations of the 1970s. They all belong to Building 3 (the *domus*) during the later phases of its development when most of the rooms had patterned floors ranging from basic bands of colour to complex schemes including figures, as well as a plain red tessellated pavement in Room 5.

The mosaic in Room 11 was the finest and paved a large apsed reception room opposite an elaborate porch. The mosaics in Rooms 4–17 have several features in common and give every appearance of being broadly contemporary. The rooms are symmetrically arranged, including two similarly shaped Rooms 9 and 16, with channelled hypocausts projecting at the rear of Building 3 and two rooms with three-sided apses at either end of the range. Room 4 towards the north-eastern end had a mosaic; the floor of the more enigmatic south-western room had been ploughed out. The design of the mosaic in Room 4, with a coarse simple chequered pavement in the apse where couches would obscure the pavement, suggests that it was a winter *triclinium* as proposed for a similar heated room with mosaics such as those at Low Ham (Somerset), Colerne (Wiltshire) and Wigginton (Oxfordshire) (see Cosh

2001, 236–7, fig. 7); these are all located at the end of the range. Rooms 1–3 (two with mosaics), may therefore represent a later addition at the south-east end of the building; and it is perhaps significant that the mosaics have no features in common with the others and, like the porticus, have borders of a different colour. Therefore, these perhaps post-date the other pavements for which coins below the mosaic in Room 8 provide a *terminus post quem* of 353 CE. Alterations and enlargements were also made to the bath-suite at the south-west end. The *frigidarium / apodyterium* (Room 25), adjacent to a fine octagonal plunge-bath (Room 26), was successively paved by mosaics of which the later has stylistic affinities with the majority of pavements in the main building. The shrine or temple-like structure in the south-west range of the villa (Building 6) might have had a mosaic originally.

No close parallels for the mosaics can be cited from other sites in the region; although some motifs are comparable with those on some Durnovarian Group pavements (Smith 1969, 109–13), there is insufficient stylistic evidence to attribute the Dewlish mosaics to that group (see below). The mosaic panels were executed in dark grey, white and red and only on the figures were other colours introduced. The standard of workmanship was not high, except on the figures – the leopard and antelope panel in Room 11 is among the finest drawn examples on any fourth-century pavement. Perhaps this and other lost figures were prefabricated away from the site; differences in the mortar of the bedding support this theory.

METHOD

The descriptions of the mosaics below, arranged in order of room numbers, are adapted from the entries in the corpus of Romano-British mosaics (Cosh and Neal 2005). The Mosaic numbers following the Room number refers to the entry in that volume, 164 being the site number for Dewlish. In a similar way to the corpus, each entry begins with details of date of discovery, dimensions (room panel and tesserae), dating, status and main references in other publications.

ROOM 1. MOSAIC 164.1 (FIGS. 9.1 (PLAN) AND 12.1)

Dimensions: room 2.50m by 4.80m. Tesserae: red, white and dark grey, 20mm; border: grey, 40mm. Post 350 CE. Reburied (Putnam 1971, 160).

The south-eastern half of this room was excavated, revealing part of a mosaic with a central rectangular panel of red and white chequers, edged in dark grey, with a surrounding white band. It has a broad grey limestone border in coarser tesserae.

ROOM 3. MOSAIC 164.2 (FIGS. 9.1 (PLAN) AND 12.2)

Dimensions: room 6.60m by 2.15m. Tesserae: dark grey, white and red, 19mm; border: grey, 40mm. Post 350 CE. Reburied (Putnam 1971, 157–60, fig. 21).

This fragmentary mosaic, predominantly of coarse grey limestone tesserae, is relieved by a 0.48m wide band of smaller white tesserae down the centre, decorated with linear tangent circles of dark grey and red each with four internal arcs of the same colours developing a central white concave square. This design is related to intersecting circles, but here the elements are separate. Beneath the floor were

Figure 12.1   Room 1 (164.1). Photograph: R2404.

coins of Helena and Constans giving a *terminus post quem* of 345 CE.

ROOM 4. MOSAIC 164.3 (FIGS. 9.1 (PLAN), 12.3, 12.4 AND 12.5)

Dimensions: room (including apse) 10.30m by 6m; Panel A: about 4.5m square. Tesserae: dark grey, white and red, 15mm; border and apse: red and white, 28mm. Post 350 CE. Panel A residual fragments lifted and stored; Panel B reburied (Putnam 1971, 157–60, fig. 20).

Room 4 had a channelled hypocaust separated during the excavations by a baulk from a three-sided apse to the north-west. In the main part of the room the mosaic (Panel A) had been almost completely destroyed by stone robbers, whereas Panel B in the apse was virtually untouched.

PANEL A (Fig. 12.4) – Part of a broad border of coarse red tesserae survived by the south-western wall of the room, with traces of a band of simple guilloche

Figure 12.2   Room 3 (164.2). Photograph: R2410.

which appears to turn at right-angles some distance short of the apse. The coarse tessellation outside this continues parallel to the south-west wall, perhaps indicating that there was originally a rectangular panel between Panel A and B, but this is conjectural because the rows of red tesserae of the borders do not always run parallel to the panels on other floors at this site. Towards the centre, bridging a hypocaust channel was a fragment with another band of simple guilloche parallel to the first, and two dark grey double fillets and part of a row of wave pattern of distinctive open type that also occurs in Room 17. The mosaic also has close affinities to those in Rooms 11 and 16 (for instance, the identical form of the guilloche).

PANEL B (Fig. 12.5) – By contrast, the apse is floored in chequers of coarse red and white tesserae, with a red band beside the north-west wall. It is unusual in that the tapering side walls cut obliquely across the chequer design as though built over a floor from a previous phase (see Chapter 9). It is not known how far south-east the chequer design extends. However, the chequers are set at a slight angle, which suggests that the plan of the room was not perfectly

symmetrical. The poor-quality mosaic of the apse (as opposed to the fine wall-painting) may indicate that it was covered by furniture, such as couches, and that the room may have functioned as a *triclinium* presumably for winter use (Cosh 2001, 236–7).

ROOM 6. MOSAIC 164.4 (FIGS. 9.1 (PLAN) AND 12.6)

Dimensions: room 6.60m by 2m; panel 4.60m by 1m. Tesserae: dark grey and white, 13mm; border: red, 38mm. Post 350 CE. Reburied (Putnam 1971, 157, fig. 17, 18, 21; Putnam and Rainey 1976, 55, 56, fig. 6).

Room 6, a passage, has a long rectangular panel of bold simple meander with double returns in dark grey on a white ground within a dark grey linear frame and a white double fillet in larger tesserae. A border of coarse red tesserae surrounds it. The pattern is truncated by the border on the north-west side. This design is also used in the porticus (Mosaic 164.9) and the technique of surrounding the panel with a double fillet of large white tesserae is employed on Mosaic 164.10 in Room 16.

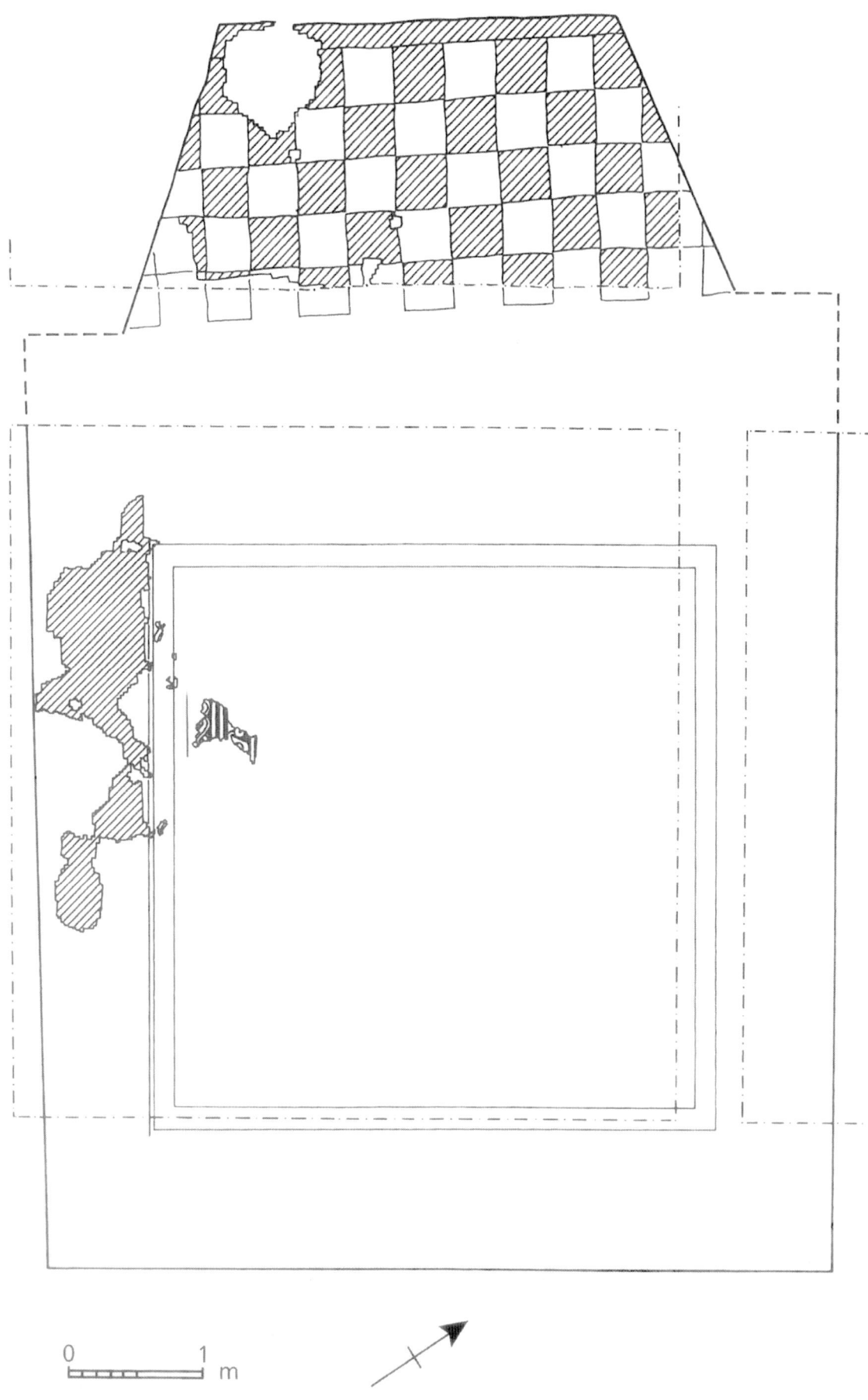

0   1 m

Figure 12.3   Room 4 (164.3) Panels A and B reconstruction drawing by S.R. Cosh.

Figure 12.4 Room 4 (164.3) The only surviving fragment of Panel A where it bridges the hypocaust channel. View to the south-west. Photograph: R2416.

Figure 12.5 Room 4 (164.3) Panel B. Photograph R2423.

Figure 12.6   Room 6 (164.4) Floor decorated by a pattern of bold, simple meander. View to south-east. Photograph: R2433.

ROOM 7. MOSAIC 164.5 (FIGS. 9.1 (PLAN) AND 12.7)

Dimensions: room 6.60m by 1.70m. Tesserae: red and white, 33mm. Fourth century. Reburied (Putnam 1971, 157; Putnam 1984, 60).

The passage or anteroom neighbouring Room 6 has a plain red tessellated floor with a 0.42m white band down the centre, all in coarse tesserae. The white band has red tesserae interspersed and ends in a ragged line where most of the north-west end of the room is repaired in red. With such extensive repair, and the floor being related in design to the neighbouring room, it is possible that Rooms 7 and 8 were originally one room.

ROOM 8. MOSAIC 164.6 (FIGS. 9.1 (PLAN) AND 12.8)

Dimensions: room 6.60m by 4m. Tesserae: red and white, 33mm. Fourth century. Removed (Putnam

and Rainey 1973, 81; Putnam and Rainey 1976, 54; Goodburn 1976, 361).

This mosaic, in coarse tesserae, consists of bands of red and white, the red bands nearest the walls being wider than those in the centre. It was patched in antiquity with red tesserae, which obscures parts of the white bands. When the mosaic was removed three coins, one of Constantius II, were found giving a *terminus post quem* of 353 CE.

ROOM 9. MOSAIC 164.7 (FIGS. 9.1 (PLAN) AND 12.9)

Dimensions: room 3.10m by 4.70m. Tesserae: dark grey, white and red, 10mm; border: red, 32mm. Post 353 CE. Reburied (Putnam 1971, 160).

The mosaic was constructed over a channelled hypocaust, which had been extensively robbed; consequently little survived, except along the

Figure 12.7 Room 7 (164.5) View to south-east. Photograph: R2455.

Figure 12.8 Room 8 (164.6) View to south-east. Photograph: R2452.

north-west wall. It comprised of a rectangular panel which can be reconstructed as a dark grey linear grid, probably five squares wide, with each square divided diagonally and shaded in red and white to give the effect of a chessboard pattern of triangles. The mosaic is unusual in that it is executed in finer tesserae than might be expected for such a simple design. It has a border of coarse red tesserae. Chessboard patterns of triangles occur at many sites, but normally incidental to or bordering the main scheme. Perhaps the most significant example is from Pitney, Somerset (Cosh and Neal 2005, Mosaic 211.2), a mosaic possibly attributable to the Durnovarian Group, but the colours differ and it is not imposed upon a grid as in the mosaic under discussion.

Figure 12.9 Room 9 (164.7) View to north-east. Photograph: R2465.

ROOM 11. MOSAIC 164.8 (FIGS 9.1 (PLAN) AND 12.10; PAINTING AND RECONSTRUCTION BY S.R. COSH; FIGS. 12.11, 12.12, 12.13 AND 12.14)

Dimensions: room 10.20m (max.) by 7.35m. Tesserae: dark grey, white and red, figured work only: grey and brown, 13mm; border: red, 25mm. Post 353 CE. Leopard and gazelle compartment lifted and kept at Dewlish House until recently, the eastern corner fragment was lifted and placed in the Dorset Museum; remainder reburied (Figure 12.10: painting by S.R. Cosh from preserved parts, photographs and plan; Putnam and Rainey 1973, 81–6, figs. 6–8; Wilson 1973, 315, fig. 14, pl. XXXIIA-B; Putnam 1984, pls p 60–1; Johnston 1994, 298–302, fig. 4–10; Ellis 1995,171, figs. 4–5, pl. I; Ling 1997, 263, pl. XXIII; Cosh 2000, 12–14, figs. 1–5; Witts 2000, 299–301, pl VIII; Witts 2016,13, 18, 22, 166, figs. 3, 18 and 184.)

Room 11 is bipartite and divided by responds separating an apse at the north-western end; it may have been a summer *triclinium* or main reception room (Ellis 1995, 171; Witts 2000, 299–301; Cosh 2001, 226–8). The black rectangular area (Panel A) had been largely destroyed. By contrast, the apse (Panel B) is well preserved.

PANEL A – Although the large, almost square panel has been reconstructed by Johnston (1994, 298, fig. 4) as a five-by-five grid, this is uncertain as almost the entire centre was destroyed, and such a grid formed by an irregular arrangement of rectangles and squares seems unlikely. More probably it had an almost square central panel, perhaps with a circle (see below), surrounded by alternate square and rectangular compartments, the square ones being located in the corners and midway along each side (Fig. 12.10). The scheme is drawn in simple guilloche in dark grey, red and white (as is all guilloche on this mosaic). Parts of three squares survived in the corners, all with guilloche mats unusually edged in red. Only one corner of the square midway along the north-east side remained, and contains a circular red band edged in dark grey within which can be seen figurative work, perhaps the shoulder of an inward-facing bust; this would be one of four and perhaps represented Winds or Seasons.

The one surviving spandrel is emphasized by a single red line. The best preserved of the rectangular compartments, with their red linear frames, contains a fine rendition of an antelope pounced upon by a leopard and with blood dripping from a wound (Fig. 12.11). The animal has been identified as a Dorcas gazelle from North Africa (Putnam and Rainey 1973, 84 n9). This scene is also inward-facing, as are those in all the other surviving compartments.

The two rectangular compartments on either side of the postulated bust are very fragmentary. One shows the right leg of a man who is taking up a typical spear-bearing stance; part of a spear can be seen and the top of his left brown boot survives. There is brown ground line or shadow outlined grey in front of each foot. He stands before a tree of which the lower trunk and basal leaf remain; in front of him is part of a bush, or possibly part of a trailing cloak (Fig. 12.12). The pose is similar to a panel on a mosaic from nearby Frampton identified as Cadmus slaying a serpent (Henig 1984, 146) but a mythological interpretation here does not fit well with the hunting theme of the antelope and leopard panel. However, a hunter taking up a similar stance and confronting a leopard appears on the large apsed mosaic from Frampton (Cosh and Neal 2005, Mosaic 168.2), but at Dewlish there seems insufficient space to show the quarry. The other rectangular compartment has what appears to be a trunk and basal leaf of a tree in the centre. The tips of two possible hooves can be detected to the left of the tree with a ground line or shadow of brown outlined grey similar to that beneath the antelope. Burning on this compartment makes the interpretation of some parts and the isolated fragments difficult. Deer with trees in the background are typical of this area, notably on Durnovarian Group mosaics, and this may be another example, but more likely it is a boar as the legs appear to be short. The animal is perhaps meant to be viewed in conjunction with the hunter panel (but separated by the medallion in the axial compartment).

Only the eastern corner of the central panel survived. The linear frame is this time dark grey with an additional two rows of grey on the north-east side. Such adjustment would seem unnecessary

Figure 12.10 Room 11 (164.8) Panels A and B painting and reconstruction by S.R. Cosh.

Figure 12.11   Room 11 (164.8) Panel A. Detail of leopard attack on a Dorcas gazelle. Photograph: R2544.

Figure 12.12   Room 11 (164.8) Panel A. Fragmentary depiction of a hunter in spear-throwing stance. Photograph: R2540.

Figure 12.13   Room 11 (164.8) Panel A. Remnant of a scene that might have depicted a triton. Photograph: R2542.

in a rectangular compartment and may indicate a spandrel created by a central circle, and the axis of the figure or motif at 45 degrees seems to support this view (Fig. 12.10). Three slightly curved spikes point to the corner, flanked by thick, tapering curved elements, one slightly invading the frame – perhaps more evidence of difficulties caused by poor geometry. Johnston (1994, 302) has argued that this represents the wing, neck and body of a gryphon (Fig. 12.13). In this case the three-spiked feature would represent a wing; but such an inept depiction is hardly in accordance with the remarkably realistic portrayal of the leopard and its prey in the adjacent panel. If this were a spandrel, then the gryphon would be upside-down for it is normal for figures and motifs to face into the corners of the room (except occasionally where they lie very close to the

corners). More likely it represents the lower portion of one of four bicaudal tritons or anquipedal giants supporting a circle as on a pavement from Horkstow, Lincolnshire (Neal and Cosh 2002, Mosaic 53.1); the fish-tail or serpentine legs would have coiled into the angles of the spandrel and the arms would be upraised to support a central medallion (Cosh 2000, 12–13). In this respect it would resemble a fourth-century mosaic from Trier (Parlasca 1959, 1–2, tafel 53), which also has trees and running animals at the margin, although the workmanship is quite different; other examples are from Soissons (Stern 1957, no. 71, pl. XIX) and Avenches (Gonzenbach 1961, no. 5.3 II).

PANEL B – Between the responds, and separating the large square panel from the apse, is a narrow rectangular panel of which only the north-east end

Figure 12.14   Room 11 (164.8) Panel B, the apse mosaic, view to the north-west. Photograph: R2531.

Figure 12.15   Room 12 (164.9) The corridor or porticus mosaic. Photograph: R2515.

survived (Fig. 12.10). It comprises a scroll with red leaves with central red and white circles, emanating from sheaths. This was presumably repeated along its entire length originally, although it is possible that it sprang from a central feature and therefore the scroll in the missing part of the panel would have been a mirror image. The apse is a slightly irregular semicircle, which is reflected in the shape of the panel, divided radially to develop five compartments and with a flattened semicircle (lunette) at the base, all drawn in simple guilloche (Fig. 12.14). In the lunette is a cantharus from which emerge two dolphins, and traces of a foliate motif, perhaps springing from the base. The cantharus has a heavily gadrooned bowl shaded red, brown and white, with a plain body and a wide mouth. Its handles are mostly obscured by the dolphins whose tails are hidden in the dark grey depth of the cantharus; their bodies are brown, grey and white with red fins. The cantharus and dolphins may represent a fountain of a stylized pool, often found in dining room either symbolic as here or real (Cosh 2006, 4–8).

Elsewhere in the apse only dark grey, red and white tesserae are used. The five segment-like compartments, framed by a dark grey double fillet, contain highly stylized 'candelabra' surmounted by a circle, with tendrils and leaves; the central and the outside ones have small faces at their bases (cf. mosaics from Keynsham (Cosh and Neal, 2005 Mosaic 204.10) and Thruxton, Hampshire (Neal and Cosh 2002, Mosaic 324.1). The motifs are not well executed and are clumsily twisted to fit the compartment, occasionally intruding into the frame. The southernmost two appear to be different with red interlacing circles edged in dark grey, perhaps by another hand. Surrounding the semicircle is a foliate scroll, similar to that on the chord panel except lacking sheaths, and a coarse red border.

Summary

The workmanship displayed in the figured panels is good, but elsewhere the same standard is not maintained and errors abound, leading to the possible conclusions that either the master mosaicist was responsible only for figured work or that the figured compartments were prefabricated. The hunting scene, the foliate scroll and the general scheme is reminiscent of the work of the Durnovarian Group but such an attribution is far less certain than with other mosaics assigned to that group. The figured work, especially where it can best be judged in the antelope and leopard compartment, is exceptionally realistic, and certainly by a different hand from the creatures with their distinctive bulging musculature at Frampton and Hinton St Mary (Dorset) and Cherhill (Wiltshire). The error in the geometry of Panel A is also exemplified at Frampton and Hinton St Mary, both products of the Durnovarian Group, but many mosaics demonstrate errors in layout and on balance the mosaic's attribution to that group is doubtful. The scheme of the apse is not dissimilar from that at Whatley, Somerset (Cosh and Neal 2005, Mosaic 222.1) and the scheme of panel A, as well as the form of scroll, is similar on a mosaic from Halstock, Dorset (Cosh and Neal 2005, Mosaic 170.1). A coin of Constantine II was found below Room 8's pavement, which is contemporary with the construction of the sidewalls along Room 11 and therefore providing a *terminus post quem* for this pavement of 353 CE.

ROOM 12. MOSAIC 164.9 (FIGS. 9.1 (PLAN) AND 12.15)

Dimensions: room 3m by over 25m (probably at least 30m). Tesserae: dark grey, white and red, 20mm; border, grey and brown, 35mm. Post 353 CE. Reburied (Putnam and Rainey 1973, 81, 84 fig. 5, 10; Putnam and Rainey 1976, 54, 56, fig. 6).

Along the south-east side of the building is a long porticus with a mosaic extending as far as Room 19 where steps lead to a lower flagged area near the baths. Although the south-west end was ploughed out and the north-eastern end unexcavated, it would seem to consist of a continuous panel of simple meander with double returns in dark grey and red on a white ground. It was bound by bands of white, dark grey and white, and by a border of grey with some brown interspersed. One of the elements of the meander is elongated perhaps as a compensation or correction. The design is a more elaborate version of that in Room 6 which may have been the inspiration for it if it belonged to a later phase of mosaics contemporary with Rooms 1 and 3.

Figure 12.16 Room 16 (164.10) Photograph: R2736.

ROOM 16. MOSAIC 164.10 (FIGS. 9.1 (PLAN) AND 12.16)

Dimensions: room 3.50m by 5m. Tesserae: dark grey, white and red, 12mm; border: red, 35mm. Post 353 CE. Reburied (Putnam 1974, 89, fig. 7–8; Wilson 1974, fig. 21).

The mosaic, paving a room with a channelled hypocaust , was mostly destroyed by stone-robbing in antiquity. Against the north-west and north-east walls are fragments of the coarse red border and parts of a rectangular panel in finer tesserae, formed by a double fillet of white, and simple guilloche outlined dark grey with red and white (x2) strands. Towards the centre of the north-west side this encloses fragments of a linear scroll with a central circle outlined dark grey and concentrically shaded red, white and dark grey. Although no leaves survive, it probably closely resembled the foliate scroll in Room 11. The northern corner shows that this motif did not continue the full length of the panel for there is a right-angle formed by a single row of red (as in the spandrels in Room 11) in which is a dark grey linear V-shape pointing towards the corner but not in line with it; a single *tessera* suggests a dark grey line parallel on the narrow side. The similarity to Room 11's mosaic indicates their probable contemporaneity, while the technique of surrounding the guilloche by a double fillet of larger white tesserae also occurs in Room 6 and the laying of rows of coarse tesserae at right angles rather than parallel to the panel is matched in Rooms 17 and 25.

ROOM 17. MOSAIC 164.11 (FIGS. 9.1 (PLAN) AND 12.17)

Dimensions: room 6.60m by 2.50m. Tesserae: dark grey and white, 12mm; border: red, 35mm. Post 353 CE. Reburied (Putnam 1974, 89).

A fragment of mosaic survived in the west corner. This has areas of coarse red tesserae of the border and the corner of a finer panel comprising a band of wave pattern forming a right angle within which are bands of white (×6) and dark grey (×4). The wave pattern is of the same open type as in Room 4 and can thus be considered contemporary. The coarse red tessellation, with evidence for burning, is laid with rows at right angles to the panel rather than parallel as is normal; this technique can also be observed in Rooms 16 and 25. The mosaic paves a passage, and the same sequence of white and dark grey bands suggests that it originally may have resembled the pavement of Room 6, another passage. The neighbouring Room 18 to the south may have also had a mosaic but was completely ploughed out.

ROOM 25, MOSAIC A. MOSAIC 164.12 (FIGS. 8.1 (PLAN) AND 12.18; FIG. 12.19 PAINTING AND RECONSTRUCTION BY S.R. COSH)

Dimensions: room 6.10m square. Tesserae: dark grey, white, red, yellow and grey, pale grey, 10mm. Fourth century. Preserved in Dorset Museum (Putnam and Rainey 1975, 59, 62, fig. 6, 7; Putnam and Rainey 1976, 55, 57, fig. 7; Goodburn 1976, 361).

This is the earlier of the two mosaics from Room 25. They had both subsided in antiquity and Mosaic A was levelled with hardcore to bed Mosaic B. The surviving fragment shows the northern corner of

Figure 12.17 Room 17 (164.11) A fragmentary wave pattern border but the principal image has been obliterated. Photograph: R2718.

Figure 12.18 Room 25 mosaic A (164.12) The earlier of two mosaics from this room. Subsidence caused this floor to be replaced within a relatively short time frame. Photograph: R3453.

Figure 12.19   Room 25 mosaic A (164.12) partial reconstruction by S.R. Cosh.

the design. The outermost surviving border is a spaced double latchkey-meander executed in dark grey and red on a white ground, the latchkeys being upright on the north-east side and recumbent on the north-west side. The spaces formed are square, of which parts of three survive: one being a guilloche mat with strands alternately shaded in red and white, and grey and white, unusually edged in red; of the other two, traces in the corner may be an inward-pointing heart-shape in one, perhaps part of a stylized flower, while the other has a red pelta, possibly part of a swastika-pelta of unconventional form, both in red linear frames. Within this is a band of right-angled Z-pattern, with the elements shaded alternately in red, yellow and white, and grey, pale grey and white, enclosing two adjacent panels. In the angle is a spaced swastika-meander with single returns enclosing at least one linear square with a small central square, all in dark grey on a white ground; it is in a rectangular dark grey linear frame with an additional dark grey line on the north-east side. Only a right angle of three-strand guilloche, with two strands in red and white (x2) and one in grey and white (×2), remains of the other panel.

The workmanship is not high and the design seems to contain several adjustments, such as the extra line in the spaced swastika-meander panel and the changes of colour in the double latchkey-meander, and clumsy cornering in the right-angled Z-pattern and the double latchkey-meander that required a dogleg. The unusual red margin on the guilloche mat and the red frames are matched in Room 11 so it is quite possible the two floors are contemporary, dating to after 353 CE. However, otherwise the mosaic is of quite different character to others at Dewlish (for instance, in its greater use of colour in repetitive motifs), and the later floor has closer affinities to the others. Therefore, an earlier date is possible.

ROOM 25, MOSAIC B. MOSAIC 164.13 (FIGS. 8.1 (PLAN) AND 12.20)

Dimensions: room 6.10m square. Tesserae: dark grey, white, red, brown, dark red and yellow, 18mm; border: red, 25–30mm, 40–45mm. Post 353 CE. The greater part is preserved in Dorset Museum

Figure 12.20 Room 25 mosaic B (164.13). Superimposed upon mosaic A (164.12), this pavement comprises a maritime scene of sea beasts. Photograph: R3299.

(Putnam and Rainey 1975, 59–62, fig. 7; Putnam and Rainey 1976, 55–57; Goodburn 1976, 361; Putnam 1984, 61; Witts 2016, 58–68, 166–7, figs. 134, 157, 185).

A large fragment was discovered in the north corner of the room sealing Mosaic A; three small fragments were found to the south-west. The design appears to comprise a very broad white band, enhanced by a single dark grey fillet near the margins, framing a square or rectangular panel of which only a band of red edged with dark grey forming a right angle remains. The broad white band contains a marine scene of sea-beasts, each outlined in dark grey and shaded brown and white, with tails, fins and streamers in red. Working anti-clockwise first is the cloven hoof and foreleg of an otherwise lost creature. Forward of and above this is a fierce-looking dolphin with a coiled tail and serrated red streamers. This appears to be chasing a sea-leopard, its head turned to confront the dolphin. It has a gaping mouth, red streamers behind the head, dark grey spots on its forequarters formed by single tesserae, forelegs with two elongated and clawed toes, and a coiled body with red excrescences and a tail with three red flukes (only two survive).

At the corner and at right angles to the sea-leopard, which it partly obscures, is a creature with similar hindquarters but with cloven hooves and a head with a curled horn indicative of a sea-ram. It also turns its head to look backwards. Ahead of the sea-ram is a fragmentary creature that may be connected with the depiction of a 'human' figure of which only the upper body, part of the head and a flying cloak over the right shoulder survive. The figure, perhaps a Cupid riding a sea-creature, is outlined in dark grey and is shaded dark red, yellow and white.

Of the other fragments, one shows the foreparts of a creature with the chest and forelegs outlined dark grey and shaded red, yellow, white and with some grey on the body. Directly above this a largely white fragment has loops of dark grey infilled red, and a trace of yellow; this seems to be the hair of a human head indicating the rider of the creature or, given its position, the head of a centaur. A small fragment exists at the threshold of Room 26 showing that fine white tessellation, edged in dark grey, continued through into the room. On the south-east side of the mosaic is a red border of coarse red tesserae, which, here at least, is laid unusually with rows at right angles to the wall, with the exception of three rows closest to the panel that are executed in slightly larger tesserae. This technique is also noted Room 16. The coarse red tessellation extends beyond the line of the wall in the north corner perhaps indicating an opening to Room 26.

The workmanship is quite good, even though relatively large tesserae are employed. The creatures are lively and imaginatively drawn. It clearly post-dates Mosaic 164.12 below and a tentative date of *c.* 370–80 CE was given by the excavator (Putnam and Rainey 1976, 57). It was in use long enough to require a mortar repair to a worn area near the doorway. Panels with sea-creatures are not uncommon, especially in bath-suites for which it is apposite, and are found in south-west Britain, for example from

Bath (Cosh and Neal 2005, Mosaic 188.6) and from Bromham, Wiltshire (Cosh and Neal 2005, Mosaic 234.2). However, the only other example in Britain to include cupids or nereids is the second-century example from Dyer Street, Cirencester (Lysons 1817, ii pl. VII). Although this is not a typical product of the Durnovarian Group, the black-edged red band is also found at Fifehead Neville (Cosh and Neal 2005, Mosaics 167.1–167.2), Hemsworth (Cosh and Neal 2005, Mosaics 171.1–171.2), and Low Ham, Somerset (Cosh and Neal 2005, Mosaic 207.4) which are all assignable to it; it also occurs in Room 11. The dolphin, particularly the shape and internal loops, is reminiscent of Durnovarian workmanship; it could be a late example of their work or merely shows influence.

It is interesting to note that one of the Fifehead Neville mosaics featuring black-edged red bands similarly lacks guilloche work, but the sea-creatures are not comparable. The scheme, as well as the inclusion of a sea-beast panel, occurs at Whatley, Somerset (Cosh and Neal 2005, Mosaic 222.1), which also lacks guilloche, but has no other significant affinity.

ROOM 26. MOSAIC 164.14 (FIGS. 8.1 (PLAN), 12.21 AND 8.7)

Dimensions: room 6.20m wide, octagonal bath 3.60m across. Tesserae: dark grey and white, 13–15mm; bath: white and red. Fourth century. Reburied (Putnam and Rainey 1975, 59, 60 fig. 8).

Room 26 was the later *frigidarium* of the bath-suite and contains a large octagonal cold plunge bath (*piscina*); the floor of the bath is executed in white tesserae with a red band at the edge, partly obscured by quarter-round moulding and thus probably intended as a key rather than as decoration. The floor of the room itself is lost except for a small fragment in a semicircular recess in the west corner. This consists of a band of white close to the wall, a row of dark grey inward-pointing stepped-triangles on a white ground and a repair in coarse red and blue-grey tesserae. Putnam and Rainey (1975, 59) suggest that this was a niche for a statue although it is difficult to see why this should have occasioned

Figure 12.21   Room 26 (164.14) A surviving fragment of mosaic from the frigidarium or cold plunge bath. Photograph: R3319. See also Fig.8.7.

repair. The use of slightly larger white tesserae than dark grey ones led to small irregularities in the stepped-triangles.

BUILDING 6 (THE 'SHRINE'). MOSAIC 164.15

Dimensions: structure 7m square. Late fourth century (Keen 1980b, 113–4).

A large number of fine tesserae from the topsoil down slope of the possible shrine implies that this building might also have had a mosaic, but convincing evidence is absent. A late fourth-century date for Building 6 is assumed.

DISCUSSION

Ignoring those wholly executed in coarse tesserae, the mosaics from Dewlish can be divided into at least three groups, probably representing the work of three or four sets of craftsmen on at least three separate occasions.

A   The earlier mosaic of Room 25.
B   Rooms 4, 6, 11, 16 and 17; possibly the later mosaic in Room 25, and Room 9.
C   Rooms 1 and 3, and the *porticus* mosaic.

The polychrome nature of the geometric mosaic found below the later mosaic in Room 25, distinguishes it from the main grouping of mosaics (B) where the colours used in the geometric elements restricted to black, white and red. The coarse borders are red whereas the presumed later grouping (C) has pale blue-grey borders around simple patterns. In the group B mosaics, the guilloche is rather loose, as is the near identical wave-crest design in Rooms 4 and 16.

Room 11's mosaic was discussed in detail by Anne Rainey (Putnam and Rainey 1973, 81–86) concluding that it is attributable to the so-called Durnovarian School or Group of mosaicists with a notional base in Dorchester; the same must apply to most of the others at Dewlish which are stylistically similar (Rooms 4, 6, 16 and 17). She adds the caveat that some features resemble 'Durnovarian' work rather than being identical to it and some features are not exclusive to that group. The attribution depends on what is understood by the Durnovarian Group. One of the reasons David Smith proposed the group was the preponderance of marine and hunting scenes in the area, and in his final thoughts on the matter he identified virtually all mosaics in the South West and South Wales as products of that Group (Smith 1984, 369–72), on which basis the Dewlish mosaics can be attributed. However, identifying a Group largely by subject matter rather than style and technique is unsatisfactory. Mosaics from Hinton St Mary and Frampton, Dorset, for example, are certainly by the same craftsmen as they have dozens of features in common, while the same can be said for the mosaics of Fifehead Neville and Hemsworth, Dorset; but – other than a frequently-used scheme and the presence of dolphins – the mosaics from the two pairs of sites have almost nothing in common. Therefore, it can be said that while the same subject matter and the use of foliate scroll were popular in the area in the fourth century, different groups of craftsmen were responsible.

Apart from the foliate scroll and the dolphin in Room 11, the feature which most resembles the 'Durnovarian' work at Hinton St Mary and a mosaic with similar features at Withington, Gloucestershire (Cosh and Neal 2010, Mosaic 455.4), is the unusual form of wave-crest pattern in Rooms 4 and 17. The figured work on the later pavement in Room 25 differs markedly from that in Room 11 (and 'Durnovarian' work elsewhere) and the use of a red band edged in black – reminiscent of mosaics from Fifehead Neville and Hemsworth, but with no other stylistic comparisons – means that it is possibly not by the same craftsmen. In other words, it is unsafe to attribute the Dewlish mosaics to any particular groups, though influence cannot be ruled out, and the mosaics very much fit in with the style and subject matter favoured in the general area.

THE ROMAN COINS

by James Gerrard, with coin identifications by Richard Reece

The excavations produced 111 bronze coins, and these were identified by Richard Reece. One hundred and three coins could be dated to within an individual reign or numismatic period and of the remainder five were illegible but of late Roman date, two are missing and one was a penny of George V.

Coins provide one of the few intrinsically datable objects that commonly occur on Romano-British sites and as such they are of great importance in establishing the chronology of relative archaeological sequences. At Dewlish few of the coins came from sealed archaeological contexts but those that

are provide a *terminus post quem* for a number of significant developments in the construction and modification of the villa building. Where relevant these coins are discussed, and their significance is assessed in relation to the site's stratigraphy. This report is primarily concerned with what the coins can reveal about the nature of coin supply and activity to the site.

Dr Reece helped to pioneer the statistical analysis of Roman coin finds from archaeological excavations and one of his most important contributions was the publication of coins from 140 Roman sites in Britain

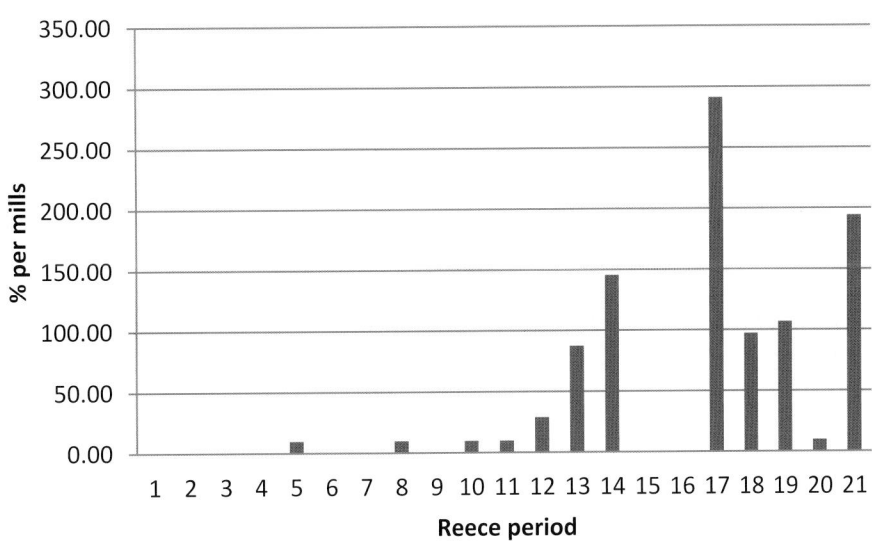

Figure 13.1 Histogram of coin finds (% per mills values) from Dewlish Roman villa by Reece (1990) period.

Table 13.1 The Roman coins from Dewlish by Reece (1990) periods

Date	Reece Period	No. of coins	% per mills
to 41	I	0	0.00
41–54	II	0	0.00
54–69	III	0	0.00
69–96	IV	0	0.00
96–117	V	1	9.71
117–138	VI	0	0.00
138–161	VII	0	0.00
161–180	VIII	1	9.71
180–193	IX	0	0.00
193–222	X	1	9.71
222–238	XI	1	9.71
238–259	XII	3	29.13
259–275	XIII	9	87.38
275–294	XIV	15	145.63
294–317	XV	0	0.00
317–330	XVI	0	0.00
330–348	XVII	30	291.26
348–364	XVIII	10	97.09
364–378	XIX	11	106.80
378–388	XX	1	9.71
388–402	XXI	20	194.17
Illegible		5	
Missing		2	

(Reece 1990). This provided an important body of data against which site finds can be compared and includes the statistical information for the Dewlish coins (Reece 1990, No. 103). For convenience's sake this is repeated here as Table 13.1 and Figure 13.1.

In Figure 13.1 the coins have been presented as a histogram in accordance with Reece's (1990) methodology. The first and second centuries are barely represented and this suggests no or very little activity before *c.* 200 CE. The early third century (Reece Periods 10–12) is poorly represented but this is typical of British sites. Indeed, the presence of single coins in Periods 10 and 11 and three coins in Period 12 is interesting and might suggest that occupation began in the middle of the third century. Periods 13 and 14 represent the debased *antoniniani* and barbarous radiates of the late third century, which were often lost on a truly enormous scale. However, the peaks in these periods are surprisingly overtopped by Periods 17 and 21, which is an unusual pattern.

The early fourth century (Periods 15 and 16) produced no coins. These periods (representing the reformed coinage of the Tetrarchy and Constantine) are always under-represented in Britain. Given the small total number of coins from the site the absence of coins in these periods should not be taken as marking a break in occupation.

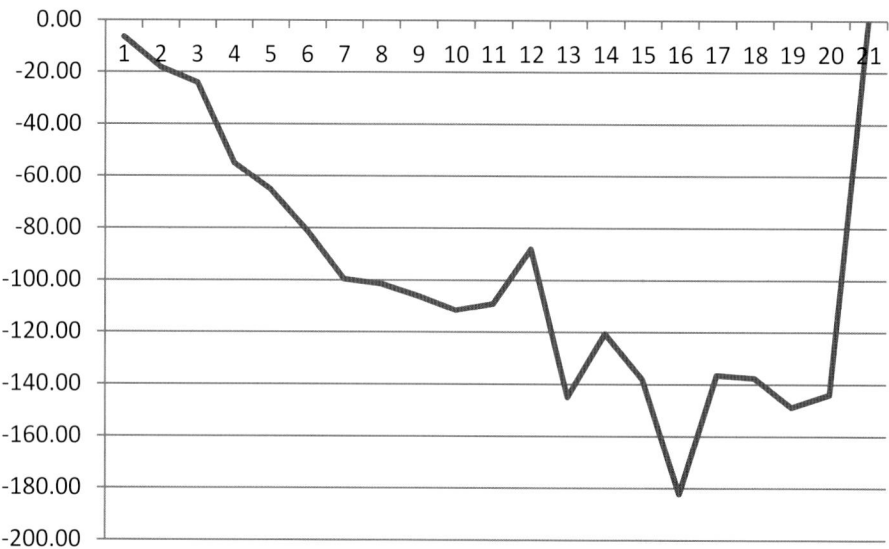

Figure 13.2 The coins from Dewlish Roman villa as cumulative per mills values subtracted from the British mean (Reece 1995).

Period 17 is the highest peak followed by equal totals for Period 18 (fallen horseman copies) and Period 19 (House of Valentinian). Period 20 is represented by a single coin of Magnus Maximus and then the final period (21: House of Theodosius) by a significant spike in loss. The ratio of Valentinianic coinage to Theodosian coinage is almost 1:2 and this is the inverse of what might be anticipated as a 'normal pattern'.

These patterns are thrown into sharper relief by converting the per mills value into cumulative per mills and subtracting them from the British mean (for the methodology see Reece 1995). This shows below average loss until Periods 11 and 12 which moves incrementally upwards against the mean, followed by a nosedive to the sharp upwards movement in Period 17, a trend which continues until Period 21 (Fig. 13.2). Reece's (1995, Fig. 25) analysis showed that this placed Dewlish alongside a number of other West Country sites including Ilchester, Cirencester and Somerton.

Current research is clearly demonstrating that the supply of coinage to Britain during the Roman period was a far from even phenomenon: it varied across both time and space. The West Country in the late fourth century seems to have been in receipt of late fourth century coinage in far greater numbers than other regions of Britain (Moorhead 2001; Walton 2012). The reasons for this phenomenon are unknown. However, sites that produce a high ratio of Theodosian (388–402 CE) to Valentinianic (364–378 CE) coins are relatively few, but include Caerwent, Colchester House in London (Gerrard 2011) and most exceptionally Richborough (Reece 1990). At Dewlish these Theodosian coins strongly suggest that activity continued until at least the end of Roman coin use at some point in the first third of the fifth century.

14

THE ROMAN GLASS

by Denise Allen

TOTAL ASSEMBLAGE

Of the 907 fragments of Roman glass, the great majority (763 fragments) is window glass including the earlier 'cast' matt-glossy variety (135 fragments) and the late Roman 'broad' or 'cylinder-blown' variety (628 fragments). The remainder comprises 137 vessel fragments, 6 beads and one tessera. There are also 4 'glassy lumps' which may have been produced by glass melting, either deliberately or accidentally, or may be the by-product of some other industrial activity. There are 8 post-medieval/modern fragments.

ORGANISATION OF THIS CHAPTER

In the following paragraphs, the glass fragments are listed individually or in groups where characteristics suggest that they are from the same vessel, or other item such as window glass. Each fragment or fragment group is itemised within a four-column structure, which reads from left to right in accord with the following example:

Site Grid Square (trench):   J2
Context Number: (4)
Small Find Number (SFN):   1501
Remarks: 1 handle fragment

In cases where a confident identification can be made of vessel type or beads etc., the itemisation of those objects is prefixed by a number from the series 1 to 40 inclusive.

Context records were retrospectively abandoned for the trial trench excavation seasons 1969 and 1970, therefore glass objects for these years cannot be assigned a specific grid square or context number. For this reason, the grid square and context number columns have been left blank as appropriate. In 1978, a series of trial trenches was opened to the south of the site grid. These trenches produced three glass fragments recorded as being from TTII.

VESSELS

Cups and bowls

Fragments from 21 different cups and bowls have been identified: 15 are of colourless or greenish-colourless glass, representing forms which were popular during the second and thirds centuries, and 6 of the yellow-green glass which is characteristic of the late Roman period, especially the fourth century.

Three rims are easily identifiable as representing two of the commonest cups in use during the later second to mid-third centuries: No 1 can be identified as a 'Cylindrical cup with fire-rounded rim and trailed decoration' (Price and Cottam 1998, 101–3, fig. 38), sometimes known as the 'Baldock type' after a fine complete specimen found at that site; Nos 2–3 belong to a similar group, but with simple 'fire-rounded rim and double base-ring' (Price and Cottam 1998, 97–99), often referred to as 'Isings 85b' (Isings 1957, 102–3, form 85b).

There are a few small body fragments from a 'convex cup without-turned fire-rounded rim' and pinched points, or nipples (Price and Cottam 1998, 112–113, fig. 45), discussed in detail with reference to examples from Brougham, Cumbria, and very popular during the third century (Cool 1990, 170–171).

Nos 4–8, 10–12 and 18–20 are all colourless cups, some with wheel-cut and incised lines, which cannot be closely identified or dated, but from within the late first to third centuries. It is possible that No 19 may be the base of an 'Indented beaker with concave base' (Price and Cottam 1998, 85–86, fig. 28), popular from *c.* 65/70 CE to the early second century, but indented vessels in various shapes and sizes were popular over a long period.

Typical late Roman drinking vessels are also quite well represented, made of the yellow-green, 'high iron, manganese and titanium' (HIMT) glass commonly produced in the fourth century (Freestone 2005; Paynter *et al* 2011, 14). The outflared, cracked off and unworked rims of nos 13–14 are characteristic of the common 'Conical beakers with straight or curved rim' (Price and Cottam 1998, 121–3, fig. 50), as is base fragment no 21. The slightly larger diameters and indents of nos 15, 16 and probably 17 suggest they represent 'Convex bowls with indents', characteristic of the later fourth century (Price and Cottam 1988, 128–129, fig. 53).

1   P95 (4) SFN 434
     Rim fragment of a cup of colourless glass; cylindrical body. Rim outflared slightly and fire-rounded and thickened, horizontal self-coloured trail below rim. Diameter of rim *c.* 100mm.
2   M95 (17) SFN 648
     Rim fragment of a cup of colourless glass. Rim turned inward very slightly and fire-rounded and thickened, diameter *c.* 60mm.
3   G2 (7) SFN 845
     Rim fragment of a cup of colourless glass. Rim turned inward very slightly and fire-rounded and thickened, diameter *c.* 90mm.
4   E4 (8a) SFN 1184

Rim and body fragments, probably from the same cup of colourless glass. Rim outflared very slightly, cracked off and polished smooth; horizontal wheel-incised lines beneath. Diameter of rim *c.* 100mm.
5   O93 (16) SFN 542
     Two fragments, including one rim, of a cup of colourless glass. Rim outflared slightly and cracked off flat, horizontal wheel-cut line beneath. Diameter of rim *c.* 100mm.
6   G5 (4) SFN 897
     Rim and base fragment of a cup of colourless glass; Rim outflared and cracked off flat, two horizontal bands of wheel-abraded lines beneath. Base flattened and very slightly concave. Diameter of rim *ca* 100mm; diameter of base *c.* 70mm.
7   M2 (8) SFN 375
     Rim fragment of a cup of very bubbly colourless glass. Rim outflared and cracked off flat, diameter *c.* 110mm.
8   N94 (11) SFN 723
     Rim fragment of a cup of very bubbly greenish colourless glass. Rim outflared and cracked off flat, diameter *c.* 80mm.
9   P4 (25) SFN 381
     Six fragments, including one from just beneath the rim, of a cup of colourless glass; some flaking post-mortem. Rim outflared, edge now missing; rounded body, with parts of three pinched out nipples extant. Diameter of rim *c.* 90mm.
10   E4 (8a) SFN 889
     Many fragments probably from the same cup of greenish colourless glass. Rim outflared slightly and cracked off flat, diameter *c.* 120mm.
11   B5 (3) SFN 901
     Rim fragment of a cup of greenish colourless glass. Rim outflared and cracked off flat, with wide horizontal wheel-cut groove beneath. Diameter of rim *c.* 100mm.
12   D4 (1) SFN 898
     Rim fragment of a bowl of good quality greenish-colourless glass. Rim outflared and cracked off flat and polished, sides slope steeply inward, diameter of rim *c.* 200mm.
13   E6 (7) SFN 365
     Rim fragment of a cup of yellow-green glass. Rim outflared and cracked off flat, horizontal wheel-abraded line beneath. Diameter of rim *c.* 80mm.
14   G1 (2) SFN 867
     Rim fragment of a cup, yellow-green glass, similar to 13 above, diameter *c.* 80mm.
15   D6 (14) SFN 178
     Rim and body fragments of a bowl of yellow-green glass. Rim outflared slightly and cracked off flat, horizontal wheel-abraded lines beneath. Sides have been pushed in whilst still warm and pliable to form oval indents. Diameter of rim *c.* 120mm.
16   C4 (2) SFN 1173

Rim fragments of a bowl, yellow-green glass, similar to 15 above, with the edge of an oval indent extant. Diameter of rim *c.* 120mm.

17   D6 (12) SFN 883
      Body fragment of yellow-green glass with an oval indent very similar to no 14 above.

18   J2 (6) SFN 368
      Base fragment, probably from a conical cup of greenish colourless glass; sides taper downward, base flattened, diameter *c.* 40mm.

19   F5 (13) SFN 907
      Base fragment, probably from a conical cup with indents, greenish colourless glass; sides taper downward, with evidence of two indents, base concave, diameter *c.* 30mm.

20   K3 (9) SFN 359
      Base-ring fragment, probably from a cup of colourless glass. Fine, solid base-ring, probably folded from the underside of the vessel, diameter *c.* 60mm.

21   G4 (4) SFN 896
      Base fragment, probably from a conical cup of dark yellow green glass; sides taper downward, base flattened, diameter *c.* 30mm.

Base and body fragments, vessel type unknown

The forms of the nine fragments, nos 22 to 30, cannot be identified, but they illustrate the range of glassware once present on the site. The applied turquoise blob on fragment 22 is typical of the decorative range for finer table wares during the fourth century – it could be from a conical beaker similar to three from Barnsley Park Villa, Gloucestershire (Price 1982, 175, 177, nos 2, 13, fig. 59) or a more elaborate jug or flask.

22   D4 (2) SFN 22
      Body fragment, yellow-green glass, with an applied oval blob (18 x 14mm) of deep turquoise glass.

23   E5 (14) SFN 888
      Base fragment of a cup, bowl or possibly flask of yellow-green glass; bulbous body, slightly concave base, *c.* 70mm.

24   D6 (11) SFN 885
      Base fragment, as above, diameter *c.* 50mm.

25   M96 (4) SFN 646
      Base-ring fragment of blue-green glass – tubular base-ring, folded from the underside of the vessel, diameter *c.* 60mm.

26   O99 (10) SFN 827
      Base-ring fragment of blue-green glass tubular base-ring, folded from the underside of the vessel, diameter indeterminable.

27   A4 (3) SFN 906
      Base-ring fragment of blue-green glass tubular base-ring, folded from the underside of the vessel, diameter *c.* 60mm.

28   J5 (3) SFN 134
      Body fragment of colourless glass – bulbous body, with two vertical ribs extant, possibly optic-blown or pinched from the vessel wall.

29   H4 8 129
      Body fragment of a vessel of bubbly pale green glass. Apparently cylindrical body, with applied self-coloured spiral trail. Diameter of body *c.* 80mm.

30   H4 (8) SFN 129
      Body fragment of a vessel of blue-green glass, very fine applied self-coloured spiral trail, diameter of body *c.* 90mm.

Unguent bottles and flasks

The form of glass container best represented on the site are the blue-green bottles which were so common during the first and second centuries, 28 fragments in all. Those whose body shape can be identified seem to come from square bottles, which were the longest-lived of these forms (Price and Cottam 1998, 194–198, figs. 196–197). After they had more or less disappeared from circulation, at the end of the second century, the colourless bottles and bottle-jugs which replaced them were never as numerous, and there must have been a major change in the way that liquids were transported and sold. Five fragments of colourless bottles or bottle jugs are represented here, which could have come from a variety of forms in use in the third and fourth centuries (Price and Cottam 1998 e.g. 181–2, 202–209).

Just one smaller unguent bottle is presented, by fragment no 22, which may be from a 'Conical unguent bottle' of the late first or second century (Price and Cottam 1998, 172–4, fig. 77).

31   K2 (1) SFN 308
      Rim fragment of a bottle-jug or flask of colourless glass. Vertical rim cracked off flat, diameter *c.* 30mm.

32   M96 (7) SFN 623
      Cylindrical neck fragment from a flask or unguent bottle, colourless glass. Diameter of neck *c.* 20mm.

33   M96 (3) 595
      Base fragment of an unguent bottle of blue-green glass. Base slightly concave, with central pontil mark, diameter of base *c.* 25mm.

Bottles – blue-green

P95	(1)	SFN 423	1 tiny fragment, square bottle corner
P92	(2)	SFN 465	1 handle fragment
O92	(10)	SFN 541	1 square bottle corner
N92	(2)	SFN 634	1 square bottle corner
M93	(2)	SFN 690	1 handle fragment
N92	(9)	SFN 756	1 square bottle corner
N92	(12)	SFN 757	4 square bottle body fragments incl. a corner
O99	(1)	SFN 767	1 square bottle body fragment
O99	(1)	SFN 768	1 neck fragment
O99	(1)	SFN 772	1 base fragment, prismatic bottle
O99	(3)	SFN 788	1 handle attachment fragment
O99	(2)	SFN 809	1 neck fragment
N100	(4)	SFN 810	1 neck fragment
E4	(8a)	SFN 887	1 handle fragment
N93	(2)	SFN 903	8 fragments, some joining, square bottle body fragments
Unstratified		SFN 905	1 shoulder fragment, square bottle
N92	(2)	SFN 909	1 square bottle corner fragment
O5	(1)	SFN 1071	1 body fragment, prismatic bottle

Bottles/flasks colourless

M95	(17)	SFN 643	1 handle fragment
N93	(6)	SFN 645	1 handle (?) fragment (possible)
O99	(10)	SFN 817	1 cylindrical body fragment

Indeterminate blue-green fragments (25 fragments)

D5	(6)	SFN 009	1 fragment
L2	(1)	SFN 303	1 fragment (mould-blown?)
O1	(3)	SFN 325	1 fragment, wheel-abraded lines
P95	(5)	SFN 443	1 fragment
R95	(2)	SFN 447	1 fragment
R96	(7)	SFN 459	1 fragment, burnt
O96	(1)	SFN 503	1 fragment
O95	(1)	SFN 506	1 fragment
O95	(3)	SFN 522	2 fragments
O96	(2)	SFN 532	1 fragment
N95	(1)	SFN 555	1 fragment
N92	(1)	SFN 603	1 fragment
M93	(3)	SFN 655	1 fragment
N92	(2)	SFN 675	1 fragment
M93	(2)	SFN 690	1 fragment
M93	(3)	SFN 696	1 fragment
N92	(2)	SFN 699	1 fragment
M92	(3)	SFN 719	1 fragment
G2	(7)	SFN 845	1 fragment
N93	(13)	SFN 892	1 fragment
L2	(32)	SFN 844	1 fragment

D7	(8)	SFN 902	1 fragment
P93	(4)	SFN 1113	1 fragment
O5	(6)	SFN 1073	1 fragment

Indeterminate colourless fragments (29 fragments)

H5	(13)	SFN 136	4 fragments, horizontal wheel-cut lines
D6	(14)	SFN 179	1 fragment, greenish-colourless
D6	(14)	SFN 184	1 fragment, greenish-colourless
N4	(1)	SFN 2093	1 fragment
H2	(1)	SFN 305	1 fragment, very fine colourless trail
L3	(8)	SFN 340	1 fragment, abraded
M2	(6)	SFN 392	1 fragment
E6	(5)	SFN 407	1 fragment
P93	(9)	SFN 428	1 fragment
TT3	(2)	SFN 486	1 fragment
TT3	(2)	SFN 487	1 fragment
O95	(1)	SFN 496	1 fragment, greenish-colourless
N96	(4)	SFN 600	1 fragment
M93	(7)	SFN 728	1 fragment
G100	(2)	SFN 866	1 fragment
D100	(7)	SFN 873	1 fragment
E5	(15)	SFN 886	2 fragments, wheel-abraded lines
Q93	(1)	SFN 893	1 fragment
D4	(1)	SFN 898	1 fragment, greenish-colourless
F4	(10)	SFN 899	1 fragment with trail
E4	(14)	SFN 904	1 fragment
E5	(13)	SFN 908	2 fragments
N3	(22)	SFN 1067	1 fragment
N5	(3)	SFN 1063	1 fragment

Indeterminate yellow-green fragments (18 fragments)

C4	(2)	SFN 1012	1 fragment
E4	(7)	SFN 1015	2 fragments
L2	(1)	SFN 304	1 fragment
K2	(1)	SFN 309	1 fragment
P93	(2)	SFN 422	1 fragment
O96	(1)	SFN 503	1 fragment
N94	(5)	SFN 584	1 fragment, wheel-incised lines
N94	(12)	SFN 591	1 fragment
N92	(2)	SFN 694	1 fragment
N92	(9)	SFN 734	1 fragment
M93	(3)	SFN 744	1 fragment, wheel-incised lines
G99	(2)	SFN 834	1 fragment
F2	(11)	SFN 853	1 fragment
E4	(8a)	SFN 889	2 fragments
M2	(1)	SFN 1105	1 fragment
C5	(2)	SFN 1177	1 fragment

Indeterminate dark green fragment

H5   (13)   SFN 136   1 fragment

BEADS

There are 6 beads of the small blue and green variety which occur often on late Roman sites, but which have a long period of circulation and therefore cannot be closely dated (Guido 1978, 92–97, fig. 37, 4–5, 12–13).

34.   F5   N/A   SFN 1896
Small biconical bead, blue glass, max. diameter 4mm, length 4mm

35.   04   N/A   SFN1206
Small cylindrical bead, green glass, max. diameter 4mm, length 10mm.

36.   D6   (14?)   SFN 169
Small cylindrical bead, green glass, max. diameter 5mm, length 4mm.

37.   P95   (1)   SFN 435
Small, roughly square-sectioned bead of blue glass, length 4 mm; width 3mm.

38.   P96   (4)   SFN 440
Small cylindrical bead of blue glass, diameter 2 mm, length 2 mm.

39.   D96   (8)   SFN 520
Small, roughly square-sectioned bead of blue glass, length 5 mm; width 2mm.

TESSERA

This may be a tessera from a mosaic, or it may be a small block of glass intended for re-use – the regularity with which individual glass tesserae turn up have led to the suggestion that this may be an alternative explanation for their presence.

40.   O98   (4)   SFN 796
Possible tessera of very bubbly, poor quality green glass, irregular cube, c. 8 × 8 × 5mm.

POSSIBLE GLASS WASTE

The significance of these lumps is obscure, and it is extremely uncertain as to whether they may be the product of glass-working, some other manufacturing process such as metal-working, or glass or glaze melted accidentally in a fire (Paynter *et al* 2011, 24–25).

E3   (7)   SFN 910   Two irregular lumps of melted vitreous material, with green glaze or glass coating ceramic or clay, *c.* max. length *c.* 25mm.
P94   (8)   SFN 911   1 lump similar to above.
L4   (6)   SFN 152   1 lump similar to above, max length *c.* 22mm.

WINDOW GLASS

Two manufacturing techniques were used for window glass in the Roman period, both of which are represented here. 'Cast', matt-glossy panes are thought to have been made by manipulating a flattened disc of glass into a square (Allen 2002, 102–109, figs. 8.1–6 on experiments by Mark Taylor and David Hill), and seem to have been used until the end of the 3rd century. From about 300 CE 'broad glass' or 'cylinder-blown' panes appear in the archaeological record. These are thinner, with two glossy surfaces and often with elongated bubbles within the glass (Allen 2002 109–110, fig. 8.9). These later panes are more numerous in this assemblage from Dewlish. There are quite substantial fragments of both varieties, including edge fragments, both the rounded edges formed during manufacture of the panes, and grosed (i.e. re-worked) edges. These are formed by breaking the edges of the glass to form a straight 'nibbled' edge, and this is now traditionally done using a pair of flat-edged pincers, which is the likely method in the Roman period too.

Cast Matt-Glossy (all blue-green unless otherwise stated in list)

158 fragments, of which 141 are blue-green, and 17 colourless. 11 have rounded edges and 5 have grosed edges.

Most fragments are 3–4 mm thick, but some are slightly thinner at 2–3mm, and some are as thick as 5mm. Some fragments have traces of plaster or mortar adhering, usually to the matt surface, at the edge of the pane. This presumably remains from where the glass was fitted into a wooden frame, or perhaps directly into an opening in the wall.

A4	(3)	SFN 1001	1 fragment
G5	(4)	SFN 1028	17 fragments, including 3 edges and 1 grosed edge
G5	(9)	SFN 1029	4 fragments, including 2 edges
H4	(13)	SFN 1041	1 fragment
H4	(21)	SFN 1042	1 fragment, edge
H5	(2)	SFN 1043	2 fragments
D5	(3)	SFN 1044	3 fragments
H5	(13)	SFN 1045	1 fragment, edge
H5	(17)	SFN 1046	1 fragment, edge
H5	(2)	SFN 1047	1 fragment, edge
N5	(9)	SFN 1065	2 fragments
O3	(2)	SFN 1068	3 fragments, including 1 edge
N2	(1)	SFN 1072	2 fragments
P4	(11)	SFN 1074	1 fragment
E4	(27)	SFN 1076	1 fragment
H2	(10)	SFN 1081	5 fragments
J2	(2)	SFN 1083	1 fragment, grosed edge
J2	(6)	SFN 1084	1 fragment
K2	(1)	SFN 1086	2 fragments
K3	(2)	SFN 1088	1 fragment
L2	(5)	SFN 1094	2 fragments
L2	(10)	SFN 1095	2 fragments, including 1 edge
L2	(15B)	SFN 1096	2 fragments
L2	(33)	SFN 1097	1 fragment
M2	(5)	SFN 1102	1 fragment
M2	(6)	SFN 1103	19 fragments, from at least two panes, including 5 edges, 4 grosed edges, some white plaster adhering to some fragments
M2	(8)	SFN 1104	1 edge fragment
O93	(9)	SFN 1108	1 fragment
P93	(2)	SFN 1112	1 fragment
P95	(3)	SFN 1116	1 edge fragment, colourless
P96	(1)	SFN 1117	1 fragment
Q92	(2)	SFN 1119	1 fragment, colourless
R91	(4)	SFN 1121	1 edge fragment
TT1	(2)	SFN 1124	1 fragment
TT3	(2)	SFN 1125	1 edge fragment
M92	(3)	SFN 1126	1 fragment, colourless
M96	(3)	SFN 1136	2 fragments, one of them colourless
N92	(2)	SFN 1137	7 fragments, including 5 colourless
N96	(8)	SFN 1145	1 fragment
N97	(6)	SFN 1152	1 fragment, colourless
O97	(3)	SFN 1153	1 fragment, colourless
O98	(5)	SFN 1154	1 fragment
O99	(2)	SFN 1155	1 fragment
O100	(3)	SFN 1156	1 fragment
O100	(5)	SFN 1157	2 fragments
F2	(14)	SFN 1158	1 edge fragment
F2	(19)	SFN 1159	1 fragment
G1	(4)	SFN 1160	2 fragments, including one edge
G2	(1)	SFN 1163	1 fragment, colourless
G100	(1)	SFN 1165	1 fragment
O100	(7)	SFN 1168	2 fragments
F3	(2)	SFN 1188	1 fragment
G3	(14)	SFN 1193	1 fragment
H4	(21)	SFN 1196	1 fragment
H4	(10)	SFN 1197	1 fragment, edge, some plaster adhering
M94	(5)	SFN 1200	1 fragment
N5	(10)	SFN 1205	6 fragments
N93	(4)	SFN 1206	1 fragments, edge
N93	(8)	SFN1207	2 fragments, 1 of them colourless
N93	(10)	SFN 1208	1 fragment
N93	(10)	SFN 1209	1 fragment, colourless
N94	(13)	SFN 1210	1 fragment
P92	(2)	SFN 1214	1 fragment
O92	(9)	SFN 1216	1 fragment, edge
O100	(6)	SFN 1217	1 fragment, edge, thick plaster adhering to matt side
O100	(5)	SFN 1218	1 fragment
E4	(22)	SFN 1182	1 fragment

Blown window glass

246 fragments with two glossy surfaces, mostly shades of yellow-green, with gradations into blue-green, and many bubbles within the glass – these are often elongated. Streaky surfaces with some brownish staining, some flaking or dense iridescence. 52 have a heat-rounded and sometimes slightly thickened edge; 22 have grosed edges. Most fragments are about 2mm thick, but some are up to 3 mm thick. Some are shattered or cracked internally, which sometimes looks like etched decoration but is not.

Unstratified		SFN 1000	2 fragments
A4	(3)	SDN 1001	3 fragments, including 1 grosed edge
A4	(7)	SFN 102	3 fragments, including 1 edge
A4	(5)	SFN 1003	27 fragments, including 3 edges
E5	(3)	SFN 1004	1 fragment
E4	(14)	SFN 1005	5 fragments
B4	(4)	SFN 1006	12 fragments, including 2 grosed edges, 1 edge
B4	(10)	SFN 007	1 fragment
D5	(6)	SFN 1009	2 fragments
E5	(12)	SFN 1010	1 fragment
C5	(10)	SFN 1011	2 fragments

E5	(5)	SFN 1013	2 fragments	J3	(1)	SFN 1085	3 fragments
E4	(8a)	SFN 1014	20 fragments	K2	(1)	SFN 1086	3 fragments including 1 edge
E4	(8a)	SFN 1014	5 fragments				
D4	(9)	SFN 1016	2 fragments, including 1 large edge	K2	(2)	SFN 1087	3 fragments including 1 edge
E3	(13)	SFN 1018	1 fragment	K3	(2)	SFN 1088	2 fragments
E3	(13)	SFN 1019	1 fragment	K3	(6)	SFN 1089	2 fragments
E3	(13)	SFN 1020	1 fragment	04	(2)	SFN 1090	20 fragments, possibly from the same pane, including 1 with grosed edge
E3	(13)	SFN 1021	1 fragment				
F5	(7)	SFN 1022	22 fragments, including 2 edges	K3	(18)	SFN 1091	1 fragment
G5	(4)	SFN 1028	1 fragment	L2	(1)	SFN 1092	37 fragments, possibly from the same pane, including 2 edges
G5	(14)	SFN 1030	1 fragment				
G5	(20)	SFN 1031	1 fragment	L2	(2)	SFN 1093	2 fragments, including 1 edge
D3	(7)	SFN 1032	1 fragment				
D6	(7)	SFN 1033	1 fragment	K3	(7)	SFN 1098	4 fragments, including 2 edges
D6	(10)	SFN 1034	1 fragment				
D7	(7)	SFN 1035	1 fragment	L3	(2)	SFN 1099	2 fragments
D7	(8)	SFN 1036–1040	8 fragments including 1 edge	M2	(1)	SFN 1100	33 fragments, including 1 edge
D5	(3)	SFN 1044	3 fragments	M2	(3)	SFN 1101	11 fragments
J5	(3)	SFN 1048	2 fragments	M2	(6)	SFN 1103	2 fragments
M5	(12)	SFN 1049	2 fragments	N2	(1)	SFN 1106	9 fragments including 1 edge
L4	(8)	SFN 1050	2 fragments, including 1 edge				
H4	(3)	SFN 1051	1 edge fragment	O2	(1)	SFN 1107	1 edge fragment
D6	(6)	SFN 1052	4 fragments, including 2 edges	O94	(2)	SFN 1109	4 fragments
				P93	(1)	SFN 1111	1 fragment
M3	(2)	SFN 1053	3 fragments including 1 with grosed edge	P93	(2)	SFN 1112	2 fragments
				P94	(2)	SFN 1114	1 fragment
M4	(3)	SFN 1054	2 fragments, including 1 with possible grosed edge	P95	(1)	SFN 1115	2 fragments
				P95	(3)	SFN 1116	1 fragment
M5	(7)	SFN 1055	1 fragment	P96	(1)	SFN 1117	1 fragment
M5	(8)	SFN 1056	1 fragment	P96	(3)	SFN 1118	2 fragments
E5	(15)	SFN 1058	1 edge fragment	Q93	(2)	SFN 1120	1 fragment
N4	(2)	SFN 1059	3 fragments	R95	(6)	SFN 1122	1 fragment
N4	(12)	SFN 1061	3 fragments including 1 edge	T95	(3)	SFN 1123	1 fragment
				M93	(1–4)	SFN 1127–9	7 fragments including 2 edges and 1 with grosed edge
N4	(22)	SFN 1062	3 fragments including 1 edge				
N5	(7)	SFN 1064	2 fragments	M94	(2)	SFN 1131	2 fragments
N5	(9)	SFN 1065	4 fragments, including 1 edge	M95	(3)	SFN 1133	3 fragments including 1 edge
O3	(2)	SFN 1068	4 fragments, including 1 with grosed edge	M95	(6)	SFN 1134	3 fragments
				M95	(18)	SFN 1135	1 fragment
N4	(3)	SFN 1069	1 fragment	M96	(3)	SFN 1136	1 fragment
O4	(1)	SFN 1070	1 fragment	N92	(2)	SFN 1137	4 fragments
D3	(1)	SFN 1075	2 fragments	N96	(4)	SFN 1144	1 fragment
E6	(5)	SFN 1077	3 fragments, including 1 with grosed edge	M98	(3)	SFN 1147	2 fragments, including 1 edge
E6	(7)	SFN 1078	2 fragments, including 1 with grosed edge	M98	(8)	SFN 1148	1 fragment
				N1	(3)	SFN 1149	1 fragment, including 1 edge
H2	(1)	SFN 1079	5 fragments	N98	(6)	SFN 1150	3 fragments, including 1 edge
H2	(9)	SFN 1080	1 fragment				
H2	(10)	SFN 1081	3 fragments	N100	(4)	SFN 1151	1 fragment
H3	(1)	SFN 1082	4 fragments	G1	(4)	SFN 1160	2 fragments including 1 edge
J2	(2)	SFN 1083	1 fragment				

G2	(1)	SFN 1161	1 fragment
G2	(2)	SFN 1162	5 fragments including 1 edge
G99	(6)	SFN 1164	1 fragment
B4	(1)	SFN 1170	5 fragments including 1 edge
B5	(3)	SFN 1171	3 fragments including 1 grosed edge
C5	(2)	SFN 1172	16 fragments including 1 edge
C5	(4)	SFN 1175	15 fragments
C5	(4)	SFN 1176	9 fragments including 1 edge
C5	(2)	SFN 1177	6 fragments including 1 edge
D7	(7)	SFN 1178	4 fragments, including 1 edge
D8	(10)	SFN 1179	1 fragment
D7	(12)	SFN 1180	1 fragment
E4	(22)	SFN 1181	1 fragment
E6	(2)	SFN 1183	1 fragment
E4	(8)	SFN 1185	42 fragments, including 2 edges and 3 grosed edges
E5	(13)	SFN 1186	36 fragments, including 1 edge
E5	(15)	SFN 1187	2 fragments, both grosed edges
F3	(2)	SFN 1188	1 fragment
G2	(1)	SFN 1191	3 fragments, including 1 edge
G3	(1)	SFN 1192	2 fragments, including 1 edge and 1 grosed edge
G100	(1)	SFN 1194	5 fragments including 1 edge, 1 grosed edge
H4	(8)	SFN 1195	1 fragment
D5	(3)	SFN 1215	2 fragments
M94	(5)	SFN 1200	5 fragments
M93	(7)	SFN 1201	1 fragment
N3	(2)	SFN 1202	2 fragments
N5	(7)	SFN 1203	30 fragments, including 4 edges, 3 grosed edges
M93	(9)	SFN 1204	1 fragment
N5	(10)	SFN 1205	17 fragments, including 2 edges
N95	(1)	SFN 1211	1 fragment
N95	(14)	SFN 1212	1 fragment
N96	(2)	SFN 1213	1 fragment
R2	(1)	SFN 1219	1 fragment
TTII	(3)	SFN 1220	3 fragments, including 1 edge
F5	(12)	SFN 1189	1 fragment
F5	(12)	SFN 1190	1 large fragment, with 2 grosed edges meeting at a square corner

MODERN/POST-MEDIEVAL FRAGMENTS

N4	(5)	SFN 227	1 green fragment
L2	(1)	SFN 302	1 pale blue fragment
O2	(2)	SFN 409	1 pale blue fragment
M3	(1)	SFN 843	1 colourless fragment
M3/F2	(4)	SFN 854	1 blue bottle fragment
N3	(2)	SFN 895	1 blue bottle fragment
O5	(1)	SFN 900	1 green fragment
M2	(1)	SFN 1100	1 window fragment.

15

THE ROMANO-BRITISH POTTERY

by Rachael Seager Smith

Overall, 20,200 sherds, weighing 220.230kg, were recovered. Although a handful of later prehistoric sherds and in the region of 100 sub/post-Roman sherds were identified, the assemblage was predominantly of Romano-British date, spanning the period from the mid/late second to fourth centuries CE. Small quantities of first and early second century CE material, mainly from the trial trenches, were also included.

CONDITION

The ceramic assemblage was predominantly derived from layers, with small amounts from structural elements of the villa and the few cut features identified across the site. Four vessels had been deliberately deposited, set into the floors of Rooms 17 and 24. Overall, however, the condition of the assemblage was generally poor. Most sherds had suffered at least moderate surface abrasion and some edge damage, while many of the rims were broken at or above the neck/shoulder junction, hampering the precise recognition of form. The mean sherd weight for the assemblage as a whole was just 10.9g (most Romano-British sites in southern Britain achieve means of between 10g and 20g). Comparable data is not available for most of the other Dorset villas but the Bucknowle villa, for example, showed a considerably higher figure (25g; Light 2009, 127, table 13). By way of comparison, the mean weight for a group of 11 villas

in Hampshire was 15.12g, with the individual sites varying from 5.67g to 28.65g, although only one was below 12.57g (Dicks 2007, 76, table 6).

HISTORY AND METHODS

In common with many other sites excavated during the 1960s and 1970s, the Dewlish villa buildings were recorded with reference to an alpha-numeric grid superimposed over the structural remains. The features and deposits identified within each 5m x 5m grid square were then assigned individual 'context' numbers, the sequence in each square beginning again at 1, while a series of unique numbers (1–51) were assigned to the 'rooms' identified within the buildings. During subsequent phases of post-excavation analysis, the entire pottery assemblage was recorded by a variety of students, working under the supervision and guidance of Bill Putnam. Within each grid-square and context, the pottery was divided into eight 'fabric families' (Black Burnished ware, samian, New Forest wares, Oxfordshire wares, Alice Holt wares, amphorae, mortaria (excluding any New Forest/Oxfordshire products) and Other) and quantified by the number and weight (to the nearest 5g) of pieces, with a separate note of the number of rims, bases and body sherds present within each group. All data were recorded using a pro-forma record sheet for each context. The vessel forms and decorative motifs were listed with reference to the Wessex Archaeology's type series (Seager Smith and Davies 1993) and other standard corpora (such as Fulford 1975a and Young 1977). The condition of the material from the square/context as a whole was also scored on a sale of 1 (freshly broken) to 5 (much abraded) and other details such as the number of pots wholly or partially reconstructed, drawing and photographic reference numbers recorded. The paper records have been retained within the archive but the basic quantified information was subsequently entered into an Excel spreadsheet for each grid line and then summarised into a single spreadsheet for the assemblage as a whole.

While a standard technique of its time, one of the main disadvantages of the alpha-numeric grid system of recording is that a square can examine more than one room or feature, while different squares can also examine the same feature or deposit. Although for this site, the stratigraphic relationships between contexts within the same room and grid square were generally well described, correlations between the deposits even in adjacent rooms/squares were rarely made. This has made it difficult to assemble wider context groups and a considerable proportion of the ceramic assemblage is therefore effectively unstratified, while securely stratified groups are rare. During a rapid scan of the whole assemblage undertaken in 2010 by the present authors to check and up-date the earlier quantified records and to assess requirements for any additional post-excavation analysis, three groups of material were considered to warrant further, more detailed study. These consisted of:

- the assemblages from so-called 'cold-stores'(pit-shafts) O100 (1143 sherds, 23.491kg) and P4 (975 sherds, 22.586kg);
- four deliberately deposited vessels, three set into the floor in Room 17 (H4, contexts 19, 20 and 21) and one from Room 24 (D7, context 7), totalling 262 sherds, 5.518kg;
- the Late Iron Age/Early Roman assemblages from three trial trenches excavated in 1976 (808 sherds, 7.366kg) – recorded to maximise information about this poorly-understood phase of the site's development.

Subsequent stratigraphic analysis identified another 68 sealed groups scattered across the site and the

pottery from these (2890 sherds, 27.046kg) was analysed to provide dating evidence to inform the structural sequence. These groups are not discussed in detail here, although the results of this analysis have been incorporated into the overall discussion of this assemblage.

Overall, then, in addition to the samian, examined in its entirety and reported upon separately by J.M. Mills (Chapter 16), 6078 sherds, weighing 86.007kg (30% of the assemblage by sherd count, 39% by weight), were subjected to more detailed fabric and vessel form analysis using an abbreviated version of Wessex Archaeology's standard recording system for pottery (Morris 1994). All the sherds were assigned to fabrics of known source or type (e.g. south east Dorset Black Burnished ware; New Forest parchment ware) or to a "catch-all" fabric group based on predominant inclusion type and colour (e.g. greywares; oxidised sandy wares). Within each fabric, the pieces were then sorted into "sherd families" – individual rims, bases, groups of joining sherds or, indeed, any group of sherds sharing certain characteristics, such as unidentifiable jar rim fragments or a mass of undiagnostic body sherds – and quantified by sherd count, weight (to the nearest whole gramme) and estimated vessel equivalence (EVE). The EVE quantification presented in Tables 15.2–7 below have been calculated excluding pieces represented by less than 5% of the diameter of the vessel. Vessel types were identified from rims only and were assigned form types with reference to the Wessex Archaeology type series (Seager Smith and Davies 1993) and other standard corpora (such as Fulford 1975a and Young 1977). Other details, such as cross-context joins, the presence of perforations, graffiti and evidence for use, re-use and repair were also noted. All this information was recorded in an Excel workbook which forms part of the archive.

COMPOSITION OF THE ASSEMBLAGE

The overall composition and distribution of the assemblage, based on the original Bournemouth University quantifications contained within the archive, is summarised in Table 15.1. Overall, half the assemblage by sherd count (10094 sherds, 98.832kg) was found in the area of Buildings 2, 6 and 1/7 (Grid lines M92–99, N92–95, N96–100, O91–95, O96–100, P92–99 and Q92–96, with a further 26% (5174 sherds, 63.179kg) from Building 3 (grid lines A–H, J and K) and 16% (3256 sherds, 42.120kg) from Building 4 (grid lines L, M1–5, N1–5, O1–5 and P3–4). The remainder derived from the trial trenches and grid lines R, S and T.

Over 80% of the assemblage was originally categorised as Black Burnished ware (Table 15.1). Although the various Black Burnished ware fabrics (e.g. Tomber and Dore 1999, 127, pl. 100, DOR BB1 and 129, pl. 102, SOW BB1; Gerrard 2010, 2, SEDOWW) were not separately quantified within the assemblage as a whole, the recently recorded material indicated that the vast majority occurred in the 'standard' south east Dorset BB1 fabric (Gillam 1976, 58; Williams 1977, 189; Tomber and Dore 1999, 127, pl. 100, DOR BB1), from the Wareham/Poole Harbour kilns. In total, only 16 sherds of south western Black Burnished ware (SOW BB1) were identified amongst the recently recorded material. It is probable that these wares were equally poorly represented in the assemblage as a whole, because its chronology is largely outside that of these wares (SOW BB1), which, in Dorset, declined rapidly in importance from the early/mid-second century CE onwards. At least five of the SOW BB1 pieces, including two bead rims and a handle (Rooms 8, 25, 42 and 51), derived from comparatively small, handled jars/beakers (WA 9), while a body sherd from an indented jar/beaker (WA 28), came from Room 25 (M3 context 14). Both these forms are amongst the few in these wares known to have been made into the later third and possibly the fourth century CE. The indented vessel finds parallels in a fourth century CE context at Alington Avenue (Seager Smith 2002, 103, fig. 48, 60) and the Bucknowle villa (Light 2009, 147).

The recently recorded material also indicated that the Late Iron Age version of the Wareham/Poole harbour fabric (*Durotrigian*-style black burnished ware; Brailsford 1958), mainly derived from the trial trenches, was included in Black Burnished ware group. South East Dorset Orange Wiped Wares (Gerrard 2010, 2, SEDOWW), mostly used for storage jars and of late fourth to early fifth century CE date, also formed a small, but significant, proportion of the assemblage from the two pits and the sealed

groups and are therefore likely to be more widely represented with the assemblage as a whole. These wares are more fully discussed below.

The Black Burnished ware vessel forms comprised the usual range of common and rarer types typically found in the Dorchester region (Seager Smith and Davies 1993, 229–249). The three most common and widely distributed Late Roman types – everted rim jars (WA 2 and 3), shallow, straight-sided dishes (WA 20) and dropped flanged bowls/dishes (WA 25) – dominated the assemblage, but other forms from each of the main vessel categories were also represented:

Jars: WA 1, 4, 6, 7, 8, 9, 11, 12, 18, 38, 47 and 67

Open bowls: WA 13, 15, 16, 32, 33 34, 36, 40, 73 and 75

Straight-sided bowls and dishes: WA 21, 22, 23 and 24

Miscellaneous: WA 10 (beakers), 19 (colander), WA 26 (lid), WA 27 (tankard), WA 28 (indented beaker), WA 29 (flagon) and WA 30 (*patera*)

Within the assemblage as a whole, the sizes and proportions of the vessels conform to those outlined by Gillam (1976) and Davies and Hawkes (1987), while the techniques of surface treatment and decoration follow the generalized 'rules' described elsewhere (Farrar 1973, 76–8; Gillam 1976, Williams 1977; Seager Smith and Davies 1993). However, sherds from an unusually deep, straight-sided bowl (Fig. 15.1) found in Rooms 26 and 27 (N5, contexts 7, 9 and 10), probably represent a variant of the common and normally shallow 'dog-dish' form (WA 20), while pieces from a thick, heavy variant of the dropped flanged bowl/dish form (WA 25) came from Rooms 1, 2 (A4, context 1) and 6 (D4, context 9; Fig. 15.2), and may be from the same or similar vessel(s). Although not sufficiently complete to be assigned to a particular form, a thick, heavy flange fragment from Room 13 (G2, context 8) is most likely to be from a large bowl/dish form and WA types 25, 69, 75 and 81 are all possibilities. The final unusual form was represented by a ribbed, strap handle and a group

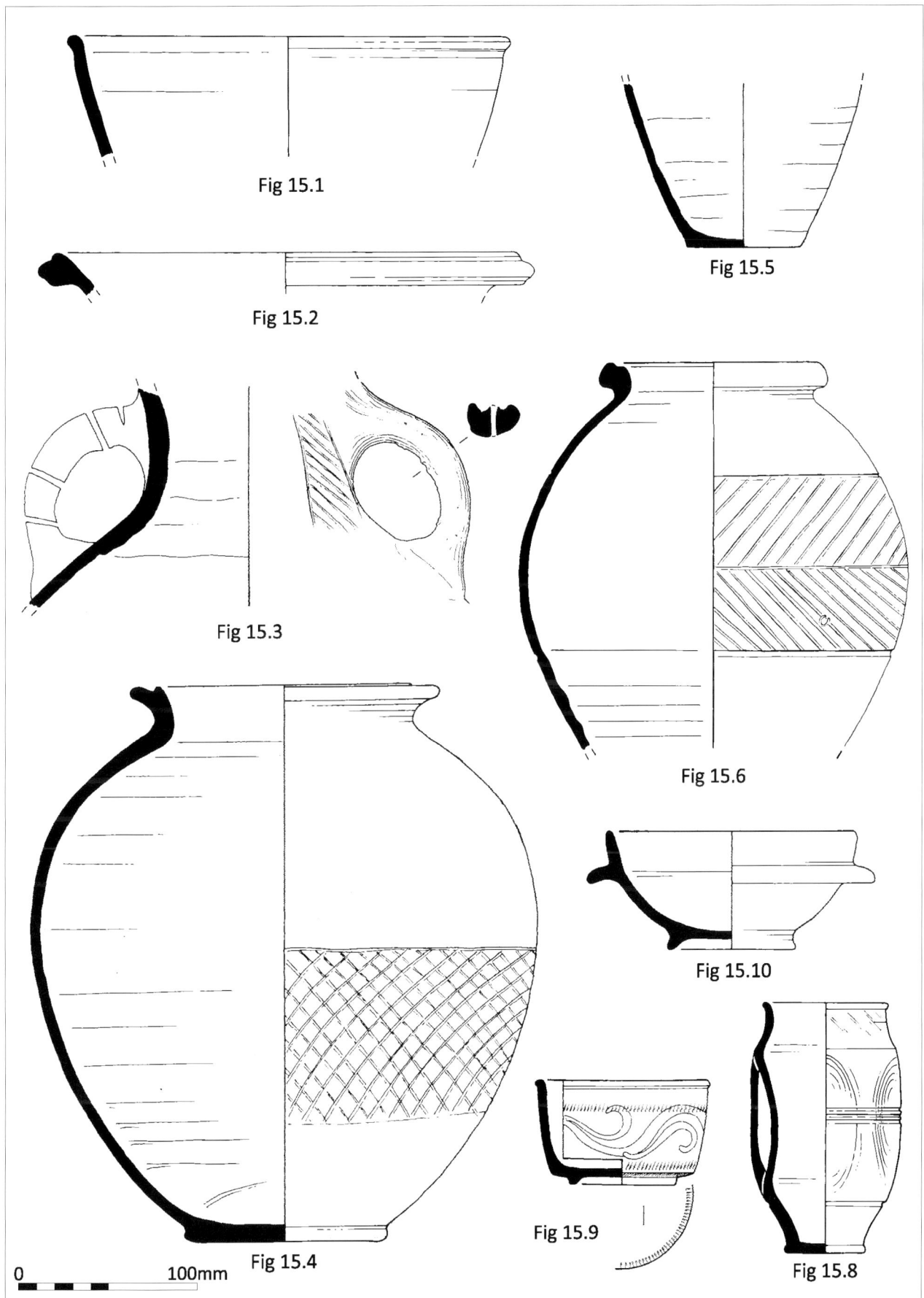

Figure 15.1   (this page and the next five pages) The Romano-British pottery. Drawings: David Watt.

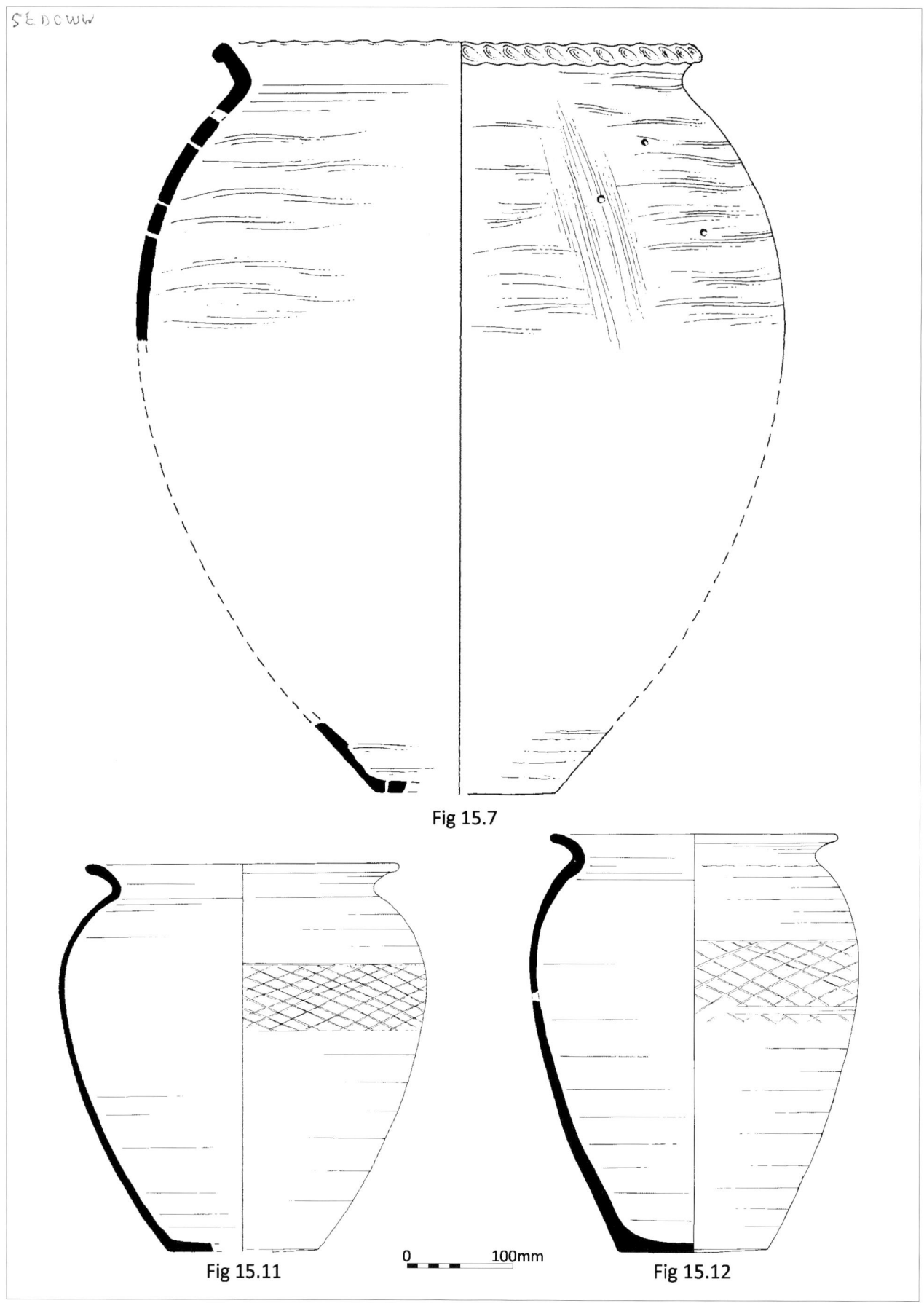

Fig 15.7

Fig 15.11

0 ⸱⸱⸱⸱ 100mm

Fig 15.12

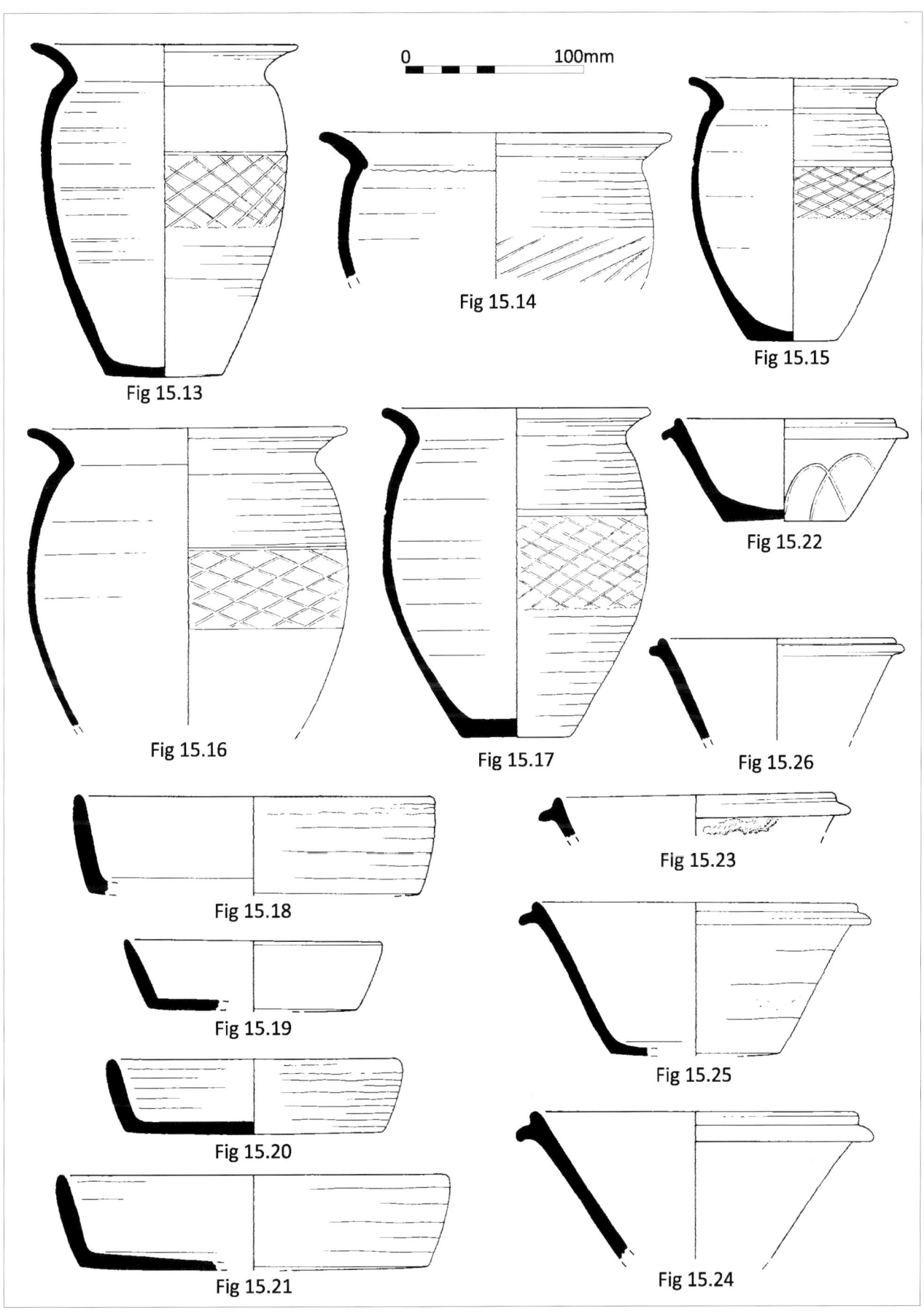

Fig 15.14

Fig 15.13

Fig 15.15

Fig 15.16

Fig 15.17

Fig 15.22

Fig 15.26

Fig 15.18

Fig 15.23

Fig 15.19

Fig 15.25

Fig 15.20

Fig 15.24

Fig 15.21

0   100mm

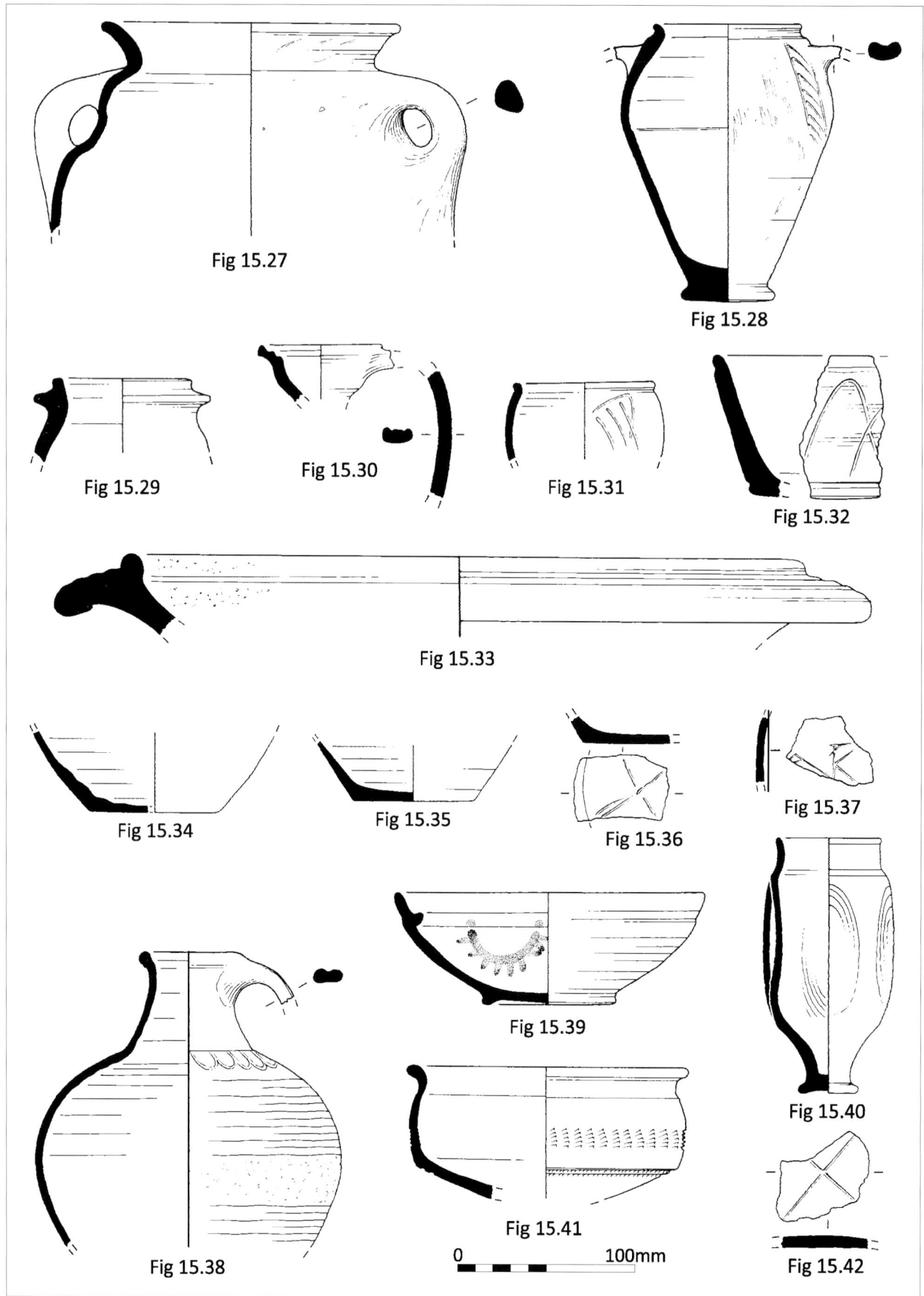

Fig 15.27

Fig 15.28

Fig 15.29

Fig 15.30

Fig 15.31

Fig 15.32

Fig 15.33

Fig 15.34

Fig 15.35

Fig 15.36

Fig 15.37

Fig 15.39

Fig 15.40

Fig 15.38

Fig 15.41

0   100mm

Fig 15.42

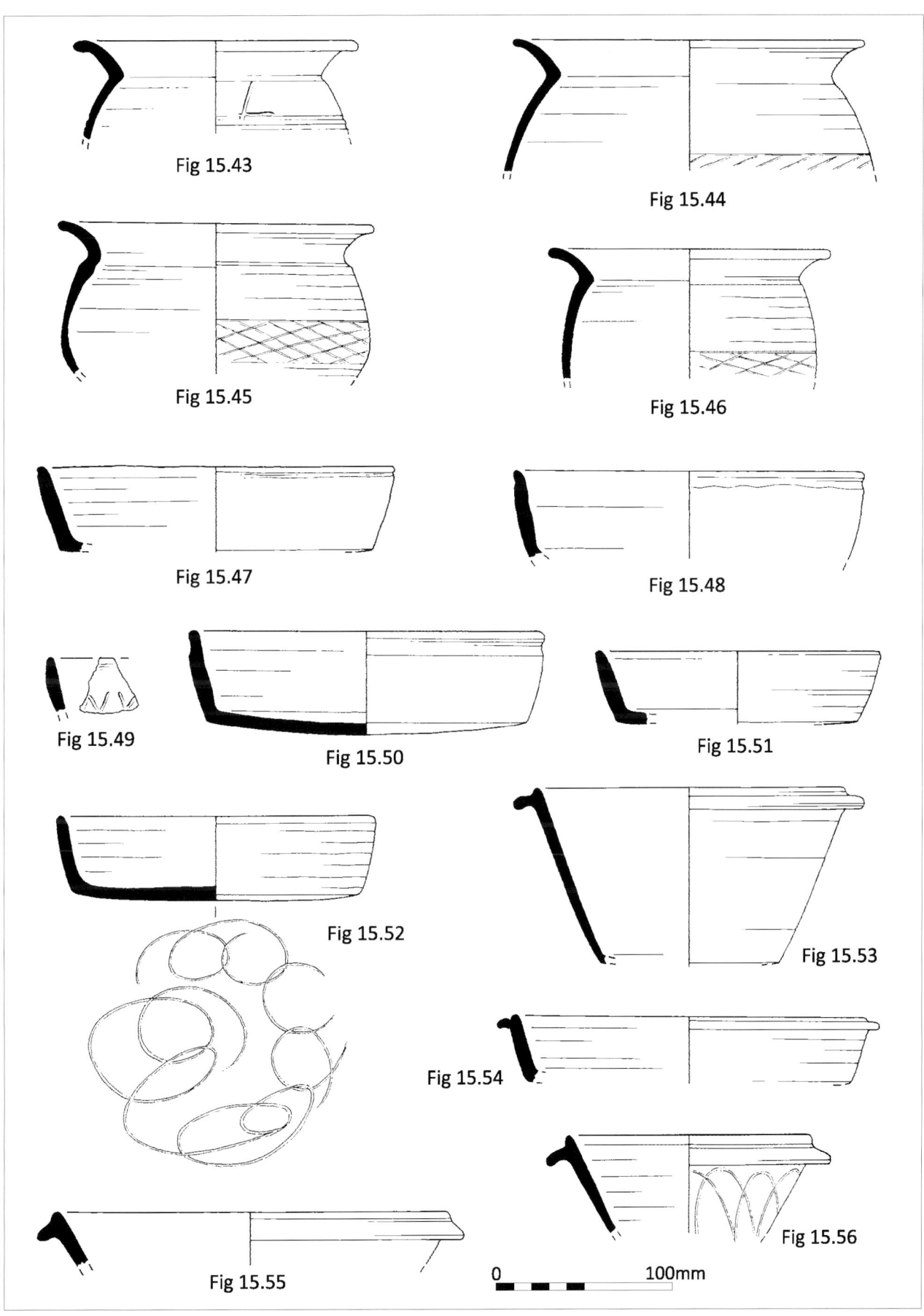

Fig 15.43

Fig 15.44

Fig 15.45

Fig 15.46

Fig 15.47

Fig 15.48

Fig 15.49

Fig 15.50

Fig 15.51

Fig 15.52

Fig 15.53

Fig 15.54

Fig 15.56

Fig 15.55

0   100mm

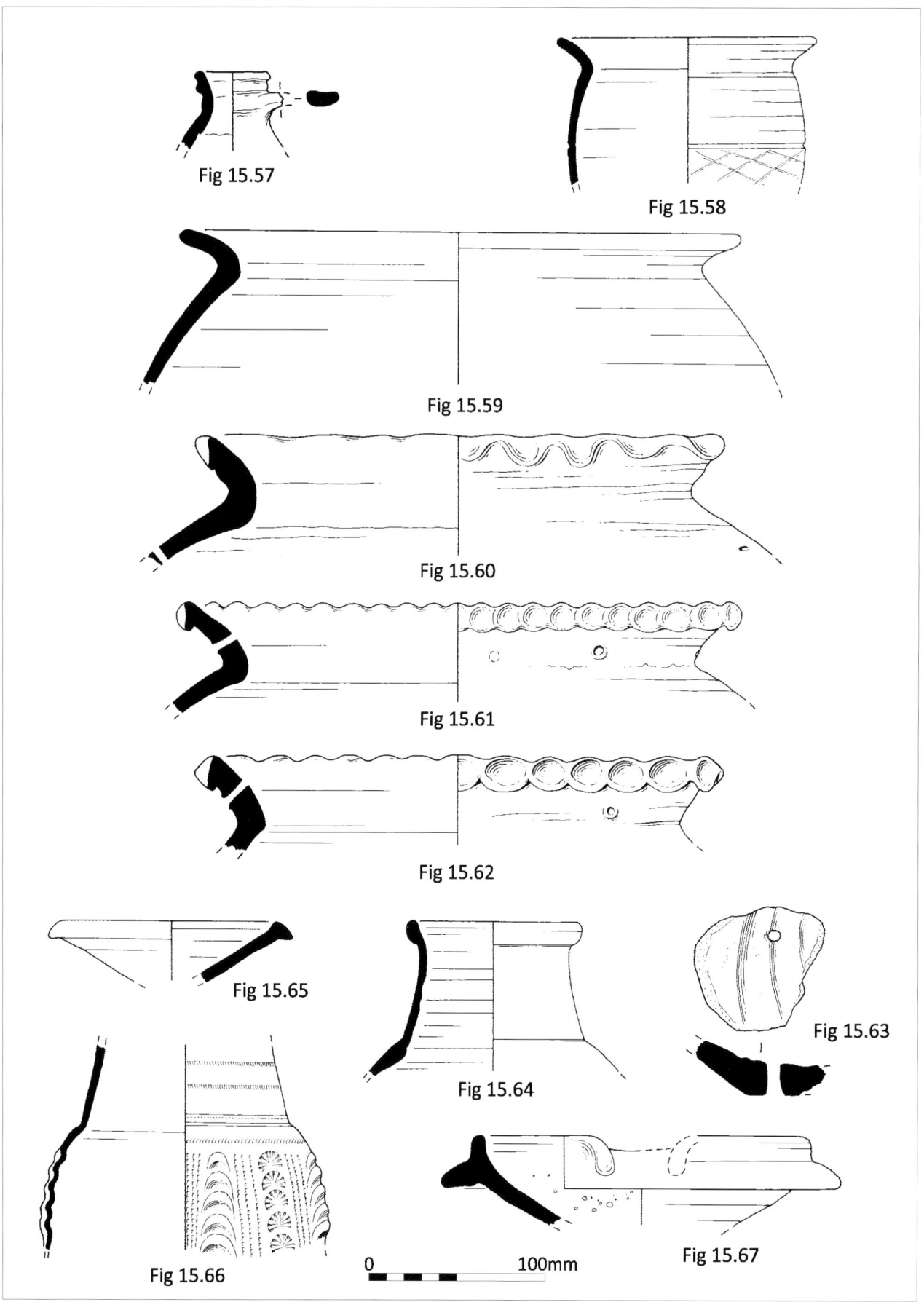

Fig 15.57

Fig 15.58

Fig 15.59

Fig 15.60

Fig 15.61

Fig 15.62

Fig 15.65

Fig 15.64

Fig 15.63

Fig 15.66

Fig 15.67

0 100mm

of associated body sherds from a flagon or jug (WA 29) from Room 21 (K4, context 9). Although these vessels form part of the standard Black Burnished ware range, this example is exceptional in that the handle (Fig. 15.3) has small, pre-firing perforations of the type more commonly associated with medieval jugs, presumably serving the same dual purposes of aiding firing and providing a decorative element to the vessel. Surface treatments and associations with other, more diagnostic, sherds suggest that all these uncommon forms are of Late Romano-British date.

In general, the earliest, first century BC – first century CE forms (e.g. WA types 1, 6–8, 13, 15, 16, 34 and 73), came from the trial trenches/. The distribution of first to early/mid third century CE vessel forms (e.g. WA 1, 2, 6, 8, 16, 23, 27, 29, 36 and 38) across the villa buildings themselves provided some slight indication of rubbish disposal being behind and in front of Buildings 2 and 2A (squares L95 and 96, P93 and P94), whist that from Building 3 seems to have gone to either side (squares A4, G–M2 – G–K5 area). It may also be of some significance that the sherds recorded as being from the colander (WA 19; M96 context 6 and R91 context 5) and *patera* (WA 30; N92 context 8) forms were from contexts associated with the southernmost building. Although both forms could have been used for a wide variety of domestic, culinary or even industrial purposes, they are sometimes interpreted as being associated with religious/ritual practices, for hand washing (Cool 2006, 47), for example, or in the preparation, pouring or collecting of libations (Woodfield 2005, 209), associated with household or public shrines.

Continental imports were scarce with samian representing just 0.5% of the assemblage by sherd count (see Mills, Chapter 16). Other imported tablewares were limited to sherds from Rhenish beakers made in Central Gaul and the Trier area and exported to Britain during the period from *c.* 150–250 CE. At least 20 sherds (weighing less than 75g) belonging to these fabrics were originally quantified amongst the 'other fabrics'. Two sherds were found in the vicinity of Room 35 (P95 contexts 1 and 7) while most were associated with Buildings 3 (Rooms 5, 12, 13 and 15), Building 4 (Room 25) and Buildings 1/7 (Rooms 42, 45 and 50). All four sherds (5g) from the sealed groups (M3 context 35; N93

context 8; N96 context 16 and R95 context 7) were in the slightly later (*c.* 180–250 CE) Moselkeramic (Trier) fabric and included one with rouletted decoration, but the pieces were too small to permit the more detailed identification of vessel form. Similar beakers also occurred in third century CE contexts at the Bucknowle (Light 2009, 142) and Halstock (Poulsen and Draper 1993, 120, fig. 43, 27) villas, at Tarrant Hinton (Draper 2006, 85) and residually, in fourth century CE deposits, at Greyhound Yard, Dorchester (Seager Smith and Davies 1993, 213).

The range of amphorae was similarly restricted and sherds from these vessels represented only 0.1% of the assemblage by sherd count. The assemblage included the ubiquitous, globular-bodied Dressel 20 vessels in standard Baetican fabrics (BAT AM 1 and 2; Tomber and Dore 1998, 84–5), used to transport olive oil from southern Spain from the middle first century CE until at least the middle of the third century CE. In addition, Gallic wine carried in the distinctive, flat-bottomed Pèlichet 47/Gauloise 4 amphorae (Peacock and Williams 1986, 142–3, class 27) may also have reached the villa. These amphorae had a long life, being imported from the middle of the first century CE, to the late third or possibly early fourth century CE, although it should be remembered that amphorae of all types were also extensively traded in their own right as empty containers. Slight concentrations in the distribution of amphorae were apparent in the vicinity of Rooms 31 and 40 (N99, contexts 2, 3, 4, 6, 14; O99 contexts 2 and 5), with a smaller group from Room 46 (N92 contexts 2 and 6). The sherds from Room 40 included part of a Dressel 20 rim (N99 context 3; rubble SE of wall 5).

Early Roman imported mortaria were also absent. However, a single rim from a moderately large vessel imported from Soller, Kreis Düren, Lower Germany (*ca* 170 – 230 CE) was found residually in pit P4 (Fig. 15.33). Locally, other vessels of this type occur in Dorchester (Seager Smith and Davies 1993, 222, WA 316). This overall paucity of imported wares is entirely consistent with the predominantly late Roman date of the assemblage as a whole, which falls outside the main period of ceramic importation.

The New Forest products represented 8.5% of the assemblage by sherd count (Table 15.1) and included all the principal fabrics made in this region – colour-coated wares, red-slipped and parchment wares (Fulford 1975a, 24–6, fabrics 1a–b, 2a) as well as sandy grey coarsewares (Fulford 1975a., 85). Although vessel forms were not quantified, indented beakers (type 27) appear to have been the most common type among the colour-coated wares (Fulford fabric 1a), with smaller numbers of plain (type 44) and decorated (type 49) bag-shaped beakers, globular-bodied beakers (types 33, 35, 36 and 41), cups (type 53), flagons (types 11), jugs (types 18 and 20) and jars/bowls (type 57). The indented beakers included one more or less complete example (Room 32; O97 context 7), with a capacity of c. 250ml. The red-slipped ware bowl forms were restricted to the most common types produced in this fabric (types 59, 61–63, 65, 67, 72, 73 and 76). The parchment wares included pieces from internally-flanged (type 89) and carinated (type 90) bowls as well as mortaria (types 102–107), while the sandy greywares included dropped flanged (type G6) and wide-mouthed (type G15) bowls, shallow, straight-sided dishes (type G19), jugs (types G20 and 21), lids (type G23), jars (types G30, G31 and G35) and storage jars (type G40). Although some of the New Forest forms were made throughout the period of production from the third quarter of the third century CE through to the late fourth century CE, the majority of forms found here (types 11, 18, 33, 35, 35, 36, 41, 44, 49, 57, 59, 61, 62, 65, 67 and 72) have more restricted, specifically fourth century CE, dates. The stamp decorated bowls (types 73 and 75), too, belong within the period c. 345–380 CE, while forms such as the parchment ware carinated bowls (type 90) and wide-mouthed greyware (type G15) bowls probably post-date c. 350 CE.

Unsurprisingly, given the distances involved and without easy overland or water routes, products of the Oxfordshire industry occurred in far smaller quantities (Table 15.1). Red-slipped ware bowls predominated and included types based on samian forms 31, 36 and 38 (Young 1977, types C45, C47, C51 and C53) made from c. 240/270 – 400 CE, as well as a wide range of more specifically fourth century CE forms (Young 1977, types C52, C61, C70, C75, C78, C79, C81 and C83). A few colour-coated ware beaker sherds from this region were also identified, including part of an indented beaker (Young 1977, type C20; c. 270–400 CE) from the topsoil overlying Rooms 34

and 35 (P95 context 1) and a globular-bodied beaker with impressed comb decoration (Young 1977, type C29; c. 270–360 CE) from Room 38 (O93 contexts 9 and 16). Whiteware, white colour-coated ware and red-slipped ware mortaria (Young 1977, types M18, M21, M22, WC7, C97 and C100), spanning the period from c. 240–400 CE, were also present. Despite the differences in quantity, the pattern of supply from the Oxfordshire and New Forest industries reflected the strengths of each; red-slipped ware bowls and mortaria were predominantly from Oxfordshire, being of superior quality to their New Forest counterparts, while beaker, flagon and jug forms made in the hard, durable New Forest colour-coated wares were preferable to the softer, more easily abraded Oxfordshire versions.

In addition to the Rhenish wares, the 'other fabrics' (Table 15.1) included a few unsourced oxidised (orange, buff, white-slipped red wares) and grey sandy ware sherds of Romano-British date as well as pieces of later prehistoric, medieval and post-medieval/modern date. Two sherds (<30g) recorded as being of Bronze Age date were found in E3 context 7 and G4 context 14, while four 'Iron Age' sherds (<50g) were recovered from K3 context 20, L2 context 19 and O99 context 9. Only two of these (from Room 22; K3 context 20) have been re-examined, comprising a body sherd from an Early Iron Age, carinated, fineware bowl in a fine, red-finished, sand and flint-tempered fabric and a grog-tempered sherd, probably of Late Iron Age/Early Romano-British date. The condition of both pieces suggested that they were residual.

Although present in only negligible quantities, the miscellaneous Roman fabrics formed part of the standard range seen in the area. The sandy grey coarsewares were numerically dominant within this group; most were probably New Forest products described above although one or two of the thick-walled storage jar sherds may have been from the Alice Holt industry (Lyne and Jefferies 1979, 34–51, classes 1, 4 and 10). The recently recorded material indicated the presence of a few grog-tempered body sherds and a handful of greyware pieces probably made in Somerset and/or east Devon between the second and fourth centuries CE (Holbrook and Bidwell 1991, 171; Seager Smith 1999, 310–12, fabrics

Q121 and Q122). These wares also occur in Late Roman contexts in Dorchester (Seager Smith 2008, 7, table 1; Seager Smith forthcoming). The oxidised wares consisted of plain body and base sherds from wheelmade flagon forms, along with smaller numbers from bowls and beakers.

A small (4g), plain body sherd in a fine, dark coloured, sandy fabric with rare to sparse organic inclusions (up to 5mm long) could be of early medieval date, probably fifth – seventh century CE, although the possibility that it was of Iron Age date could not be completely excluded. It was found in Room 12 (K3 context 9), alongside ten other pieces of Late Roman date. The medieval sherds (24 sherds, <260g) included jar rims and glazed jug sherds, all of local origin. The post-medieval/modern material (68 sherds, <950g) was of 18th–20th century date, and included salt glazed stoneware and Bellarmine jug fragments as well as one or two pieces of clay tobacco pipe and modern drain pipe. Most of the medieval and post-medieval material derived from the topsoil and layers immediately beneath it.

RE-USE AND REPAIR

Evidence for re-use and/or repair was not consistently recorded for the assemblage as a whole, although comments were sometimes included in a free-text notes field on the original Bournemouth University recording sheets. This information has been incorporated into this section, although most of the observations made here are based on the recently recorded portion of the assemblage.

Internal residues were noted on only three vessels, one probably of early to mid-first century CE date and the other two, both from pit-shaft P4, belonging within the late third or fourth century CE. One of these, part of a dropped flanged bowl (Fig. 15.20), has deposits of iron smithing slag on the interior and broken edges of the sherd. Its size and shape probably preclude any direct role (to hold water for quenching, for example) in the metallurgical process, but it could have been used for more domestic or culinary purposes by the metalworkers themselves and damaged in an accidental spillage, perhaps, or it might simply indicate the disposal of metallurgical

waste in the same areas as domestic rubbish during the late third or fourth century CE. A second vessel from this feature (context 19), a Late Roman Black Burnished ware jar, represented by body sherds with wiped surfaces and obtuse-angled lattice decoration, had deposits of limescale on the inside.

The early to mid first century CE vessel was found in Trial Trench 2 (TT2, contexts 2 and 9) and was made in the coarse, gritty *Durotrigian*-style black burnished ware fabric. This flat, jar-type base has limescale on its interior surface, extending through five, post-firing perforations set in a quincunx arrangement in its base. Three other jar bases with post-firing perforations, but without residues, were also recorded. One of these, again in the *Durotrigian*-style fabric and from Trial Trench 2 (context 15), had a single, central perforation (15mm across) while the others, from cold-store O100 (context 6) and Room 22 (K3 context 15), both had several smaller holes (4–5mm across). Although not closely datable, these two pieces were both of later, definitely Roman, date and the example from the so-called 'cold-store' may have had as many as five perforations, again in a quincunx arrangement. Such post-firing perforations are comparatively common in Britain, occurring during all four centuries of Roman rule (e.g. Fulford and Timby 2001, 294), although in Dorset, the practice is most frequently associated with the Late Iron Age/Early Romano-British period. Considerable care must have been required to drill the holes without breaking the whole pot and their creation clearly indicates the intentional adaption of a vessel to suit some purpose other than that for which it was originally made. In some instances, especially during the Late Iron Age/Early Romano-British period (e.g. Seager Smith 1997, 115), close associations between the perforations and internal limescale or other organic 'food' residues have been observed, suggesting that the residues relate to the use of the vessel after the holes were made. Such purposes are, however, likely to have been many and varied; it is easy to imagine such vessels used as plant-pots, for example, or, with a cloth lining perhaps, used to drain, strain or filter solids from liquids in a wide variety of industrial and domestic contexts. Other suggestions include their use as timing devices (filled with a material such as sand and then a liquid, which drips through in a pre-determined amount of time), while some may have been holed as part of wider chthonic rituals, to deliberately separate them from their previous function, perhaps prior to their deposition in deep pits, wells or other significant contexts (Fulford and Timby 2001, 295–6).

Small, post-firing perforations, probably indicating repair with metal staples or organic ties, were noted on a carinated sherd probably from a stepped lid found in Room 25 (M2 context 19) and a jar shoulder sherd from pit-shaft P4 (context 10). Both were made in the standard south-east Dorset Black Burnished ware fabric, the jar sherd exhibiting the slip and surface wiping characteristic of a Late Roman date. Once broken, a New Forest colour-coated ware beaker base from 'cold-store' P4 (context 19), may have been trimmed down and re-used as a small, shallow cup but in general, the villa assemblage was too fragmentary and abraded for evidence of such re-use and repair to be apparent. Two re-used sherds, however, both of Black Burnished ware, were also noted. One, from Room 29 (O5 context 6), had been trimmed and smoothed to form a flat disc; the second (pit-shaft O100) had been made into a oval shape, approximately 55 × 50 × 10mm. Items such as these are generally been interpreted as gaming pieces, counters or weights, but recent research has suggested that some, known throughout the Greco-Roman world as '*pessoi*', may have been used for cleaning the buttocks and anal area after defecation (Papadopoulos 2002; Charlier 2012).

SELECTED GROUPS

Deliberately deposited vessels

Three vessels were found set into the floor in Room 17 (H4, contexts 19, 20 and 21) and are presumably contemporary with its use. These vessels consisted of a more or less complete flanged rim jar (Fig. 15.4; context 19) and a jar base, probably from an everted rim form (Fig. 15.5; context 20), both in south east Dorset Black Burnished ware and a narrow-necked jar with a slightly cupped rim (Fig. 15.6; contexts 19 and 21), in a sandy greyware fabric probably made in the New Forest *c.* 270–350 CE (Fulford 1975a, 100, fig. 35.2). The flanged rim jars can reach a

considerable size (the largest known, from Colliton Park, Dorchester (Farrar 1977, 218, fig. 14.3, 32), has a capacity of over 50 litres), and were part of the repertoire of the south east Dorset potters from *c.* 250 CE onwards (Seager Smith and Davies 1993, 231; Holbrook and Bidwell 1991, 106, type 28), although the type seems most common in fourth century CE deposits (e.g. Farrar 1977, 218, fig. 14.3, 32–34; Fulford 1975b, type 154.1–3; Lyne 2012, 216, class 12). The jar base can only be given a later third – fourth century CE date. The function of these three vessels remains unclear, although similarly late vessels, including a flanged rim jar with comparable 90° burnished-line lattice decoration, were found set into the floor, possibly as storage vessels, of a Late Roman building in Charles Street, Dorchester (Wessex Archaeology 1989, 28–9, structure 1609, figs. 33, 11–17, fig. 34, 18 and 19), while others occur at Tarrant Hinton (Graham 2006, figs. 14 and 16) and at Bucknowle, where three third century CE jars, one of storage jar size and two smaller, one containing a small amount of carbonised grain, had been set into a floor (Light and Ellis 2009, 35). Other sherds from these deposits in Room 17 included a part of an everted rim jar (WA 2/3), a jar base fragment and four body sherds, all in oxidised, possibly slightly burnt, south east Dorset Black Burnished ware fabrics and likely to be of late third – fourth century CE date.

The fourth deliberately deposited vessel was a rope-rimmed storage jar (Fig. 15.7) made in South East Dorset Orange Wiped Ware (Gerrard 2010, 2, SEDOWW), found in Room 24 (D7 context 7) and broadly associated with Theodosian coins. Rims, bases and body sherds were recovered, 62 pieces (2901g) in all, although its profile was not fully reconstructable and it is possible that further sherds may occur in surrounding contexts. Approximately 30% of the rim (diameter of 460mm) and 12% of the base (diameter 180mm) survived; both surfaces were heavily wiped and there were traces of an off-white wash coating the exterior, while the interior of the base was heavily pitted and abraded, perhaps through wear. The vessel had the small (2–3mm across), square, angled, pre-firing perforations characteristic of this form through its walls and underside of the base, but none were noted around the rim/neck and not enough of the base survived to indicate whether this vessel had been made with

Table 15.1 Overall composition and distribution of the assemblage (number of sherds and weight in grammes)

Grid line	Black Burnished ware		Samian		New Forest wares		Oxfordshire wares		Amphora		Mortaria		Other fabrics		Overall total		
	No.	Wt.	No.	Wt.	No.	Wt.	No.	Wt.	No.	Wt.	No.	Wt.	No.	Wt.	No.	Wt.	Mean wt.
A	177	1920	1	5	8	55							10	145	196	2125	10.8
B	119	1775			5	25	1	35	7	285			5	320	137	2440	17.8
C	20	190											2	10	22	200	9.1
D	457	4578			11	130	2	50					75	3085	545	7843	14.4
E	954	11135	1	10	60	389	8	190					12	185	1035	11909	11.5
F	322	3985	1	50	14	215	7	140					4	45	348	4435	12.7
G	465	5755			48	445	7	115					29	520	549	6835	12.4
H	671	8610	3	5	68	400	3	115					49	645	794	9775	12.3
J	604	6345	10	210	49	575			1	495			3	15	667	7640	11.5
K	831	9225	2	25	43	672							5	55	881	9977	11.3
L	569	5465			17	220			2	370			5	55	593	6110	10.3
M1–5	1047	8375	6	175	74	470	1	5					5	20	1133	9045	8.0
M92–99	1382	10670	12	165	71	675	42	475					10	75	1517	12060	7.9
N1–5	288	2835			23	205	3	85					3	40	317	3165	10.0
N92–95	2556	19515	21	470	243	2410	9	225	2	225			5	45	2836	22890	8.1
N96–100	1395	11695	9	90	155	2920	3	30	8	595			4	60	1574	15390	9.8
O1–5	167	1885	6	20	4	30	2	250					1	5	174	2170	12.5
O91–95	848	6640	6	20	111	900	7	30					4	20	976	7610	7.8
O96–100	1619	21940	8	120	472	8895	22	885	3	120			17	230	2141	32190	15.0
P3–4	927	18810	1	5	103	2015	7	385			1	415			1039	21630	20.8
P92–99	717	5697	1	15	102	1320	51	305					3	20	874	7357	8.4
Q92–96	170	1285	1	5	4	30							1	15	176	1335	7.6
R,S,T	562	5155	3	35	25	219	11	110					3	15	604	5534	9.2
Test trenches	1037	9635	15	120	9	655	2	100					9	55	1072	10565	9.9
Totals	17904	183120	101	1525	1719	23870	188	3530	23	2090	1	415	264	5680	20200	220230	10.9
%	88.6	83.1	0.5	0.7	8.5	10.8	0.9	1.6	0.1	0.9	0	0.2	1.3	2.6			

Table 15.2 Summary of the assemblage from Pit-shaft P4

Fabric	Total no.	Total wt. (g)	Rim form code	No. sherds assigned to form	Max no. vessels	EVE
South-east Dorset black burnished ware	754	18356	WA 2	186	2	1.55
			WA 2/3	20	20	0.99
			WA 3	103	9	3.56
			WA 4	1	1	0.43
			WA 9	21	1	0.90
			WA 10	2	2	0.19
			WA 11	1	1	0.15
			WA 20	30	21	1.87
			WA 25	40	24	3.96
			WA 29	2	1	0.89
			WA 36	1	1	-
subtotal:	*754*	*18356*		*407*	*83*	*14.49*
South-east Dorset orange wiped ware	5	139	body sherds only	-	-	-
Greywares	30	397	FUL G20	22	1	1.00
New Forest parchment ware	11	218	FUL 89	11	1	0.05
New Forest colour-coated ware	36	1215	FUL 27	16	5	2.01
			FUL 53	1	1	1.00
Local red slipped ware	11	383	imit form 38 bowl	11	1	1.00
Soller mortaria	1	417	WA 316	1	1	0.08
Total	848	21125		469	93	19.63

a large central hole like some examples of this form (e.g. Seager Smith 1997, fig. 198, 13; Lyne 2012, fig. 154.8 and 155.1, .3 and 3). The earliest occurrences of SEDOWW are currently dated to *c.* 330–350 CE (Gerrard 2010) and at Bestwall, a post-370 CE date is suggested for the introduction of the rope-rimmed storage jar form (Lyne 2012, 216, fig. 149, class 13.2). The function of these vessels remains unclear, but they are a consistent feature of the latest Roman deposits in and around Dorchester and on the Isle of Purbeck, with rare examples further afield in Devon and Somerset, and it is probable that they continued to be made, used and deposited into the early fifth century CE (Gerrard 2010). Recent excavations at High Post, to the north of Salisbury (Jones 2011, 61, fig. 27, 30) and at Durrington (Wessex Archaeology 2012), in Wiltshire have identified sherds from vessels of the same form but made in sandy greyware fabrics, probably from the New Forest, and of similar very late or early sub/post- Roman date.

Pit-shaft ('cold-store') P4 and associated layers

This feature yielded 848 sherds (21.125kg) of pottery with a mean sherd weight of 25g; the composition of the assemblage is summarised in Table 15.2. Products of the south east Dorset Black Burnished ware industry represented 90% of the assemblage by sherd count, the remainder being sandy greywares (3%) and a small range of tablewares from the New Forest and an unsourced, but probably local, red slipped ware workshop (7%) as well as the Soller mortaria rim sherd described above. Overall, jar forms predominated (39% by EVE), with bowls/dishes at 25%, beakers/cups at 16% and flagon/jug forms at 10%, while shallow dishes were comparatively infrequent in this assemblage, representing only 9% of the forms by EVE.

The lowest investigated fills (contexts 24 and 25) of this feature contained sherds from six more or less complete vessels. The site archive includes reference to these layers containing "masses" (i.e. distinct groups) of pottery, most found close to the edge of the feature, especially its south-west face, but full details of their relative positioning *etc.* were not recorded and it remains unclear whether or not these pots were deliberately deposited. In all, 272 sherds, 8496g, were recovered, the six vessels comprising an indented beaker (Fig. 15.8; Fulford 1975a, 50, type 27) and a cup with white-painted decoration (Fig. 15.9; Fulford 1975a, 60, type 53), both in New Forest colour–coated ware, a local, red slipped ware flanged bowl imitating samian form 38 (Fig. 15.10) and three everted rim jars in the standard south east Dorset Black Burnished ware fabric (Fig. 15.11–13). Two of the jars (Fig. 15.11 and 15.12) had fairly squat, globular profiles, while the third (Fig. 15.13) had the more attenuated shape characteristic of Gillam's forms 12–14 (1976, 63–4, fig. 2). All three have the surface treatments and decoration characteristic of mid/late third – fourth centuries CE (Woodward 1987, 83–4). Both New Forest forms were made throughout the life of the industry (*c.* 270–400 CE), although there is some evidence to suggest that decorated cups mostly belong within the first half of the fourth century CE (Fulford 1975a, 60). A fourth century CE date is also most likely for the red slipped ware bowl (Fig. 15.3). The fabric of this vessel is broadly comparable to that of the Oxfordshire bowls, although it contains more sand and less mica than the typical products of this region. Similar wares have been identified in fourth century contexts at Greyhound Yard (Seager Smith and Davies 1993, 225, LRSW.3, fig. 121, 4 and 5), for example, and while still unsourced, these vessels are likely to be from Dorset workshops, perhaps representing further late off-shoots of the Oxfordshire industry (cf. Bird and Young 1981, 303–9).

Although more fragmentary, re-fitting sherds were noted among the material from the main fills (contexts 16–23) of this feature. Overall, 576 sherds (12629g; 13.62 EVE) were recovered from these layers, with the greatest quantity (197 sherds or 34%; 4922g), being from rubble layer 19. The Black Burnished wares were dominated by the standard range of Late Roman vessel types – everted rim jars (Fig. 15.14–17), shallow, plain rimmed dishes (Fig. 15.18–21) and dropped flanged bowls/dishes (Fig. 15.22–26). One of the everted rim jars has

diagonal burnished lines in the decorative band around its girth, a motif considered to date from *c.* 340 CE onwards (Lyne 2012, 222). Only four of the plain rimmed dishes were decorated; evidence from Portchester suggests that the use of arcading on dishes was already being abandoned by the end of the third century CE (Lyne 2012, 213). Two of the dropped flanged bowl/dish rims were from undecorated vessels, generally considered to be of fourth century AD date (Holbrook and Bidwell 1991, 109, type 46.3a and b), and two others were from vessels with very narrow, almost residual flanges (e.g. Fig. 15.26), a variant of the form dated to the last quarter of fourth century CE at Exeter (Holwell and Bidwell, 109, type 47) and present in final Roman assemblages dated to *c.* 370–420+ CE at Bestwall (Lyne 2012, 213, class 6/10–12). The minority forms, all known to continue into the fourth century CE, consisted of single examples of an everted rim jar with countersunk handles (Fig. 15.27), a handled beaker (Fig. 15.28), a flanged rim jar (Fig. 15.29) and a well-burnished cup-mouthed flagon with a narrow strap handle (Fig. 15.30) as well as rims from two small bead rim beakers (e.g. Fig. 15.31). One other piece, from an imitation samian form 29 bowl (Fig. 15.32), found in context 19, is, however, likely to be residual. Bowls of this type are generally considered to be of late first or early second century CE date, although the interlocking hoop decoration on this example is more characteristic of the flat-rimmed bowls and dishes (WA 22) of the period after *c.* 120 CE, perhaps suggesting a slightly later, mid/late second century CE date for this vessel. The Soller mortarium (Fig. 15.33), also from context 19, is again likely to be residual and these two distinctive pieces may therefore be highlighting the presence other, less diagnostic, residual sherds.

Although represented by base sherds only, two of the Black Burnished ware jars from these layers (cross-context joins, layers 17 and 19) were clearly wheel-made (Fig. 15.34 and 35). While outside the handmade tradition normally associated with the Wareham/Poole Harbour potters, wheel-thrown vessels in otherwise standard Black Burnished ware fabrics have also been recognised in Late Roman contexts at Poundbury (Seager Smith 2011, 100, pl. 5.9) and at the former County Hospital site in Dorchester (Trevarthen 2008, 40), including some from the same

Table 15.3   Summary of the assemblage from contexts 6, 10, 11, 12, 14 and 15 sealing Pit-shaft P4

Fabric	Total no.	Total wt. (g)	Rim form code	No. sherds assigned to form	Max no. vessels	EVE
South-east Dorset black burnished ware	112	1236	WA 2	1	1	0.23
			WA 2/3	2	2	0.05
			WA 3	3	3	0.29
			WA 10	1	1	0.15
			WA 20	2	2	-
			WA 25	5	4	0.24
subtotal:	*112*	*1236*		*14*	*13*	*0.96*
South-east Dorset orange wiped ware	6	52	body sherds only	-	-	-
Greyware	1	3	body sherd only	-	-	-
New Forest colour-coated ware	5	30	Fulford 27	1	1	0.07
Oxon colour-coated ware	3	140	Young C78	3	1	0.22
Total	127	1461		18	15	1.25

layer as the large Theodosian coin hoard probably put together and deposited in the first quarter of the fifth century CE (Cooke 2007, 65). Other pieces of interest include a Black Burnished ware body sherd (Fig. 15.36), with two letters, probably part of a literate graffito, cut into its exterior surface, while a jar base from layer 19 had a scratched X graffito on the underside (Fig. 15.37). This may represent an owner's mark although it is possible that some X marks represented simplified wheel or 'double-axe' motifs which may have carried funerary or underworld meanings, or were symbolic of deities, such as Fortuna, and good luck.

The fabrics and forms from other sources included five plain body sherds of South East Dorset Orange Wiped Ware (layers 16, 17, 19 and 21). Most of the sandy greywares came from a single jug with a collared rim (Fig. 15.38), probably made until at least *c.* 350 CE in the New Forest (Fulford 1975a, 96, type G20), while other products of this industry included an internally flanged Parchment Ware bowl (Fig. 15.39; Fulford 1975a, 72, type 89) and at least four colour-coated ware indented beakers (e.g. Fig. 15.40). Overall, a date in the second half of the fourth century CE seems likely for the deposition of these layers, the frequency of cross-context joins suggesting rapid, probably deliberate, infilling of this feature.

A further 127 sherds, 1461g, of pottery (Table 15.3) were recovered from layers 6, 10, 11, 12, 14 and 15

overlying pit-shaft P4. The small size and abraded condition of these sherds (average weight 11.5g) was comparable with that of the villa assemblage as a whole, and provided stark contrast to the large, well-preserved and often refitting, sherds from pit-shaft P4 itself. Chronologically, however, there was little to separate these two groups. Small quantities of South East Dorset Orange Wiped Ware were present and the vessel forms were consistently late. Part (0.22 EVE) of a well-worn, stamped Oxfordshire red-slipped ware bowl (Fig. 15.41; Young 1977, 166, type C78; *c.* 340–400 CE) came from context 15 and two of the South East Dorset Black Burnished ware flanged bowls/dishes (WA 25) had the short, stubby flanges characteristic of the Exeter type 47 vessels (Holbrook and Bidwell 1991, 109). Diagonal burnished line decoration was also noted on two of the everted rim jars (WA 3) and three other groups of jar body sherds, while two joining body sherds from a jar decorated with an external groove (context 10) were wheel-thrown. Post-firing scratched X graffiti were also noted on two vessels (Fig. 15.42 and 43).

Pit-shaft ('cold-store') O100

The assemblage from this feature is summarised in Table 15.4. With a mean weight of 20.5g, the sherds were marginally smaller than those from pit-shaft P4 (23.1g overall), although not significantly more abraded. Although still dominated by the south east Dorset Black Burnished wares (71% by sherd count), this feature contained a wider range of fabrics than

Table 15.4 Summary of the assemblage from Pit-shaft O100

Fabric	Total no.	Total wt. (g)	Rim form code	No. sherds assigned to form	Max no. vessels	EVE
South-east Dorset black burnished ware	817	14160	WA 2/3	34	33	1.37
			WA 3	23	11	2.31
			WA 10	3	3	0.29
			WA 11	1	1	-
			WA 18	2	2	0.38
			WA 20	43	37	2.61
			WA 25	55	41	3.90
			WA 29	1	1	1.00
subtotal:	*817*	*14160*		*162*	*129*	*11.86*
South-east Dorset orange wiped ware	250	7646	WA 2	13	3	0.56
			WA 12	10	7	0.39
Greyware	35	515	Fulford G6	2	1	-
			Fulford G20	8	3	1.20
			Fulford G23	3	1	0.31
Oxidised ware	1	9	body sherd only	-	-	-
New Forest colour-coated ware	23	546	Fulford 18	1	1	0.17
			Fulford 27	5	5	0.65
New Forest red-slipped ware	4	57	Fulford 63	3	3	0.30
New Forest parchment ware mortaria	2	267	Fulford 103	2	2	0.26
Oxon colour-coated ware	5	81	body sherds only	-	-	-
Oxon white-slipped red ware mortaria	2	87	body sherds only	-	-	-
Oxon red/brown slipped ware mortaria	1	44	base sherd only	-	-	-
Local red slipped ware	1	13	body sherd only	-	-	-
Pelichet 47/Gauloise 4 amphora	2	66	body sherds only	-	-	-
Total	1143	23491		209	155	15.70

pit-shaft P4, with far greater quantities of South East Dorset Orange Wiped Wares (22%, compared with 1% in pit-shaft P4 and its associated layers). By EVE, jars and bowls/dishes occurred in equal quantities (26% each), while the shallow dishes accounted for 17% overall. At 15%, the narrow-necked jug/flagon forms, which tend not to break into many pieces, were perhaps over-represented by EVE, the rims being from just five vessels or 3% of the maximum number of vessels identified overall. Of the remaining types, beakers and storage jars both represented 6% by EVE and mortaria and lids in the region of 2% each.

The Black Burnished wares were again dominated by the standard Late Roman forms – everted rim jars (Fig. 15.44–46), shallow, plain rimmed dishes (Fig. 15.47–52) and dropped flanged bowls/dishes (Fig. 15.53–56), although the majority of the jar rims were broken at or above the neck/shoulder junction (WA 2/3), preventing the precise identification of profile

shape. Only two jars were sufficiently well-preserved to show decoration; both had obtuse-angled lattice, one with a groove, one without, although jar body sherds with diagonal line decoration also occurred, notably in contexts 5 and 7. A maximum of 13 (0.72 EVE) of the plain rimmed dishes and 12 (1.86 EVE) dropped flanged bowls/dishes were decorated, mostly with burnished arcading, leaving the majority plain, with the simple wiped surfaces characteristic of the fourth century CE. Two letters, probably part of a literate graffito, were cut into the exterior surface of one of the plain rimmed dishes (Fig. 15.49), while one flanged bowl had unusual sloping flange (Fig. 15.55) and might be from a round-bodied variant (WA 69/81), sometimes supplied with one or more strap handles; although not illustrated, examples are known from fourth century CE or later contexts at Greyhound Yard, Charles Street and Colliton Park, Dorchester (Seager Smith archive). The minority forms again included small, bead rim beakers (WA

10), a flanged rim jar (WA 11) and a flagon (Fig. 15.57) as well as sherds from two round-bodied jar/bowls with everted rims (WA 18), both from context 6. One (Fig. 15.58) was clearly wheel-thrown and both were decorated with obtuse-angled lattice decoration beneath a horizontal groove. Although rare, partly because it is difficult to distinguish small pieces of this form from the ubiquitous everted and/or cavetto-rimmed cooking pots (WA 2 and 3), WA 18 vessels occur widely across Dorset and Somerset, generally in the latest Roman assemblages and often associated with Valentinianic and Theodosian coinage. This form is likely to have been introduced around 350 CE, possibly as late as 375 CE (Gerrard 2004, 69–71, table 8.1), while evidence from Bath highlights the possibility that the currency of this form and, by implication, that of the three standard late forms it is frequently found with, continued into the second or third decade of the fifth century (Gerrard 2007).

The similarly late, South East Dorset Orange Wiped Wares were present in all layers within this feature. Most derived from large jars, the rims indicating a maximum of ten vessels varying from 250–320mm in diameter, although all were relatively small pieces, resulting in the underrepresentation of these vessels by EVE (Table 15.4). Three of the rims, all from the basal fill (context 9), were from plain, everted rim storage jars (WA 2; Fig. 15.59), while the others, from contexts 5 and 6 at the top of the profile, were of the rope-rimmed variety (WA 12; Fig. 15.60–62). Storage jar base sherds, including one with pre-firing perforations (Fig. 15.63), were also noted in context 9. The other coarsewares, in sandy grey fabrics and a single body sherd in an unsourced oxidised ware (context 7), represented 3% of the assemblage by sherd count. Most of the greywares were probably from the New Forest, the recognisable forms including a flanged bowl, jugs (e.g. Fig. 15.64) and a lid (Fig. 15.65).

Together, the local red-slipped wares and products of the New Forest and Oxfordshire industries also represented 3% of the sherds from this feature. The Oxfordshire wares occurred as body and base sherds only, although these included a part of a large, brown, colour-coated ware beaker (Fig. 15.66), probably made between 340–400+ CE (Young 1977, 154, fig. 55, C30). The red slipped ware mortarium base from this industry (context 5) was noticeably worn and may even have been deliberately trimmed to form a shallow, saucer-like vessel; patches of burning on the surface of this piece hint that it might then have been used as an open lamp, in the same way as a Trier samian mortarium base found at Springhead, Kent (Seager Smith *et. al.* 2011, 120, fig. 2, 16). The more numerous New Forest wares included pieces from a colour-coated ware jug and indented beakers, red-slipped ware bowls resembling samian form 38 and parchment ware mortaria with plain, horizontal flanges (Fig. 15.67), all relatively common types within the repertoire of this industry (Fulford 1975a, types 18, 27, 63 and 103). The Pèlichet 47/ Gauloise 4 amphora sherds (**context 5**) suggest that Gallic wine reached the villa at some point during its history, although they are likely to be residual here.

While clearly of fourth century CE date, the presence of the WA 18 sherds and the increased frequency of the South East Dorset Orange Wiped Wares suggest that pit O100 filled slightly after pit-shaft P4, probably in the last decades of the fourth or even in the early fifth century CE. Within this feature, however, there were no traces of deliberate deposition, no more or less complete pots and few re-fitting sherds. Complete profiles were limited to incidental survivors, generally from relatively shallow vessels and, despite the healthy mean sherd weight (20.5g overall), fragmentation rates were comparatively high, with just 18% of the sherds assigned to form (Table 15.4) and many rims being broken at the neck/shoulder junction. Although undoubtedly derived from the villa occupation, it is likely that this assemblage had been subjected to one or more stages of mixing and manipulation prior to its deposition in this feature.

TRIAL TRENCHES (SOUTH) 1976

Although not conclusively located, the pottery from three of the four trial trenches excavated to the south of the villa in 1976 provided useful glimpses of the pre-villa, Late Iron Age and earliest Romano-British activity in the vicinity. As the descriptions of trenches 1–3 appear to have been lost, the three assemblages are considered here as single groups,

Table 15.5 Summary of the assemblage from Trial Trench 1

Fabric	Total no.	Total wt. (g)	Rim form code	No. sherds assigned to form	Max no. vessels	EVE
South-east Dorset black burnished ware	333	2475	WA 1	4	4	0.15
			WA 6	1	1	-
			WA 7	8	7	0.28
			WA 10	2	2	0.10
			WA 13	2	2	-
			WA 15	1	1	-
			WA 16	4	3	0.25
			WA 26	2	2	-
			WA 34	1	1	-
			WA 73	1	1	0.06
			jar rim frag	9	9	0.05
subtotal:	*333*	*2475*		*333*	*33*	*0.89*
Southwestern black burnished ware	2	23	base/body only			
Grog-tempered ware	2	16	plain bodies only			
Total	337	2514		333	33	0.89

although the context divisions have been maintained in the archive.

Trial Trench 1

The assemblage from this trench, summarised in Table 15.5, was highly fragmentary, illustrated by the mean sherd weight of just 7.4g and the low EVE total compared with the maximum number of vessels represented by the rims. The vast majority of sherds occurred in the standard Wareham/Poole Harbour Black Burnished ware fabric, although the vessel forms are typical of the first century BCE to first century CE 'Durotrigian' types defined by Brailsford (1958, fig. 1) – upright rimmed jars (WA 1), sometimes with countersunk handles (two examples found loose), flat-rimmed jars (WA 6), a wide variety of bead rim jars and bowls (WA 7, 10, 13, 15, 16 and 34) and lids (WA 26). The presence of a black burnished ware rim from a shallow dish or platter form (WA 73), loosely based on imported early samian or Gallo-Belgic fineware types, together with the two sherds of south-western Black Burnished ware made from the Claudian period onwards (Holbrook and Bidwell 1991, 91), however, suggest that the assemblage probably belonged within the third quarter of the first century CE.

Trial Trench 2

With the exception of a plain body sherd in an unsourced coarse sandy fabric probably of Romano-British date and a very battered Late Roman WA 25 rim, both from context 1 and likely to be intrusive, the assemblage from this trench (Table 15.6) was of Late Iron Age (c. 150 BC – 50 CE) date. The assemblage was characterised by an overwhelming predominance of sherds in the *Durotrigian*-style black burnished ware fabrics widely known in the area (e.g. Brown 1991, fabric A2). These wares share the subrounded, quartz sand temper of 'cod's roe' appearance and the same range of impurities (chalk, limestone, shale and ironstone) (Williams 1977, 198), as the later, more standardised Romano-British products of the Wareham/Poole Harbour kilns, but tend to be softer, more coarsely grained and thicker walled, with moderately smooth surfaces, often with a horizontally 'tooled' finish. Most appeared to be from jars, although diagnostic sherds were scarce and rims were limited to pieces from large flat-rimmed jars (WA 6) and bead-rimmed (WA 7) forms, both well-known *Durotrigian* types (Brailsford 1958, pl. 1, 4, 7 and 12), occasionally with scratched or finger-smeared 'eye-brow' motifs on the shoulder. The two jar bases with post-firing perforations (contexts 9 and 15) are discussed more fully above.

Table 15.6   Summary of the assemblage from Trial Trench 2

Fabric	Total no.	Total wt. (g)	Rim form code	No. sherds assigned to form	Max no. vessels	EVE
Durotrigian-style black burnished ware	131	2612	WA 6	17	4	0.83
			WA 7	4	3	0.35
			WA 26	1	1	-
sand and fine flint-tempered ware	4	22	plain bodies only			
South-east Dorset black burnished ware	1	10	WA 25	1	1	-
oolitic limestone tempered ware	1	9	plain body			
coarse sandy ware	1	2	plain body			
Total	138	2655		23	9	1.18

The four sand and fine flint-tempered sherds were similar enough to suggest that they, too, represented Late Iron Age products of the Wareham/Poole Harbour district, the sparse flint inclusions having been accidentally incorporated. Oolitic limestone-tempered wares formed a significant component of the Iron Age assemblage from Maiden Castle (Brown 1991, 186–7), for example, the Jurassic outcrops which would provide a suitable source for such vessels occurring within 7–12km of the site. The complete lack of any Romanised fabrics or forms in this assemblage, however, suggest that it is of first century BCE – early first century CE date and unlikely to have been added to after *c.* 30/40 CE.

Trial Trench 3

The assemblage from trial trench 3 (Table 15.7) was also highly fragmentary (mean sherd weight just 6.6g) and of mixed date. Although predominantly of earlier Romano-British date, residual Iron Age sherds (fine sandy ware, sand and flint-tempered and oolitic limestone-tempered wares) were recovered from contexts 2, 3, 6 and 10. These included a piece probably from an Early Iron Age red-finished fineware bowl (context 6), but the others could only be assigned a generalised Iron Age date. All 18 sherds (145g) from context 7 were, however, of Middle/Late Iron Age date, and may provide a genuine indication of the date of this deposit. They included three thick-walled body sherds (24g), probably from the same vessel, in a sand and fine flint-tempered fabric, as well as all the pieces of *Durotrigian*-style black

burnished ware. The two proto-bead rim jar sherds find extensive parallels at Hengistbury Head (Brown 1987, 208, type JC2, illus. 135 and 136), Maiden Castle (Brown 1991, 187) and elsewhere.

The Romano-British material spanned the period from the mid/late first century until at least the later second century CE, although again only standard products of the south east Dorset industry were included. Closed forms (WA 1, 2, 7 and 10) predominated, together representing 78% of the Black Burnished wares by EVE, while the round-bodied bowls (WA 13, 15 and 73) represented a further 9% and the straight-sided bowl/dishes (WA 20 and 22) 12% overall. A small footring base sherd (context 10) may have derived from a cup or small bowl copying samian form 33 (WA 54; probably of second century CE date) but no other sherds of intrinsic interest occurred amongst this group.

SUMMARY

Although predominantly of late third – fourth century CE date, the ceramics suggest that Romano-British activity on the villa site itself commenced during the mid/late second century CE and may have continued into the early fifth century CE. The earlier, Late Iron Age (*c.* first century BCE into the early decades of the first century CE) material was, by and large, confined to the trial trenches, and there appears to have been a temporal as well as a spatial hiatus between these two phases of activity.

Table 15.7   Summary of the assemblage from Trial Trench 3

Fabric	Total no.	Total wt. (g)	Rim form code	No. sherds assigned to form	Max no. vessels	EVE
South-east Dorset black burnished ware	309	2004	WA 1	8	7	0.22
			WA 2	6	6	0.40
			WA 7	2	1	0.17
			WA 10	2	2	0.22
			WA 13	2	1	0.07
			WA 15	1	1	0.05
			WA 20	4	4	0.10
			WA 22	1	1	0.06
			WA 73	1	1	0
subtotal:	*309*	*2004*		*27*	*24*	*1.29*
Durotrigian-style black burnished ware	15	121	proto-bead rim jar	3	2	0.17
sand and fine flint-tempered ware	7	53	plain bodies			
oolitic limestone tempered ware	1	10	plain body			
fine sandy ware	1	9	plain body			
Total	333	2197		30	26	1.45

The composition of the assemblage, overwhelmingly dominated by Black Burnished wares from the Wareham/Poole Harbour kilns, was typical of other villa sites in the region (Draper 2006; Light 2009) and indeed, of Dorchester itself (e.g. Seager Smith and Davies 1993; Seager Smith 1997, 2002; 2008; 2011). The paucity of imports is entirely consistent with the Late Roman date of this assemblage and known distribution patterns across southern Britain as a whole. The relatively small proportion of non-Black Burnished ware fabrics (less than 20% by sherd count) indicated that there was little room for anything other than 'specialist' vessels (such as mortaria, amphorae, fine tablewares and flagons), all the normal, everyday food preparation and storage roles being fulfilled by the Wareham/Poole Harbour industry – at least until the very end of the Roman period when a slightly wider range of fabrics reached the area. The vessel forms were predominantly utilitarian, encompassing the standard range of types characteristic of the period in this region – jars of all sizes and straight-sided bowls and dishes, together with a smaller range of less common types (flagons, lids, beakers, mortaria *etc.*). There was nothing within the ceramic assemblage as a whole to indicate status, functional specialisation or particular activity zones. Only limited evidence for re-use or repair was encountered, implying easy access to the wider market economy and a ready supply of replacement vessels. However, the comminuted nature of the assemblage and its recovery, in the main, from layers overlying the structural remains, suggests that most of the domestic and/or industrial debris originating from the occupation of the villa buildings was initially deposited in discrete middens, that were only later spread out, presumably by agricultural processes, after the abandonment of the site.

16

THE SAMIAN POTTERY

by J.M. Mills

METHOD

Notes were made of the fabric, form and date range of the sherds. Where possible, potters' stamps were identified, whilst decorated sherds were dated only on stylistic grounds. There appears to be little post-depositional degradation or abrasion of the sherds. Some heavy wear was noted internally and on foot-rings, whilst drilled holes and cut slots observed on two or three sherds suggest vessels were mended to extend the usual life of these pots.

THE ASSEMBLAGE

Fewer than 100 sherds were recovered so any interpretations based on this group of samian will not be statistically valid (Table 16.1). The overall impression is that the vast majority dates to the late Antonine period into the early third century, with bowl forms predominating. Of the 36 sherds identified to a vessel form, 12 are rouletted bowls, although many are recorded as either Dr 18/31R or Dr 31R given the apparent late second century bias in the collection most of these are likely to be form 31R. Only six cups were identified, one Dr 27, three Dr 33 and two which could not be identified to a specific form, but based on size, must be cups.

There were two sherds of first century samian from South Gaul (probably La Graufesenque), one decorated, and one the rim from a Ritterling 12

bowl, a form that is predominantly pre-Flavian. The majority of the samian is from the second century kilns of Lezoux in central Gaul; no Les Martres ware was noted. One incomplete stamp was noted on a plain bowl, as well as fragments of Doeccus i mould stamp from a decorated bowl. The latest vessels are from Eastern Gaul, a total of seven were identified, three of which were stamped. Of these two could be identified, the latest, a stamp of Paternus iii of Trier is dated *c.* 220–245 CE. East Gaulish samian is well-known from Dorchester and sites in the Dorchester hinterland excavated when the by-pass was built (Seager-Smith 1997, 226–8). East Gaul wares were also recovered at Tarrant Hinton villa (Pengelly 2006, 75–84).

The Dewlish samian assemblage is a small but valuable collection, essentially of a late second century date with a small amount of third-century ware present. This suggests that samian was available almost to the end of the period that it was exported to Britain. The few first century sherds and the presence of Central Gaulish forms 27 and 18/31 may indicate a limited amount of activity on the site in the early second century CE.

THE SAMIAN POTTERS' STAMPS

Fig. 16.1 Doeccus i (Doveccus), 11c, CG, Dr 37. [D]OVII[CC] V[S] (N92, 2) *c.* 170–200 CE.

Fig. 16.2 Iuvenis ii, die 2a or 2a', EG, Dr 31 (Lud Sa). IVU[ENISFECT] (F2, 27). Die 2a is complete as shown, whilst 2a' ends with the F. This potter is known from Rheinzabern and may have worked at Heiligenberg before working there. This sherd was too small to be certain of the exact provenance c. 170–220 CE.

Fig. 16.3 Paternianus iii, die 1a, Trier, Dr 31R (Lud Sb). PATERN[IΛVΊ] (M2, 19) c. 220–245 CE.

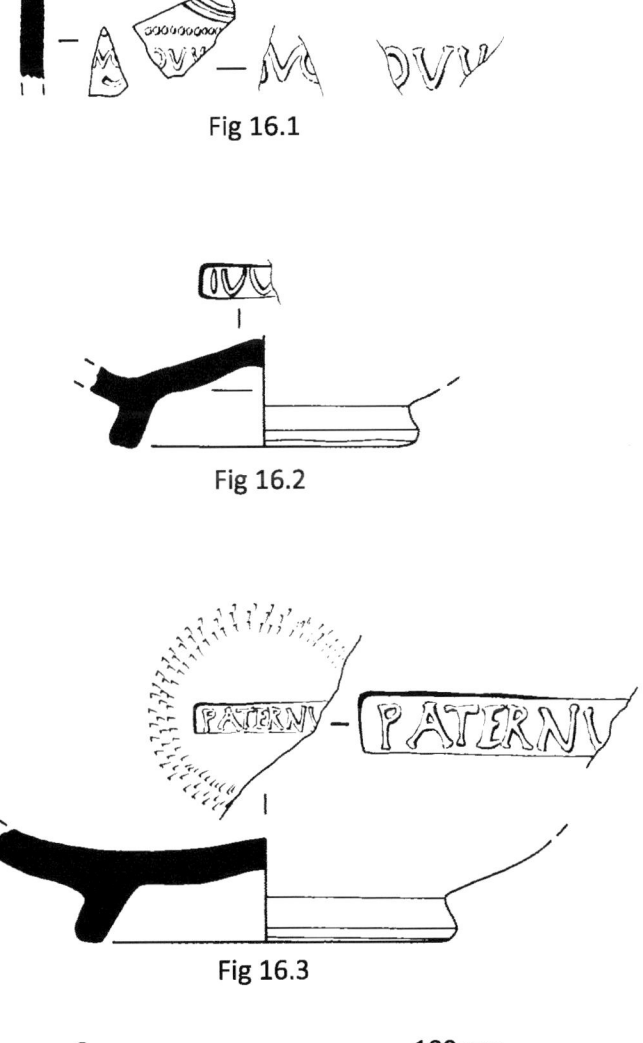

Fig 16.1

Fig 16.2

Fig 16.3

0   100mm

Figures 16.1–3   The samian potters' stamps. Drawings: David Watt.

Table 16.1 Samian wares

Gr1	Gr2	Cont.	rim	total no	wt (g)	Cnd	Fabric	Sld	Remarks	form	date min	date max	Fabric
N	94	1		1	5	3	?CG	n	dish/bowl rim,	dish/bowl	160	200	?CG
K	3	19		1	20	2	CG	y	Dr ? CG (Antonine)		140	200	CG
J	3	1		3	35	2	CG	n	18/31R or 31R (slot cut for rivet)	18/31R or 31R	140	200	CG
J	3	11		3	50	2	EG (TR) & CG	y	2 x 18/31R or 31R CG rims (120–200); 1 base angle Dr 18/31 CG 120–160;	18/31r or 31R x 2 AND 18/31	120	220	EG (TR) & CG
J	4	7		1	15	2	CG	n	Dr 33 CG rim (mid-late Antonine)	33	150	200	CG
J	4	17		2	60	2	CG	y	Dr31R poss Lezoux (165+)	31R	165	200	CG
M	2	6		2	5	3	CG	n	rim=Dr37(C2nd) no dec;base=Dr 31 CG, (C2nd)	37; 31	140	200	CG
M	2	8		1	5	3	CG	n	37 dish/bowl rim CG(2nd)	37; dish/bowl	120	200	CG
M	5	3		1	40	3	CG	n	Dr37 CG crab O.2156 not sure of potter Antonine	37	140	200	CG
M	92	2		1	10	4	CG	n	18/31R or 31R (2nd C)	18/31R or 31R	120	200	not seen this time
M	92	3		5	120	3	CG	n	18/31 dish CG (2nd C)	18/31	120	160	not seen this time
M	92	11		1	10	4/2	CG	y	bowl CG Antonine)	bowl	140	200	CG
M	92	14		1	5	5/3	CG	n	27	27	120	200	CG
M	93	2		1	10	3	CG	n	Dr31R base angle	31R	165	200	CG
M	95	16		2	5	3	CG	n	Dr 33 CG (Antonine) body	33	140	200	CG
M	97	5		9	35	?	CG	?	dish/bowl CG (2nd C) rim	dish/bowl	120	200	CG
N	92	2		2	10	4	CG	n	SF740 Dr 37 in dec stamp Doeccus 11c	37	170	200	CG
N	92	12		1	10*	?	CG	n	rim =?Dr31 CG (Antonine)	31	150	200	not seen this time
N	93	2		1	50	4/5	CG	n	Dr 31R CG base	31R	165	200	CG
N	93	6		3	160	3/3	CG	n	Dr 31R CG 3 joining shds, patch of slip worn off inside wall	31R	165	200	CG
N	94	15		1	5	3	CG	n	18/31R or 31R	18/31R or 31R	120	200	CG
N	94	32		1	15*	?	CG	?	Dr 37 Mercator II	37	160	180	CG
N	97	3		1	5	3	CG	n	18/31 dish/bowl rim,CG (2ndC)	18/31	120	200	CG, not seen this time
N	97	11		1	5	3	CG	n	foot-ring, bowl	bowl	140	200	CG
N	98	6		2	30	4/2	CG	n	18/31R or 31R, slip worn off rim	18/31R or 31R	140	200	CG
N	98	14		1	5	3	CG	?	33	33	140	200	CG
O	92	10		1	5	3	CG	n	chip C2nd		120	200	CG
O	100	3		2	20	4	CG	n	37 – DEC ? Casurius leaves??	37	160	200	CG

Gr1	Gr2	Cont.	rim	total no	wt (g)	Cnd	Fabric	Sld	Remarks	form	date min	date max	Fabric
Q	96	3		1	5	5	CG	n	chip CG		120	200	CG
TT	3	2		4	5	4	CG	n	2xCG dish –2 vessels	2 x dish	120	200	CG
TT	3	3		6	25	4	CG	n	?Dr 33 or 46 CG not stamped, int base worn; 1 x dish (R-), 4 x body chips (Form not known)	33/46; 1x dish	120	200	CG
TT	4	2		3	75*	?	CG	n	base Dr31CG stamp] И ;2 x rims Dr18/31R or 31R	31; 18/31R or 31R x 2	165	200	CG
	XV	1		1	15	4	CG	n	plain footring 'bowl' CG	bowl	140	200	CG
		sum		67	875								
N	93	8		1	5	3	CG or EG	y	dish/bowl rim,	dish/bowl	160	220	CG or EG
N	94	9		3	100	3	?EG	?	lge dish +plain ftring,drilled repair hole; broken across stamp . Could be Lud Tb cf New Fresh Wharf 2.166 (Bird 1986)	?Lud dish	160	220	?EG
N	95	8		1	10	4	?EG	n	37 rim, no dec	37	180	230	?EG
R	91	4		2	15	3	EG	n	probably 31R body – both sherds prob same vessel	31R?	170	220	EG
F	2	27		1	50	?	EG (Rheinz)	y	Dr 31 stamped base IVV[luvenis ii	31	170	220	EG (Rheinz)
J	3	11		1	50	2	EG (TR) & CG	y	Dr31R Trier base heavily worn foot (late C2nd – e C3rd); 2 x 18/31R or 31R CG rims (120–200); 1 base angle Dr 18/31 CG 120–160;	31R	120	220	EG (TR) & CG
M	2	19		2	135	3	EG(TR)	y	Dr31R stamp EG Paternus iii	31R	220	245	EG(TR)
O	92	9		2	15	2/2	Rz and CG	y	1 x CG body, 1 x EG base , ?cup form-footring worn, no stamp. ?RZ (could draw if late C2nd = stuff important	cup?	170	220	Rz and CG
		sum		12	375								
TT	2	1		1	10	4/5	SG – La Graufesenque	n	SG Ritterling 12 C1st 50–90)	Ritt 12	50	90	SG – La Graufesenque
O	100	6		4	35	2/2	?SG	y	4 x oxford; 1 x SG Dr 30? dec	30?	50	100	?SG
		sum		5	45								

SMALL FINDS

Compiled by Maureen Putnam with analyses by Iain Hewitt
and illustrated by Jonathan Milward, Tilia Cammegh and David Watt

INTRODUCTION AND METHOD STATEMENT

The scope of this report refers to finds that were designated as being of particular interest and therefore retained as material archive during the excavations of 1969–1979, during which time each of these items was allocated a unique Small Finds Number (SFN) and recorded in a site register which is part of the Dewlish Roman villa archive (BU100DEW0130). The materials in question include objects of copper (CuA), iron (Fe), lead (Pb), shale, and worked bone. These categories are dealt with in discrete sections in the paragraphs that follow under three headings: Metals (copper, iron and lead), Shale, and Worked Bone including a substantive section on bone pins. Where appropriate, individual items were examined macroscopically using a ×8 hand lens. Measurements were obtained using a dial calliper calibrated in millimetres.

This report will not provide an exhaustive list of finds because many of the examples are in a fragmentary state and/or in poor condition making them difficult to identify with confidence, and the Special Finds Register contains some ambiguities. Here, emphasis will be given to the objects that can be identified with reasonable confidence and will indicate their significance to the interpretation of site. Throughout this chapter sealed contexts are designated by an asterisk (e.g. 8*).

METALS

The Copper Alloy (CuA) objects

A total of 103 copper alloy objects, including multiple same object fragments, was excavated from c. 80 contexts across the site of the villa between 1969 and 1979. Only 21 of the contexts that contained copper artefacts were designated as sealed (i.e. 26.3%). Many of the copper finds were scattered in the topsoil and subsoils that had been disturbed by medieval agricultural activity and by the two 18th century excavations recorded by Hutchins (see Chapter 1). These episodes of disturbance probably account for the poor condition of many of the copper finds from Dewlish. Table 17.1 shows sub-groupings of the 103 CuA finds by use (function) categories. Most of the artefacts can be regarded as objects of personal adornment such as bracelets, or tools for grooming such as sets of tweezers. The CuA artefacts are indicative of middle to high status. If this premise is accepted, then the distribution of the copper artefacts across the site is a matter of potential significance that requires further consideration.

Table 17.2 records the distribution of the CuA finds across the villa site. Essentially, the 1969–1979 excavations were exercises in wall-chasing: sections of wall were revealed by trial trenching and these features were followed across the site by subsequent trenches until all elements of a specific building or feature were defined. This strategy confined

Table 17.1   CuA Small Finds by function category

Object function category	Number of objects	Percentage of total (103)
Bracelets	9	8.7
Brooches	1	1.0
Hasps and fittings	2	1.9
Nails and tacks	4	3.8
Pins	3	2.9
Plates and binding strips	22	21.3
Rings	8	7.8
Strap ends	1	1.0
Studs	8	7.8
Tweezers	3	2.9
Utensils (miscellaneous)	6	5.8
Wire lengths	2	1.9
Unidentified fragments	34	33.0
Totals	103	100

Table 17.2   Sealed CuA deposits by Building number or feature

Building/Feature no and name	Sealed CuA Contexts	Percentage of Total (21)
Building 1 (Small Villa)	1	4.8
Building 2/2A (Aisled Building)	2	9.5
Building 3 (*Domus*)	10	47.6
Building 4 (Bath House)	2	9.5
Building 5	-	-
Building 6 (Shrine/Temple)	-	-
Building 7	-	-
Pit-shaft O100	3	14.3
Pit-shaft P4	-	-
Buildings 1 and 2 overlap	2	9.5
Buildings 1 and 7 overlap	1	4.8
Totals	21	100

the archaeology of the site to the footprint, or the immediate vicinity of built structures, therefore the distribution of finds of all categories was virtually absent from the largely unexcavated courtyard of the villa and areas beyond its curtilage. The archive is also bereft of artefacts of all categories (including surface finds), from the area of the unexplored east range of the villa. Arguably, these limitations diminish the significance of artefact distribution plots.

Limitations aside, Table 17.2 gives details of the distribution of CuA finds associated with each of the seven excavated component buildings of the villa and the two pit-shafts from which several discarded objects were recovered. The picture is complicated by the multiple episodes of building development at Dewlish that resulted in two notable instances of foundation overlap as redundant buildings were demolished and replaced, making the provenance of artefacts from these areas difficult to determine unless they were retrieved from a secure context. Nonetheless, the fact that 47.6% of copper finds were recovered from the footprint and the immediate environs of the *domus* (Building 3), and a further 9.5% from the bath house (Building 4), demonstrates that a total of 57.1% of these artefacts were associated with the two buildings of highest status. By contrast,

copper was entirely absent from Building 5 (of uncertain function), Building 6 (probably a shrine) and Building 7 (a barn or store, perhaps also a workshop). The absence of copper artefacts from these buildings is arguably unsurprising.

Illustrated CuA finds

The fifty most securely identifiable finds have been illustrated. Each object is listed by its unique Small Find (SFN) number followed by a brief description that includes distinguishing characteristics, measurements in millimetres and its location within the Dewlish site grid by alphanumeric grid trench code and bracketed context number (e.g. A1(4)).

SFN523   Penannular **bracelet** with 5 linear incisions at each knurled end. Outer diam. 55mm, inner diam. 47mm. Context O92(9*). Fig. 17.1a.

SFN513   Penannular **ring** fragments (×3), two with rolled ends 34.4mm diam. O94(4). Fig. 17.1b.

SFN109   **Bracelet** fragment 18mm long with 'stepped' decorative detail. F3(2). Fig. 17.1c.

SFN742   Twisted wire **bracelet** with bent hook type clasp. External diam. 6.5mm. N93(7). Fig. 17.1d.

SFN821   **Bracelet** in two fragments decorated with three-line bands. 46mm approx. diam. M98(8). Fig. 17.1e.

SFN804   **Bracelet** fragment decorated with bands and punch marks. 47mm long × 4mm wide. M99(1). Fig. 17.1f.

SFN402 **Bracelet** in sub-circular form, clasp incomplete. Oblique and banded line decoration. Max. diam. 53mm. D3(2). Fig. 17.1g.

SFN128 Curved strip, probably a **bracelet** fragment. Decorated with punched bands and diagonal lines. *c.* 50mm × 5mm. K4(3). Fig. 17.1h.

SFN416 **Bracelet** fragment of twisted wire, part of clasp present. 50mm × 4.5mm. Fig. 17.1i.

SFN236 Signet-type **Ring** *c.* 20mm internal diam. Corroded. Unstratified. Fig. 17.1k.

SF7N11 **Ring** *c.* 20mm diam. of twisted wire with circular bezel 8.5mm diam. of wire in spiral form. N92(2). Fig. 17.1l.

SFN806 Headless **Pin** formed into a sub-circular ring. O99(2). Fig. 17.1m.

SFN562 **Ring** with no visible joint. Perhaps a part of a larger object. External diam. 19mm, internal diam. 14.2mm. M95(1). Fig. 17.1n.

SFN861 **Ring** sub-hexagonal in shape. External diam. 20mm × 3.6mm max. width. O100(7*) sealed within pit-shaft deposits therefore probably a discard. Fig. 17.1i.

SFN136 **Tweezers** with one side bent. Chain attachment loop at top. 50mm long. Max. width 7.11mm, min. width 3mm. Unstratified but recovered from the footprint of Building 3. Fig. 17.2a.

SFN001 **Strap end** sub-triangular in shape. 50mm long × 30mm max. dimensions. Unstratified, but a similar example was found at Bestwall quarry, Wareham, Dorset which was in a (Ladle 2012, 938) medieval context. C5(1). Fig. 17.2d.

SFN350 **Tweezers** 40mm long gripping ends turned inwards. Top loop for chain attachment. Max. width 6mm. Corroded. P4(20*). Recovered from fills of a pit-shaft therefore probably a discard. Fig. 17.2e.

SFN263 Implement with hook at one end and tapering to a point at the other. Possibly a dual-purpose **tool**. Length 108mm × width 5mm. N5(9). Fig. 17.2b.

SFN462/3 Curved 155mm length of 10mm gauge **wire** found in two parts. R96(7*). Fig. 17.2c.

SFN505 **Chain link** 22mm long shaped from 3mm gauge wire. O96(7). Fig. 17.2g.

SFN378 **Bell-like** object with loop for chain attachment. 26mm diam. D3(2). Fig. 17.2f.

SFN123 Decorative fastening probably a **hasp** component of a larger object. 23mm in length. E3 (20*). Fig. 17.2h.

SFN092 **Hasp**, sub-triangular in form. Max. length 19mm. Probably relatively modern. Unstratified. Fig. 17.2i.

SFN282 **Fibula** fragment, curved with ridge embellishment. Length 24mm. Unstratified. Fig. 17.2j.

SFN111 **Bracelet** formed from a CuA strip 9mm wide

bent into a sub-circular shape with overlapping ends. Decorated with two faint lines along entire length of strip. F3(8). Fig. 17.2k.

SFN361 Oval **plate** with one end broken. As seen, 35mm long × 8mm max. width. 2 × t-shaped rivets attached, each 7.5mm diam. K3(18*). Fig. 17.3a.

SFN002 Rectangular **strip** 41mm × 22mm with torn or corroded edges. Two holes 3.8mm diam. One of which contains a rivet. Unstratified. Fig. 17.3b.

SFN012 Rectangular **plate** 30mm × 23mm perforated centre by a square hole of 5.5mm sides. E5(13). Fig. 17.3c.

SFN099 **Plate** in two parts, combined dimensions 68mm × 15mm, with three holes. Repeat chevron pattern on longer sides. G5(20*). Fig.17.3e.

SFN014 **Binding strip** 9mm wide with sides of 39mm as measured from the scallop decorated spine. A single punched hole on each side. Unstratified. Fig. 17.3d.

SFN687 **Binding strip** with rib decorated spine measuring 42.3mm × 22mm. Two flat T-shaped rivets of 2.5mm diam. *in situ.* N95(15). Fig. 17.3f.

SFN108 Penannular **tube**. Length 40mm × 8mm. F3(2). Fig. 17.3g.

SFN067 **Strip**, curved in section, 59mm × 5.5mm with double band decoration at one end. E3(13*). Fig. 17.3h.

SFN566 **Stud** with domed head 8.5mm diam. with square shank 13.5mm long. M95(3). Fig. 17.3i.

SFN658 **Stud** with domed head and square **sectioned** shank 12mm long. N92(2). Fig. 17.3j.

SFN713 **Stud** with 8mm diam. head, shank 14mm long. N92(2). Fig. 17.3o.

SFN679 **Nail** fragment with flat asymmetric head. Shank 11mm long. N92(2). Fig. 17.3p.

SFN629 **Stud** with domed head 7mm diam. Shank of square section, bent at tip. N92(2). Fig. 17.3l.

SFN654 **Nail** with convex head of 6mm diam. Shank 14mm long. G3(25*). Fig. 17.3m.

SFN750 **Stud** with head 8mm diam. Square sectioned shank 14mm long. N92(2). Fig. 17.3k.

SFN601 **Stud** with misshapen domed head 7.5mm diam. Square sectioned shank 12mm long. N93(2). Fig. 17.3n.

SFN223 **Nail** fragment of irregular shape *c.* 9mm × 5mm. O5(7*). Fig. 17.3q.

SFN560 **Stud** with misshapen head 7mm diam. Shank of square section 4mm long. M96(5). Fig. 17.3r.

SFN813 **Pin or peg** with head of 3.5mm diam., shank 19mm long. M99(2). Fig. 17.3s.

SFN805 **Nail** with oblique head and square sectioned shank. O100(1). Fig. 17.3t.

SFN006 **Wedge** roughly rectangular and drawn to a point at one end. 44mm long. E4(2). Fig. 17.3u.

SFN003 **Wedge** of square section with chisel-like end. 29mm × 5mm. E4(2). Fig. 17.3v.

SFN011 **Tack** with domed head of 19.8mm diam. and short pointed shank of 8mm length. E5(13). Fig.17.3w.

SFN320 **Ligula**, olivary type, probably had a dual purpose in the process of preparing medicines (Milne 1907). Length 155mm. 'Spoon' end 25mm long × 8mm wide decorated with simple lines. Probe at opposite end (Ward 1912, 208). Recovered from fills of pit-shaft P4(17*). On loan at Dorset Museum. Fig. 17.4 (BU100DEW0223).

SFN758 **Spoon** (lost). Scale on archive photo indicates a total length of 150mm with scoop measuring with scoop measuring *c.* 35mm long × 8mm wide. Conjunction with shaft decorated with 3 bands. Opposite end forms a point, possibly a probe. Fig. 17.5 (R3904).

The Ferrous (Fe) objects

Approximately 250 Ferrous objects were recorded but most of these items are in a parlous condition after of 50 years in storage in various locations in some of which environmental controls were not rigorous. Consequently, less than half of the Fe items (120 or 48%) are recognisable with reasonable confidence, conservation methods having been applied to a limited number of examples all of which are at the Dorset Museum. Nails were numerous across the site having been used for a host of constructional purposes including roof tiling and joinery. Manning (1986, 134–7) devised a classification of types of which Types 1a and 1b are common at Dewlish. Nails of Type 1a ranged from 137mm to under 20mm in length, 190 nails of this type being 60mm long. Twelve nails from Dewlish were Manning's Type 2 with shafts that are square in section. At Dewlish, nails were not always retained at the end of the excavation seasons. Most of the ferrous objects were found in unsealed contexts.

For the above reasons, illustration of the ferrous objects has been restricted to what is currently recognisable or where a suitable archive drawing or photograph is available. A summary of the 120 identifiable ferrous objects and object groups (excluding nails) is presented as Table 17.3.

Table 17.3 Identifiable ferrous objects by category

Object Category	Quantity	Percentage of total (120)
Bindings	18	15.0
Buckles	1	0.8
Cleats	14	11.7
Hobnails	45	37.5
Knives	7	5.8
Latch lifts and door components	25	20.8
Metal working equipment	1	0.8
Rings (functional)	4	3.3
Stylii	3	2.5
Tool fragments	2	1.7
Totals	120	100

Illustrated Ferrous finds

SFN616 Joiner's **pinch dog** a similar type to staples joining timbers but varying in size. Length 505mm, with a strong stem. N94(15). Fig.17.6.

SFN561 Double spiked **loop** for attaching to woodwork or masonry to provide a ring or loop. Manning (1985,129–130) suggests that if these loops were driven into relatively thin wood, the spikes might project on the reverse side, but that they could still be made secure by hammering the spike ends over. Length 55mm, diameter of ring 30mm. M94(2). Fig. 17.6.

SFN106 **Door latch** in 5 parts. F3(8).
1. Slightly tapering bar, rectangular 135mm long × 15mm wide, 12mm thick. Fig. 17.6a.
2. Similar to 106a but 88mm long × 15mm wide × 5mm thick broken at narrow end. Fig. 17.6b.
3. Similar but tapering. 18mm at widest, broken end, 86mm long. Fig.17.6c.
4. Rectangular 4 mm thick × 10mm wide × 54mm long, broken at both ends. Fig. 17.6d.
5. Rectangular, broken at one end, 4mm thick × 12mm wide × 60mm long. Fig. 17.6e.

SFN467 **Door latch**. Missing but 1:1 scale drawing survives. Fragment of fitting plate 150 × 70mm thickness not recorded, with a 10mm diameter hole in a right-angled corner, together with a bent lever 250mm long with a further separate length of 45mm. One end of the separate lever leads into two bent prongs 12mm wide, 70mm long, the other end splaying into a 45mm triangular plate. Found in a dense pile of broken, burnt, regular pieces of pink and white mortar and limestone roof tile. Two further plates – 10 × 5mm and 20 × 10mm and 4 nails. Probably part of a heavy associated with room 33, Building 2/2A. P96(23). Figs. 17.7 (drawing) and 6.3 (photograph R3756).

SFN346   **Stylus** fragment, point missing. Manning (1985, 85, fig. 24 type 1 or 2. Length 53 mm. L2 16. Fig. 17. Photograph R 2494. A second example, SFN205 measures 98mm long Fig. 17.6.

The Lead (Pb) objects

Twenty-six lead objects were recorded from the site of the excavations twelve (46.2%) of which were found in sealed contexts (E3(22), D6(14), (D7(8), P4(19), P4(18), P4(23), L2(27), M2(6), K3(18), N96(16), O100(5) and M3(35). However, four of the sealed contexts listed were within two pit-shafts (O100 and P4) and these represented deposits of rubbish over a period of years. Table 17.4 shows the 26 lead objects by category. None of the items can be confidently identified by function but two objects (7.6%), both from sealed contexts, have interesting characteristics:

SFN125   A **ring** attached to a shaft broken at the end. A half lozenge pattern c. 6.5mm wide, on the exterior of the ring with an internal diameter 22mm. The shaft is 78mm long and roughly 4mm square in section. Found in rubble below the mosaic floor laid in Room 8. E3(22*). No available illustration.

SFN329   **Disc** 80mm diameter, 8mm thick with pie crust edge decoration and inserted triangular pieces on the edge. The under-side is rougher and pitted more than the top surface. Found within an ashy layer in pit-shaft P4. P4(18*). No available illustration.

The remaining 24 lead finds are variously described in the small finds register as being in a part 'molten' state prior to deposition, or as being offcuts, fragments, or strips (Table 17.4). This suggests that most, if not all of the lead finds represented scrap metals that were intended for reheating and re-use. The distribution of the lead is in a very obvious cluster of 15 items (53.7%) in and around Building 4, the bath house. Of this number, 7 (27%) were recovered from the robbed course of the drain

Table 17.4   Lead small finds by category

Description	Number of objects	Percentage of total (26)
Disc	2	7.7
Fragment	8	30.8
Off-cut	3	11.6
Plug	1	3.8
Ring	1	3.8
Strip	11	42.3
Totals:	26	100

from the octagonal cold plunge bath in grid square N5. By inference therefore, much of the lead from Dewlish was associated with the plumbing needs of the baths and the evidence from the plundered drainage trench indicates that lead was in demand for reprocessing.

Discussion of the metal finds

The evidence for the re-working of scrap lead prompts a review of the evidence for metal working at Dewlish. Specifically, three groups of finds invite comment:

SF343   A **tuyere** found with a blow hole in slag debris with a complete crucible recovered from rubbish deposited in pit-shaft P4, context 18* (monochrome photographs: The Ancient Monuments Laboratory G.A.S 177, 178, 179, 180. The **crucible** measures 80mm external height; the uneven interior is 17mm max. depth. (monochrome photographs: The Ancient Monuments Laboratory G.A.S 177, 178, 179, 180. Photographs R 3988- 3993. Fig. 17.9.

SF839   **Crucible fragment** was also found in the O100 pit-shaft, context 6*.

SF630   **Slag** spread over area 50 × 35 and 10mm deep. N93(7). Other deposits were encountered in small amounts in grid trenches O96 2, 4 and 6 and in an area of burning in P96.

At the end of the 1975 excavation season, the tuyere and crucible from pit-shaft P4 (SF343) were despatched to the Ancient Monuments Laboratory (AML) which produced a short report that was subsequently published in the interim report for that year (Putnam 1976, 54; Biek, L. BU100DEW0223). The full text of Biek's report is as follows,

Both crucible and tuyere are in an unusually good state of preservation, the crucible being complete and virtually undamaged. From the vitreous residues on its surface it was clearly used for melting copper alloy, and probably in casting small 'bronze' objects. The tuyere, and the small fragment of another one found with it, could well have been employed in the same process. However, there is no obvious evidence of this, and indeed a somewhat indefinite pointer to iron smelting instead. But it is always difficult to tell without thorough investigation of all associated material, and in the absence of any features in the ground, and large quantities of waste, it is not possible to be more specific at this stage.

The context in which the tuyere and crucible were found comprised what was described as 'ash' but Biek's statement indicates that none of this matrix was sent to the AML for investigation. If samples were taken, then they are no longer available for analysis and a crucial strand of evidence has been lost. Nonetheless, we are left with the strong possibility that the casting of copper alloy objects did take place at Dewlish and an 'indefinite pointer' to iron smelting (Biek). The spread of slag noted in context N93(7) was, at the time of excavation, associated with the 'small villa' or 'Priest's House' but this is a complex area of overlapping building phases and it is quite possible for this material to have been associated with Building 1 (late second century), Building 2/2A (third century) or Building 7 (fourth century) as indicated in Chapter 5, this volume. A further deposit of slag from grid trenches P96 and O96 (contexts 2, 4 and 6) can be confidently placed in the multi-purpose Building 2/2A (Chapter 6). In sum, the potential for metal-working activity at Dewlish is intriguingly sound but after 50 years confirmatory evidence is absent.

SHALE

Bituminous Kimmeridge shale is an oil-shale of dark brown colour that was sourced from the beds known as the Kimmeridge Ledges close to Clavell's Head, Dorset (*c.* BNG 391285, 77597; SY920777; Fig. 10.2). Kimmeridge Shale, locally known as 'blackstone' or 'Kimmeridge Coal' has been exploited as a raw material for the manufacture of objects of personal adornment, furnishings and other decorative items during the Iron Age and Romano-British periods of Britain. Shale is relatively soft and was lathe-turned

from the Late Iron Age onwards (Arkell, 1978, 68–9; Calkin 1954, 45–7).

The Dewlish shale assemblage has been a fragile resource. A total of 39 items are listed in a Bournemouth University condition assessment inventory dated to April 2014. Nine of the shale finds listed were deposited in the Dorset Museum (DM) during the 1970s but a further 10 (*c.* 25%) of the shale artefacts that were recorded in the Small Finds Register could not be found and others were in a poor state of preservation. Shale and jet from non-waterlogged environments (such as Dewlish) can be expected to be considerably degraded and fragile (Watkinson and Neal 1998, 49), a threat that has significantly diminished the size and range of the original assemblage over a period of 40 plus years. The threat of degradation is likely to have been exacerbated during the years when the material archive was out of store during the first post-excavation project (1999–2008; Chapter 3). Of the remaining artefacts, 14 were deemed worthy of record in 2015, and these are produced as drawings in Figures 17.1–3 and listed immediately below.

Illustrated shale finds

SFN135   **Spindle whorl** fragment, 250mm diam. with central hole 7mm diam. J5(6). Fig.17.10.

SFN166   **Armlet** curved fragment 20mm long × 5mm oval section. D6(14*). See also SFN172. Fig. 17.10.

SFN172   **Armlet** curved fragment 12 mm long × 5mm thin oval section. D6(14*). Probably part of SFN166. Fig. 17.10.

SFN207   **Armlet** curved fragment 40mm long, round section 4mm. O4(2). Fig. 17.10.

SFN260   **Armlet** curved fragment 44mm long, oval section 6mm diam. P4(11). Fig. 17.10.

SFN269   **Armlet** curved fragment 15mm long, sub oval section 5mm diam. N5(7). Fig. 17.10.

SFN284   **Spindle whorl** fragment, 25mm diameter, central hole 4mm diam. M3(2). Fig. 17.10.

SFN298   **Spindle whorl**, 40mm diam. M3(15*). Fig. 17.10.

SFN574   **Disc** in two fragments 15mm thick together comprising an arc, perhaps of a plate of *c.* 125mm diam. The inner edges are slightly angled showing chisel or gouge marks. On the outer edge are 3 incised grooves of varying depth. P4(11). Fig. 17.10.

SFN578   **Fragment** of sub-triangular shape tapering

from a flat edge to a break line. Dimensions: 55mm at widest point, 50mm in length by 6mm thick. Chamfered edges bearing saw marks with a drilled hole of 5mm diam. The reverse side is flat but roughened suggesting that it was not meant to be seen. N93(4). Fig. 17.11.

SFN733   **Armlet** in 2 fragments, one being 81mm long and the other 20mm long. N92(9). Fig. 17.10.

SFN819   **Armlet** fragment 35mm in length. Unstratified. Fig. 17.10.

SFN855   Sub-circular **lathe waste** (i.e. 'Coal Money' fragment) of 30mm diam. and 2 × chuck holes each of 10mm diam. P2(11). Fig. 17.10.

Not listed   Square **tile** measuring 140mm × 140mm with chamfered edges. Found in Room 31 (Building 2) amongst flint and plaster rubble. O98(5). Fig. 17.11.

The surviving shale assemblage includes some interesting examples, but it is a much-depleted resource that is of limited interpretative value.

WORKED BONE

A total of 32 objects of worked animal bone was recovered from the eleven seasons of excavation. Five of these artefacts form a miscellaneous group and a further 27 constitute an assemblage of bone pins.

Miscellaneous objects

Of the five objects in this group only a peg was found in a sealed context (SFN398) which was in close association with two bone pins, SFN386 and 387 (see below). The context in question was sealed beneath the mosaic pavement of the *apodyterium*, Room 25, which is a mid-to late fourth century feature and so the best that can be said is that the peg is earlier than that. SF401 is possibly a large knife handle. It was found amongst the demolition rubble associated with Room 23A, part of the Annexe of Building 3, the *domus*. The Annexe is a late fourth or early fifth century construct which shows evidence of having functioned as a kitchen and associated administrative facilities (see Chapter 9). The conjectural bone knife handle might be of similar date.

SFN401   Antler (knife?) **handle**, sawn at root end. 176mm long, with 2 parallel straight cut sides 19 ×

14mm long, and a drilled hole 11mm interior diam. E6(7). Fig. 17.12.

SFN398   **Peg**, roughly 12mm diam., overall 3 length 9mm, with longitudinal cuts ending in a broken shaft 5mm length. L2(32*). Fig. 17.12.

SFN382   Bone **handle** fragment, sub-ovoid, overall length 48mm, with carved a bound leather design. Two drilled holes 4mm diameter, one at each end. O2(2). Fig. 17.12.

SFN198   Decorated **spindle whorl** fragment, 25mm diameter, with central drilled hole 6mm diam. surrounded by 3 rings carved in relief on the surface. Evidence of re-working around the circumference that has reduced the original size. D7(7). Fig. 17.12.

SFN203   Undecorated **spindle whorl** of 20mm diam. overall with central drilled hole of 8mm diam. and 15mm deep. Unstratified. Fig. 17.12.

Bone pins

The 27 bone pins have been classified in accordance with the typology devised by Crummy (1979, 157–63) and enhanced by the same author with additional illustrated examples four years later (1983, 19–25). The results of this process are shown in Table 17.5. Seventeen of the Dewlish pins (Figs 17.13 and 17.14) conformed to Crummy's illustrated examples (Types 1 to 6 inclusive) but a further 9 pins could not be matched to these categories with confidence but more readily belonged in the catch-all Type 7: 'pins with individually styled heads.' Six of these pins had undecorated conical heads though in one example the cone may have been worn or mis-formed whereby it resembled a rectangular form. Conical-headed pins were noted by Stacey as being present in the assemblage from Greyhound Yard, Dorchester (1993, 184). In Table 17.5, the Dewlish conical-headed pins have been recorded at Type 7a. A single pin (SFN 806) was provided with an inverse conical head with a bow-sided shaft, entered in Table 17.5 as Type 7b. Stacey also noted two pins with a deeply cut spiral-form head which are represented by similar but not identical examples from Dewlish (SFN387 and 639). If anything, they are related to Crummy's Type 2 decorated conical form but there is no true cone in evidence and the spiral design is well executed with sides that taper towards a lost point. These examples are entered as Type 7c. As Stacey has observed Type 7 pins represent an assemblage variation from the Colchester forms that provide the basis for Crummy's

Table 17.5 Dewlish Roman villa worked bone pin types (*denotes derived from a sealed context)

Type number	Small Finds Number	Type Totals	Percentage of Total (27)
1		-	-
2		-	-
3	363, 373*, 386*, 469, 484*, 521*, 582, 614, 615,741, 779, 794, 833*, 870, 880	15	55.6
4	419	1	3.7
5	736	1	3.7
6		-	-
7a	397*,576, 593, 777, 789, 840*,	6	22.2
7b	806	1	3.7
7c	387*, 639	2	7.4
Headless pins	611	1	3.7
Totals		27	100

typology. At Dewlish, as at Greyhound Yard, Type 7 denotes instances of a south-west regional style.

The Crummy typology includes a postulated life-span for bone pins by type:

Type 1: *c.* 70–200/250,
Type 2: *c.* 50–200/250,

Type 3: *c.* 200 to late fourth/early fifth century,
Type 4: *c.* 250 to late fourth/early fifth century,
Type 5: *c.* 250 to late fourth/early fifth century,
Type 6: *c.* 200 to late fourth/early fifth century.

Eight of the Dewlish Bone pins are from sealed contexts. Five of these stratified pins belong in Type 3 and the Crummy date range would not be incompatible with the contexts in which they were found. The remaining three stratified pins have been assigned to Type 7 which does not have a postulated life span assigned to it. SFNs 387 and 840 and were sealed beneath fourth century mosaic floors of the *apodyterium* (Room 25) in Building 4. A *terminus ante quem* cannot be offered. SFN397 was sealed beneath a scatter of roof tiles and under bedding for the mosaic floor in Room 8, Building 3. A third century/ early fourth century date is probable, and this can be regarded as an indicative but provisional date for the conical headed pin type referred to above.

Comparison with the assemblages from other published Roman villas in Dorset (Lucas 1993; Graham 2006; Light and Ellis 2009) has not provided the critical mass to elucidate further with regard to bone pin types and their chronology in the region. A detailed study of the distribution of bone pin types throughout the villa country of south-west England and south Wales is overdue, for this would provide a geographical counterbalance to the work of Crummy in Colchester and the county of Essex.

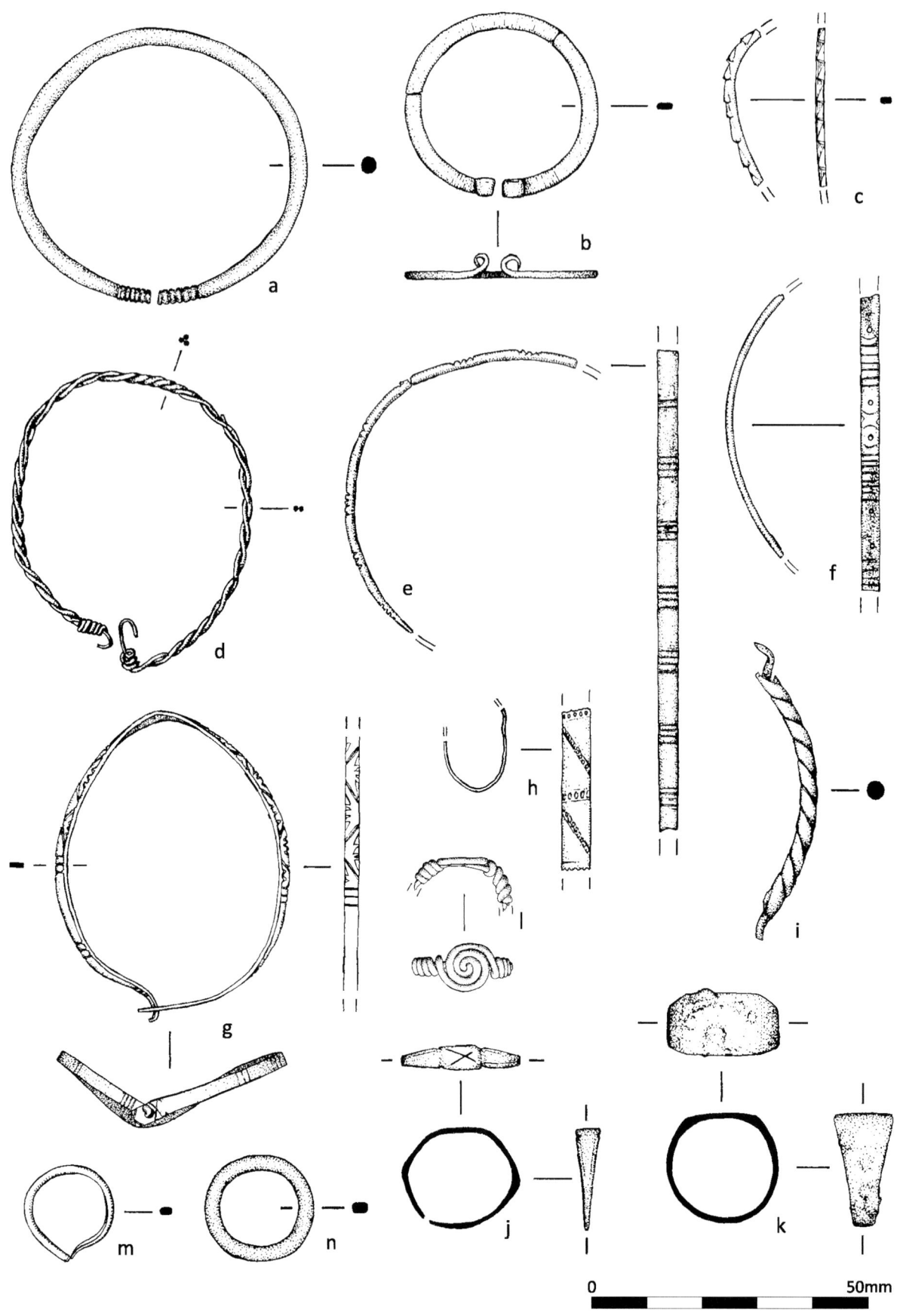

0   50mm

Figure 17.1   Copper alloy (CuA) small finds. Drawings: Jonathan Milward.

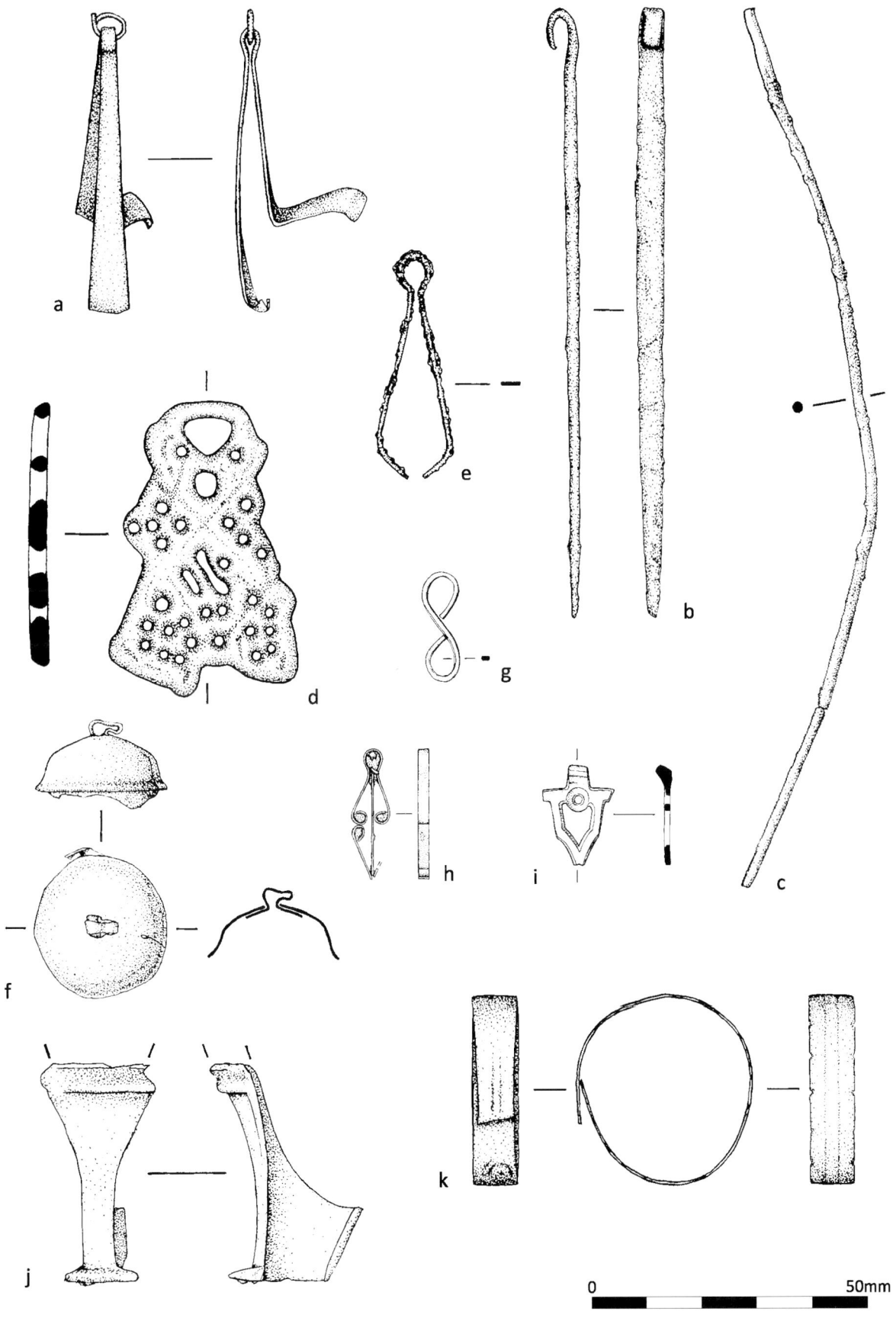

Figure 17.2   Copper alloy (CuA) small finds. Drawings: Jonathan Milward.

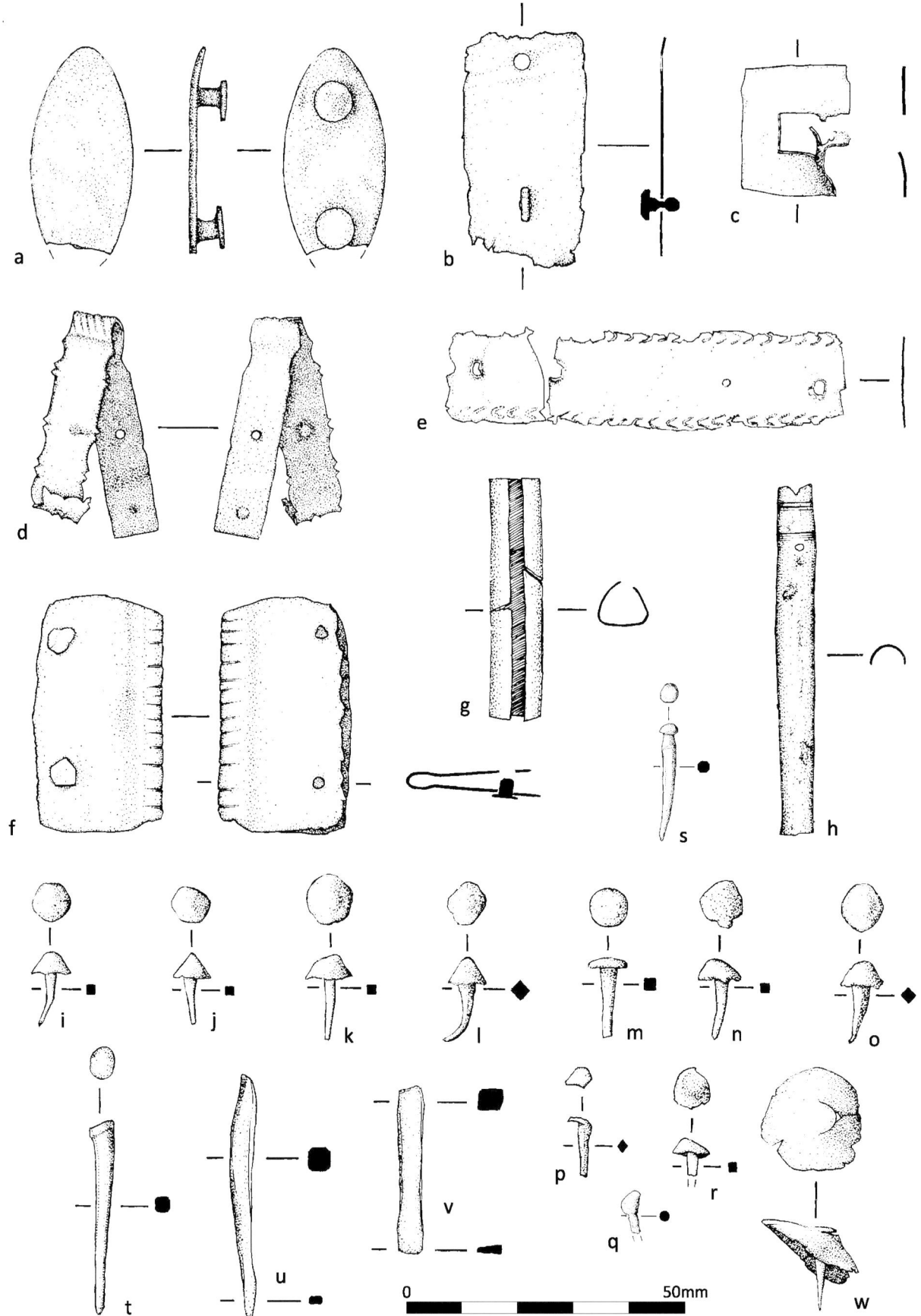

Figure 17.3   Copper alloy (CuA) small finds. Drawings: Jonathan Milward.

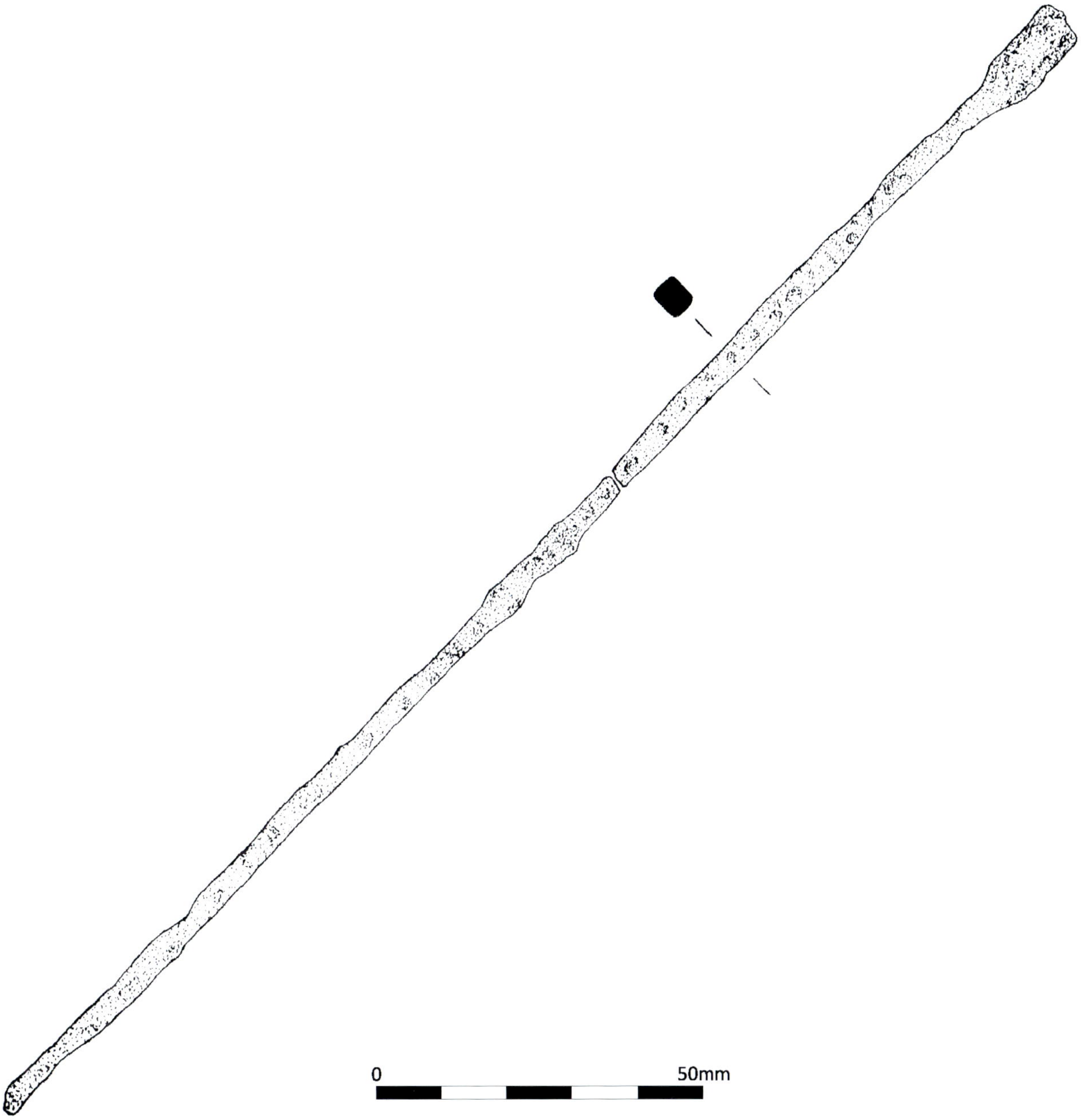

Figure 17.4   Ligula, SFN 320. Drawing: Jonathan Milward.

0   50mm

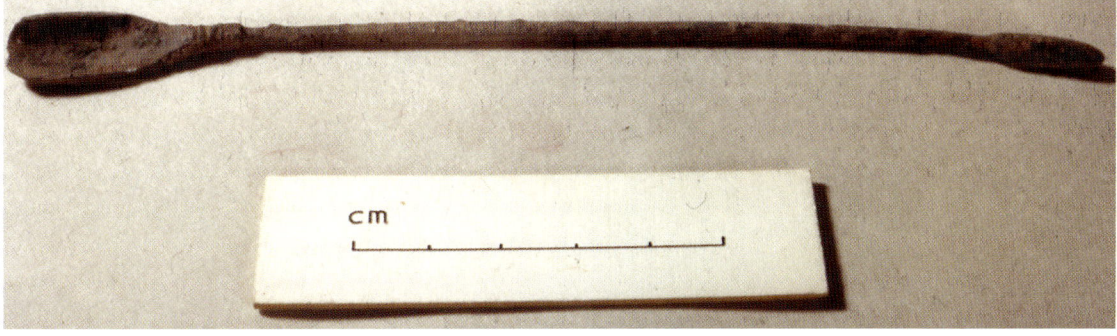

Figure 17.5   Spoon. Photograph: Photograph: R3904.

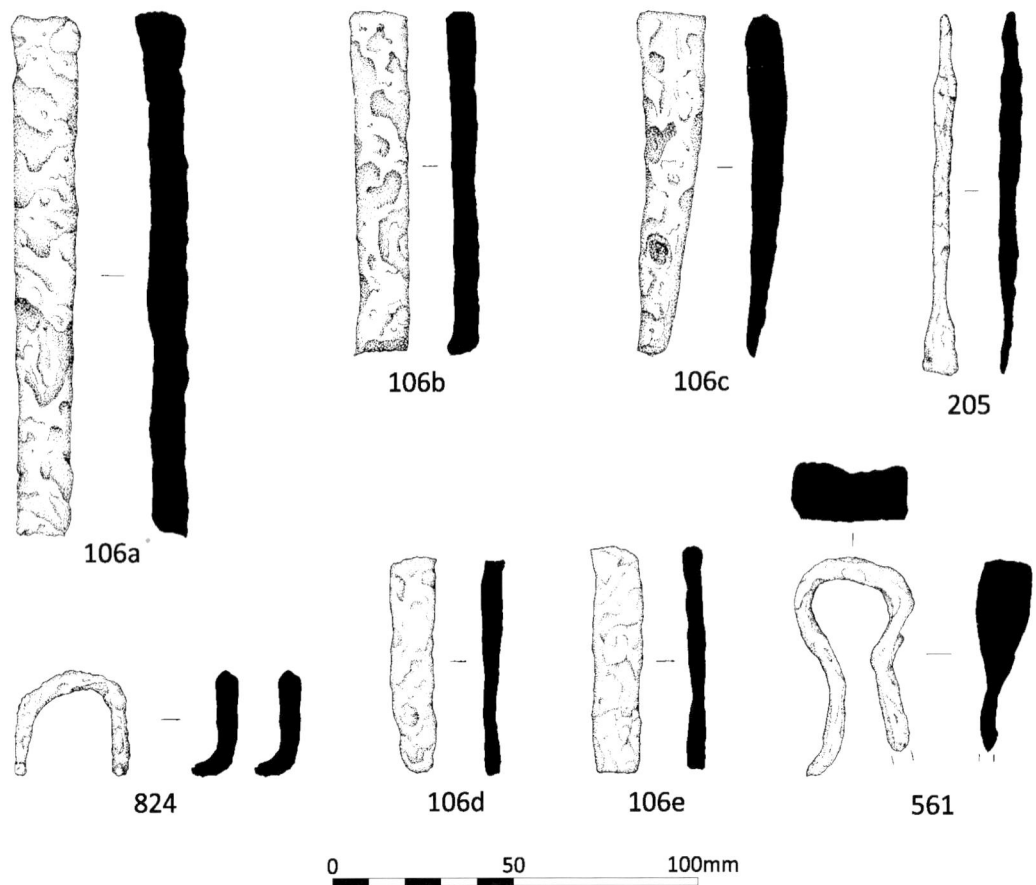

Figure 17.6　Iron (Fe) small finds. Drawings: Tilia Cammegh.

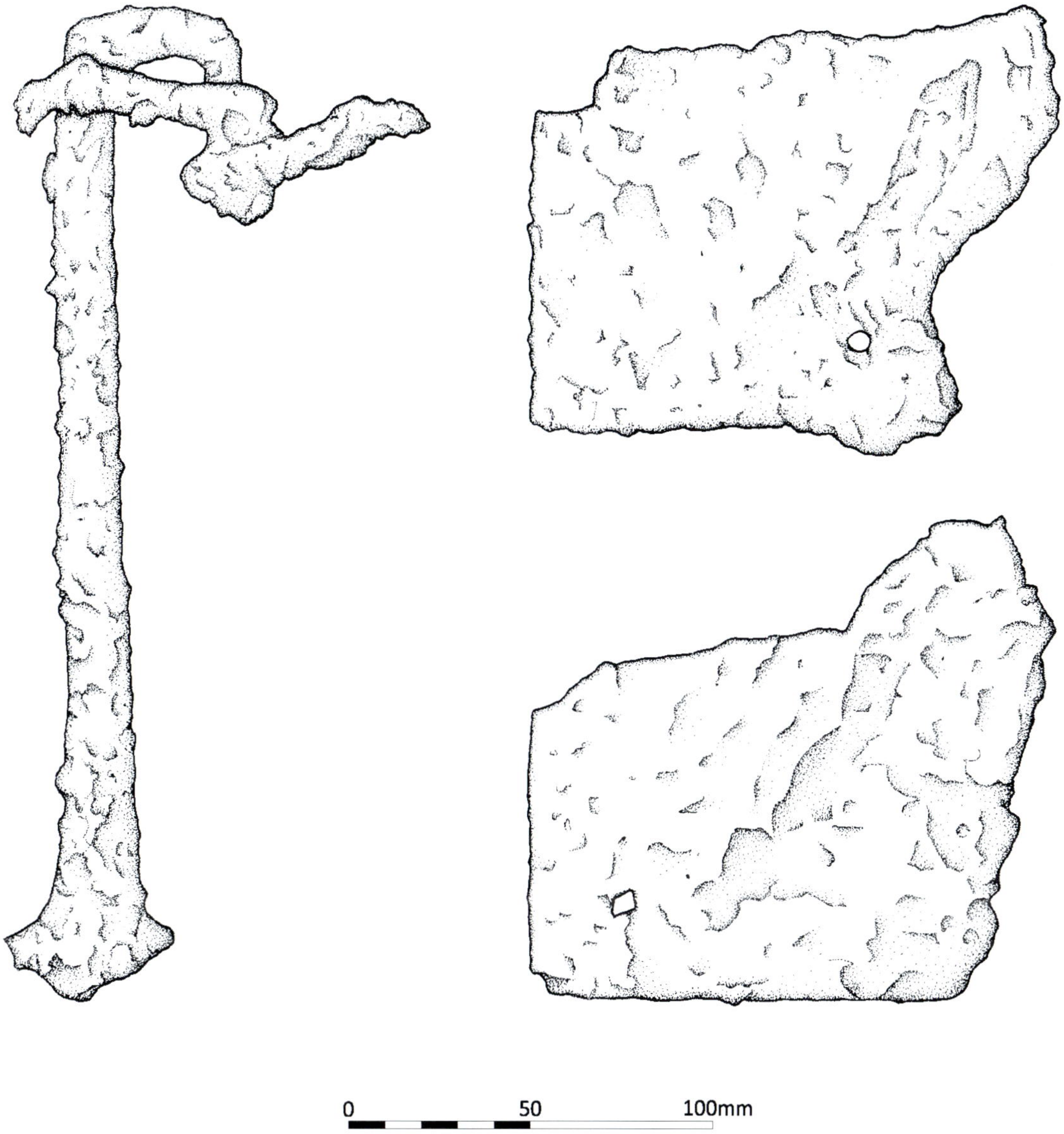

0   50   100mm

Figure 17.7   Iron heavy duty door latch, SFN 467 (see also Fig. 6.3). Drawing: Jonathan Milward.

CM

Figure 17.8   Stylus. Photograph: R2494.

Figure 17.9   Crucible and tuyere. Photograph: R3988.

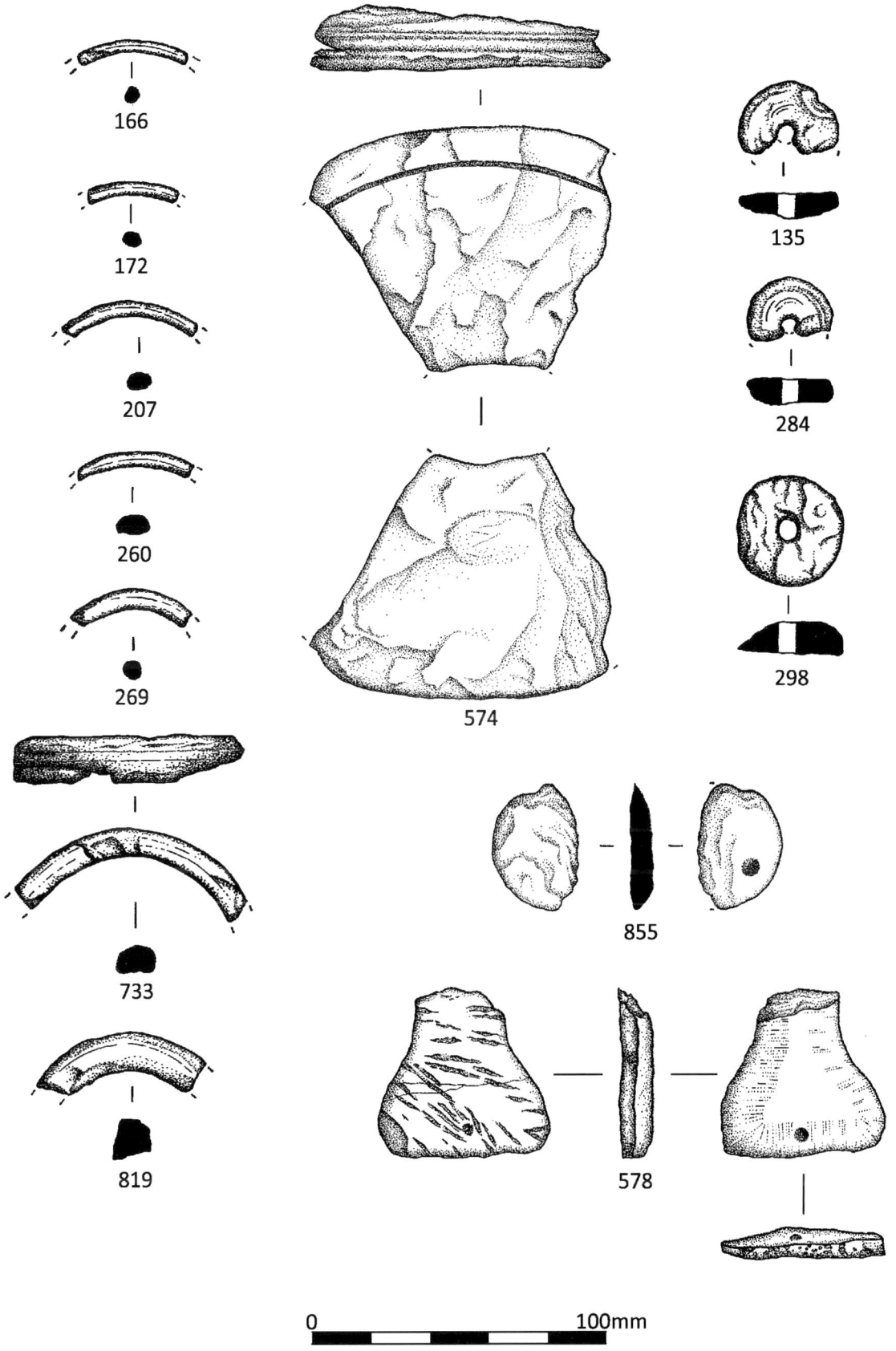

Figure 17.10 Shale objects. Drawings: Tilia Cammegh.

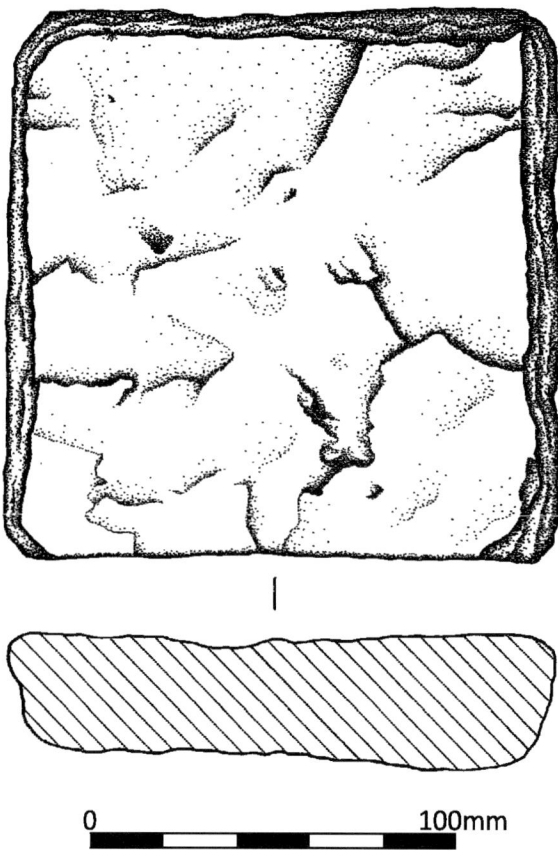

Figure 17.11   Shale tile from Room 26, Building 4, found amongst rubble in Room 31, Building 2. Drawing: Tilia Cammegh.

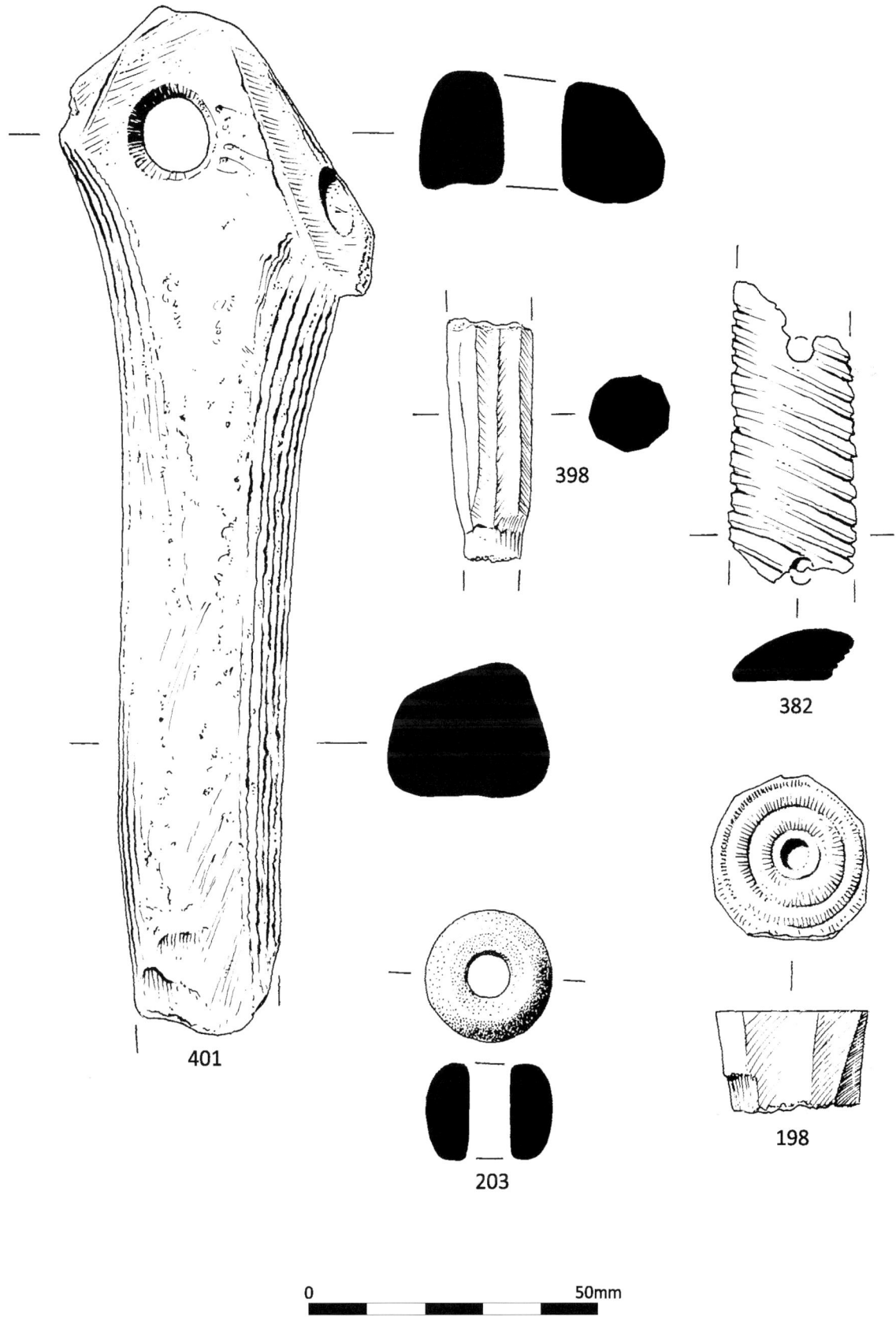

Figure 17.12 Worked bone. Drawings: David Watt.

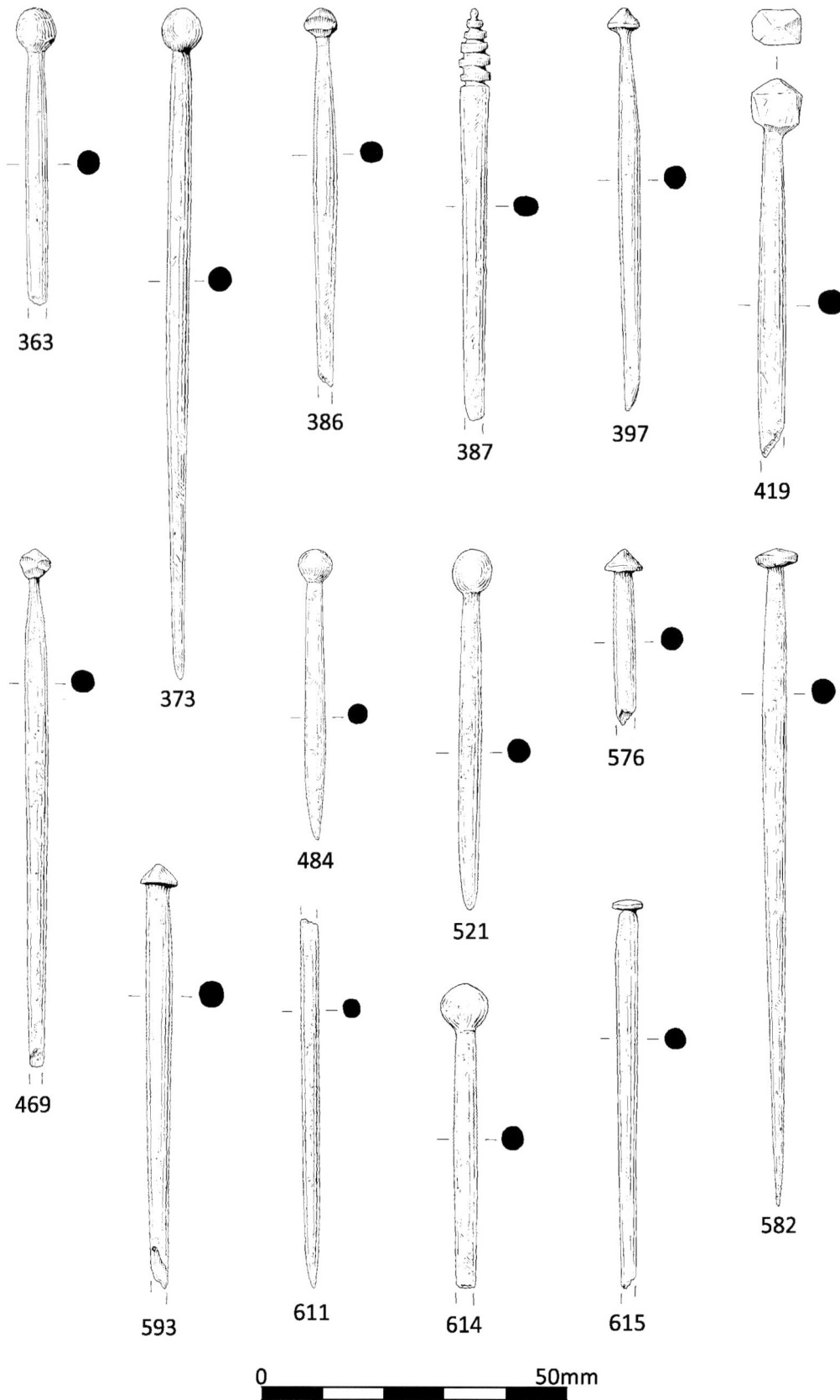

363

386

387

397

419

373

484

521

576

469

593

611

614

615

582

0   50mm

Figure 17.13   Bone pins. Drawings: David Watt.

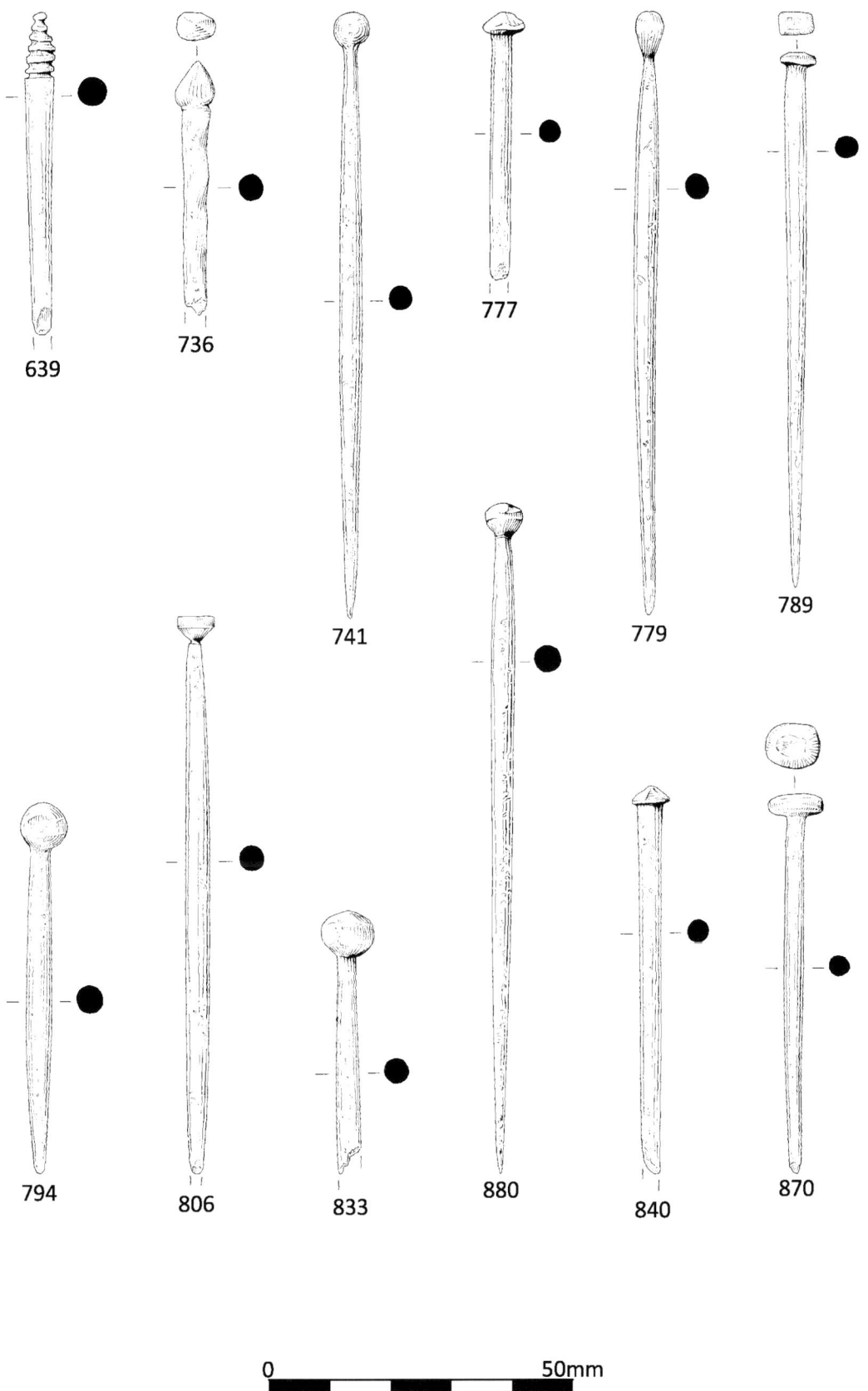

Figure 17.14 Bone pins (continued). Drawings: David Watt.

18

ANIMAL BONES

by Mark Maltby with Grace Clark

ANIMAL BONE IDENTIFICATION AND RECORDING

All the bones and teeth recovered from the excavations were identified and recorded by the authors in the Zooarchaeology Laboratory of Bournemouth University using its modern skeleton reference collection where necessary. Some of the wild bird and mammal bones were identified by Sheila Hamilton-Dyer, who also confirmed identifications of some of the other unusual specimens. Each bone was recorded individually onto a relational database (Microsoft Access). The following data were recorded where appropriate for each specimen: context; species; anatomical element; zones of bone present; approximate percentage of bone present; gnawing damage; erosion; weathering; concretions; burning (charring and calcification); epiphyseal fusion data; associated bone group; other comments including observations of pathology. Separate tables linked to the main table by an individual identification number were created for butchery, metrical and tooth ageing data. Tooth eruption and wear descriptions for cattle and sheep/goat followed Grant (1982). Estimates of mandibular age followed Jones and Saddler (2012) for cattle, Jones (2006) for sheep and Bull and Payne (1982) for pig. Measurements were selected from those recommended by Driesch (1976). All fragments, including loose teeth, limb bone shaft fragments, rib heads and vertebral bodies were recorded to species level where possible.

In the animal bone database, the context information was converted to a 7-figure alpha-numeric coding system. The first three figures represent the grid co-ordinates (e.g. G04), the next two digits refer to the context and the final two to the room number. Thus, context G04(04)11 refers to bones found in Grid G4; context (4); Room 11. The last two digits of contexts not assigned to rooms are given as 00. Although all the bones were recorded by individual context, it was decided to carry out only limited intra-site analysis, as the complexities of phasing meant that many of the bones would have been redeposited during various building developments and abandonment.

INTRA-SITE STUDIES

The following section provides a summary of the animal bones found in each room and in deposits outside the buildings.

Building 3

Room 4
Two unidentified mammal fragments were the only bones recorded.

Room 5
A small fragment of cattle femur was the only bone recorded.

Room 6

A total of 21 fragments were recovered. These included a cattle tibia fragment and a chicken scapula. A complete femur and tibia probably belonged to the same adult cat. Wild species were represented by a red deer tibia fragment and a porcine scapula and pelvis that were sufficiently large to be considered to be from wild boar. A toad femur and rodent tibia were also recorded.

Room 7

Seventeen bone fragments were recorded of which only a piglet mandible and a dog humerus were identified.

Room 8

Seven bone fragments included a cattle femur, a pig fibula, a femur of a neonatal pig and a chicken coracoid.

Annexe corridor 10

Fifteen bone fragments were recovered. Five, including three loose teeth, belonged to sheep/goat. A cattle tibia fragment and seven bird bones were also recorded. Two of the bird bones belonged to chicken, and there was one each of woodcock and a member of the thrush family. Three bones were from a barn owl.

Room 11

A total of 39 bone fragments were recorded, of which ten were unidentified. The 16 cattle elements included a complete metatarsal, three substantial portions of scapulae and three calf mandible fragments. Eight sheep/goat elements included a largely complete specimen of a sheep metatarsal and a lamb femur. The three pig elements included a mandible fragment from a large individual, possibly a wild boar. A dog ulna and an ulna of a rook or crow were also found.

Corridor 12

A substantial faunal assemblage of 290 bone fragments was recovered. These included 152 unidentified mammal fragments. Cattle provided 46 of the identified elements including seven loose teeth and four fragments from at least three radii. A largely complete pair of adult cattle mandibles was recovered from K2 (10). The 31 sheep/goat elements included 11 loose teeth. A complete radius and

metatarsal both belonged to adult sheep. At least four different mandibles and tibiae were represented. Pig (28 fragments) was also well represented. These included a large mandible probably from an adult wild boar. Four other porcine fragments came from either large domestic stock or possibly wild boar. Horse, dog and red deer were each represented by three fragments. These included two mandibles of adult dogs and an antler fragment. Five bird bones included three of chicken. Two bones of mole were probably intrusive. The 17 amphibian bones include nine identified as toad.

Room 13 (porch)

Thirty-two bone fragments were recovered, of which 15 were unidentified mammal. Bones of sheep/goat, cattle, pig and horse were identified (Table 18.1). The only largely complete bone was a cattle scapula.

Room 14

Only seven bone elements were recovered including a substantially complete femur of a young adult cow, the metatarsal of a neonatal calf and a radius of a lamb.

Room 15

Fifty-four bone elements were recorded including 11 unidentified mammal fragments and two unidentified bird bones. Sheep/goat elements (23) were the most commonly identified. These included 17 bones from the lower spine, pelvis and upper hind limbs of an immature large male sheep from H5 (3). Context H5 (13) produced the left metatarsal and five associated phalanges of a sub-adult cow. A pair of metacarpals may have been from the same animal. No butchery marks were observed on either of these groups. A complete metacarpal of an adult bull or ox was also found in H5 (3). Three pig bones and a dog tooth were also found.

Room 16

Thirteen animal bone fragments were recovered including six of cattle, four of sheep/goat and one of pig.

Room 17

Thirteen animal bone fragments were recorded, ten of which were identified. Sheep/goat, cattle, horse, red deer and hare were recorded (Table 18.1).

Room 18

Sixty-four bone fragments were recorded including 30 of unidentified mammal. Sheep/goat provided 21 elements including a fairly complete mandible and tibia. The eight cattle elements included two ribs of a neonatal mortality. Two bones of duck and one each of pig and chicken were also recovered.

Room 19

An adult sheep/goat radius and ulna were the only bones recovered.

Room 20

Only two bones were recorded: a cattle hyoid and a humerus of a small wader.

Room 21

A total of 59 fragments were recorded, of which 21 were from unidentified mammals. Cattle and sheep/goat both provided 17 fragments. Most of the cattle elements were from young animals and included a pair of metacarpals and an associated first phalanx of a calf. There were also two bones of a neonatal calf. Six of the sheep/goat elements were loose teeth. Mandibles of a pig and a dog and two dog loose teeth were also recovered.

Room 22

Thirteen of the 24 elements were from rodents including a short-tailed vole mandible. Five amphibian bones included at least two of toad. There was also a badger maxilla and a weasel humerus. The only elements of domestic mammals were a largely complete cattle mandible, a pig metapodial and a lamb scapula.

Room 23A

Ninety bone fragments were recovered including 51 unidentified mammal fragments. Sheep/goat provided 35 elements including 25 ribs and vertebrae from an adult skeleton found in E6 (12). No evidence for butchery was recorded on these bones. Only one bone each of cattle and pig were identified. An astragalus and calcaneus of an adult red deer were also recorded.

Room 24

Forty-four bone fragments were recovered including 16 unidentified mammal fragments. The identified material was quite diverse. It included eight bones from at least two chickens and seven elements of pig including two canines of domestic males and a mandible of a neonatal piglet. Sheep/goat, cattle, hare and red deer were also represented in small numbers (Table 18.1).

Building 4

Room 25

This area produced a large faunal assemblage of 291 fragments including 117 unidentified mammal fragments. Sheep/goat were the most commonly identified. Their 76 elements included 16 bones of the lower right forelimb of an adult sheep in M3 (07). There were also 19 loose teeth, nine fragments from at least four metatarsals and six vertebrae, four of which were butchered. The 23 cattle elements included five scapula fragments, one of which was from a young calf. Most of the 11 pig elements came from the head or lower limbs. Small numbers of horse, dog, cat, red deer, toad and rabbit were also recorded (Table 18.1). There is the possibility that the rabbit tibia from M3 (02) was intrusive. The 39 small mammal bones included four that were identified as short-tailed vole. Six unidentified fish bones were also recovered along with 11 bird bones, which included elements of chicken, goose and duck, a member of the pigeon family and a small corvid.

Room 26

A substantial assemblage of animal bones was recovered consisting of 221 fragments including 42 assigned to unidentified mammals. Sheep/goat dominated the domestic mammal assemblage. Their 66 elements included eight bones from the lower right hindlimb of a lamb in M4 (6). No butchery marks were recorded on bones in this group. The sheep/goat assemblage included eight vertebrae, 16 loose mandibular teeth, and nine and six fragments from at least five tibiae and radii respectively. The 13 cattle elements included a fairly complete metatarsal and four loose teeth. The seven dog fragments incorporated a substantial portion of a skull including a maxilla from M4 (6). Four elements of horse, three pig metapodials and part of a red deer skull were also discovered. Small mammals and amphibian bones formed a substantial proportion of the assemblage, most of them coming from M4 (4).

The 69 small mammal bones included seven field vole mandibles and teeth and a water vole mandible. The 14 amphibian bones included at least four of frogs. The two bird bones came from a chicken and a member of the thrush family.

Room 27
A large assemblage of 225 animal bones was recovered including 53 of unidentified mammals. Amphibians, mainly from N3 (17), provided 76 bones, of which at least 49 were from frogs and four from toads. Three small mammal bones included two short-tailed vole mandibles. Sheep/goat were the most common of the larger mammals. Their 36 elements included two fairly complete sheep metacarpals and metatarsals. The 21 cattle elements included all six phalanges and the distal portion of a metatarsal from N3 (4). All the bones in this associated group were charred. Two other cattle second phalanges and a centroquartal, as well as a kitten femur were also charred in this deposit. Eight pig bones included four tibiae: one of these was a complete bone from a sub-adult domestic pig; one of the other tibiae was much larger and probably belonged to an immature wild boar. Twelve bones were positively identified as dog and two vertebrae were either from a dog or fox. Two bones probably from the same adult male polecat were found in N5 (10). Two tibiae of rabbits were also identified: one from N3 (2) was from an immature animal; the second from N4 (2) was from an adult. Both could have been intrusive. At least four of the eight bird bones belonged to chickens. There was also a goose tarsometatarsus and a humerus of a member of the thrush family.

Room 28
A total of 35 animal bones were recovered including nine unidentified mammal fragments. Five of the 11 sheep/goat elements were loose teeth. Cattle, horse and dog and short-tailed vole were each represented by a single element. The 11 bird bones belonged to a partial skeleton of an adult goose found in N4 (23). The presence of medullary bone in a tibiotarsus indicated that this was a female in lay.

Room 29
Ninety-two bone fragments were recovered including 34 from unidentified mammals. Sheep/goat elements

(24) were the most commonly identified. These included five metatarsals, two of which were substantially complete. The nine cattle bones included a largely complete mandible and radius. Four of the eight dog bones belonged to at least one neonatal puppy. Pig, horse, cat, duck and thrushes were each represented by a single bone. At least five of the six small mammal bones belonged to short-tailed voles and at least two of the amphibian bones came from frogs.

Room 30
This area produced the largest faunal assemblage from the villa comprising 391 well preserved fragments including 128 from unidentified mammals. The majority of the bones came from Pit-shaft P4. The identified material was dominated by sheep/goat, which provided 129 elements. These included 20 rib heads and 13 vertebrae. These bones are quite fragile and their high numbers attest to the good preservation of this assemblage. Many of them bore butchery marks. Similarly, seven fragments from at least six different maxillae were recovered. Normally maxillae survive much less well than mandibles but in this assemblage they were found in roughly equal numbers (9 mandible fragments came from at least five jaws). Metatarsals were the best represented limb bone providing 12 fragments from at least ten different bones. There were also at least seven different metacarpals. Eight tibia fragments came from at least five bones. The cattle assemblage was much more fragmented. Its 29 bones included three from foetal or neonatal animals. Pig (10) and horse elements (4) were present in small numbers. The 27 cat bones came from at least three adults. Most of the bones came from partial skeletons located at P4 (24) and P4 (19). P4 (24) also produced 14 bones of hare. Most of these could have been from the same adult skeleton but at least two hares were represented by three tibiae. A red deer antler tine was found in P4 (14) and three fish fin rays were found at P4 (10).

The pit produced an unusually rich bird assemblage consisting of 45 bones, of which 30 were identified as goose. Twenty-four of the bones came from an adult goose skeleton located at P4 (23) and P4 (24). Bones of the breast, both wings and legs were represented. Thick deposits of medullary bone in the shafts of the leg bones testified that this was a female that died during the laying season. P4 (24) also produced five very porous leg bones of a young gosling. A second gosling was represented by a slightly smaller porous tarsometatarsus in P4 (25). Seven of the nine chicken bones were tarsometatarsi. Six of these were from adults. The absence of spurs indicated these belonged to at least three hens. The seventh tarsometatarsus belonged to an immature bird. Four other avian species were represented by a single bone: a crow humerus was found in P4 (19); a carpometacarpus of a female goshawk was recovered from P4 (18); a tarsometatarsus of a young pigeon (squab) was found at P4 (8); and most of a skull of a woodcock survived in P4 (23).

Buildings 2 and 2A

Room 31

Although 65 bone fragments were recovered, only 23 were identified. Seventeen of these belonged to sheep/goat including a metatarsal of a neonatal lamb. Three cattle elements included a complete metacarpal of an adult. A horse tooth and a humerus of a woodcock were also recorded.

Room 32

Fifty-seven bones were recorded including 24 unidentified mammal fragments. A partial skeleton of an immature chicken from O97 (7) provided 26 bones. All parts of the body were represented. Small numbers of sheep/goat and cattle were also present (Table 18.1).

Room 33

Forty-three bone fragments were recorded, of which 17 were identified. Sheep/goat, cattle and dog were represented (Table 18.1). Three bird bones were unidentified, although one could have belonged to a very young chicken.

Room 34

Sixty-five bone fragments were recovered, of which 36 belonged to unidentified mammals. Most of the identified elements (22) were from sheep/goat including seven loose teeth and a fairly complete mandible and metatarsal. Three pig teeth, a red deer antler fragment, and tibiotarsi of a chicken and a member of the thrush family were also recorded.

Room 35

This area produced a large assemblage of 315 bone fragments, of which 152 belonged to unidentified mammals. Sheep/goat elements (64) were the most commonly identified. These included 17 loose teeth, seven mandibles, tibiae and metatarsals. At least four animals were represented by the axis (second cervical vertebra). The 51 cattle elements included 13 loose teeth, a fairly complete metacarpal and a group of six ribs from R95 (7). The 24 pig elements included two ribs, which either came from large domestic pigs or possibly wild boars. The six dog elements included the skull and both maxillae of an adult from R95 (12) and a femur and tibia of an adult dog from R96 (7). Red deer, frog/toad and rodent were each represented by a single bone. The 11 bird bones included seven from chickens, and one each from duck and pigeon.

Room 36

Seventeen of the 28 animal bone fragments from this area were identified. Seven belonged to sheep/goat and four to cattle including a second phalanx of a neonatal calf. Horse and cat were each represented by a single element. Two bones of duck and two of chicken were also identified, the latter including a humerus of a young chick.

Room 37

Only six of the 19 bone fragments recovered were identified. Cattle, sheep/goat and pig were each represented by two elements.

Room 38

Only seven of the 26 bone fragments recovered were identified. Five of these belonged to sheep/goat and there was one element each of cattle and chicken.

Room 39

Twenty-three fragments were recovered including 14 from unidentified mammals. Cattle and sheep/goat were both represented by three elements, toad by two and a member of the thrush family by one.

Building 6

Room 40

This area produced 124 bone fragments, of which 62 were unidentified. Most of the identified elements belonged to sheep/goat (30) and cattle (21). These included a mandible of a neonatal lamb, a complete cattle metatarsal and a largely complete cattle metacarpal. There were six pig elements and two fragments of red deer metatarsal. A right tibia and three associated metatarsals of an adult female otter were found in N 98 (6).

Room 41

Forty-two bone fragments were recovered, of which 17 were unidentified. Most of the identified elements belonged to sheep/goat (12) and cattle (10). Two elements of pig and one of horse were also identified.

Buildings 1 and 7

Room 42

This area produced quite a large bone assemblage of 147 fragments including 89 unidentified mammal fragments. Sheep/goat elements (30) were the most commonly identified including nine loose teeth. Cattle (14), pig (6) and horse (2) were also present. These included the sawn shaft of a horse metatarsal. A largely complete red deer scapula was also recovered. Chicken (2) and duck were also identified.

Room 43

Thirty-seven bone fragments were found in this area including 17 from unidentified mammals. Sheep/goat (7), pig (5), cattle (2), cat and red deer were identified. Three bones from at least two species of duck were also recorded.

Room 44

Ninety-two bone fragments were found in this area including 62 from unidentified mammals. Unusually, pig was the most commonly identified. Twelve elements included five maxilla fragments. The eight sheep/goat elements included two substantial portions of radii of immature sheep and a metapodial of a neonatal lamb. One of the four cattle elements (a tibia) was also from a neonatal calf. The two dog bones included an ulna of a miniature breed. A radius and ulna came from the same adult cat. A horse tooth and a red deer metatarsal were also recorded.

Room 45

This area produced a large bone assemblage of 193 fragments including 99 of unidentified mammals. Sheep/goat elements (41) were the most frequently identified. Their 41 elements included 13 loose teeth and six mandible fragments from at least four jaws. Seven tibia fragments also came from at least four different bones. The 24 cattle elements included a substantially complete radius of an adult and a humerus of a neonatal calf. Pig elements (20) were also quite well represented. The three elements of horse included a complete thoracic vertebra. The mammal assemblage was completed by a dog ulna, a cat tibia and a roe deer metatarsal fragment. Two bones of chicken and one of a small passerine were also recorded.

Room 46

This area also produced a large bone assemblage of 158 fragments including 103 of unidentified mammals. The 30 sheep/goat elements included 12 loose teeth, a largely complete sheep metatarsal, a skull fragment of a hornless sheep and a femur of a neonatal lamb. Ten cattle fragments included five of scapulae. Horse, cat, dog and red deer (antler) were each represented by a single element. Four bones of chicken and one of duck were also identified.

Room 47

Thirty-eight bone fragments were recovered but only 12 were identified. Sheep/goat, cattle, pig and duck were present in small numbers (Table 18.1).

Room 49

This area produced a large bone assemblage of 235 fragments including 159 of unidentified mammals. The assemblage was dominated by pig cranial elements. Their 51 elements included five mandible fragments, six maxilla fragments and five fragments from other parts of the skull. There were also 19 loose teeth. Some of these cranial elements may have belonged to the same pigs but at least three animals were represented. One very large canine could have belonged to a wild boar but most of the other pig elements were smaller and were from domestic stock. Elements of sheep/goat (11) and cattle (9) were also present. These included a femur of a foetal calf. Two fragments of red deer and three bones of badger were also identified. At least two of the badger bones from M94 (5) belonged to the same adult.

Room 50

Only five of the 37 bone fragments found in this area were identified to pig, sheep/goat and cattle (Table 18.1).

Room 51

Only six of the 28 bone fragments retrieved from this area were identified. Sheep/goat, cattle, horse and pig were recorded (Table 18.1).

Other Contexts

Assemblages found in contexts not associated directly or indirectly with rooms provided 415 bone fragments, of which 201 were unidentified. Most of the assemblages came from contexts in N100 and O100, the latter co-ordinate being the location of a pit-shaft. Sheep/goat provided 84 elements. The most common bone was the tibia with 17 fragments from at least 11 different bones. Ten metatarsal fragments came from at least five different bones, nine mandible fragments belonged to at least seven different jaws and there were nine fragments from at least six radii. There were also nine loose teeth. The 78 fragments of cattle included ten humerus fragments from at least six bones. Three of these were substantially complete, as were a femur, a tibia, four vertebrae and two scapulae. A complete metacarpal was also recovered. Six of the cattle bones belonged to neonatal calves.

Seventeen horse elements included a largely complete humerus. Only eight pig elements were recovered including two from neonatal piglets. The four dog bones included an atlas and axis from the same individual and a complete tibia from an adult. Three bones of red deer and two of hare were also identified along with two bones of small rodents, at least one of which was from a short-tailed vole.

Nine of the 17 bird bones belonged to chickens, including two tarsometatarsi of adult hens and one of a cockerel. Two ulnae belonged to younger chickens. Three bones of duck were recorded, two of which were the size of mallards and the other was a good match for teal. Two bones of pigeons and one from a member of the thrush family were also recovered.

OVERALL SAMPLE SIZE AND BONE PRESERVATION

Animal bones were recorded from 358 contexts. They provided a total of 4,245 individual specimens (NISP), of which 1,961 were unidentified mammal fragments. Bones were found in 46 rooms. Over 200 fragments were recovered from contexts from Rooms 25–27, 30, 35 and 49. Over 400 fragments were recovered from contexts not associated with rooms (Table 18.1)

Assemblages from each context were assigned to one of five preservation grades. Although only five assemblages were allocated to the highest grade (excellent preservation), 70 (19%) had good preservation, in which most bones had sound surface condition but some had suffered gnawing damage. Bones in these assemblages provided 28% of the total NISP counts. Two hundred and three contexts (57%) produced moderately-preserved assemblages, which accounted for 52% of the total NISP counts. Bones in these contexts generally had fair surface preservation but included significant numbers of slightly weathered specimens as well as gnawed bones. A total of 81 assemblages (23%) were assigned to the quite poorly preserved category. These contained high numbers of eroded and weathered fragments, which provided 14% of the total fragments. None of the assemblages were very poorly preserved.

Only 89 fragments (2%) were burnt. These were mainly unidentified mammal fragments but they also included several elements of cattle, sheep/goat, cat, horse and pig (Table 18.2). Amongst the identified elements, 193 were recorded as eroded. However, 536 were recorded as weathered, indicating that bones were often exposed to the elements before final burial. The weathering damage, however, was generally slight. Gnawing damage was observed on 99 mammal elements indicating that some bones were accessible to dogs. Many (258) of the bones had modern breaks. Fragments of the same broken bone were recorded as a single specimen. In general, however, the assemblage was well preserved. Fifty-six bones had a shiny ivoried surface, indicative of very good preservation conditions.

Table 18.1   Number of individual specimens (NISP) of animal bones

Room	Cattle	S/G	Pig	Horse	Dog	Cat	Deer	Hare	OM	Small M	Amph	Bird	Fish	Unid M	Total
4														2	2
5	1														1
6	1		2			2	1			1	1	1		12	21
7			1		1									15	17
8	1		2									1		3	7
10	1	5										7		2	15
11	16	8	3		1							1		10	39
12	46	31	28	3	3		3			2	17	5		152	290
13	5	10	1	1										15	32
14	2	1												4	7
15	14	23	3		1							2		11	54
16	6	4	1											2	13
17	2	4		1			1	2						3	13
18	8	21	2									3		30	64
19		2													2
20	1											1			2
21	17	17	1		3									21	59
22	1	1	1	1					2	13	5				24
23	1	35	1				2							51	90
24	4	4	7				1	3				9		16	44
25	23	76	11	1	3	1	1		1	39	1	11	6	117	291
26	13	66	3	4	7		1			69	14	2		42	221
27	21	36	8		12	2			6	3	76	8		53	225
28	1	11		1	1					1		11		9	35
29	9	24	1	1	8	1				6	6	2		34	92
30	29	129	10	4		27	1	14			1	45	3	128	391
31	3	17		1								2		42	65
32	1	5										27		24	57
33	5	11			1							3		23	43
34		22	3				1					3		36	65
35	51	64	24	4	6		1			1	1	11		152	315
36	4	7		1		1						4		11	28
37	2	2	2											13	19
38	1	5										1		19	26
39	3	3									2	1		14	23
40	21	30	6				2		4					62	125
41	10	12	2	1										17	42
42	14	30	6	2			1					5		89	147
43	2	7	5			1	1					4		17	37
44	4	8	12	1	2	2	1							62	92
45	24	41	20	3	1	1	1					3		99	193
46	10	30	5	1		1	1	1				6		103	158
47	3	6	2									1		26	38
49	9	11	51				2		3					159	235
50	1	2	2											32	37
51	2	2	1	1										28	34
Other	78	84	8	17	4		3	2		1		17		201	415
Total	471	907	235	49	54	39	25	22	16	136	124	197	9	1961	4245

S/G = sheep/goat; OM = other mammals; Small M = small mammals (rodents etc); Amph = frog and toad; Unid M = unidentified mammal

Table 18.2   Animal bone preservation data

	Cattle	S/G	Pig	Horse	Dog	Cat	Red Deer	Hare	Bird	Total
Burnt	11	7	1	1		2			1	23
Eroded	57	89	21	5	8		5	1	7	193
Weathered	162	247	74	18	8	2	12		13	536
Gnawed	38	41	11	7	1		1			99
Ivoried	4	20	3	1		5	2	3	17	55

S/G = sheep/goat
Counts = number of individual specimens (NISP)

Table 18.3   Mammal bone frequencies

	NISP	ABG	%	% exc ABG	% Dom	% C:S:P	% S:P	%H:C
Cattle	471	19	25.9	26.6	27.6	29.6		
Sheep/Goat	907	66	49.9	49.6	51.3	55.0	78.2	
Pig	235		12.9	13.8	14.3	15.4		
Horse	49		2.7	2.9	3.0			9.8
Dog	54	8	3.0	2.7	2.8			
Cat	39	24	2.1	0.9	0.9			
Red Deer	24		1.3	1.4				
Roe Deer	1		0.1	0.1				
Hare	22		1.2	1.3				
Rabbit	3		0.2	0.2				
Dog/Fox	2		0.1	0.1				
Badger	4		0.2	0.2				
Otter	4	4	0.2	0.0				
Polecat	2		0.1	0.1				
Weasel	1		0.1	0.1				
Total	1818	121	1818	1697	1638	1528	1076	501

Totals exclude small mammals
NISP = number of individual specimens
ABG = number of bones in associated bone groups
% = % including bones in ABGs
% ex ABG = % excluding bones in associated bone groups
% Dom = % of domestic mammal bones (excluding ABGs)
% C:S:P = percentage of cattle, sheep/goat and pig (excluding ABGs)
% S:P = percentage of sheep/goat of total sheep/goat and pig (excluding ABGs)
% H:C = percentage of horse of total cattle and horse (excluding ABGs)

CATTLE

Cattle were the second most common species identified providing 26% of the identified mammal NISP counts (Table 18.3). Three associated bone groups (ABGs) accounted for only 19 of their 471 elements. Two of these groups consisted of foot bones and the third was composed of six ribs. Although none of the bones in these groups bore butchery marks, they could have been discarded during carcass processing.

Excluding ABGs, cattle provided 27% of the identified mammal bones (excluding small mammals) and 30% of the total cattle, sheep/goat and pig elements (Table 18.3). Cattle elements have been outnumbered by those of sheep/goat in assemblages from most Roman rural sites in Dorset, although Dewlish has produced one of the lower percentages (Table 18.4). For example, cattle and sheep/goat were represented in fairly equal numbers at Myncen Farm (Sixpenny Handley) and in the later Roman deposits from Bucknowle villa. The assemblage from Halstock villa is unusually rich in cattle, which provided 53% of the cattle, sheep/goat and pig elements (Allen *et al* 2018). In most urban assemblages from Dorchester, cattle elements have been outnumbered by sheep/goat in the earlier Roman phases but their percentages tend to increase in later Roman deposits (Maltby 2017, 183–4), reflecting a national trend (Allen *et al* 2017). However, because of the complexities of bone deposition at Dewlish, it was not possible to investigate possible chronological changes in species abundance.

In terms of minimum numbers of animals represented, there were at least 13 cattle in the Dewlish assemblage compared with 21 sheep/goat and six pigs. This suggests that more sheep were consumed at Dewlish but in terms of carcass weight, cattle would comfortably have been the greatest source of meat.

Cattle elements are listed in Table 18.5. Loose teeth provided 14% of the total cattle assemblage, which is indicative of a substantial amount of destruction and fragmentation of the jaws. The scapula was the most common bone, forming 10% of the cattle NISP counts. At least 26 different scapulae were represented. Upper limb bones were generally well represented, together forming 28% of the cattle NISP counts. The humerus was the most common upper limb bone; 37 fragments came from at least 21 different bones. Bones of lesser meat value, however, were also well represented; 13% of the cattle assemblage consisted of mandible and other cranial fragments and metapodials and phalanges formed 17% of the NISP counts. At least 15 metacarpals and 11 mandibles were represented. The presence of substantial numbers of low-quality meat bones indicates that a lot of the cattle carcasses were processed at Dewlish itself.

This is supported by the butchery evidence. Processing marks were recorded on 42 cattle bones. Most of the marks were incisions made with fine knife blades. Other marks were created by heavier blades and saw marks were observed at the base of a horn core (Table 18.6). The fine incisions observed on first phalanges were associated with initial skinning. The same explanation could account for a similar cut on the distal shaft of a metatarsal. Incisions created during dismemberment were observed on four proximal femora, three rib heads, an astragalus, a distal humerus, an ilium, a distal femur and an atlas. Filleting cuts were noted on the shafts of two humeri, the shaft of a rib and a scapula blade. Cuts on a hyoid may have been made during the extraction of the tongue.

Superficial chop and heavier blade marks mainly associated with carcass division were observed on a scapula blade, the head of a femur, an ischium and the shaft of a radius. The heads of two femora and four pelves had been completely chopped through during the separation of the hindlimb at the hip joint. The proximal end of an ulna, a scapula blade, the distal end of a metatarsal and a cervical vertebra had also been completely severed during dismemberment. Two tibiae and a femur had filleting marks made by a heavy blade that had removed slivers of the shaft with the meat. This method of filleting is prevalent on Roman military sites and larger nucleated sites where specialist butchers were operating but generally occur much less frequently, if at all, on rural sites (Maltby 2007; 2017). They occurred commonly in assemblages from Greyhound Yard, Dorchester (Maltby 1993). Similarly, none of the cattle upper limb bones had been split longitudinally to gain access to marrow. Many Romano-British towns, including Dorchester, have produced concentrations of these bones that were sometimes processed in large numbers. They are absent or occur very infrequently in most rural assemblages (Maltby 2007; 2017). In contrast, blade marks, which had removed part of the spine, particularly at the base of the acromion, were observed on five scapulae. These were made during separation of the shoulder blade from the humerus. Shoulder blades were commonly hung for preserving meat through smoking. Although they occur more commonly on urban sites, scapulae butchered in this

Table 18.4 NISP Comparisons of mammal bone frequencies in Dorset Roman assemblages

	Period	Cow:S/G:Pig NISP	% Cattle	% Sheep/G	% Pig	% S:P	%H:C	% Wild	% Ch:S
Dewlish	Roman	1528	29.6	55.0	15.4	78.2	9.8	3.5*	6.7
Myncen Farm	Roman	223	46.2	47.1	6.7	87.5	15.6	2.8	13.2
Norden	Roman	406	38.4	37.2	23.6	61.1	1.3	0.0	0.0
St Georges Road	Late RB	198	35.9	53.5	10.6	83.5	10.1	0.0	0.0
Maiden Castle Road	Roman	208	28.3	68.3	3.4	95.3	11.9	0.5**	5.3
Fordington Bottom	Early RB	95	22.1	73.7	4.2	94.6	12.5	1.0	1.4
Fordington Bottom	Late RB	411	43.1	52.6	4.4	92.3	12.8	0.2	1.4
Alington Avenue	Roman	857	53.0	41.5	5.5	88.3	18.9	0.2	0.6
Whitcombe	Late RB	338	38.2	56.2	5.6	90.1	11.0	0.0	0.0
Poundbury	Early RB	2813	22.4	73.6	4.0	94.8	9.6	7.4	0.4
Poundbury	Late RB	1362	43.2	45.6	11.2	80.2	6.5	3.5	0.5
Bucknowle	Late RB	3152	45.2	47.1	7.7	86.0	11.0	1.7	7.2
Portland Royal Manor	Roman	6020	15.9	72.8	11.2	86.6	3.7	0.1	1.4
Barton Field, Tarrant Hinton	IA-RB	1225	23.5	69.4	7.1	90.7	29.8	3.2	0.0
Tolpuddle Ball	Late RB	886	37.2	58.2	4.5	92.3	8.3	1.2	0.6
Halstock	Late RB	2023	53.4	36.6	9.9	78.7	5.8	6.4	no data
Dorchester, Charles St	Early RB	701	28.1	58.5	13.4	81.3	2.5	0.4	
Dorchester, Charles St	Late RB	1339	33.6	48.2	18.1	72.7	2.4	0.7	
Dorchester, Wessex Court II	Early RB	942	29.8	46.1	24.1	65.7	1.8	0.6	
Dorchester, Wessex Court II	Late RB	299	40.1	36.1	23.7	60.3	4.0	0.9	
Dorchester, Charles and WC II	Roman								9.3
Dorchester, Colliton Park	Early RB	817	27.4	68.2	4.4	93.9	1.3	0.2	no data
Dorchester, Colliton Park	Late RB	614	44.1	45.4	10.4	81.3	5.9	0.0	no data
Dorchester, Greyhound Yard	Early RB	11270	33.8	40.4	25.8	61.0	1.9	0.8	16.7
Dorchester, Greyhound Yard	Late RB	6215	46.3	30.5	23.2	56.9	2.0	2.1	21.4
Dorchester, Hospital	Roman	1107	42.5	42.8	14.6	74.5	4.3	0.6	25.9

NISP totals exclude ABGs where known and exclude bones in graves

% S:P = percentage of sheep/goat of total sheep/goat and pig

% H:C = percentage of horse of total cattle and horse

Data from St Georges Road and Maiden Castle Road adapted from Bullock and Allen (1997)

Data from Fordingtom Bottom adapted from Reilly (1997)

Data from Alington Avenue adapted from Maltby (2002). Totals exclude bones from graves

Data from Portland adapted from Maltby (2009)

Data from Tolpuddle Ball adapted from Hamilton-Dyer (1999). Totals exclude bones from tanning pit

Data from Dorchester sites adapted from Maltby (2017)

Data from other sites adapted from Allen *et al* (2018)

* excluding possible wild boar

** excluding probable ABGs of dog and hare

Table 18.5 Mammal element counts

Element	NISP								MNE							
	Cattle	S/G	Pig	Horse	Dog	Cat	Red D	Hare	Cattle	S/G	Pig	Horse	Dog	Cat	Red D	Hare
Horn Core/Antler	4						4		2						1	
Maxilla	6	19	21		3				4	10	7		2			
Skull frag	16	14	14	1	2		1	1	4	6	3	1	1		1	1
Mandible	31	79	28	4	3			2	11	41	11	2	3			2
Hyoid	3	2														
Loose Teeth	64	175	48	10	9											
Scapula	49	15	7	2		1	1		26	8	6	1		1	1	
Humerus	37	26	10	1	2	6			21	22	7	1	2	5		
Radius	24	71	7	3	1	4	1	5	10	34	4	2	1	4	1	3
Ulna	14	8	12		5	3			10	6	8		5	3		
Pelvis	24	26	5	1	2	3	1		9	11	3	1	2	3	1	
Femur	27	36	5	6	6	8	2		10	22	3	4	4	8	2	
Patella	1								1							
Tibia	31	93	17	2	4	7	2	5	12	40	9	2	4	7	1	3
Fibula			7		1						4		1			
Carpals	3	5	1	2					0.5	0.83	0.17	0.33				
Astragalus	6	6	5	1			4		6	6	4	1			4	
Calcaneus	6	10	5	1	1		1		6	10	5	1	1		1	
Centroquartal	1	3	1						1	3	1					
Other Tarsals	1	1														0.75
Metacarpal	22	56	6	3	1	1		3	15	23	5	3	0.75	0.25		1
Metatarsal	17	87	4	1	3	1	6	4	10	35	4	1	0.75	0.25	2	
Metapodial	3	5	1	2	1	1										
Peripheral Mp			6	3												
Phalanx 1	20	26	5	2			1		5	6.5	1	1			0.25	
Phalanx 2	12	8	1						3	2	0.25					
Phalanx 3	6	2	1						1.5	0.25	0.25					
Sesamoids		5														
Atlas (VC1)	3	7	2	1	1											
Axis (VC2)	1	11		1	1											
Cervical Vertebrae	7	16	2	1	1											
Thoracic Vertebrae	7	22	3	1												
Lumbar Vertebrae	3	17	2			3										
Sacrum	1	3	1		1	1										
Caudal Vertebrae	2	1														
Ribs	19	50	8		6			2								
Sternebrae		2														
Total	471	907	235	49	54	39	24	22								

NISP = number of individual specimens
MNE = minimum number of different elements represented
Raw MNE counts of all phalanges and dog and cat metacarpals and metatarsals of divided by 4

Table 18.6   Cattle, sheep/goat and pig butchery evidence

	Cattle	Sheep/Goat	Pig
Horn Core	s1		
Maxilla	`	k1	
Mandible			k1
Hyoid	k1	k1	
Scapula	b5 c1 k1 t1		c1
Humerus	k3		k1 t1
Radius	c1	c1 k2 t2	
Ulna	t1		
Pelvis	c1 k2 t4	c2 k2 t1	k1
Femur	b1 c1 k5 t2	k4 t1	
Tibia	b2	k2 t1	c1
Astragalus	k1		k3
Calcaneus		k1	
Metacarpal	a1	k1	
Metatarsal	k1 t1	k3	
Phalanx 1	k2		
Atlas	k1	k1	
Axis		c3 k3	
Cervical Vertebrae	t1	a2	
Thoracic Vertebrae		a2 k1	a1
Lumbar Vertebrae		a4 k3 t2	
Sacrum			a1
Ribs	k4	k7	k1
Total	a1 b8 c4 k21 t10 s1	a8 c6 k32 t7	a2 c2 k7 t1

Totals include specimens with more than one type of butchery mark
a= axially or longitudinally severed
b= blade skim
c = superfical heavy blade or chop mark
k = incisions
t = transversely or obliquely severed
s= sawn

way have a broader distribution, which could imply that shoulder joints were sometimes traded.

Only 13 cattle mandibles provided tooth ageing evidence. This is too small a sample to reconstruct mortality profiles other than observing that cattle of all ages, ranging from newborn calves to mature adults, were represented (Table 18.7). Epiphyseal fusion data was more abundant (Table 18.8). About 90% of the early-fusing epiphyses were fused indicating that at least 10% of the bones were from calves under a year old. The cattle assemblage included 25 very porous bones from neonatal and, in a few cases, possibly foetal animals. Their presence suggests that some cattle were being bred at the settlement. Some of the others could have been from calves that supplied veal. Three-quarters of the epiphyses of the distal tibiae and metapodials were fused which indicated that only around a quarter of the cattle were younger than about 2–3 years old (epiphyseal fusion ages have a high degree of variation). In contrast, only around 35% of the latest-fusing epiphyses were fused, indicating that many of the cattle were slaughtered before old age. There is therefore a focus on the acquisition of prime beef from sub-adult and young adult animals. Comparisons of the breadth and length measurements of five complete metacarpals indicated the presence of adults of both sexes.

Withers height estimates were derived from eight complete cattle limb bones. These ranged between 104cm and 121cm, with a mean of 113cm (Table 18.9). The smallest cattle were no larger than the size of many Iron Age cattle but the largest indicate the presence of some larger stock that emerged in Roman Britain (Rizetto *et al* 2017). The range and average size of cattle is very similar to those measured at Dorchester (Maltby 2010a, 292).

SHEEP/GOAT

Half of the identified mammal bones (excluding small mammals) belonged to sheep/goat. Of the bones that allowed specific identification, none were diagnostic of goat whereas 95 were identified as sheep. Four ABGs accounted for 66 (7%) of the sheep/goat elements. These were comprised of vertebrae and ribs of an adult (Room 15), the lower spine and upper hindlimbs of an immature male sheep (Room 23), the right foot of an adult sheep (Room 25) and the right lower hindlimb of an immature sheep (Room 26). Sheep ABGs occur commonly in Iron Age and Roman sites in Wessex (Morris 2011) and interpretations need to consider the evidence of age, completeness, carcass processing, weathering and gnawing damage and the context of deposition or redeposition. Although none of the bones in these groups had evidence of butchery or animal disturbance, there is

Table 18.7   Cattle, sheep/goat and pig tooth ageing evidence

	Cattle		Sheep/Goat			Pig	
	N	Stage %	N	Stage %	Cum %	N	Stage %
Stage 1	3	23.1	1	1.6	1.6	1	7.1
Stage 2			2	3.2	4.8	1	7.1
Stage 3	3	23.1	8	12.9	17.7		
Stage 3–4			3	4.8	22.5	1	7.1
Stage 4			11	17.7	40.2	1	7.1
Stage 4–5	1	7.7	2	3.2	43.4	4	28.6
Stage 5			22	35.5	78.9		
Stage 5–6	1	7.7					
Stage 6	3	23.1	7	11.3	90.2	2	14.3
Stage 6–7			4	6.5	96.8		
Stage 7	2	15.4	2	3.2	100	4	28.6
Total	13		62			14	

Stage 1 = 4th deciduous premolars (dp4) not in wear
Stage 2 = dp4 in wear; 1st molar (M1) not in wear
Stage 3 = M1 in wear; 2nd molar (M2) not in wear
Stage 4 = M2 in wear; 3rd molar (M3) and permanent premolars not in wear
Stage 5 = M3 in wear; 4th permanent premolar (P4) not in wear (Cattle)
Stage 5 = M3 in wear; M1 at Grant (1982) wear stage g (S/G)
Stage 5 = P4 in wear; M3 not in wear (Pig)
Stage 6 = P4 in wear; M3 < Grant wear stage k (Cattle)
Stage 6 = M1 at Grant wear stages h–m; M2 at Grant wear stage g (S/G)
Stage 6 = M3 at Grant wear stages a–b (Pig)
Stage 7 = M3 at Grant wear stages k–m (Cattle)
Stage 7 = M1 and M2 at Grant wear stages h–m (S/G)
Stage 7 = M3 at Grant wear stages c–g (Pig)

no conclusive evidence to suggest that any of these depositions were ritually motivated.

Excluding ABGs sheep/goat provided 55% of the total cattle, sheep/goat and pig NISP counts (Table 18.3). Comparing other sites in Dorset, sheep/goat outnumbered cattle in 13 out of the 16 rural and seven of the nine urban assemblages (Table 18.4). Therefore, the dominance of sheep/goat at Dewlish confirms their regional importance, particularly as recovery and preservation biases will have favoured the NISP counts of cattle. For example, 19% of the sheep/goat assemblage consisted of loose teeth (Table 18.5). Higher percentages of loose teeth reflect poorer preservation. Small bones such as the carpals, tarsals and phalanges are poorly represented, which reflects retrieval bias. As is usually the case in archaeological samples, larger bones of higher density were prominent in the Dewlish sheep/goat

assemblage. This included 93 fragments from at least 40 tibiae, 87 fragments from at least 35 metatarsals and 79 fragments from at least 41 mandibles. Vertebrae and ribs were quite well represented, not just in ABGs.

Butchery marks were recorded on 48 sheep/goat bones (Table 18.6). Most of these consisted of fine knife cuts mainly inflicted during disjointing. Eight vertebrae had evidence for the division of the carcass into roughly two equal sides. Two vertebrae had been severed transversely to divide the backbone into sections. Four upper limb bones had also been severed during dismemberment. However, cleavers and other heavy blades were utilised much less frequently than in cattle carcass processing.

Ageing data derived from 62 mandibles (Table 18.7) indicated that at least 56% of the jaws belonged to

Table 18.8 Cattle, sheep/goat and pig epiphyseal fusion evidence

Cattle

Early Fusing	U	J	F	Total	%F
Radius P			14	14	100.0
Scapula D		1	16	17	94.1
Acetabulum	2		4	6	
Humerus D	1		7	8	
1st Phalanx P	3		15	18	83.3
2nd Phalanx P	1		10	11	90.9
Total	7	1	66	74	89.2

Later Fusing	U	J	F	Total	%F
Tibia D		1	2	3	
Metacarpal D	1	1	8	10	80.0
Metatarsal D	2		5	7	
Metapodial D				0	
Total	3	2	15	20	75.0

Latest Fusing	U	J	F	Total	%F
Ulna P	1			1	
Femur D		2	2	4	
Radius D	1		3	4	
Humerus P	2	1		3	
Femur P	3	4	4	11	36.4
Calcaneus P	3		1	4	
Tibia P	2			2	
Total	12	7	10	29	34.5

Sheep/Goat

Early Fusing	U	F	Total	%F
Radius P	1	13	14	92.9
Scapula D	1	6	7	
Acetabulum		5	5	
Humerus D	3	13	16	81.3
1st Phalanx P	3	21	24	87.5
2nd Phalanx P		8	8	
Total	8	66	74	89.2

Later Fusing	U	F	Total	%F
Tibia D	8	19	27	70.4
Metacarpal D	9	4	13	30.8
Metatarsal D	13	8	21	38.1
Metapodial D	2	1	3	
Total	32	32	64	50.0

Latest Fusing	U	F	Total	%F
Ulna P	1		1	
Femur D	8	1	9	
Radius D	6	6	12	50.0
Humerus P	3		3	
Femur P	9	4	13	30.8
Calcaneus P	6	4	10	40.0
Tibia P	3		3	.
Total	36	15	51	29.4

Pig

Early Fusing	U	F	Total	%F
Radius P	1	3	4	
Scapula D		1	1	
Acetabulum	1	1	2	
Humerus D	1	1	2	
2nd Phalanx P	1		1	
Total	4	6	10	60.0

Later Fusing	U	F	Total	%F
1st Phalanx P	3	1	4	
Tibia D	6	3	9	
Fibula D	3	1	4	
Metacarpal D	2		2	
Metatarsal D	3	1	4	
Metapodial D		1	1	
Peripheral Mp D	3	1	4	
Total	20	8	28	28.6

Latest Fusing	U	F	Total	%F
Ulna P	3		3	
Femur D	1		1	
Radius D	3		3	
Humerus P	3		0	
Femur P	1		1	
Calcaneus P	4		4	
Tibia P	2	1	3	
Total	14	1	15	6.7

P = proximal; D = distal; U = unfused; J = fusing; F = fused

Table 18.9 Cattle and sheep measurements

Cattle	Measurements (mm)	Mean	sd	cv
Astragalus Bd	36.3 36.6 37.1 40.1	37.5		
Astragalus GLl	57.0 59.0 61.3 61.7	59.8		
Humerus BT	65.0 76.1 77.4 77.7 89.0	77.0		
Humerus HT	36.9 43.6 45.4 45.5 54.3	45.1		
Metacarpal Bp	47.0 47.6 50.6 50.6 55.2 60.0 62.7 63.7	54.7	6.7	12.2
Metacarpal Bd	51.2 53.6 59.3 62.5 67.5	58.8		
Metatarsal Bp	42.1 43.4 43.8 46.6 47.5	44.7		
Scapula LG	47.5 55.1 55.5 55.6 56.9	54.1		
Withers Ht (cm)	103.5 108.4 110.9 110.9 113.3 114.5 119.9 120.6	112.8	5.7	5.1

Sheep	Measurements (mm)	Mean	sd	cv
Humerus BT	27.0 27.5 27.5 27.7 27.8 30.2	28.0		
Humerus HT	16.9 17.4 17.7 17.9 18.5 19.6	18.0		
Metacarpal Bp	18.5 18.7 19.0 19.9 20.6 22.6 24.0 24.5	21.0	2.4	11.4
Metatarsal Bp	16.9 17.1 17.2 17.3 18.0 18.3 18.7 18.9 19.9 20.1 20.4 21.0	18.7	1.4	7.5
Metatarsal Bd	19.9 20.7 21.7 23.2 24.4	22.0		
Radius Bp	27.2 27.8 28.4 28.6 29.1 29.4 30.3 32.3	29.1	1.6	5.5
Radius BFp	25.6 26.1 27.6 27.8 27.9 29.1 31.3	27.9		
Tibia Bd	22.2 22.2 22.5 22.8 23.1 23.3 23.3 23.5 23.5 23.6 23.8 23.9 24.0 24.0 24.1 24.4 26.0	23.5	1.0	4.3
Withers Ht (cm)	52.3 56.8 58.6 59.4 61.3 61.9 63.1 64.9 68.3	60.7	4.7	7.7

Bd = distal breadth; GLl = greatest lateral length
BT = breadth of distal trochlea; HT = greatest height of distal trochlea
Bp = proximal breadth; BFp = breadth proximal articular surface
LG = length glenoid cavity
Withers height estimated from length measurements of complete limb bones
sd = standard deviation; cv = coefficient of variation

sheep which were slaughtered in their second (Stage 4 – at least 18%), and particularly, their third and fourth years (Stage 5 – at least 36%). In addition, at least 13% of the mandibles were from sheep aged between 3–12 months old (Stage 3). Only 21% of the mandibles belonged to sheep over four years of age. If the mortality profile is representative of regional practices, it indicates that sheep husbandry was focused mainly on meat production, although wool would have been obtained from any sheep that survived the annual culls.

The results of the mandible ageing analysis were broadly supported by the less reliable epiphyseal fusion evidence (Table 18.8). Only 11% of the early-fusing epiphyses had not fused indicating that

relatively few lambs were represented. However, eight very porous bones of young lambs were recorded including those of neonatal mortalities, whose presence could suggest that some sheep were being reared at the villa. Alternatively, very young suckling lambs could have been consumed as a luxury food, particularly if their mothers were being exploited for milk. Half of the epiphyses of the distal tibiae and metapodials were fused. Many of these would have been from sheep that they were younger than two years old, although fusion is commonly delayed in castrated animals (Popkin et al 2012). Only 29% of the surviving late-fusing epiphyses had fused indicating that most sheep were slaughtered before full skeletal maturity. The focus on the culling of sheep between two and four years of age was also apparent at Greyhound Yard, Dorchester, where the proportion of sheep ages between two and four years increased in later Roman features (Maltby 1993, 323–4).

Withers height estimates indicated that the stature of sheep varied between 52cm and 68cm with an average of 61cm (Table 18.9). The range was similar to the complete sheep bones measured in Dorchester, although the average height there was lower (58.1cm), although over half of those dated to the later Roman period measured over 60cm (Maltby 1993, 324). Average breadth measurements of the tibia, radius and metatarsal from the two sites were all broadly similar (Maltby 2010a, 294–5). One example each of a horned and hornless skull was recorded. Therefore the sheep at Dewlish included some sheep no larger than Iron Age stock but also others that were from larger types.

PIG

Excluding ABGs, pig elements provided 14% of the identified mammal and 15% of the total cattle, sheep/goat and pig NISP counts. They contributed 22% of the total sheep/goat and pig elements (Table 18.3). On most rural settlements in Roman Dorset, pigs contributed less than 20% of the sheep/goat and pig totals and in several cases less than 10%. In contrast, pigs have usually formed higher percentages of assemblages from Dorchester, particularly in sites in central areas of the town (Table 18.4). This again reflects a national pattern with pigs being generally better represented in Roman military sites and major urban centres than on rural settlements, reflecting both dietary preferences and economic status (King 1984).

Loose teeth provided 20% of the pig elements again showing quite a high degree of destruction of jaws. Other cranial elements formed 27% of the assemblage. At least 11 different mandibles were represented (Table 18.5) A high percentage of cranial elements is typical of most archaeological pig assemblages because they survive better than most postcranial bones. The tibia was the best represented limb bone, forming 7% of the NISP counts.

Butchery marks were observed on 14 pig bones. As in the case of sheep/goat, these mainly consisted of fine incisions (Table 18.6). These included disarticulation marks on three astragali, a mandibular ramus, a distal humerus, an ischium and a rib head. Two vertebrae had been axially severed during separation of the trunk into sides. One humerus had been severed through the distal end during separation from the radius/ulna and superficial chop marks were recorded on a scapula blade and the shaft of a tibia.

Only 14 pig mandibles provided ageing evidence (Table 18.7). They mainly belonged to pigs culled in their second (Stages 4–5) and third years (Stage 6). This is typical of pig mortality profiles in Romano-British sites. Four mandibles belonged to fully grown pigs, some of which were over three years of age (Stage 7). The few jaws of younger pigs included one neonatal mortality (Stage 1). This was one of four very porous bones of very young piglets. The epiphyseal fusion evidence confirmed that very few fully adult pigs with fused late-fusing epiphyses were represented (Table 18.8). Most pigs were culled within the first three years.

Eleven out of the 14 canines belonged to boars, which could imply that they were preferentially selected for consumption at the villa. However only two of these were embedded in jaws and retrieval bias probably favoured the recovery of the loose larger male canines.

Domestic pigs are generally smaller than wild boar although there can be a substantial amount of overlap (Evin et al 2014). Although most of the pig elements at Dewlish were smaller than wild boar, ten bones and teeth were unusually large and worthy to be considered to be wild boar. Unfortunately most of these were not measurable but a mandibular third molar (greatest length 40.2mm), a mandibular second molar (greatest length 25.0mm), a tibia (distal breadth 34.1mm) and two scapulae (greatest lengths glenoid process 44.5mm and 41.2mm) were all significantly larger than any of the measured pig bones from Greyhound Yard, Dorchester (Maltby 1990). The tibia may have been from a large domestic pig but the others are more likely to have belonged to wild boar.

HORSE

It is assumed although not proven that all the equid bones belonged to horse but the presence of mules cannot be ruled out. They provided 3% of the mammal NISP counts and 9% of the total cattle and horse elements (Table 18.3). Horses generally tend to be better represented on Roman rural and suburban sites than on urban sites (Maltby 2016) and this is the case in Dorset, where they often form over 10% of rural assemblages but less than 6% in all the assemblages from Dorchester (Table 18.4). Loose teeth formed 20% of the horse elements. The femur was the most common bone with six specimens from at least four different bones (Table 18.5).

Although their bones were found fairly commonly, there was no conclusive evidence that horseflesh was consumed by humans. No skinning or butchery marks were observed and their bones were generally much less fragmented than those of cattle. One metatarsal shaft had been sawn through transversely. This was probably an offcut from bone working. However, seven horse bones had evidence of canid gnawing indicating that their remains were sometimes accessible to dogs (Table 18.2).

There was only a limited amount of ageing evidence but there was no evidence for the presence of young foals. Only one of the loose teeth was unworn and the crown height of a worn mandibular third molar gave an estimated age of 9–10 years (Levine 1982). The only unfused limb bone was a distal radius. Eleven other epiphyses had fused including five from late-fusing femora. Horses would have been valued for riding and as pack animals and therefore could expect a longer life than species exploited mainly for meat.

DOG AND CAT

Dog elements provided 3% of the identified mammal NISP counts (Table 18.3). A small ABG consisting of four neonatal puppy bones was recorded from Room 29 and parts of a skull and jaws of an adult were found in Room 35. Loose teeth provided 17% of the dog assemblage. Six fragments from at least four femora and parts of five different ulnae were present (Table 18.5). None of the dog bones had evidence for carcass processing. In addition to the ABG from Room 29,

two other bones of neonatal puppies were recovered. Twenty other ageable dog bones including three mandibles belonged to adults. A tibia with a greatest length of 196mm came from quite a large dog with an estimated shoulder height of 58.1 cm (Harcourt 1974). In contrast an ulna with an olecranon length of only 18.9mm belonged to a miniature type, reflecting the diversity in dog sizes in the Roman period (Clark 1995). The large number of gnawed bones (Table 18.2) showed that dogs kept at the villa had common access to butchery and kitchen waste.

Cats provided 2% of the total identified mammal fragments, although 24 of their bones in Pit-shaft P4 formed ABGs (Table 18.3). Most of the cat remains consisted of the major limb bones with the largest bones, the femur and the tibia being the best represented (Table 18.5). No evidence for carcass processing was found. Most of the cat bones were from adults but two unfused bones came from kittens. Cats would have been kept as companion animals or rodent exterminators. They have been found usually in small numbers in several Roman bone assemblages from Dorset, including Dorchester (Maltby 1993; Grimm 2008), Poundbury (Buckland-Wright 1987) and the villas at Bucknowle, Tarrant Hinton and Halstock (Allen *et al* 2018).

OTHER MAMMALS AND AMPHIBIANS

Excluding the possible bones and teeth of wild boar, other mammals provided 3.5% (excluding small mammals and ABGs) of the identified mammal bones (Table 18.3). If the ten potential wild boar elements are included, this figure rises to 4%. This a relatively high percentage compared to other Roman sites in Dorset (Table 18.4). All but one of the assemblages from Dorchester have produced fewer than 1% wild mammal elements and the same is true for many of the rural settlements. However, wild mammals have tended to be better represented in villa assemblages such as Dewlish, Myncen Farm, Halstock and Tarrant Hinton, indicative of greater dietary diversity and participation in social hunting. The highest percentage of wild mammals from Dorset sites comes from Poundbury, which apparently produced an exceptional number of roe deer bones (Buckland-Wright 1987).

Red deer were the most common of the wild mammals forming over 1% of the identified mammal NISP counts (Table 18.3). Their remains included four antler fragments (Table 18.5), one of which was a sawn offcut of worked antler. Most of the bones came from the hind limb including six fragments of metatarsals. A deep blade mark was recorded on a pelvis. Roe deer was represented by a single metatarsal and there was no evidence for the recently introduced fallow deer, which has been found on a few high-status Romano-British sites (Sykes *et al* 2011).

Hares provided over 1% of the identified mammal NISP counts (Table 18.1). Most of their elements consisted of the larger limb bones that had a better chance of recovery. The tibia and radius were the best represented (Table 18.5). These included a radius with fine knife cuts. Hares have been found in small numbers in several Roman assemblages from Dorset. Three bones of rabbit were identified. These are likely to have been more recent intrusions but rabbits have been confirmed to be present at a few Roman sites (Sykes and Curl 2010), so it is just possible that the rabbits from Dewlish could be of Roman origin.

Badger, otter, polecat and weasel were represented in small numbers. Three metatarsals and a tibia of an adult female otter were found in Room 40. Three of the four badger bones from the area of Room 49 probably belonged to the same skeleton. Room 22 produced another badger bone and one of a male weasel. Two bones of a male polecat were found in Room 27. None of the bones displayed evidence of butchery, although they all may have been collected for their pelts. Although it is feasible that the badger and weasel bones may have been more recent intrusions, it is very unlikely that otters or polecats would have inhabited the immediate vicinity. Otters and polecats have not been recorded on any of the Dorset assemblages listed in Table 18.4, although four polecat/ferret bones were identified in a late Iron Age/Early Roman phase at Fordington Bottom (Reilly 1997). Ten badger bones were recorded from Greyhound Yard, Dorchester (Maltby 1993).

A total of 136 bones of small mammals were recovered from the excavations, mainly from Rooms 25 and 26 (Table 18.1). Two mole limb bones from Corridor 12 were probably intrusive. Attempts at rodent speciation were limited to mandibles, skulls and some loose teeth. Twenty of these elements belonged to short-tailed vole, and one to water vole. Although some of these rodents may have been intrusive, most of the bones came from well-sealed deposits and are likely to be of Roman origin. The short-tailed vole is found commonly in grassland and other open habitats and can form a significant part of the diet of barn owls, which were also identified at Dewlish (Table 18.10). No bones of mouse or rats were identified. A total of 124 amphibian bones were identified including 76 from Room 27 (Table 18.1). Most of the 56 bones identified as frog came from the deposit in Room 27. A total of 18 bones of toad were found in seven of the rooms.

BIRDS

A total of 197 bird bones were recovered from the Dewlish excavations, of which 173 were identified and 69 were from ABGs (Table 18.10). 50% of the identified bird bones belonged to chickens including 26 bones from the skeleton of an immature bird in Room 32. Excluding all ABGs, chickens provided 58% of the identified bird bones and 7% of the total chicken and sheep/goat NISP counts. The chicken and sheep/goat ratio can be compared with other Roman assemblages. Generally, higher percentages of chickens have been encountered in towns than on rural sites. Most farmstead assemblages have less than 1% chicken and very few have over 5%. Although most villa assemblages have fewer than 10% chicken, they have tended to produce higher percentages than farmsteads and a few have levels of over 20%. In contrast, chickens have provided over 10% of the total sheep/goat and chicken bones in most urban assemblages and in many cases this figure rises above 20% (Maltby *et al* 2018). The results from Dorset largely fit this pattern (Table 18.4). Most of the assemblages from Dorchester have over 15% chicken, whereas 11 of the 15 rural assemblages have less than 2% chicken. Three of the four assemblages that have produced more than 5% chicken are from villas including Dewlish. Chickens were first brought to Britain during the Iron Age but, despite evidence for an increase in abundance during the Roman

Table 18.10   Bird bone frequencies

	NISP	ABG	%	% exc ABG	% Ch:S
Chicken	86	26	49.7	57.7	6.7
Goose	46	40	26.6	5.8	
Mallard-sized Duck	12		6.9	11.5	
Medium-sized Duck	4		2.3	3.8	
cf Teal	1		0.6	1.0	
Woodcock	3		1.7	2.9	
Wader	1		0.6	1.0	
Pigeon/Dove	5		2.9	4.8	
Goshawk	1		0.6	1.0	
Barn Owl	3	3	1.7	0.0	
Rook/Crow	2		1.2	1.9	
cf Jackdaw	1		0.6	1.0	
Thrushes	7		4.0	6.7	
Small Passerine	1		0.6	1.0	
Unidentified	24				
Total	197	69	173	104	901

NISP = number of individual specimens

ABG = number of bones in associated bone groups

% = % including bones in ABGs but excluding unidentified bird bones

% ex ABG = % excluding bones in associated bone groups and unidentified bones

% Ch:S = % of chicken of total chicken and sheep/goat (excluding bones in ABGs)

period, they remained a rare commodity. During this period, they may have been regarded as an exotic, perhaps luxury, commodity, which is reflected by their greater abundance on high status rural and urban sites. Their special status is also reflected in funerary practices, as it is not unusual for their bones to be found in graves even on settlements where they formed very small proportions of the rest of the assemblage, for example at Alington Avenue and Maiden Castle Road (Maltby 2002; Bullock and Allen 1997).

In addition to the bones in the ABG, five porous bones came from immature chickens including one very young chick. The presence of bones of young chickens indicates that they were being kept at Dewlish. As expected, the largest elements dominated the chicken assemblage with the tibiotarsus and tarsometatarsus represented by 15 bones each (Table

18.11). Seven of the tarsometatarsi were found in Pit-shaft P4, which indicates that the feet were detached from the rest of the carcass during butchery.

Eight of the adult tarsometatarsi had no spurs and belonged to hens, whereas only three had spurs and were probably from males. One tarsometatarsus with no spur was unusually large (greatest length = 80.6mm). This bone was slightly porous and could have been from a male that was culled before the spur had fully developed. A knife cut near the proximal indicated that the foot had also been detached. Other unspurred tarsometatarsi were usually under 70mm in length, typical of the small size of chickens in this period (Table 18.12). Adult hens would have been able to supply eggs. However, none of the shafts of 12 broken femora and tibiotarsi had any evidence of medullary bone, which is formed by hens in lay.

Forty-six bones of geese were identified, 40 of which belonged to three ABGs, two from Pit-shaft P4 and one from Room 28 (Tables 18.10 and 18.11). The most complete ABG consisted of 24 bones from the breast, wings and legs of an adult in Pit-shaft P4. The presence of thick deposits of medullary bone in the femora and tibiotarsi indicated that the goose had died during the laying season. A radiocarbon date (1810 ± 30 BP – Beta Analytic – 543096: Appendix 2) confirmed that the skeleton was of mid-late Roman date. Eleven bones of a second adult goose were found in Room 28. Evidence for medullary bone was also found in a tibiotarsus of this ABG. These are very rare finds, as to the author's knowledge, no other example of Roman geese in lay have been reported. Pit-shaft P4 also produced five leg bones of a young gosling and a tarsometatarsus of a second gosling of similar age. Their presence strengthens the evidence that domestic geese were being kept at Dewlish at some stage. The sizes of the geese bones fall into the range of greylag/domestic goose (Table 18.13).

Bones of geese have been found in small numbers on some Romano-British sites. Most of them are the size of greylag geese. There has been discussion about whether any geese were kept in captivity in Roman Britain (Albarella 2005). However, some Romano-British geese bones are larger than wild greylag and are likely to have been domestic birds (Poland 2018). Of the Dorset sites listed in Table 18.4, goose bones

Table 18.11 Bird elements counts (NISP)

Element	ABG Chicken	Other Chicken	Total Chicken	ABG Goose	Other Goose	Total Goose	Total Ducks
Skull	1	1	2				1
Maxilla	2		2				
Mandible	2		2	2		2	
Sternum	1		1	1		1	
Furcula	1		1	1		1	1
Coracoid	2	6	8	1		1	
Scapula		3	3	2		2	2
Humerus	2	3	5	2		2	3
Radius	2	2	4	3		3	4
Ulna	2	7	9	2		2	3
Carpometacarpus	1	1	2	2		2	1
Wing phalanx				3		3	
Pelvis	1	3	4	1	1	2	
Synsacrum		3	3	1		1	
Femur	2	3	5	4		4	1
Tibiotarsus	2	13	15	4	2	6	1
Fibula	1		1				
Tarsometatarsus		15	15	5	3	8	
Foot Phalanx				1		1	
Vertebrae				3		3	
Ribs	4		4	2		2	
Total	26	60	86	40	6	46	17

Table 18.12 Chicken tarsometatarsi measurements

GL	Bp	Bd	SC	Comments
63.5	11.5	11.4	5.7	No spur
63.7	10.9	11.5	6.1	No spur
64.0	11.6	11.1	5.6	No spur
66.2	11.9	11.2	6.2	No spur
67.7	11.3	11.3	5.5	No spur
	12.8			Spur
70.6	13.5	12.9	6.2	No spur
73.7	14.4	12.3	6.2	No spur
	13.5			No spur
78.2	12.9	12.2	6.3	Spur
		13.3		Spur length 17.9
80.5	13.6	13.5	6.7	No spur young

All measurements in millimetres
GL = greatest length
Bp = greatest proximal breadth
Bd = greatest distal breadth
SC = minimum diameter of shaft

have only been recorded at St Georges Road (Bullock and Allen 1997), Portland Royal Manor (Maltby 2009) and the Greyhound Yard and Charles Street sites in Dorchester (Maltby 1993; 2010). Significantly a hatched goose egg was recorded at the Dorchester Hospital site (Siddell 2008) indicating that some geese were being kept in the Roman town.

Seventeen bones from at least three species of duck were identified at Dewlish (Table 18). One tibiotarsus (distal breadth 5.5mm) was a good match for teal. Twelve of the bones were from large ducks comparable in size to mallard. Four were from medium-sized ducks similar in size to wigeon and pochard. All the bones were from adult birds and there is no evidence that any of the ducks were kept in captivity. In Dorset ducks have also been found in small numbers in Roman deposits from Myncen Farm (Allen et al 2018), Portland Royal Manor (Maltby 2009), Poundbury (Buckland-Wright 1987) and from

Table 18.13   Goose measurements

Pit 4 ABG	GL	Bp	Dip	Bd	Did	Dd	SC
Coracoid	78.4						
Humerus		37.3		24.0			
Radius	150.0			10.9			5.3
Ulna	159.0	16.2	20.2		16.2		8.3
Femur	81.5	20.7		20.1		16.0	8.6
Tibiotarsus	149.5			18.0			8.8
Tarsometatarsus	89.2	19.1		18.5			8.5

Other	GL	Bp	Dip	Bd	Did	Dd	SC
Radius	152.0			10.9			
Tarsometatarsus		20.0					
Tarsometatarsus	88.0	18.2		19.2			8.8

All measurements in millimetres   Bp = greatest proximal breadth   Did = greatest diagonal at distal end
ABG = associated bone group   Dip = greatest diagonal at proximal end   Dd = greatest distal depth
GL = greatest length   Bd = greatest distal breadth   SC = minimum diameter of shaft

most of the sites in Dorchester (Maltby 1983; 2010a; Hamilton-Dyer 1993; Grimm 2008).

Three bones of woodcock were recorded. Woodcocks have been found on many Romano-British sites including Greyhound Yard, Dorchester (Maltby 1993) and they seem to have been the most commonly hunted of the waders (Maltby 2010a). A humerus of a smaller wader was also recovered. This was the size of a redshank or snipe but could not be further identified. Five bones of the pigeon family were recorded including one bone of a squab. Pigeons may have been kept in captivity in Roman Dorchester (Maltby 1993) but they could also have been captured on fowling expeditions or have been nesting nearby. Similarly, the barn owl, which was represented by three bones from Corridor 12 may have been a bird that was a resident at the site.

The female goshawk carpometacarpus from Pit-shaft P4 is a rare find of this species in Roman Britain. There are several possibilities to explain its presence. The first is that the bird was attracted to the villa as a predator of some of the animals kept there, such as geese and chickens. Another possibility is that it was exploited for its feathers. Butchered wing bones of eagles (Holmes 2018) and other birds of prey including buzzards (Maltby 2013) have been found on several Romano-British sites. A third possibility is that the

bone was from a bird kept for falconry. Although Poole (2018) has noted that falconry is not generally regarded to have been practised in Roman Britain, he reminds us of the discovery of a sparrowhawk tarsometatarsus along with bones of the thrush family in a well at Great Holt Farm, Boreham, Essex. It was suggested by Murphy et al (2000) that this could have been a bird that was used in falconry or as a decoy to capture small birds. As noted below, several bones of the thrush family were also discovered at Dewlish.

The corvid family was represented by three wing bones, two of rook or crow and one of a smaller species, possibly a jackdaw. All three bones belonged to adults. These birds may have been attracted as scavengers and may have been nesting nearby.

Seven bones from birds of the thrush family were recovered. Several species may be represented. Although these may have been bones of birds that were resident near the villa, it is possible that some of these birds were captured for food. One bone of a smaller passerine was also recorded.

FISH

Only nine fish bones were recovered. Unfortunately, these mainly consisted of fin rays, which could not be speciated. However, many fish bones may have been overlooked during hand excavation.

DISCUSSION

The bone assemblage from Dewlish has provided insights into the relationships between the human inhabitants of the villa and the animals they kept and exploited. Because of the complexities of deposition, it is not possible to trace changes in animal exploitation during the life of the villa and we must be cautious about statements that imply continuity throughout its occupation. Overall, however, although more sheep than cattle were slaughtered, beef would have been the main source of meat. Although beef and lamb were the mainstays of the meat supply as elsewhere in Roman Britain (King 1984; 1999; Maltby 2016; Allen *et al* 2018), the inhabitants at Dewlish had a more diverse meat diet than many of their contemporaries who lived in farming settlements in Dorset. They also ate more pork and poultry, but not to the same extent as many of the people who lived in Dorchester. Most of the meat they ate were from near full grown or fully-grown stock killed in their prime rather than in old age. Less frequently, the Dewlish residents ate veal, suckling pigs and young lambs, which were possibly regarded as luxury foods. Despite the relatively frequent finds of horse bones, there is no conclusive evidence that horseflesh was eaten by humans but some of their carcasses were made available to dogs. Some of the cattle and sheep were no larger than those found on Iron Age sites in the region but there were also some larger animals reflecting the acquisition of new stock and/or better feeding regimes.

The villa inhabitants did acquire, either directly or indirectly, the captures of the chase or wildfowling expeditions more frequently than most people who lived in Dorchester or in lower status rural settlements. Consequently, they occasionally supplemented their diet with venison, wild boar, hare, ducks, waders, pigeons and possibly smaller birds. Otters, polecats, and possibly badgers and weasels may have been hunted for their pelts.

Many of the domestic stock were probably slaughtered and butchered locally using both fine knives and heavier blades, but carcass processing was not as intensive or as systematic as encountered in Dorchester, where the supply of beef particularly was in the hands of specialist butchers. However, several of the cattle scapulae at Dewlish had evidence of being butchered in a similar manner to those in Dorchester and it is possible that some smoked shoulders of beef were imported to the villa.

There is evidence from offcuts that a small amount of horn- bone- and antler-working took place at the villa but it does not seem to have been a major activity. Wool would also have been obtained from many of the sheep before they were slaughtered but the mortality evidence suggests it was not the main focus of their exploitation. Similarly, the ageing and sexing profiles did not indicate that dairy production was a major component of cattle and sheep husbandry.

The presence of a few bones of neonatal cattle, pigs and sheep suggests that some domestic stock may have given birth in the villa precincts. There is also evidence that chickens and, more unusually, geese and perhaps even rabbits were kept there at some point, although the latter may have been more recent intrusions. Cats and dogs, including miniature types, were also kept at the villa. Dogs had easy access to food waste and would also have assisted in herding flocks and possibly in the chase. Horses may also have been used in hunting as well as more mundane transport duties. Goshawks may even have been used in the hunting of small game.

Animals therefore played a diversity of roles in the lives of the human occupants of Dewlish. They served as sources of food and income, and as companions in the household, yards, fields and hunting grounds. They would also have played a symbolic role in their belief systems. Although in this assemblage there were no incontrovertible examples of ritual depositions involving animals, some of the contents of Pit-shaft P4 may be worthy of such consideration. Multiple ABGs in some wells and deep pits have been interpreted in this way in Dorchester, for example (Woodward and Woodward 2004), although other explanations for some of these depositions also need to be considered (Maltby 2010b).

NON-ADULT HUMAN BONES

THE BURIALS FROM ROOMS 5, 8 AND 32, BY ANNA ROHNBOGNER

Background

Human burials were located in three distinct areas of the villa complex. The high level of fragmentation and commingling proved challenging during skeletal analysis, particularly as the remains could not be observed *in situ*. The minimum number of individuals was eight. The minimum number of individuals was calculated for burials 2 and 3 based on stages of skeletal development where applicable, and the siding of element or fragment counts. Ageing was undertaken using Fazekas and Kosa's (1978) method based on long bone length, as well as dental development outlined by Demirjian *et al* (1973), Ubelaker (1989) and Schaefer *et al* (2009). The determination of sex remains problematic in non-adult individuals and was therefore not attempted. 'Perinate' denotes a newborn that died at around 38–40 weeks gestation, 'neonate' is used for those aged between birth to one month, whereas 'foetus' describes any individuals younger than 37 weeks gestation. The term 'infant' is used to refer to non-adults below the age of one year old (Lewis 2007).

Burial 1 D4 (13), Room 5 (Fig. 19.1)

Burial 1 contained the remains of a perinate, aged 39–40 gestational weeks (Demirjian *et al* 1973; Fazekas

and Kosa 1978). The preservation of the bones was good with minimal taphonomic damage. Most of the major long bones, the cranium and bones of the pelvic and pectoral girdles were present. Epiphyses and the small bones of the hands and feet were largely missing, and some elements exhibited post-mortem breaks. A supratrochlear spur/supracondyloid process on the distal portion of the right humerus superior to the medial epicondyle was observed (Finnegan 1978, Buikstra and Ubelaker 1994). This type of proliferative bone growth occurs in infants as well as adults and is suggested to be an inherited non-metric trait (Robb and Rogers 2009, 157).

Burial 2 F3 (8), Room 8 (Fig. 19.2)

Burial 2 contained the skeletal remains of at least two infants. Preservation was reasonably good and taphonomic damage was limited to post-mortem breaks of fragile flat bone fragments and epiphyses. The burial holds the remains of a foetus, aged 29–30 gestational weeks with around 75% of the skeleton present. We have to bear in mind that these may also be the remains of a baby that was small-for-gestational age, rather than a pre-term birth, as it is currently not possible to differentiate between the two using ageing methods based on diaphyseal lengths (Lewis and Gowland 2007). One right true rib, a sphenoid and left temporal pars squama also suggest the remains of a perinate in burial 2, as the elements were at a more mature developmental

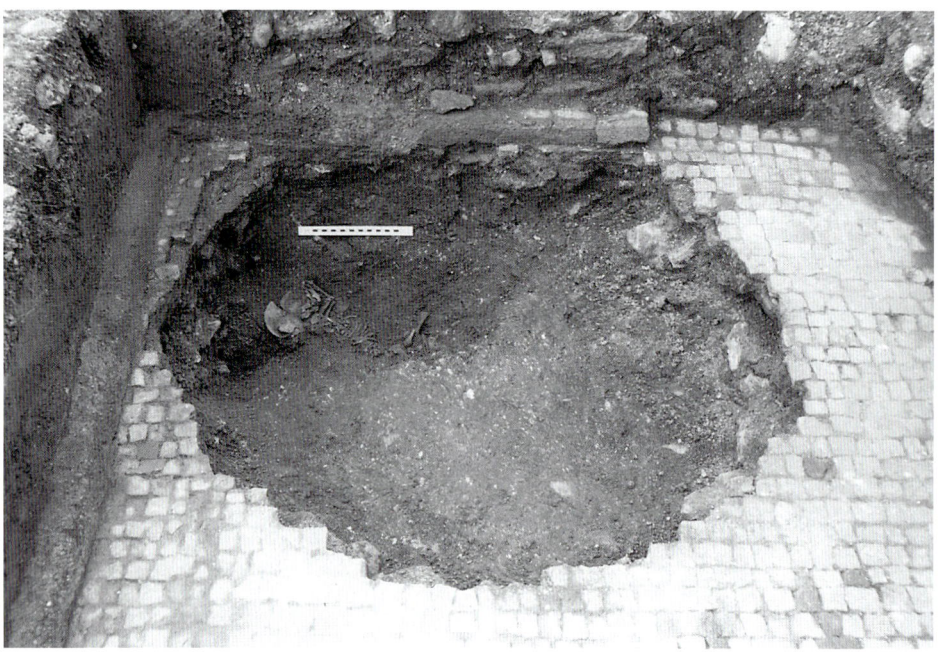

Figure 19.1   Burial 1: west corner of Room 5. Photograph: Bill Putnam (DH71DHA).

Figure 19.2   Burial 2: south corner of Room 8. Photograph: R2567.

stage than those of the foetal individual. The surface and general mass of the perinatal sphenoid and its fused left wing were poorly defined and exhibited a high level of porosity, possibly indicative of scurvy (Brickley and Ives 2006). However, widespread new woven bone deposits, pitting and porosity are a sign of healthy regular bone growth that is deposited rapidly within these young infants (Shopfner 1966; Kwon *et al* 2002; Rana *et al* 2009). Distinguishing bony changes as a result of vitamin C/D deficiency or infection is therefore inherently difficult in neonates, especially since the perinate in burial 2 is very poorly represented.

Burial 3 O97(6), Room 32

Burial 3 was disturbed by ploughing which resulted in the scattering of bones over a small area. Tooth marks were found on various bones, alongside animal bone including rib fragments and a maxilla, most likely from a rat or similar sized rodent. As a result burial 3 may have been disturbed throughout rather than only superficially via ploughing. The high degree of commingling and fragmentation, alongside significant taphonomic damage to the skeletal elements in burial 3 made analysis challenging. There was a high level of fragmentation, mostly including flat bone and long bone shaft fragments. The minimum number of individuals was five, including two non-adults and three perinates. The perinates were aged around 39–40 weeks gestation (Demirjian et al 1973; Fazekas and Kosa 1978). Each perinate is represented by 75% of the skeleton with most of the major limb bones present, along with bones of the pectoral and pelvic girdles, cranial elements, vertebrae and ribs. All three individuals were at the same developmental stage considering long bone measurements, tooth development and epiphyseal fusion. No pathological conditions or non-metric traits were found on these newborns. The non-adults are represented by one long bone shaft fragment, vertebrae and sacral fragments, at distinctly more advanced developmental stages than the perinates. There are two axes, both at the same stage of epiphyseal fusion, indicating a minimum number of two non-adults. The stages of vertebral epiphyseal union suggest an age of around three years old (Schaefer et al 2009, 119–121). No pathologies or non-metric traits were observed.

Discussion and conclusion

Generally, the ages-at-death of the majority of individuals were around full term, conforming with those recovered from other rural and villa sites across Roman Britain (Macdonald 1977, 35–36; Everton and Leech 1981; Everton 1982; Scott 1991, 1999; Waldron et al 1999; Esmonde Cleary 2000). None of the individuals exhibited any signs of trauma or

pathology and we cannot make any inferences about their causes of death. The perinates may have been stillborn, died shortly after birth or were even the victims of infanticide as often speculated for infant assemblages in the osteoarchaeological literature (Mays 1993, 2003; Mays and Faerman 2001; Gowland and Chamberlain 2002; Bonsall 2013). Current theories on intramural burials of those aged 1-year old and below stipulate a distinct burial rite, rather than infanticide or exposure. It may have been the case that those dying within the first year of life were rendered somewhat different from the rest of the community and therefore required burial away from the main cemetery area and closer to the sphere of the living (Moore 2009; Gowland et al 2014; Millett and Gowland 2015). However, the two 3-year-olds slightly diverge from this common burial practice as they exceed the general age profiles of intramural infant burials in Roman Britain. Perhaps the working population at Dewlish followed separate rites following the death of young children within their community, and it was not only infants who warranted intramural burial. The age distribution in Burial 3 also evokes more general questions, including when exactly Romano-British children were deemed suitable for burial in the communal cemetery.

ADDITIONAL HUMAN REMAINS IDENTIFIED DURING THE COURSE OF POST-EXCAVATION ANALYSIS, BY HOLGER SCHUTKOWSKI AND GABRIELLE DELBARRE

During 2019, the skeletal remains of six non-adult individuals came to light during the examination and analysis of the Dewlish Roman villa animal bones assemblage at Bournemouth University (Maltby and Clark, Chapter 18). These remains were in addition to those that were previously known to have been excavated during the 1969 – 1979 fieldwork seasons which are the subject of Rohnbogner's report above. The six additional skeletons had been excavated from three rooms (32, 35 and 36 in Buildings 2 and 2A) and a pit-shaft that was partially sealed beneath Room 30 in Building 4 (the bath house suite). The remains were analysed individually, separated by the burial location and/or stages of skeletal development (Table 19.1).

Table 19.1   Individuals excavated at Dewlish Roman villa recovered during faunal remains analysis.

Context number	Room/ feature	Individual	Bone inventory	Maturity stage
P4 (12*)	pit-shaft	1	Left radius and 4 metacarpals.	Perinate
P4 (19*)	Pit-shaft	2	Left scapula, 4 CV 9 TV, 2 LV, 11 Right ribs, 10 Left ribs Left and right humeri, Right radius, Left ulna, Left and right ilia, Left and right femora, Right tibia, Left (fragment, proximal) and right fibulae	Perinate – 40 weeks
098 (4)	32	3	Right and Left humeri	Foetus – 22–24 weeks
097 (6)	32	4	Mandible	Infant – under one year old
P92 (6)	36	5	1st rib, left	Perinate
Q96 (1)	35	6	Left proximal tibia	Perinate

(CV = cervical vertebra, T V= thoracic vertebra, L V= Lumbar vertebra. * denotes a sealed context)

Ageing of the remains was undertaken using Fazekas and Kosa's (1978) method focusing on long bone length and dental development using van Beek (1983). 'Foetus' describes any individuals younger than 37 weeks gestation. 'Perinate' refers to a newborn who died at around 38–40 weeks gestation. 'Neonate' is used for those aged between birth to one month. 'Infant' is used to refer to non-adults below the age of one year old (Lewis 2007, Scheuer and Black 2000). The pelvis being present with a sufficient degree of completeness, sexing was determined using Schutkowski (1993) for individual 2. Sexing was not attempted for the other five individuals as their developmental stage was unsuitable for sex determination and/or the remains were fragmented, and sexually dimorphic areas were absent.

With the exception of Individuals 3 (foetus) and 4 (infant), all the skeletons are those of perinates. The bones of Individuals 1 and 2 are well preserved and present minimal taphonomic damage (grades 0–1 in Brickley and McKinley 2004). Whist retaining their general morphology, the bones of all other individuals present cortical surface erosion which prevented observations from being made (Brickley and McKinley 2004, grades 3–4). All the skeletons are incomplete, five of them being represented by five or less bone elements all of which are postcranial, with the exception of Individual 4 which is represented by a fragmented mandible. None of the six individuals shows evidence for pathology and/or trauma and no non-metric traits were observed.

Only Individuals 1 and 2 were recovered from sealed contexts. In the case of Individual 1, skeletal development stage and taphonomy could suggest that the left radius (P4 (12)) may be an antimere of the right radius of Individual 2 (P4 (19)) and therefore potentially represent the same individual. Both individuals were recovered from within a 5m deep pit-shaft, the mouth of which was within the sub-walls footprint of Room 30. Analysis of the pit-shaft fills indicates that it was used for the deposition of rubbish from the kitchens and elsewhere on the villa site, and it seems that the human remains were disposed of along with the household waste. However, the contexts from which Individuals 1 and 2 were excavated, 12 and 19 respectively, are very distinct. Context 12 was ash and charcoal and was amongst the upper fills of the pit-shaft, whereas context 19 was a layer of 'mortary' rubble c. 50cm deep. From their depositional contexts it is therefore concluded that these skeletal remains represent two different individuals of matching perinatal developmental stage. Both Individuals 1 and 2 were excavated from amongst animal bones and were thus misidentified as faunal remains by the excavators.

Represented solely by postcranial bone elements, Individual 2 is the most complete and well-preserved skeleton (grades 0–1 in Brickley and McKinley 2004) of a full-term female perinate infant. The skeleton of Individual 2 does not show evidence for trauma or pathology. It is not possible to determine whether the baby was still-born or died within a month of birth, but in light of the other perinatal remains found in this assemblage, a high rate of infant mortality during the birth process, or shortly afterwards, is conceivable. While infanticide has been documented for this period, there is no evidence on this skeleton that suggests that this was the case (Mays 2001, Bonsall 2013). In the light of the good preservation and completeness of the postcranial bone elements, the absence of skull, atlas and axis (cervical) vertebrae is noticeable. This could result from a range of aetiologies, from possible depositional process (e.g. these bone elements 'fell' further down inside the shaft if the perinate was thrown in headlong), to intentional severance (with possible disposition of the bones elsewhere) or damage inflicted during the process of excavation.

The taphonomy of Individual 4 (O97 (6)) and the fragmentation of the mandible suggest that it could belong to one previously excavated individual from the same context (Rohnbogner, above, Burial 3). However, its developmental stage as infant does not correspond to any of the maturity stages of the other individuals from Burial 3 (two early childhood c. 3 years old individuals, and three perinate individuals). This suggests that this mandible probably represents an additional individual from this commingled burial, thus bringing the minimum number of deposited individuals to 6. Whether the Room 32 commingled deposit was a single event, or a multi-episode sequence is unknown.

The non-adult remains from the Dewlish Roman villa have been afforded virtually no comment in the published literature to date (see Putnam 2002, 22–23; Putnam 2007, 97–116). Three 'burials' that were recorded in the excavation records were regarded as representing just three individuals (BU100DEW3060). The number of non-adult remains from the site was expanded to a minimum of eight by Rohnbogner's osteological report for the second post-excavation project (see above). The remains identified from a further six contexts discussed here has increased the total number of individuals to 14. Potentially, other deposits of non-adult remains were missed during the 1969–79 excavation seasons, and it is important to bear in mind that the north-east range of the villa was not excavated in modern times, if at all.

Comparison of the results of the Dewlish field programme with those from published Dorset villa excavations provides some interesting data. The Bucknowle villa revealed 60 infant burials (Robb and Rogers 2009, 156–8) whilst the Tarrant Hinton villa yielded eight individual non-adult skeletal deposits (Mays 2006, 163–4). Paradoxically, the publication of the fieldwork at the Halstock villa contained no specialist human osteology report (Lucas 1993). This brief review of the comparative figures indicates inconsistencies in the archaeological record thus demonstrating that there is further work to be done regarding the presence of non-adult human remains from Roman villas in Dorset and the South West region.

ARCHAEOBOTANICAL ASSESSMENT AND ANALYSIS OF ENVIRONMENTAL SAMPLES FROM DEWLISH ROMAN VILLA: BUILDINGS 2 AND 2A

by Lisa Gray

INTRODUCTION AND RATIONALE FOR ASSESSMENT AND ANALYSIS, BY IAIN HEWITT

Environmental samples were recovered throughout the eleven seasons of excavations, in most cases from areas of burning such as hearth sites and stoke holes (see, for example, Chapter 6). Details of the sampling strategy are not known but it did include collection from contexts that were not designated as sealed as was the case with four of the seven available samples that were submitted for assessment. Collected samples were bagged, boxed and stored as a component of the Dewlish Roman villa archive, a resource that was initially stored at Weymouth College of Education and subsequently at Bournemouth University and, during the first post-excavation project (PEP1), at Chebbard Farm where they were effectively abandoned (Chapter 2). By chance, the boxed samples that are the subject of this assessment, were rediscovered in 2013 amongst the assemblage of painted wall-plaster and architectural stone fragments but these represent a small proportion of the total number of samples that was collected throughout the course of the 1969–79 field work. The chequered storage history of the environmental samples raised questions as to their viability for scientific analysis and therefore it was deemed prudent to submit the samples for assessment in the first instance. The assessment process identified two samples as being worthy of

analysis. Both samples were from unsealed contexts, but they were collected in close proximity to ovens or kilns within the footprint of Building 2 and are regarded as being relevant to these features. The results of the analysis of these samples are described in Part 2 below.

THE ASSESSMENT

Assessment was undertaken to determine the abundance, diversity and potential of the plant macro-remains and to inform decisions about further work.

Methods

The submitted samples have been stored in plastic food bags sealed with twist grips (Hewitt 2015, BU100DEW0359). They appeared to have been kept dry and undisturbed and the plant remains in them survived intact. It is likely, though, that any un-charred or un-mineralised plant remains had not survived over 40 years of storage. The samples from contexts 10A, 10B and 20 soaked and gently bucket floated in a 1 litre measuring jug. The rest appeared to have been ineffectively floated but were probably unprocessed samples that had dried out enough to allow the plant remains to be scanned. These samples were scanned using a binocular stereo-microscope with magnifications of between 10 and 40 times. The quality of preservation, diversity of plant remains, mollusca and bone were recorded as were any artefactual remains. A magnet was passed over the flots to retrieve any hammerscale.

Results

Six of the seven samples that were submitted for assessment were recovered from areas of burning associated with ovens or kilns in Buildings 2 and 2A (see Chapter 6). The Plant Macro-remains that were identified in all seven samples are summarised in Table 20.1.

Quality and type of Preservation

The details of the preservation conditions are unclear but the underlying geology is chalk with loam above, which was ploughed and so aerated (Hewitt 2015, BU100DEW0359). None of the samples came from waterlogged deposits and modern root/rhizome fragments were frequent indicating preservation conditions of aerated and most likely pH neutral soils. These preservation conditions favour charred and mineralised plant macro-remains (Campbell *et al* 2011, 5) and this is apparent in the archaeobotanical remains recovered from these samples. Sampling was undertaken by non-specialists and so contamination may have occurred (Hewitt 2015, BU100DEW0359). Most of the plant macro-remains in these samples have been preserved by charring. Charring occurs when plant material is heated under reducing conditions where oxygen is largely excluded leaving a carbon skeleton resistant to decay (Boardman and Jones 1990, 2; Campbell *et al* 2011, 17).

Plant remains present

The two samples from context 8 were particularly good with regards well-preserved and abundant cereal grains and lesser quantities of chaff and seeds. These samples appeared to have been poorly floated, but it seems that none of these samples had been processed (*pers. comm.* Hewitt 2015). The grains were dominated by those of barley and spelt. The barley grains were straight. No barley chaff was visible at this stage so identification of these barley grains to two- or six-row varieties was not possible. The seeds

observed during scanning for assessment were one of wild radish (*Raphanus raphanistrum* L.) and bedstraw (*Galium* sp.). The chaff fragments were fragments of spelt glume.

All but samples from grid square P95 contexts 10A and 10B contained fragments of charred wood larger than 4mm. Fragments of this size are easier to break to reveal the cross-sections and diagnostic features necessary for identification and are less likely to be blown or unintentionally moved around the site (Asouti 2006, 31; Smart and Hoffman, 1988, 178–179). Most of these appeared to be fragments of young oak or sweet chestnut. Young oak often lacks the multiseriate rays that are clear to the naked eye or low magnification in oak. Epi-luminating magnification would be necessary for a clearer identification. The samples from context 20 contained fragments of charred wood that had diffuse porosity and were clearly not oak or sweet chestnut. The two samples from grid square P95, context 10A and B were botanically unproductive.

Faunal and inorganic remains present

Samples from grid O93 and P95 contained moderate number of terrestrial snails. A fragment of un-charred mammal bone was found in the sample from grid P95, context 6. Fragments of pottery or ceramic building material were found in samples from grid O96, context 8. Fragments of burnt flint were present in the context 10A from grid P95. Magnetic material was detected in the sample and this might be hammerscale, but further testing would be necessary before a confident identification can be made.

Abundance, diversity and potential

The most interesting samples came from grid O96, context 8. Ethnographic research amongst traditional European farming communities has shown that grain rich samples with very few chaff fragments and seeds of similar size as the grains are evidence of grain crops ready for storage or milling that were accidentally charred during drying (Hillman 1981; Van der Veen 1989). Further analysis on the material from this context was recommended.

Table 20.1 Plant macro-remains from Dewlish Roman villa samples as listed

Grid code & context number	Room Number	Sample description	Charred grains		Charred chaff		Charred Seeds			Charred wood >4mmØ			Charred wood <4mmØ	Modern root/rhizomes	Details - main and significant taxa
			A	D	A	D	A	D	P	A	D	P	A	A	
096 (8)	34	ES34a Burnt material near oven/kiln	3	1	3	2	3	1	3	3	3	3	3	-	Many well-preserved barley (*Hordeum* sp.) and spelt wheat (*Triticum spelta* L.) grains and lower numbers of well-preserved cereal chaff and seeds. Many fragment of well-reserved charred wood, mostly oak/sweet chestnut (*Quercus/Castenea sativa*).
096 (8)	34	ES34b Burnt material near oven/kiln	3	1	3	-	1	1	3	3	3	3	3	-	Many well-preserved barley (*Hordeum* sp.) and spelt wheat (*Triticum spelta* L.) grains and lower numbers of well-preserved and seeds. Many fragment of well-reserved charred wood, mostly oak/sweet chestnut (*Quercus/Castenea sativa*).
P96 (4B)	34	Burnt material and clay/stone tiles	-	-	-	-	-	-	-	3	-	-	3	2	Useful for charred wood
P95 (6)	34	Burnt material with charcoal on the line of a wall	-	-	-	-	--	-	-	3	-	-	3	-	Useful for charred wood (contains burnt material)
093 (20)	38	ES41 Charcoal/soot: sealed context	-	-	--	-	-	-	-	3	-	-	3	-	Useful for charred wood, not just oak/sweet chestnut in this sample
095(10A)	34/39	Burnt material with flint at base from stokehole between rooms. Sealed context.	-	-	-	-	-	-	-	-	-	-	3	-	Just charred wood flecks
095 (10B)	34/39	Grey, finely powdered substance containing silt and minute pieces of chalk from stokehole between rooms. Sealed context.	-	-	-	-	-	-	-	-	-	-	3	3	Just charred wood flecks

Key to Estimated Quantities: A = abundance [1 = occasional 1–10, 2 = moderate 11–100, and 3 = abundant>100; D = diversity [1 = low1–4 taxa types, 2 = moderate 5–10, 3 = high; P = preservation [1 = poor (family level only), 2 = moderate (genus), 3 = good (species identification possible).

Table 20.2 Plant macro-remains (by number present) from two samples from Dewlish Roman villa

Grid trench code		P96	O96
Context		4b	8
Charred Cereal Grains			
Avena sp.	oat	-	7
Hordeum vulgare L. (hulled straight grain)	barley	106	180
Hordeum vulgare L. (hulled twisted grain)	barley	5	11
Hordeum sp. (poorly preserved grain)	barley	31	46
Triticum spelta L.	spelt	215	484
cf. *Triticum spelta* L. (distorted)	spelt	-	2
Triticum sp. (fragments)	indeterminate wheat	-	113
Indeterminate grain tissue	-	3	3
Charred Cereal Chaff			
Avena sp. (awn fragment)	oat	-	1
Avena sp. (floret base)	oat	-	1
Avena sp. (lemma/palea fragments)	oat	-	45
Hordeum vulgare L (poorly preserved rachis segments)	barley	-	6
Triticum spelta L. (glume base)	spelt	73	16
Triticum spelta L. (glume fragment)	spelt	9	108
Triticum spelta L. (spikelet fork base)	spelt	26	26
Triticum spelta L. (rachis fragments)	spelt	3	6
Triticum sp. (glume base)	indeterminate wheat	14	
Triticum sp. (awn fragment)	indeterminate wheat	2	27
Triticum sp. (spikelet base)	indeterminate wheat	9	34
Detached embryos	-	-	5
Indeterminate cereal (culm node)	-	1	1
Indeterminate Poaceae (stem fragment)	indeterminate grass	-	7
Charred Seeds			
Poaceae	indeterminate grass	-	1
Raphanus raphanistrum L. (fruit)	wild radish	1	-
Raphanus raphanistrum L. (fruit fragment)	wild radish	1	6
Polygonum aviculare L. (fruit)	knotgrass	4	5
Rumex acetosa/crispus/obtusifolius	common sorrel/curled dock/broad-leaved dock	-	3
cf. *Anagallis arvensis* L.	scarlet pimpernel	-	2

ANALYSIS

The samples selected for analysis were from burnt material near the oven kiln, sample P96 (4B) and O96 (8). Whilst the site record did not designate these contexts as sealed, analysis of this context had the potential to provide a spotlight on the economy of the villa estate. Therefore, this section lists the sample contents and consider taphonomic issues and any economic and ecological information they provide. Both samples were examined in their entirety, using magnification of ×10–×40. It was confirmed that the remains had all been preserved by charring.

Results

Both samples produced assemblages dominated by cereal grains and chaff (Table 20.2). Spelt (*Triticum spelta* L.) grains were the most frequent grains and spelt glumes and glume bases were the most frequent type of chaff. As commented above, ethnography indicates that grain rich samples with very few chaff fragments indicate grain crops ready for storage or milling (Hillman 1981; van der Veen 1989). The ratio of grains to chaff for sample P96 (4B) and for O96(8) is 2:1 so grains do dominate the samples indicating that they are likely to be remnants of the final processed product ready for drying. The seeds and chaff could have arrived in the deposits as contaminants of the cleaned grain or have become mixed with accidentally charred grain as kindling or, simply, thrown onto a fire (Jones 1981, 107). The use of chaff for fuel in drying kilns is often asserted (van der Veen 1989, 310–311).

Grains of hulled barley (*Hordeum vulgare* L) were also present in both samples. The ratio of straight: twisted grains for sample P96 (4B) was 21:1 and for sample O96 (8) 16:1. The ratio of straight: twisted grains for six rowed barley should be 2:1 (Ros *et al* 2014, 569) so if 6-rowed barley was present the straight grains clearly outnumber the twisted grains but it would not be wise to make a definite identifications of 6-rowed barley here because the rachises in sample O96 (8) were too poorly preserved to help with this identification. Ethnographic studies in traditional farming communities have demonstrated that twisted barley grains tend to be sieve out of 6-rowed barley crops leaving more straight grains in the final processing stage than twisted (Jones 1996, 181).

Charred seeds were scant but ruderals and segetals that are likely to have grown among cereals. Wild radish (*Raphanus raphanistrum* L.) prefers nutrient rich habitats, lime free, sandy and loamy soils and is common in Spring cereals and roadsides (Hanf 1983, 255). Knotgrass (*Polygonum aviculare* L.) is also found in spring cereals, preferring sandy and humic loams (Hanf 1983, 303) and common in a range of disturbed, nutrient rich environments (Grime *et al* 1990, 264).

Discussion

Assuming that this largely cleaned assemblage was charred whilst being deliberately heated, we may ask if that was in the process of being dried for storage or sprouted for malting. If beer were being brewed one would expect to see germinated grains in the assemblages (Carruthers, 2011 and Hillman, 1982). None of the spelt grains exhibited sprouted embryos or grains with dorsal grooves (Carruthers 2011, 364). It is more likely that these grains are remnants of grains being dried in a corn drier prior to grinding and milling as soft grain can clog up the querns (van der Veen 1989, 303). This would mean that these grains seem more likely to be being prepared for bread-making than beer. Van der Veen's study of charred grain assemblages from Roman-period corn driers lists the several sites that produced charred assemblages similar to that recovered from the Dewlish sample. These included County Hall, Dorchester, Poxwell, Dorset, Farmoor, Oxfordshire, Wasperton, Warwickshire and Welton Wold, Humberside (van der Veen 1989, 310–312).

21

DISCUSSION AND SYNTHESIS

by Iain Hewitt and illustrated by Jonathan Milward

'There is a rich man whose land yielded heavy crops.

He debated to himself: "What can I do? I have not the space

to store my produce. This is what I will do", said he: "I will

pull down my storehouses and build them bigger. I will collect

in them all my corn and other goods, and then say to myself,

'Man, you have plenty of good things laid by, enough for many

years: take life easy, eat, drink and enjoy yourself."'

(from Luke 12, 16-20 [New English Bible, 1961]).

INTRODUCTION

The Dewlish archives do not include a research proposal for the villa excavations. There is no evidence of questions that underpin an overarching aim supported by strategic objectives. At the outset (1969) Bill Putnam was aware of the sketchy details of the two 18th century investigations at the site as recorded by Hutchins, but there is no reason to believe that this information was paramount to his motives for launching the field project. Given the background to the introduction of the teaching of archaeology to the Weymouth College of Education (WCE) curriculum, it seems certain that the impetus for the launch of the Dewlish project was purely opportunistic: a gilt-edged chance to provide a long-term field research programme to provide an experiential learning environment for student teachers (Chapters 2 and 3). Essentially, the excavation programme was a product of its time.

After the death of Bill Putnam in 2008, the responsibility for the publication of the Dewlish excavations passed to Bournemouth University (BU), where the material and paper archive had been in store since it became the intellectual property of its predecessor, the Dorset Institute of Higher Education (DIHE) which had absorbed WCE in the mid-1970s. In the absence of an inaugural research proposal for the 1969–79 fieldwork, the launch of a new post-excavation project in 2010 (PEP2) determined that the principal thrust had to be to investigate the findings of the field and research programme at this large and important Romano-British villa site, and to publish, with the aim to complete in ten years. To recap, this entailed:

1   Assessment of the state of completion of Bill Putnam's own publication project (PEP1, 1999–2008).
2   Evaluation of the content of previously commissioned specialist contributions and to enhance and supplement this pool of information as appropriate.
3   To synthesise the available data and to publish a coherent account of the development of the villa complex.

4   To formulate research questions and guidance for future investigations at the Dewlish villa site (see below, Future Research: a suggested agenda).

ESSENTIAL BACKGROUND

The excavation of a large Roman villa was a major commitment for a provincial college of education such as Weymouth at a time of transition in the teacher training sector (see Chapter 2). Annual interim reports of the excavations were published, the most detailed accounts appearing during the first seven years of the eleven season project. Rapidly changing circumstances determined that these provisional statements of progress unwittingly trivialised the evidence which, as circumstances dictated, were not worked up into a full report. As the years slipped by, the interim reports stood as the only readily available sources for researchers to use. As director, Bill Putnam did publish some broad post-excavation descriptions of the villa and its development, but they borrowed heavily from the original interim reports (e.g. Putnam 2002, 20–23; 2007, 97–116). These post-excavation publications were not reflective and provided no revisions of the original interim interpretations. By way of example, there were three missed opportunities for important retrospective comment:

1   Room 4 (Building 3) with its channelled hypocaust was first excavated in 1971 and described in the interim report for that year (Putnam 1972, 160). A year later, during the 1972 season, a trial trench was excavated to test the relationship between Room 4 and the adjacent Room 3 (see Chapter 9). This revealed an earlier stokehole for the Room 4 hypocaust thus demonstrating that the room had a constructional history of at least two phases. No mention was made of this development in the relevant interim report (Putnam and Rainey 1973, 81–6) or in subsequent publications.

2   Building 4, the villa's bath house, was the subject of field investigation in the 1974 and 1975 seasons. Interim publication included a phase-shaded scale plan drawing of the bath house showing the cold plunge bath (Room 26) and the *apodyterium* (changing room; Room 25) to be 'first period' components of the suite. In 1979, the final year of the Dewlish field project, a small-scale re-examination of the bath house that included the south-west wall

of Room 25, demonstrated that the sequence of construction needed to be revised with Rooms 25 and 26 being the latest phase of Building 4 rather than the earliest (Chapter 8). No interim report was published for 1979 and no revised phasing for the bath house was placed in the public domain.

3   The south-east ends of Buildings 2 and 2A were dug in 1976. This included two internal walls of Building 2 (the 'aisled barn') that were thought to represent the footprint of Room 39 which was not mentioned specifically in the interim statement for that season (Putnam 1978, 55) but it is numbered as a room on the site plan dated 1999 (Fig. 2.3). Building 2 cut the foundations of Building 1 and Building 7 cut both Building 1 and Building 2. Excavation of this complex interface zone in 1977 provided evidence that Room 9 was not a room in the accepted sense (Chapter 6). It was not a social space but had the characteristics of a kiln or drying facility. Initial impressions were never reconsidered.

The above examples are not an implied criticism of the excavator, but they are indicative of the limitations of interim reports which, if not amplified by a reflective and detailed discussion in a subsequent full report inevitably lead to misinterpretations and misunderstandings.

In 2012 the present post-excavation and publication project (PEP2) produced a draft report that was essentially an expanded version of Bill Putnam's published Dewlish interim papers, but this script was abandoned as deeper trawling of the site archive revealed evidence of complexities and inconsistencies in the development of the Dewlish villa, such as those alluded to above, that needed to be understood and explained. In addition, the gradual flow of new and revised specialist reports significantly enhanced the available evidence, providing new interpretations and alternative lines of enquiry.

This report represents the Mark II version of the PEP2 output. It is underpinned by the original site archive and takes into full consideration the ideas of Bill Putnam. However, the present post-excavation project has included a reassessment of the available evidence and this process has raised a number of issues and questions that will be discussed in the paragraphs that follow.

DEWLISH: CATEGORISATION AND CHARACTERISTICS

Throughout this chapter the main or principal residential building of the villa complex is sometimes referred to as the *domus* (house/home) or 'main house', which at Dewlish is Building 3.

The Dorset Historic Environment Record (HER) has categorised Dewlish as, 'A large and elaborate fourth century style corridor villa which represented the final stage in a series of alterations and rebuilds' (DC 1 040 011 – MDO 985). This statement requires clarification. The corridor feature concerned is a characteristic of Building 3. This building does have a south-east corridor-facade (Room 12) which defines it as a house type, but it does not describe the whole of the villa complex as a villa type (Figs 3.4 and 3.5; Collingwood and Richmond 1969, 135–53; Perring 2002, 72–79). Furthermore Building 3 was a multiphase structure, but the corridor was not its latest feature and in origin it was not of fourth century date (Chapter 9). Loose use of terminology has also benighted the villa at Sparsholt, Hampshire, whereby the main house had a corridor but more specifically it is described by Perring as being 'a portico villa with pseudo-pavilions and central reception rooms' (2002, 74 fig. 24d). However, the authors of the Sparsholt monograph report describe their site as a 'courtyard villa' (Johnston and Dicks 2014, 82), a description that would not find favour with Dark and Dark who point out the subtle distinction between 'villas with courtyards' (such as Sparsholt) and villas at which 'a single building itself forms a courtyard' (1997, 45). For the record, Dark and Dark classify Sparsholt not as a courtyard villa but as a 'corridor house', this being a specific reference to the main house (Dark and Dark 1997, 46, plan f).

These inconsistencies argue that the generally accepted criteria for categorising the main house within a villa complex do not constitute a robust method for categorising these buildings in particular, or Romano-British villas in the general sense. In the case of Building 3 at Dewlish, to describe it as a 'corridor style villa', grossly oversimplifies the intricate history of the development of the associated buildings that comprise the plan of the villa complex, and neither does it provide any meaningful indication of the evolution and function of the building itself and how it compares with buildings of similar function on other villa sites. By way of an example, it is useful to compare Dewlish with another Dorset villa site, Park Farm, Iwerne Minster.

The Park Farm villa

The villa at Park Farm was excavated in 1897 by General Augustus Pitt-Rivers but, like Dewlish, the site report was not committed to print until fifty years later (Gray 1947, 50–62). A useful digest of the principal findings with a site plan and photographs has been published by the Royal Commission on Historical Monuments, England (RCHME 1972, 40–41, pl. 48). The plan of the villa buildings is reproduced as Figure 21.1.

The Park Farm villa comprised two known buildings that shared a south-west to north-east alignment: a main house or *domus*, and a structure that superficially resembles an aisled barn, but without an aisle, and with no evidence of holes or bases for aisle-posts (Fig. 21.1, left; RCHME 1972, 40). This building shares some similar features with Building 2 at Dewlish which was also aisleless until a single aisle was added along with other modifications during the latter part of the third century CE. The two buildings are broadly contemporary and both were sited within a landscape that produced evidence of numerous pits that have been ascribed to the Pre-Roman Iron Age on the basis of datable associated artefacts. It has been inferred that an Iron Age settlement was situated to the north-west of the Park Farm villa as was certainly the case at Dewlish. In the first and second centuries CE, the landscape of both sites was re-planned in a way that is illustrated by Millet (1990, 121, fig. 50, citing Riley 1980) by the creation of ditched fields and the digging of pits that were sub-rectangular in plan. At Dewlish, the replacement of an irregular pattern of enclosures of late Pre-Roman Iron Age date by a network of small square or rectangular fields of the first to second centuries CE was documented by Keen, citing Bill Putnam, following a series of trial trench excavations in 1976 and 1978 (1978, 54–55).

At Park Farm, a second building, the *domus*, shares a number of characteristics with its counterpart

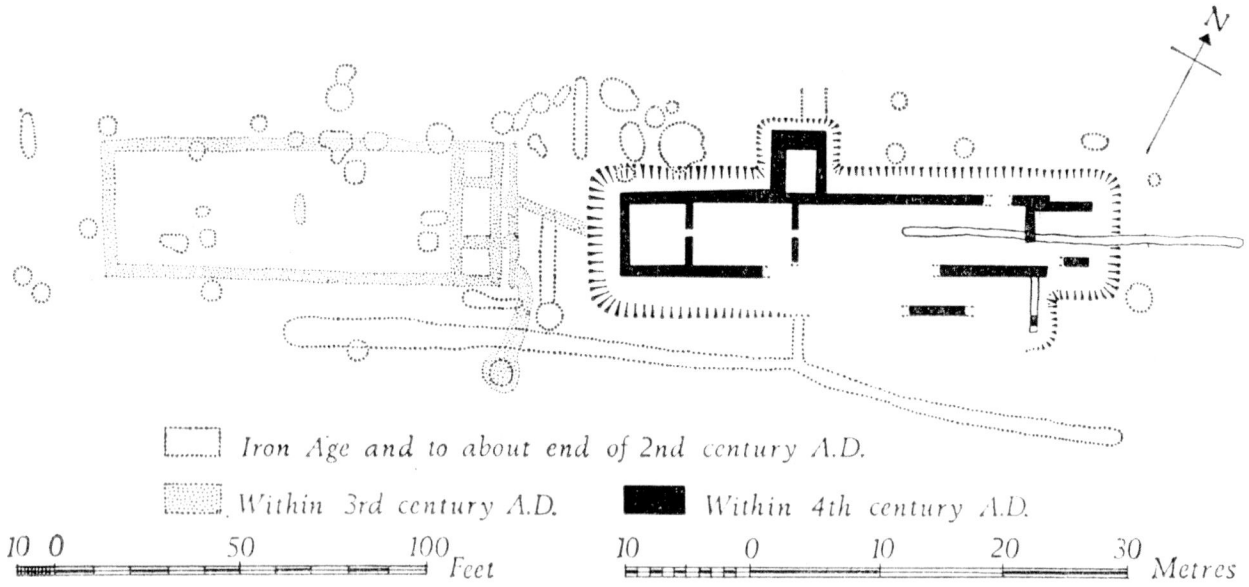

Figure 21.1   Park Farm villa, Iwerne Minster, Dorset (adapted from RCHME 1972, 40–41).

at Dewlish, Building 3. Prior to construction, both sites needed to be levelled in order to cope with undulating terrain (Fig. 21.1, right). In the case of Building 3 at Dewlish, the essential groundworks involved the dumping of waste material for the creation of a level building platform (Chapter 9). Conversely, site preparation at Park Farm took the form of a terrace that was cut into the natural slope of the land, but the purpose was the same: the creation of a level site for the digging of foundation trenches and the construction of walls and floors.

The similarity of the plan of the Dewlish and the Park Farm *domus* buildings is striking. Both have a length to breadth ratio of 3:1 or greater; they conform to the row or strip building format with internal sub-divisions. Both houses have an identical facade orientation towards the south-east and on this elevation a full length corridor identifies the buildings as members of the 'corridor house' group. Other features are shared by both of these *domus* buildings, and in the interests of brevity these are summarised by category in Table 21.1 below.

Divergence between the Dewlish and Park Farm buildings only becomes strikingly apparent in category 11 of Table 21.2: there is no evidence of later fourth century CE aggrandisement at Park Farm such as mosaic pavements, hypocausts, window glass,

Table 21.1   Concordance of Putnam (PEP1) and BU (PEP2) phases for Dewlish Roman villa (see Figs 3.4 and 3.5)

Phase nos: PEP1 (Putnam)	Phase nos: PEP2	Dates CE
N/A	1	Late 2nd to early 3rd centuries (Building 1)
1.1; 1.2	2	3rd century (Buildings 2 and 3)
N/A	3	Later 3rd century
1.2	4	Late 3rd–4th centuries
2.0	5	Early to mid-fourth century
3.1	6	Mid-to late fourth century
N/A	7	Late 4th to early fifth centuries
3.2 and 3.3	8	Mid-fifth century and later
0.0	X	Unphased features

or the presence of an axial hall or reception room of elevated status such as Room 11 at Dewlish (see below). There was no associated bath house suite or further extensions to the core *domus* building. The north-west elevation additional room was not demolished as a precursor of new structural developments unlike the similar Room 14 at Dewlish which was swept away in advance of the construction of the Room 11 apse (Chapter 9). From the available evidence, Park Farm was not occupied beyond *c.* 360 CE (RCHME 1972, 41) whereas at Dewlish, social and economic activities continued into the fifth century CE. Both Dewlish and Park Farm were 'corridor houses' at similar times in their respective architectural histories, but this term does not take account of the significantly different outcomes to their respective development pathways.

PROBLEMS OF CLASSIFICATION

It is not part of the present remit to devise a new method for the classification of Romano-British villas, but it is important to make the point that the commonly used framework based upon the pioneering work of Collingwood and Richmond (1930; revised 1969) requires reconsideration. Some of the limitations of the classificatory systems have been identified by McCarthy (2013, 50). This is a lesson that the Dewlish villa makes clear: many of the typologies and terminologies are misleading and they inhibit understanding of the archaeological evidence from Romano-British villa sites. Each individual villa has a distinct identity at different snapshots in time, but these identities are subject to change as time passes in accord with the fluctuating needs, aspirations and the economic resources of the owners and occupiers. There is a tendency for Romano-British villa studies to fixate on 'typical' plans that are relevant only at a particular point in time in their development (e.g. Percival 1976; Smith 1977), but adherence to this mindset can obscure the subtle changes to the building stock and the variation to the social context that this implies. A classificatory system based upon comparable developmental pathways and chronology is likely to serve better than a simplistic grouping of approximately dated plan types.

Collingwood and Richmond point out that in Latin the word 'villa' means a farm (1969, 135) but in the archaeological sense, 'villa' is a word that has wider connotations and this simple definition is now regarded as being anachronistic. Wacher points out that that 'villa' is a term that applies to the *whole* farm estate and should not be applied only to the residential building at the centre of the complex (1998, 115). Dark and Dark extend the definition to include farms or country estates, whilst pointing

out that in relation to Roman Britain, villas are defined by the presence of 'prestige' and 'romanised' attributes including mosaics and baths (1997, 43). Comparison of the development of the Dewlish villa with that of Park Farm indicates that a villa cannot be defined by a single architectural feature (such as a corridor) in a particular building. Some villas do not evolve beyond the establishment of a simple farmhouse whilst others, such as Dewlish, develop extensively from, perhaps, a single unit of accommodation over a period of 200 to 300 years. There is an imperative need to be inclusive and comprehensive in our approach to villa studies taking account of the individual peculiarities of each site rather than treating them as an amalgam of architectural elements.

There are many uncertainties regarding the development of the Dewlish villa, but it is clear that from the earliest known Roman phase of the site that there was a sequence of modification, demolition, replacement, enhancement and aggrandisement with no apparent hiatus. It is important to emphasise that absence of an interruption in the occupation of the villa is the principal difference between Bill Putnam's phasing (PEP1) and the outcome of PEP2, this publication. No evidence from the site, including the coinage, supports an occupational discontinuity (Gerrard with Reece, Chapter 13). Furthermore, the evidence derived from the building stock is actually indicative of continuity, as portrayed in Figures 3.4 and 3.5 the rationale for which is embedded in Chapters 4 to 9 inclusive. For at-a-glance comparison of the building phases see Table 21.2.

THE DEWLISH VILLA PLAN AND ITS COMPONENT BUILDINGS

It was by chance that Bill Putnam's first season of excavation at Dewlish (1969) involved the setting out of a single trench at the north-east end of the site of Building 3. No geophysical equipment had been available to the excavator which meant that the position of this inaugural evaluation cut was probably determined by the presence of surface artefact scatters, but the precise details are not clear. A mosaic pavement was soon revealed and this determined that in the following year a second

Table 21.2   Comparative characteristics of Dewlish villa Building 3 (*domus*) and the Park Farm (Iwerne Minster) *domus* building

	Characteristic	Dewlish	Park Farm
1	Iron Age settlement evidence	Yes	Yes
2	Third century CE construction date	Yes	Yes
3	Pre-construction ground works	Yes	Yes
4	Row / strip building plan	Yes	Yes
5	Internal subdivisions (rooms)	Yes	Yes
6	Corridor facade	Yes	Yes
7	South-east facing facade	Yes	Yes
8	North-west room attached	Yes	Yes
9	Internal painted wall-plaster	Yes	Yes
10	Evidence of associated Romano-British agricultural activity	Yes	Yes
11	Later 4th century CE aggrandisement	Yes	No

evaluation trench would be set out that would intersect with the first at right angles (Fig. 2.1). This second trench confirmed that a high status Roman building had been found and that the positions of its principal walls could be inferred. Thus, the starting point for a larger scale investigation had been determined. It was also during the second evaluation year that a series of test pits was excavated in an attempt to determine the position of other buildings within the villa complex (Chapter 2). These test pits were positioned at measured distances and at various compass points from the site TBM for 1970. One of the pits indicated the remains of Building 4, the bath house, whilst two others fixed the location of Buildings 2 with 2A. Of the test pits that were dug to the south and east of the TBM, none showed convincing evidence of building foundations or floors, and therefore it was presumed that there was no archaeology in these areas. Consequently, the strategy for the next nine seasons had been determined. Building 3 with Building 4 occupied full attention from 1971 through to and including 1975, and again in the final season, 1979. Just three seasons, 1976–1978, were devoted to the excavation of Buildings 1, 2 with 2A, 5, 6 and 7 collectively in addition to three series of trial trenches that were set out broadly to the south and west of the villa complex.

That first fateful decision made in 1969 determined that no time would be devoted to exploring the

north-east through to the south side of the villa. The perception was that the Dewlish villa plan was an inverted 'L' – shape (i.e. north-west and south-west ranges only), and that is the notion that has prevailed until relatively recently. Bill Putnam launched his Dewlish post-excavation and publication project in 1999 with the conviction that the villa comprised just two ranges (see Fig. 2.3). As a separate and unrelated development, in 2001 two Bournemouth University undergraduate student dissertations involved geophysical surveys of the Dewlish villa site. The results of this fieldwork demonstrated the presence of a north-east range of some substance which formed the third side of a courtyard (Fig. 21.2). The existence of this previously unsuspected building range dramatically alters any previous notions of what type of villa Dewlish might be and the economic and social structures that might apply (see below). This further undermines adherence to the evidence of simplistic single phase snapshot villa plans that are relevant only within a limited chronological framework for the site. In addition, the student surveys also showed traces of rectilinear structures to the north-west of Building 3 and field investigation of these is likely to bring about further revisions to preconceived notions about the site. More recently, a further Bournemouth University geophysical survey has been carried out at the site which confirms and enhances the earlier survey outcomes (Cheetham, forthcoming).

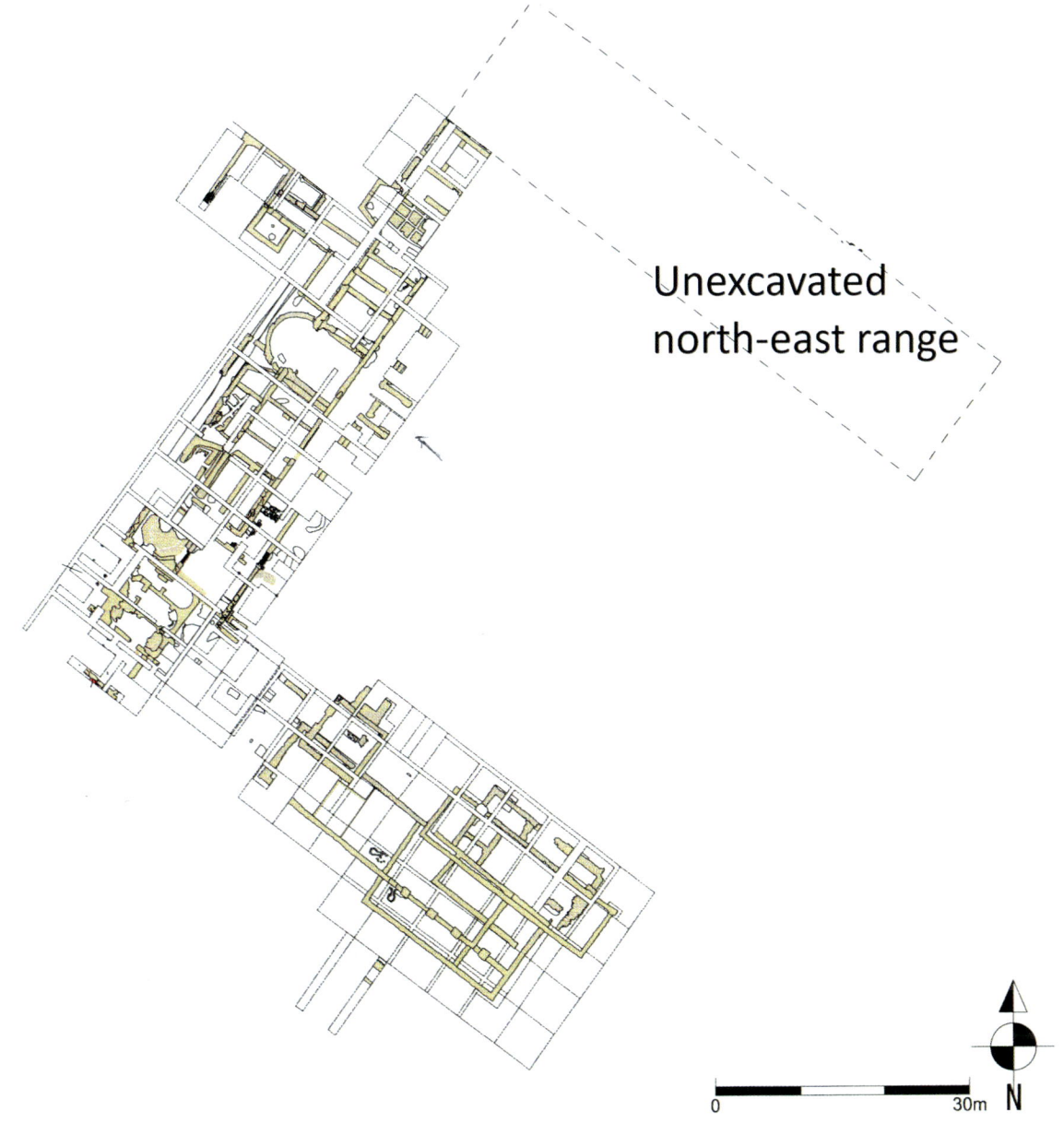

Figure 21.2 Dewlish villa plan showing the location of the unexcavated north-east range.

Building 1

The origin of the Dewlish villa probably dates to the Late Pre-Roman Iron Age (Chapter 4). Of the seven buildings that were all or partially excavated between 1969 and 1979, Building 1 dates to around the second century CE, although it was not identified as a separate entity from Building 7 (i.e. part of the 'Priest's House') by the excavator. Associated artefacts place Building 1 as being the earliest known component of the villa complex. The building stood parallel with the south-west perimeter of the villa's courtyard until it was demolished to make way for Building 2 during the

third century CE. It is not known if Building 1 stood alone as the first Dewlish *domus* or if it was part of a group of buildings that has not been revealed by excavation or geophysical survey to date (Fig. 21.4). Nonetheless, the Putnam excavations did uncover several concentrations of demolition material across the villa site including rubble contained within the building platform of Building 3. Some of this debris might have been from Building 1 itself, but that is not demonstrable, and it is feasible that a predecessor *domus* stood on the site of Building 3 at the same time that Building 1 was functioning.

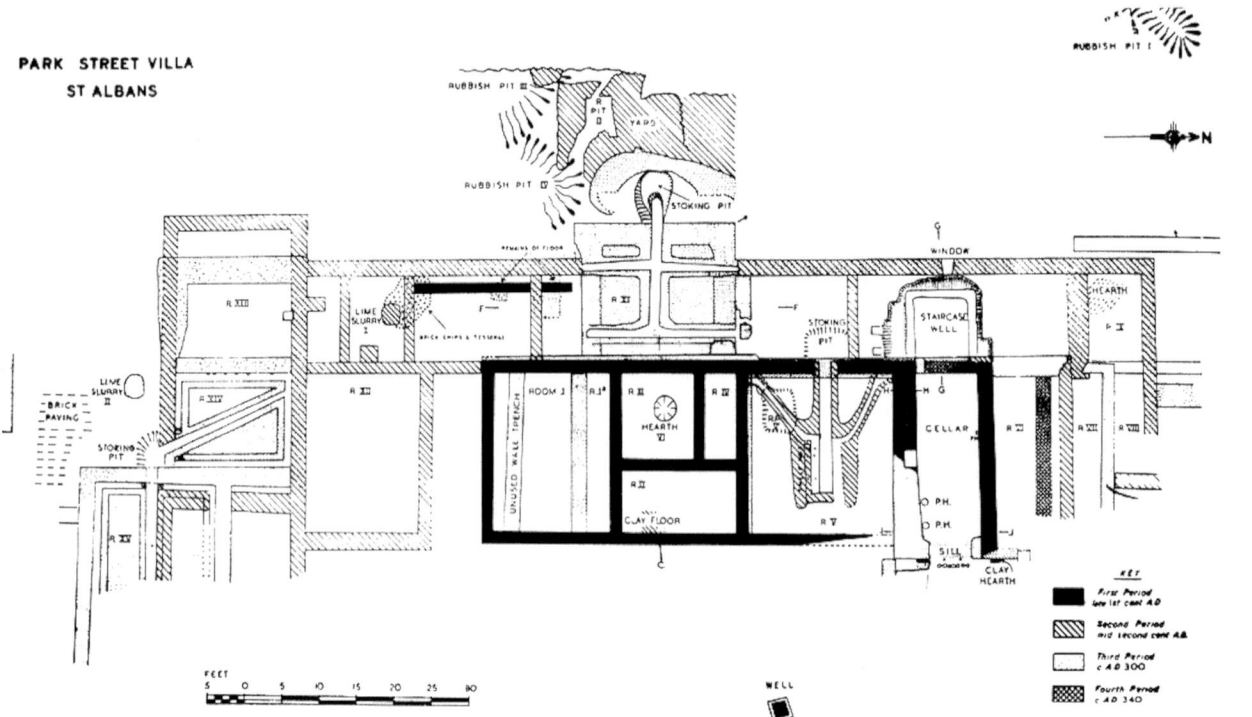

Figure 21.3 Park Street villa, St Albans, Hertfordshire: plan of the First Period cottage house (O'Neil 1971).

Based upon the available evidence, Building 1 was a single phase structure although there are indications that it stood on the site of earlier features (Chapter 5). In layout and size (Figs. 3.4 and 3.5), the building conforms to the description of a 'cottage house' such as the First Period (earliest) structure at Park Street, St Albans, Hertfordshire which also overlies pre-Roman features (Dark and Dark 1997, 44; O'Neil 1971, figs. 2 and 3. but here represented by Fig. 21.3).

Buildings 2 and 2A

Buildings 2 and 2A (Chapter 6) were two components of a single structure that represent separate episodes of construction, both within Phase 2 of the development of the Dewlish villa complex (Figs. 3.4, 3.5 and 6.1). It is important to stress though, that this structural dichotomy had the effect of transforming Building 2 from one category of building type to another once the elements of 2A were added.

In its unmodified form Building 2 was not an aisled building although examples of these are recorded from a number of sites in Dorset including Buildings 4 and 5 at Halstock (Lucas 1993) and Building 4 at Tarrant Hinton (Graham 2006). Examples of aisled buildings are widespread elsewhere, notably at Brading (Building 2), Isle of Wight (Cunliffe 2013). The distribution of this building type is not confined to any specific region of the Romano-British villa landscape. An example of an aisled building at Lodge Farm, North Warnborough, Hampshire, has been the subject of a paper by Wallace (2018, 331–254). In considering the purpose and development of this example, the author has stated that in origin, this building represented a vast internal open space within which a series of structural phases are manifest, including a number of divisions or partitions with wattle and plaster walls which defined rooms that contained features such as hearths (Cunliffe 2018, 231 and 248). Given that Building 2 at Dewlish was not an aisled house (or barn), it is important to consider whether Wallace's observations have relevance.

Smith (1997, 15) states that Romano-British aisled houses appear to have originated as a type of long house that provided a multi-purpose shelter

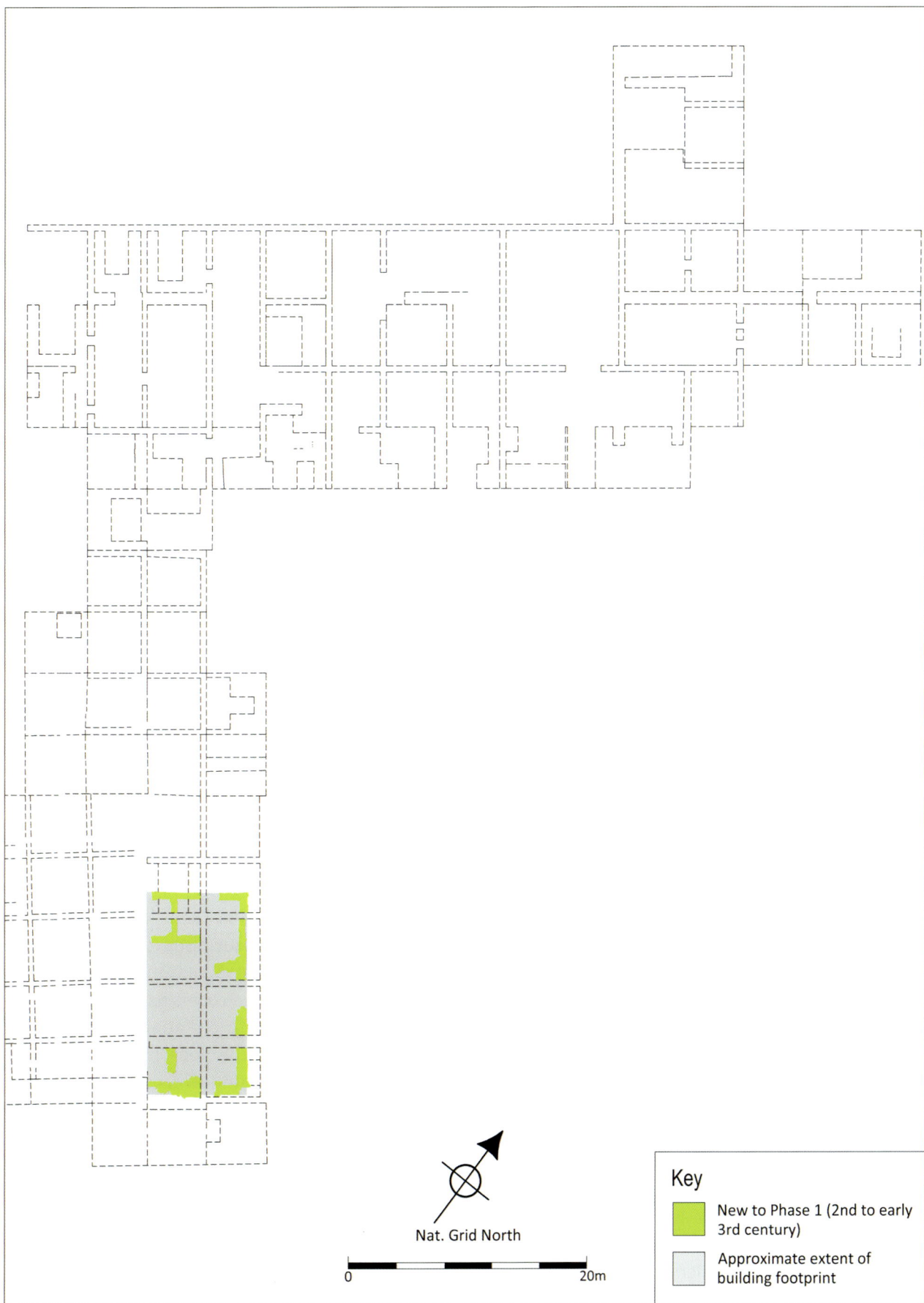

Nat. Grid North

0   20m

Key

New to Phase 1 (2nd to early 3rd century)

Approximate extent of building footprint

Figure 21.4 Dewlish villa Phase 1: location of Building 1 within the site grid. Jonathan Milward.

for family stock and crops. This is an apposite description of Dewlish Building 2 which could have been a featureless internal void at the outset, but within which the north-west accommodation suite of three rooms was added in a similar way as that described by Wallace (2018). It is also the case that Building 2 does have some of the characteristics of the long houses that are a feature of the moorlands of medieval Devon. These later long houses were the subject of a series of papers that was triggered by the excavations of E.M. Minter at the medieval settlement of Houndtor (Devon) as reported by Beresford (1979, 98–159). In a follow-up paper Beresford lists five characteristics of the long house of which three are worthy of note in respect of Dewlish Building 2, specifically the presence of:

1   a byre (accommodation for cattle known as a shippon) indicated by the presence of central or lateral drains,
2   domestic accommodation separate from the byre,
3   a cross passage separating the two areas of the building as indicated by opposed doorways in the long elevations.

Building 2 comes close to satisfying the above criteria for long house status because in conformity with the term, its length is conspicuously greater than its width. Self-evidently, the building has two distinct zones of activity: the human accommodation element of three rooms formed by wattle and (painted) plaster partitions separated from an agri-industrial zone by an intervening wall. The excavated evidence does not include the presence of a cross-passage but the disturbance to this part of the villa site was so considerable that the surviving wall heights were reduced to below threshold level. There was tentative evidence of an external door on the south-west long wall of the building (Chapter 6) but no corresponding feature was identified on the opposite north-east wall. However, one might tentatively infer that a cross passage did exist because in Building 3, which in origin is also third century, a cross passage is suggested by Room 6 which connects the Room 12 corridor to the Annexe rooms via Room 10 (Figs. 9.1 and 21.5). With regard to the animal byre, there is absolutely no evidence for this in Building 2. In fact, the existence of a byre would normally be betrayed by the presence of a central or lateral

byre-drain as indicated immediately above in item 1. The purpose of the drain was to remove cattle urine from the byre, and to facilitate this process long houses were commonly situated upon a slope with the byre located at the lower end of the building. Although no such feature was detected in Building 2, the building was constructed upon a downhill slope (south-eastwards) whereas the accommodation suite of rooms was at the top end of the slope (i.e. north-west). However, the fourth century *domus* at the Park Farm villa was furnished with a central drain that might identify the north-east end of this structure as a byre (Fig. 21.1).

Examples of Romano-British buildings with byre accommodation have been identified at the rural settlement of Woodhouse Hill, Studland, Dorset (BNG 403138, 82203; SZ 01308 82203). The Studland site is important because it encapsulates the transition from Late Iron Age timber, wattle and daub roundhouse dwellings to the rectilinear form that is more readily associated with Romano-British buildings. The excavator describes it as a community of two centres or complexes and it is what is designated 'The First Complex' that is relevant here, because in the third and fourth centuries CE, two 'cottages' (A and B) were constructed (Field 1966, 146 Fig. 2). The built characteristics of both cottages comprised footings of unmortared rubble with walls of cob and internal roof supports of timber. Within a plan ratio of *c.* 2:1, the long axis walls of Cottage B were interrupted by door openings which indicated the location of a cross-passage that divided the floor space into two component rooms demarcated by a screen. The excavator surmised that because the cottage had been constructed on a gentle slope, that the lower of the two rooms had been purposed as a cattle byre. This interpretation was reinforced by the archaeology of the floor of the byre which revealed signs of 'churning', inferentially by cattle. The presence of a sump and an associated gully were thought to provide the necessary foul fluid drainage typical of a byre house.

The excavation of Cottage A uncovered structural similarities to those of Cottage B. Both were divided into discrete zones of human and animal occupation typical of the longhouse building category, but without the *c.* 3:1 length/breadth dimensions of medieval examples of this rural building type of which the Studland cottages might represent early examples.

It is not possible or safe to postulate the development of a building type that has roots in a Romano-British villa through to the twelfth century long houses of Houndtor and Hutholes on Dartmoor. Nonetheless, the excavations at Woodhouse Hill make the case for further investigation of this lineage and for suggesting that the term long house is an appropriate one for Building 2 at Dewlish even though there is no reason to believe that it was ever provided with a byre. In layout, the closest comparative match for Building 2 is the 'hall-type strip buildings' such as the example at Caerwent (Gwent) cited by Perring (2002, 57 Fig. 11g) which excavation also proved to be 'aisle-less'.

In Phase 3, the later third century CE, an aisle was constructed on the south-west elevation of Building 2 and three 'rooms' were added to the south-east of the extended structure similar to those at that were observed at the narrow elevation of the third century building at Park Farm (Figs. 21.1 and 21.6). These additions are discussed in Chapter 6 and below in respect of the villa's economy; collectively they transformed Building 2 into a single aisle building that is identified as Building 2A.

There is insufficient archaeological evidence to deduce exactly when the accommodation unit within the north-west end of Buildings 2/2A was constructed (i.e. Rooms 31,32 and 32a). This event could have occurred during the long house phase (Building 2) or after the addition of the south-west aisle (Building 2A). Similar uncertainty prevails regarding the introduction of the cereal drying facility that is represented by Room 39. Detailed plans and section drawings for these areas have not survived.

By the end of the third century CE, the accommodation suite had fallen into disuse, revealing evidence that it too had been transformed into a cereal processing area or light industrial zone. Finally, the north-west end of Building 2/2A had become a repository for building rubble that included *pilae* tiles, box-flue fragments and loose tesserae, none of which were a

feature of the building at any time during its period in use. These materials also included a shale tile of a kind that were found only in Room 26 in the bath house (Building 4) and therefore this is likely to be the source of the debris scatter (Fig. 17.2).

Building 3

The development of the *domus* was of labyrinthine complexity but it is well documented in Chapter 9 and no amplification of its phases is required here (Figs. 21.5, 21.6, 21.7, 21.8 and 21.9). The most obvious issue concerns the mosaic in Room 11, the high status axial reception chamber which included a multi-image mosaic (164.8, Panel A). A second mosaic floor adorned the Room 11 semi-circular apse (164.8, Panel B). Both mosaics are ably described by Cosh (Chapter 12) whose reconstruction painting is reproduced as Figure 12.10. This shows that Panel A survived in a partial state only when excavated in 1972 with just one rectilinear frame being sufficiently complete as to allow recognition of the image therein: a leopard attack on a Dorcas gazelle. This scene is derived from the natural habitat of north Africa, the littoral of the Mediterranean Basin. Other component images of this pavement depict fragments of hunting scenes that provided a coherent overall theme when the floor was intact.

The archaeology of the Room 11 mosaic floors

The Dorset historian John Hutchins has attributed the initial discovery of the Dewlish villa to the uprooting of a tree in the 1740s (Chapter 1). Bill Putnam explained the incomplete state of the Panel A mosaic by suggesting that it was caused by the presence of the fallen tree (Putnam 2007, 100) and that this damage was exacerbated by exposure to frost (Putnam and Rainey 1973, 81). This interpretation needs to be tempered with caution. The excavation record for Room 11 includes no convincing evidence of tree-throws and no features that suggest tree root damage (see Fig. 9.2). Furthermore, the damage to the mosaic is extensive, bordering on total, but intriguingly widespread destruction stops short of Panel B, the adjacent apse mosaic. Post-Roman prospection for sub-floor stone deposits within a hypocaust chamber can be eliminated as a possible

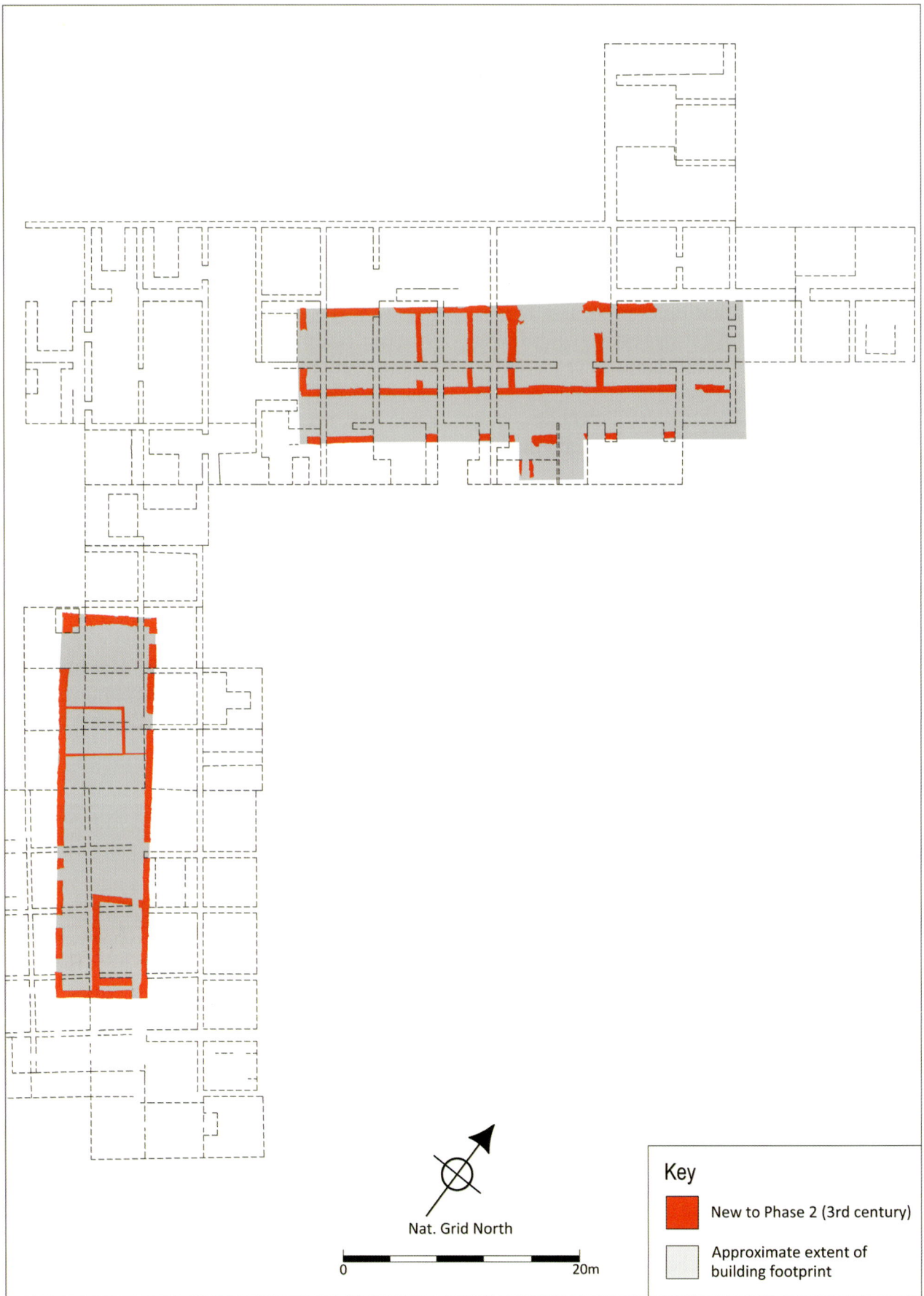

Key

New to Phase 2 (3rd century)

Approximate extent of
building footprint

Nat. Grid North

0   20m

Figure 21.5   Dewlish villa Phase 2: the relative locations of Buildings 2 and 3. Jonathan Milward.

Key

- **Retained from Phase 2 (3rd century)**
- **Retained from Phase 3 (Later 3rd century)**
- **Retained from Phase 4 (late 3rd to 4th century)**
- **New to Phase 5 (Early to mid 4th century)**
- **Approximate extent of building footprint**

Nat. Grid North

0   20m

Figure 21.6   Dewlish villa Phase 3 showing Buildings 2 with 2A and Building 3. Building 4, the bath house belongs to Phase 4 but might have been contemporary with Phase 3 in its earliest form. Jonathan Milward.

explanation for the damage because stone robbers would have become quickly aware that no hypocaust existed beneath Room 11. In short, the defacement of Panel A presents as widespread and deliberate, perhaps the work of iconoclasts, which prompts the questions, When? and Why?

In seeking answers to these questions, a conjectural scenario is provided by Perring in his analysis of the mosaics at the Frampton Roman villa, Dorset (2002, 132–39). In his preamble, Perring provides details of the followers of an early Christian heresy which became known as Gnosticism (Gk. *Gnosis* = mystical knowledge). Gnosticism was the religion of an educated elite. Perring goes on to outline what he refers to as a 'speculative review of the evidence for Gnostic imagery in late Romano-British pavements' (Perring 2002, 132–133) and the Frampton mosaics, which are of fourth century CE date like those of Dewlish, are considered, by Perring, to provide a close fit to Gnostic imagery. This included a liking for 'allegory, images and geometric patterns' (Perring 2002, 133) characteristics that can be recognised in the Room 11 Panel A mosaic at Dewlish. At its point of interface with Panel A, Panel B, the semi-circular apse mosaic, includes the image of a *cantharus* (two handled drinking cup) which also occurs in a similar context at Frampton. At Dewlish, two dolphins emerge from the *cantharus*. According to Perring, both the cup and the dolphins can be associated with Gnostic beliefs, as can hunting scenes in a metaphorical sense (Perring 2002, 134–5). Panel B survived the depredations that had befallen Panel A, but the *cantharus* had been damaged which hints at targeted desecration of an out of favour image regardless of whether it was inspired by a reaction to Gnosticism or not.

It must be stressed that there are no convincing arguments for advocating the existence of the imagery of Gnostic beliefs at Dewlish, but equally there are insufficient grounds for attributing the destruction of the pavement to tree root growth or the activities of 18th century antiquarians. Destruction of Panel A and relatively minor damage to Panel B by iconoclasts, regardless of motive, is feasible and it is an optional interpretation that needs to remain open. In connection with this hypothesis, it is perhaps a heresy to suggest that it is

regrettable that too much attention has been paid to the imagery of the Room 11 mosaics at the expense of recovering detailed archaeological evidence from the surface of the floors (for good practice on the archaeology of floors see Milek 2012). The context records provide limited information about the nature and content of the layers that sealed the floor, but there is sufficient detail to indicate that Room 11 had not been disturbed by the excavations of the 1740s and 1790s. The Putnam site plans are exclusively derived from final drawings; there is no visual record of layer by layer excavation.

What might have been overlooked during the excavation of Room 11 is a matter of conjecture, but one sub-floor feature that was recorded was a flint-filled drain 'below the fourth century mosaic', presumably beneath Panel A, because Panel B was not lifted for conservation. It is not clear though whether the words 'below the fourth century mosaic' refer to a feature that was visible in one of the destroyed areas of the pavement, or if it was observed once the surviving fragments of the mosaic had been lifted. The distinction is important because the flint-filled drain' is reminiscent of a similar feature that was identified at the Roman villa at Bradford on Avon, Wiltshire (the St Laurence's School villa).

St Laurence's villa is unusual because it has an arrangement of buildings that is intricate, and there are two that would fit the description of a *domus*, or 'main house': Building 1 (east) and Building 2 (west) (Corney 2003b, 4–20, fig. 1 and plate 8). In Building 2, the central room was bipartite, a double room, the northern part of which was provided with a semi-hexagonal apse which was paved with a mosaic that depicted dolphins associated with a *cantharus*, identical imagery to the Room 11 apse mosaic at Dewlish (Corney 2003a, plate 12, but unpublished to date as an academic report). At St Laurence's, the room that abutted the hexagonal apse, was excavated and it was noted that there was an arrangement of rubble in a circular concentration that defined a kerb at the centre of the room. Within the kerb structure, a large part of the room's mosaic floor had been 'deliberately cut away' to a depth of *c.* 0.2m and a deeper cut in the south-western arc of the kerb might have been intended to serve as a soakaway or drain (Corney 2003a, 18). The excavator dated the kerb feature, the soakaway and the deliberate damage to the mosaic to the fifth or even sixth century CE. With the exception of the kerb feature, the archaeology of the floor of the axial room of Building 2 at St Laurence's, is very similar to that of the same feature at Dewlish Room 11.

Corney's interpretation of the kerbed feature described above is that it was constructed while Building 2 was still standing and roofed and that this centrally placed feature was cut through the fourth century mosaic floor. The excavator goes on to assert that the kerbing possibly represents the perimeter of an early Christian baptistry; the shallow pit providing a drain for the water that was used in the baptismal rites (2003, 18). If this hypothesis is accepted, then the baptistry is a rare example of Christian worship at a Romano-British villa, but this interpretation is not without its detractors. At Dewlish there is no evidence of Christian affinities regardless of sect or creed.

There are similarities in the archaeological evidence from the floors in the axial rooms at Dewlish and the St Laurence's School villa, for in both cases the surface of a principal mosaic floor had been cut, possibly to make provision for a drain, or alternatively obscured an earlier feature of this description. The apparent absence of firm evidence for a surface structure associated with the drain on the floor surface of Dewlish Room 11 might be explained with reference to the differences in archaeological techniques employed. The Putnam box grid excavation strategy, by chance, determined that a 0.5m baulk passed through the centre of Room 11, separating grid columns G and F (Fig. 2.3). Variable rates of progress in the relevant grid trenches, G4 and F4 would have worked against the recognition of features common to both. Context numbers and recording were not shared between adjacent trenches, and usually only final photographs were taken, and plans drawn. The principal focus of attention would have been on the mosaic pavements with overlying features removed. Furthermore, the 1970 pre-grid 1.5m wide evaluation trench passed through the centre of Room 11 (Fig. 2.1) removing all archaeology from this part of the site prior to the more detailed

excavation of 1972. The damage had been done and details of the evidence have been lost.

One further and important similarity between Building 2 at St Laurence's School and Building 3 at Dewlish is that although both were *domus* or high status buildings, at the former site, evidence suggested that it was not primarily residential (if at all) but served agri-industrial functions as well. The Dewlish *domus* was residential, but it was also the site of a probable malting kiln (Chapter 9). This will be discussed below with regard to the villa economy.

Building 4

At Dewlish the bath house comprises two conjoined buildings. This arrangement is best appreciated with reference to Figures 3.4 and 3.5 where a suite of three baths is contained within a rectangular block (Rooms 27–29) that is colour-phased to the late third to fourth centuries CE. Building 4 was always a discrete structure, separated from Building 3 by *c.* 7.5m in linear distance. Henceforth, this component of the baths will be referred to as 'the bath suite' in order to distinguish it from the adjacent and later cold plunge bath with attached *apodyterium* (Rooms 25 and 26) that has been phased to the mid- to late fourth century CE. Even with the construction of the cold plunge rooms, the combined bath house structure remained a separate entity from the Building 3. Details of the phase by phase spatial relationship between Buildings 4 and 3 are mapped on Figures 21.7, 21.8 and 21.9.

Four sub-phases of the bath suite have been identified (see Chapter 8 and Fig. 8.1), but it has not been possible to relate these to any other developments within the whole of the villa complex with confidence. During the course of its structural development, the bath suite was provided with corner buttresses which suggests that it was distinguished by enhanced height above ground floor level. Topographically, the suite is situated at the west corner of the villa plan where it would conform to Hutchins' description of the site as being 'on the slope of a rising'. The probability that Building 4 was the site of the 1790s dig is given additional credence by his description of a 'gutter' of interconnecting red tiles that the excavations of 1974 and 1975 confirmed was a feature peculiar to the baths (Chapter 1). Since the 1790s investigation was sited with reference to that of the first field exercise *c.* 50 years earlier, it is reasonable to assume that the substantial part of the 18th century disturbance to the villa took place in the bath house area.

The inference that Building 4 was the site of the 18th century excavations is given additional support by evidence from the octagonal cold plunge bath (Room 26) the fill of which suggested to Bill Putnam that it had been 'emptied before' (BU100DEW0006, 70 and 72). Excavation revealed that the whole of the north-east side of the plunge bath had been destroyed including the adjoining floor surface (Fig. 8.7). The extent of the damage is not inconsistent with the action of tree roots and the consequences of a tree being thrown down in a strong wind. Thus, Room 26 is a good candidate for the site of the 1740s fallen tree as described by Hutchins (Chapter 1). Finds from the area of Room 26 and Room 25, specifically grid trenches M3, M4 and M5, are likely to have been redeposited as backfill and this needs to be taken into account when assessing evidence from the site (see, for example, rabbit bones identified during the course of the faunal remains project by Maltby and Clark (Chapter 18).

The octagonal shape of the Room 26 cold plunge bath has been the subject of much speculation. Plunge baths of this shape are a feature of the south-west counties of Great Britain; other examples include Lufton, Somerset and Holcombe, Devon, both of which are of fourth century CE date. Perring has argued that baths of this form acted as baptisteries associated with Gnostic religious rites (2002, 175–77; 2003, 97–128). However, Todd (2005, 307–11) and Henig (2006, 105–7) have both reconsidered the evidence for octagonal baptistery-baths and have expressed doubts that this hypothesis is valid. Furthermore, Witts (2018, 22–37) in an assessment of the evidence from Lufton, was not persuaded that the octagonal bath was a baptistery, and this is a view that is shared by the present authors regarding the octagonal plunge bath at Dewlish.

In the late fourth to early fifth centuries CE, a buttress was added to the south-east corner of Room 25/26 cold plunge component of Building 4.

That this action was taken suggests that there was a subsidence problem that needed to be remedied especially if the building reached to clerestory height. If this was the case, then the combined bath suite and cold plunge unit (Building 4) would have been conspicuous to observers approaching from the west. Perhaps this is an indication that the bath facilities were used by members of a wider community than the residents and staff of the villa. The wear and tear thus implied might explain the need for the regular repairs, modifications and upgrades that have been identified at Dewlish. At Llantwit Major, Glamorgan, the *pilae* stack of the bath-block hypocaust 'showed signs of heavy corrosion from the heat of the furnace' (Nash-Williams 1953, 115). On the evidence of site photographs, there are tentative signs that this was so at Dewlish too (see, for example, Fig. 8.5), perhaps a further indication of the heavy use that villa bath houses received. Unfortunately, the structure of the Dewlish bath house rooms and their heating system was not well preserved having been subjected to multiple episodes of post-Roman ploughing and post-medieval antiquarian excavation.

Building 5

Unlike the other component units of the villa complex this building cannot be defined by readily identifiable structural limits on the site plans (Figs. 3.4 and 3.5). In reality, 'Building 5' is a collective term that includes a number of features that were excavated in grid squares O2 and N1 to the south-east of Building 4. Recorded features include a vestigial floor of *opus signinum* set upon a foundation of heavy rubble (Chapter 8, sub-phase (i)) and at least one wall fragment (Fig. 7.1, WF10; see Chapter 7 for details). Information is otherwise sketchy, and the impression is given that the investigation of these remains was cursory. The work was carried out during the summer of 1978, the penultimate year of the Dewlish field project. In that year participant student numbers were low, and the area investigated included the north-west end of Building 2, the whole of Building 6, and a series of trial trenches to the south of the villa. This was the year in which the site camera failed, and consequently no photographic record of Building 5 can be identified with certainty, but a sequence of six unannotated slides (R3914 to R3919) are within the Putnam archive and at least one of these (R3915, not reproduced) depicts a surface that resembles the excavator's written description.

Provisionally Building 5 has been interpreted as an early phase of the bath house, but it is an area of the site that requires clarification by new excavation (see proposed future research agenda below).

Building 6

Building 6 (Chapter 7) has been variously described as a shrine or a temple on the strength of its near-square footprint that resembles the ground plan of the *cella*, the focal space or room of a Romano-Celtic temple (for illustrated examples see Woodward, A.B. 1992, 9–30). At this point, caution is required because, as Wait advises, in a Romano-Celtic context the term 'shrine' should be applied to small buildings attached to villa complexes, whilst ideally the descriptor 'Romano-Celtic temple' should be used in relation to buildings that have both a *cella* and an ambulatory (1985, 179) such as those at Springhead, Kent which were distinguished by the presence of a *temenos*, a sacred precinct (e.g. Penn 1968, 105–123), a feature that was not detected at Dewlish.

Typically, the *cella* would be central to an ambulatory, a covered walk, that in plan resembled the cloister of a medieval monastic house. At Dewlish, excavation revealed no trace of an ambulatory, but it is important to note that like Building 5, the fieldwork took place in the summer of 1978 and that therefore it was subject to the same constraints and similar outcomes. Excavation beyond the walls of the building was limited, and external features such as evidence for stone post pads, that might have provided part of the structural support for a lean-to roofed ambulatory, could have been missed. A reconstructed example of this type of Romano-Celtic temple structure can be seen at Schwarzenacker, Saarland, Germany (Johnston 1995, 429–30) and in published form at Caistor St Edmund, Norfolk (Bowden *et al* 2020, 24–7, fig. 7). Excavation was further complicated by the fact that the foundations of Building 6 cut the earlier walls of Building 2 and the site diary records the confusion of stratigraphy that this overlap caused (details in Chapter 7).

Little has been published regarding the interpretation of the evidence from Building 6. The interim report for 1978 was slender and it was a third-party account (Keen 1980b, 113–14). This source tentatively refers to Building 6 as a 'small temple' and suggests that it replaced the villa farm in the late fourth century as a focus for religious devotion.

Aside from three out of context coins that probably represent random losses or discards, there were no finds associated with the Building 6 remains that could be interpreted as votive offerings or ritual deposits. This is in marked contrast to the Romano-Celtic excavated at Badbury Rings, Dorset (BNG 396080, 102990; ST 9608 0299; Papworth 2014, 242–271). Analysis of the coins recovered from the Badbury site identified 353 examples dating from the Iron Age through to the late fourth century CE (Hammerson 2014, 264–7). Similarly, at the Brean Down Temple (Somerset) 468 Roman coins were recorded (Boon 1965, 232–7). By comparison, the total number of coins recovered from Building 6 is derisory even allowing for the relatively short chronology for its use. The apparent absence of votive finds undermines the case for interpreting Building 6 as a temple.

Putnam's suggested fourth century CE date for Building 6 is broadly accurate, but its function remains a matter of conjecture. It is possible that the foundations of the building denote the site of a late Romano-British mausoleum, similar to stone-walled examples that were identified at the Poundbury cemetery, Dorchester (Farwell and Molleson 1993, 42 fig. 33 and 44–61; Woodward, A.B. 1993, 233–235). The most complete of the stone built Poundbury mausolea was R8 (Site B) which measured 4.8m × 6.4m compared with the 7.2m × 7.4m of Building 6 at Dewlish. Both were rectangular but diverged with regard to proportions and the R8 example lacked the attached porch that was a feature of Building 6. Whilst the comparison is interesting, no firm conclusions can be drawn from it.

After 1978, the story of the 'temple/shrine' became embellished and included the assertion that the building had been destroyed by a fire (Putnam 2007, 103). Chapter 7 demonstrates that Building 6 was devoid of any evidence of conflagration, therefore

Key

Retained from Phase 2 (3rd century)

New to Phase 3 (Later 3rd century)

New to Phase 4 (late 3rd to 4th century)

Approximate extent of building footprint

Nat. Grid North

0　　　　　　　　　　　20m

Figure 21.7　Dewlish villa Phase 5. Jonathan Milward.

Key

■ Retained from Phase 2 (3rd century)

■ Retained from Phase 4 (late 3rd to 4th century)

■ Retained from Phase 5 (Early to mid 4th century)

■ New to Phase 6 (Mid to late 4th century)

□ Approximate extent of building footprint

Nat. Grid North

0   20m

Figure 21.8   Dewlish villa Phase 6. Jonathan Milward.

the circumstances of its demise remain as unclear as its intended function, however, the absence of signs of scorching, charring or charcoal/ash deposits probably confirms that Building 6 did not have an industrial purpose. Currently, it is not possible to substantiate the notion that the villa became a centre for a religious community, or that there was a change of ownership at the expense of its agricultural assets (see Putnam 2002, 20–23). If Building 6 was a shrine, then it is quite possible that it was systematically dismantled when it outlived its purpose as was the case with the temple at Brean Down, Somerset as explained by ApSimon (1965, 222—3).

Ann Woodward has observed that in many past cases, the excavators of Roman temples did not dig beneath the wall footings and floors to reveal earlier phases or versions of the structure (1992, 20). At Dewlish, due diligence was given to the search for underfloor features and this process revealed the presence of a wall fragment (Fig. 7.1, WF1) which could represent the corner of an earlier building. However, it was on the right alignment (i.e. north-west to south-east) for it to comprise part of a demolished south-west courtyard perimeter wall.

The excavation of Building 6 has raised more questions than answers and these issues will need to be investigated by a future fieldwork programme.

Building 7

Building 7 (Chapter 5) was a construction of barn-like dimensions in plan (Figs. 3.4, 3.5, 5.1 and 21.8). Evidence of doorways and associated internal partitions did not survive. This unit of the villa complex will be discussed below under the section relating to the villa economy.

THE VILLA ECONOMY

The component buildings of the Dewlish Roman villa did not exist in a vacuum. By the time of its final developmental phase in the late fourth century, the buildings had evolved into a conspicuous display of encapsulated wealth that was generated, at least in part, by the estate's own economic resources and at considerable financial cost (Perring 2002, 132).

The source of this wealth is likely to have been the network of fields within which the villa was set (RCHME 1970331–332, Plate 87 and Part 2 end map; see also Chapter 1). These fields were sampled by excavation in 1976 and 1978 (Chapter 4) and found to date to the Pre-Roman Iron Age, possibly earlier. The link between this field system, the Dole's Hill group, and the villa buildings is made manifest by the presence of associated grain storage pits (Reynolds 1979, 70–82) and the provision of cereal processing facilities in Buildings 2/2A and Building 3. These features have been considered in Chapters 6 and 9 respectively, where it has been suggested that the emphasis was upon malting rather than corn drying.

Evidence of malting has been recovered from other villa sites in the region such as Halstock (Dorset), Building 4, a similar single aisle structure in Period 2 (c. 175–300 CE), and broadly contemporary with Building 2/2A at Dewlish (Phase 2). At Halstock, an 'oven' was constructed within Building 4 Stage 1, for which malting was suggested as being a possible purpose, but there was an absence of discussion about the source of the grain that would have been required to fulfil the end product (Lucas 1993, 134–5). In similar vein Building 12 at Bucknowle villa (Dorset) (Period 4, c. 150–250 CE) contained a structure that included a furnace that was reasoned to be a cereal dryer (Light and Ellis 2009, 28–30 and 176). The excavation of this villa complex also revealed Iron Age settlement remains, but no firm link to the Celtic field system at the nearby Corfe Common was possible (BNG 397575, 80997; SY 97575 80997).

At Dewlish the link between the adjacent fields and the villa's buildings is reinforced by the sequence of construction, demolition and replacement. Above, and in Chapter 6, it has been shown that in its original form Building 2 (Phase 2) probably had a dual function: it was, simultaneously, both residential and a cereal storage and processing amenity. This second purpose seems to have outgrown itself because in Phase 3 it was extended by the addition of a single aisle and either two or three room units (Building 2A), a project that extended the footprint of the structure by approximately 50% (Fig. 21.7). This implies a growing yield from the fields, perhaps fuelled by an increased demand from the nearby town of *Durnovaria* (Dorchester). Unfortunately,

Key

- **Retained from Phase 2 (3rd century)**
- **Retained from Phase 4 (late 3rd to 4th century)**
- **Retained from Phase 5 (Early to mid 4th century)**
- **Retained from Phase 6 (Mid to late 4th century)**
- **New to Phase 7 (Late 4th to early 5th century)**
- **Approximate extent of building footprint**

Nat. Grid North

0   20m

Figure 21.9   Dewlish villa Phase 7. Jonathan Milward.

there is no published data from other Dorset villa sites that can be used as a yardstick for comparison.

Expansion continued. By Phase 5, cereal drying and/ or malting had been transferred or extended to the combined 'Rooms' 20, 21 and 22 of Building 3. This was a prelude to the replacement of Buildings 2/2A by Building 7 in Phase 6, the mid- to late fourth century (Fig. 21.8). The dimensions and absence of internal features together suggest that Building 7 was a barn. Bill Putnam's teams did collect samples during the eleven season course of the excavations but few of these have survived the intervening years and were therefore unavailable for analysis. Nonetheless, the few samples that remained were submitted for expert scrutiny and found to include grains of barley, spelt and other indeterminate wheats (Gray, Chapter 20; Table 20.2).

Significantly, the expansion in grain storage and processing provision coincided with the aggrandise-ment of Buildings 3 and 4, the *domus* and bath house respectively. The Dewlish example suggests that in some cases at least, villas were constantly evolving, a process that was conditional upon the disposable income made available from its own economic base and, in the cases of individual owners with multiple holdings, input from the surplus wealth from other estates too. Building and rebuilding were routine as increased income permitted the upgrading of the building stock to the point whereby each unit transcended the purely functional and became a repository of high status symbols of power and influence. Johnston has suggested that in some cases, these developments might signify the gradual transformation of the villa estate into the prototype medieval manor (1988, 23). If this hypothesis is accepted, then at Dewlish one might envisage the *domus* (Building 3), as the embryonic manor house complete with great hall (Room 11) and detached kitchens (the Annexe), with tithe barn (successively Buildings 2, 2A and 7) and cereal processing rights. Building 6, if accepted as a temple, shrine or mausoleum, might be seen to foreshadow the church and manor type settlements of the medieval countryside. Extension of this analogy would imply that at least a portion of a villa's economy might have been tribute based.

Communications network: roads and tracks

The above picture of an agricultural economy would not have been possible without an easily accessible market, an amenity that would have been provided by the town of *Durnovaria* (Dorchester) *c.* 10km south-west of the Dewlish villa site. The Roman military road from Shapwick (Dorset) with links to Poole Harbour, lies *c.* 3.7km due south of the villa. This is Margary's section 4e of the road that runs through the Roman town and on towards Exeter (1973, 85, Map 3.1). Hayward (Chapter 10) has suggested that this road might have been used to transport goods such as construction materials to Dewlish villa and this is entirely feasible. However, there are two complications. The first and least problematical objection is that there is no evidence of a northbound linking route from military road to villa, but future fieldwork might reveal the former presence of such a feature.

More challenging are the results of an evaluation exercise carried out on a short stretch of the Roman road at a point where it passes through Thorncombe Woods, part of Puddletown Forest, by Bill Putnam in 1968, the year before the start of the Dewlish project (Putnam 1971, 147–8). Given its close proximity to the villa, this site needs to be regarded as part of a Dewlish landscape project. Briefly stated, the excavated surface of the road betrayed no trace of wheel ruts or signs of any repairs which the transport of heavy goods would have caused. Overall, the impression given on the strength of this one sample, was that the road had been little used, a result which suggests that the military road did not metamorphose into a civil supply and trading route. Putnam mused that heavy goods were transported by water (i.e. the River Frome) to Dorchester, presumably from despatch points along the shores of Poole Harbour (Fig. 1.1). This is a matter that merits further consideration: if the military road was not the means of moving goods, then how did the villa economy work and how did heavy building materials arrive on site?

First, it is important to state that there is circum-stantial confirmation that the Shapwick-Dorchester stretch of Roman road had become an insignificant landscape feature by the end of the first century CE.

From Shapwick at the River Stour crossing point (BNG 393596, 101568; ST93596 01568) to Stinsford (BNG 371887, 91649; SY71877 91649), which lies 2km north-east of Grey's Bridge (the gateway to Dorchester), is a total distance of 26km. Along the entire stretch of this section of the road, there is no cartographic evidence that it ever comprised part of an established medieval or post-medieval route network except for a brief appearance as the spine for the village settlement of Winterborne Kingston (BNG 386231, 97567; SY86231 97567). Similarly, the road does not represent part of a parish boundary (although it bisects some) which might be an indicator of its lack of importance in the formulation of boundaries of various hierarchies since the first century CE. The reason for this neglect might have been the impracticality of moving heavy goods by road from the coast at Poole Harbour or Hengistbury Head (Christchurch) to the civitas town at Dorchester. The difficulties posed by such overland routes is a point that has been made by Selkirk (1983) in his analysis of the logistics of road transport in County Durham, but with similar implications for the Romano-British period in general.

For the Roman road to have been a reliable trade and civil communications route for Dorchester it would have required a link to a coastal port. Such a link would have been provided by the River Stour which, from the road crossing point at Shapwick, drains into Christchurch Harbour, site of the Iron Age and Romano-British settlement of Hengistbury Head. This port has been the subject of thorough investigation by Cunliffe who concludes that with the establishment of the main Roman military supply base at Hamworthy (Poole Harbour), Hengistbury declined to the status of a backwater and that it was not extensively occupied by the late third century and early fourth century CE (1987, 345–6).

An alternative and shorter overland market and general access route from Dewlish to Dorchester needs to be identified. The economy of the Dewlish villa had been established in the Late Iron Age with the setting out of the Dole's Hill field system within which the villa is situated (see above and Chapter 4). The continued use of fields of Iron Age or earlier origin implies that pre-Romano-British roads and tracks remained in use. A strong contender for an alternative Dewlish-Dorchester link route can be traced from Shailes Farm c. 250m to the north of the villa. The farm is situated on a modern road that heads south-westwards cutting through an enclosure of Iron Age date in the process (Figs. 1.1, 1.2 and 4.1). After a further 1.7km the road forms a junction with two footpaths, effectively a crossroads. The site of the Druce Farm villa is reached next (1.73km). Here the route crosses the River Piddle (perhaps the Druce villa's *raison d'etre*) and climbs as a track passing to the north-north-west of Troy Town Farm (1.3km) as a recognised ridgeway to an Ordnance Survey spot height of 128m aOD (2.1km). From here the route descends and becomes a stretch of the B3143 which it follows to conjoin with the Roman road and crossing the River Frome at Grey's Bridge into Dorchester (3.6km; for details see Table 21.3). In so doing the route will have by-passed the site of Bill Putnam's 1968 road dig in Thorncombe Wood, thus reinforcing the excavator's belief that the military road was never used for civil purposes.

Grey's Bridge was built in 1748, but it is situated within the medieval parish of Fordington, the name of which indicates that it was associated with a traditional crossing point on the River Frome (RCHME 1970, 115; Mills 1998, 74). It is also possible that this was the location of an inland river port for shallow draught craft from Poole Harbour that would have serviced the needs of Dorchester though this remains conjectural at present. Nonetheless, it is a proposition worthy of consideration because the River Frome was navigable from Poole Harbour as far as Wareham beyond the 12th century CE and the town has produced numerous Roman finds which, according to RCHME (1970a, 304) 'indicate a substantial occupation and at least one building of distinction'.

Subsequently, a large scale excavation and fieldwork programme has been carried out at the Wareham extra-mural site of Bestwall (BNG 393121, 878220; SY 931878) where pottery production took place on an industrial scale. In Field Z, 9 kilns and a dryer were identified that could be dated to c. 200–300 CE with an additional 22 kilns with a dryer belonging to the years from c. 300 CE. In her report, the excavator suggested that much of the industrial outputs from Bestwall were shipped out in small boats or punts

Table 21.3 Itinerary for Dewlish to Dorchester (*Durnovaria*) overland communications via Druce Farm, avoiding the Shapwick to Dorchester military road (*i.e.* Margary's route section 4e)

Outward bound route stretch no.	From	BNG map ref.	To	OS map ref.	Approx. distance by road/track (km)
1	Shailes Farm BM (aOD 82.87m), **Dewlish R-B villa**	376972 97506	Road dog-leg/ intersection	376020 96064	1.7
2	Road dog-leg/ intersection	376020 96064	Druce Farm	374528 95300	1.7
3	**Druce Farm**	374528 95300	Troy Town Farm	373613 94301	1.3
4	Troy Town Farm (NNW of) via River Piddle crossing point	373613 94301	Ridgeway spot height (128m aOD) SSW of Laycock Farm	371585 94349	2.1
5	Ridgeway spot height (128m aOD) SSW of Laycock Farm	371585 94349	SSW on Slyer's Lane (B3143) to junction with Roman Road from Thorncombe Wood (B3150)	370337 91019	3.6
6	(B3143) junction with Roman Road from Thorncombe Wood (B3150)	370337 91019	Grey's Bridge (Fordington, **Dorchester**)	370051 90847	0.4
Total km:					10.8

(Ladle 2012, 307–19). Presumably inland markets, such as Dorchester, were reached via the River Frome.

Ladle's vision of the Poole Harbour trade network is shared by Sunter whose investigation of the Romano-British industrial site at Norden, Isle of Purbeck, Dorset, uncovered evidence for the production of objects of shale, Purbeck Marble and chalk (BNG 39564, 82710; SY 9564 8271). Sunter proposed that stone from the Purbeck quarries was transported to quays on the southern shores of Poole Harbour (1987, 43). From here it would have been possible to transport goods to inland clients upstream of the River Frome.

Navigation beyond Wareham to Dorchester in the Roman period is not proven but the discovery of an Iron Age oak log boat in Poole Harbour reveals that the technology for river transport was available (Peers 1964, 131–4). This vessel has been dated to the third to fourth centuries BCE, or radiocarbon years 2245 +/50 BP (Historic England, PastScape. org). At 11m in length it has been calculated that it had the capacity to carry 1,723kg of cargo and four persons in less than 0.4m of water, or 18 persons in less than 0.3m of water (McGrail 1983, 37–8). The use of rafts potentially increased the carrying capacity for heavy weights such as salt, bulk pottery loads and building materials. Hypothetically, the use of traditional craft of this type not only made navigation of the River Frome beyond Wareham possible, but provided a means of transport that could have continued to service inland Romano-British settlements.

From the crossing point on the Frome at Grey's Bridge, the proposed ridgeway route to Dewlish and beyond (see above) linked the Roman town to the nearby villa estates. This underlines the economic viability of the villas of Dewlish and Druce as suppliers of farm produce to the nearest urban centre. This was a two-way process that generated wealth from the sale of agricultural surplus from the villa estates, whilst thus providing the means for acquiring the materials and expertise to install and display overt symbols of wealth in their owners' buildings. In sum, the association of the Dewlish villa's economy with the nearby routes of Roman roads cannot be substantiated and the case has been made for a credible and viable alternative, although it needs to be said that more archaeological fieldwork needs to be done with regard to the Frome navigation model. This is an avenue of investigation that needs to be extended to include other villa sites in the region and elsewhere.

Pit-shafts: a post-script on the villa economy

In this report, the term 'pit-shaft' has been assigned to pits that are sub-rectangular in plan, but which taper to a depth that generally exceeds twice the diameter of the aperture; the base is usually flat or slightly concave (Fig. 21.10). Examples of this type of feature were encountered at the Greyhound Yard excavations at Dorchester between 1981 and 1984 and in the report are referred to as 'shafts' (Woodward, P.J. *et al* 1993, 47–9 and 51). At Amesbury (Wiltshire), seven pits answering this description were identified ranging from 1.9m to 2.87m in depth (Cooke *et al* in prep.), which is comparatively shallow for this type of feature.

Two pit-shafts were excavated at Dewlish, P4 and O100, these codes identifying their relative positions on the alpha-numeric site grid (Fig. 3.5; Chapter 7, Fig. 7.4; Chapter 8, Fig. 8.2). In an interim report, Bill Putnam referred to Pit-shaft P4 as being a 'cold store', i.e. for unspecified foods, but without explanation (Putnam and Rainey, 1976, 54). A feature, also described as a cold store, was recorded at the Roman settlement at Gatcombe, Somerset, which is associated with a nearby villa (McCarthy 2013, 54, fig. 3.9). However, this feature is described in detail in the site report which makes it clear that in this instance 'cold store' was intended as a conjectural purpose for what is described as a type of sunken featured building, or SFB (Branigan 1977, 36–40; 183; 185 fig. 33). In every sense, the Gatcombe cold store was quite different to the pit-shafts referred to here, but it is likely that the idea was derived from the initial 20th century excavations of the Somerset site, which took place in 1965 and 1966 (Cunliffe 1967, 126–60).

Of the two Dewlish examples, Pit-shaft P4 was situated within the confines of the stoke hole enclosure of the bath house (Building 4). In this position it is difficult to envisage that it would have functioned as an efficient means of cold storage. Though this was probably not its original purpose, Pit-shaft P4 became a dumping facility for household refuge of various kinds including animal bones, a sample of which was sent for radiocarbon assay which confirmed a mid- to late Roman date for this part of the fill (Maltby and Clark, Chapter 18; Appendix 2). Initially, Bill Putnam judged that the Dewlish 'cold

stores' were wells but changed this interpretation without useful explanation of the reasons why, therefore it is only possible to speculate. Pit-shaft O100 (Fig. 21.10) produced tentative evidence that it might have been wood-lined (or 'steined' see below) and Hodge has explained that wells lined in this way were often square in section (1991, 52). This matches the above description of a pit-shaft, but it is conceivable that the excavator was persuaded to rule out the possibility of well-shafts by the absence of ground water at the base of these features at Dewlish, and an answer that fitted 'dry' storage had to be found. Consequently, cold food stores became the new purpose of choice. Against this notion, Hodge advises that with regard to water-divining for well digging, Roman engineers had little grasp of the necessary principles of geological science and that well-sinking tended to be a speculative task (1991, 51). It therefore follows that abortive attempts would be present in the archaeological record and by implication these would be dry.

If the Dewlish pit-shafts do represent failed well-sinking exercises, then these efforts were abandoned at an early stage in the process. At the Dorset villa of Tarrant Hinton, a well was excavated that extended to 26.5m in depth whilst the Dewlish pit-shafts reached to *c*. 5m below surface level. The Tarrant Hinton well was situated adjacent to a small bath house (Building 6) and it was provided with a wooden force pump to facilitate efficient water delivery (Graham 2006, 34, 37 and 160–1). At Dewlish, Pit-Shaft P4 was also adjacent to the bath house (Building 4) but one that incorporated a more extensive range of ablutions that probably would not have been satisfied by a water supply from a well with a pump. In Chapter 8, it has been argued that water to the Dewlish baths was supplied by an aqueduct, not a well.

Taking all of the evidence into account, it is unlikely that the Dewlish pit-shafts were wells. In ruling out this interpretation and that of 'cold stores' an alternative primary purpose for pit-shafts needs to be identified. This will require close comparison with similar features from other sites. As a starting point, the two pit-shafts from Dewlish, P4 and O100, were both close to principal buildings which suggests that there was a reason for this that a convenient store

Figure 21.10   Pit-shaft O100 surface details. Photograph: R4007.

for food does not explain. The sub-rectangular plan and the generous depth of pit-shafts are factors that need to be considered. As a working hypothesis, it is suggested here that the Dewlish pit-shafts were part of the process of building construction. Construction of walls in stone requires an aggregate, a bonding agent, and lime mortar was the medium of choice. At Dewlish, the raw material for lime making was the readily available natural chalk upon which the villa was situated (Chapter 1). The pit-shafts were not dug as quarries for chalk, a pit of any random shape would suffice for that purpose, but any chalk excavated during the digging of each pit was effectively a useful by-product. The shape of the pit was critical though

because the extended cuboid profile made it easy to line with wooden planking; Bill Putnam noted that he detected signs of this during the excavation of pit-shaft O100 although verification of the presence of this lining was elusive (Chapter 7). Recently, conclusive evidence of a lined pit-shaft was revealed during excavations carried out during the upgrading of the Dorset Museum, Dorchester (Clare Randall, pers. comm., BU100DEW0361).

The type of lime mortar that would have been used in the villa buildings was non-hydraulic lime which is produced by burning a limestone such as chalk which produces calcium oxide (CaO). This needs to be mixed with water which produces a violent chemical reaction: it is a dangerous process known as slaking (Schofield 1995,3). One use for a wood-lined pit could have been for arms-length slaking. More likely though, is that the pit was used to store the resultant lime putty which needs to be maintained in a moist state until it is used (Schofield 1995, 3). A major building project could take weeks to complete and so a safe store for preserving the workability of the bonding material would have been essential. In this sense, pit-shafts were an integral part of the villa's economy as the building stock grew and became modified and enhanced. Pit-shaft P4 was effectively sealed by Building 4 and therefore pre-dated it, and so it could not be associated with its construction, but it was suitably placed to be a lime putty supply store for the construction of the *domus*, Building 3. In similar vein, pit-shaft O100 may have provided a similar function during the erection of Building 2. Both of these buildings belong to Phase 2 in origin and together they represent the largest known single episode of construction in the developmental history of the villa. Therefore, it is feasible that pit-shafts O100 and P4 comprise an integral part of this third century building programme as safe stores for lime putty.

If pit-shafts originated as lime putty stores, then they became redundant upon the completion of a major building project. At this point, at Dewlish and in the nearby Roman town of Dorchester, these features became repositories for all manner of household waste and, for archaeologists, this has proved to be a vital function because the pits have preserved a datable stratigraphy that has provided insights into multiple dimensions of community life including the local environment, diet, disposal of the dead (see Future Research Agenda below) and the economy of the villa, town or settlement. In the case of Dewlish, the fills of the two pit-shafts provided evidence of metallurgy in the form of discarded crucibles and a tuyere (Putnam *et al,* Chapter 17). However, there is no evidence to indicate that metal working was ever a major part of the Dewlish economy which was primarily pastoral and not industrial. More likely is that the finds from the pit-shafts reveal a dimension of the workings of the villa's estate maintenance regime. There is insufficient available evidence to

suggest that the Dewlish pit-shafts were repositories for structured ritual deposits.

DECLINE AND RUIN

The demise and eventual abandonment of Romano-British villas needs to be assessed on an individual basis because local circumstances are likely to have played an important part. However, local factors might have been exacerbated by wider social and economic forces that make the process of decline and ruin a complex process to understand. Here, comment will be focused upon Dewlish with occasional reference to other published Romano-British villa sites as appropriate.

At Dewlish, as in the cases of other Romano-British villas, there is no evidence of an apocalyptic final act of destruction and such was probably not the case even allowing for the unexcavated evidence from the north-east range and elsewhere. It is worth emphasising though, that the villa was the subject of antiquarian activity on two tersely recorded occasions in the 18th century and it is certain that a significant amount of important archaeological information was lost in the process. Similar circumstances prevailed at other sites as lamented by Corney in his reappraisal and assessment of the villa at Box, Wiltshire (undated [*c.* 2012], 67–8). On the strength of the data amassed during the Putnam excavations, the Dewlish story is one of gradual decline by the end of the fourth century CE and into the fifth century CE, suggesting that the process was probably one of continuity and readjustment rather than catastrophe. Two groups of artefacts best illustrate the case: pottery and coins.

Pottery

The fabric in question is South East Dorset Orange Wiped Ware (SEDOWW), a product from the margins of Poole Harbour and the Isle of Purbeck (Dorset) and thus shared the same raw material source as Black Burnished ware (BB1). In broad terms, SEDOWW was being produced during the late fourth century and into the fifth century CE (Gerrard 2010, 219–312). A small quantity of SEDOWW was deposited in the upper fills of pit-shaft P4 along with other

Figure 21.11   Room 23A north-west external wall with adult sheep/goat sealed within the foundations. Photograph: R3472.

late pottery types, but a far larger quantity (22% as compared with 1% in P4) was derived from the contents of pit-shaft O100. A more complete example of the fabric type was a rope-rimmed storage jar found in the Building 3 Annexe, Room 24 (Chapter 9), and broadly associated with Theodosian coins (Seager Smith, Chapter 17, Fig. 15.7).

Coins

A concentration 13 of Theodosian and other late bronze coins was recovered from the component rooms of the Building 3 Annexe (Fig. 9.1 and Table 9.1). Gerrard with Reece (Chapter 13) have dated nine of these coins to 388–402 CE which places them at the end of the imperial mint coin supply in 402 CE (Esmonde Cleary 1989, 140). This spatially associated group of late Roman coins was not found in a single context but they were all recovered from sealed layers over a period of two excavation seasons and in two separate box grid trenches which makes it possible that the relationship between each of these finds was not mapped with critical accuracy. Conceivably, this Annexe group of coins constituted a late coin hoard deposit, a

possible indicator of economic turbulence in the early fifth century CE.

In Chapter 9 it has been proposed that the Building 3 Annexe group of rooms belong to the last phase of building development at Dewlish and that this component of the villa complex was of timber frame construction, at least in part (Figs. 3.4 and 3.5, Phase 7), indicatively conforming to Williams' variations 'b' or 'd' (1971, 175–6). In particular, Room 23A, a component room of the Annexe, was the source of a remarkable piece of evidence: the skeleton of an adult sheep sealed in the foundation trench fill at the base of its north-west common wall with Room 24 (Maltby and Clark, Chapter17; Fig. 21.11). The find prompted no mention in the excavation site diary (BU100DEW0006), but it is challenging not to regard this interment as a dedicatory act in the process of erecting a new building. This immured animal might be an indicator of evolving beliefs and social norms towards the end of the Dewlish villa's history of occupation. The coincidence of late pottery and coin finds from this area of the site hints that late Romano-British inhabitation of the villa was focused here.

Other parts of the villa might have been abandoned or repurposed at this time, although the presence of SEDOWW in pit-shafts P4 and O100 argues that these refuse dumps were still in use even though the nearby Building 2 had been long since demolished. In his site diary for 1971, Bill Putnam noted details of his impression that the floor surfaces of Rooms 1 and 2 had been gravelled over during a late phase of the villa's history (BU100DEW0006, 4) a possible indication of demolition following contraction.

There were obvious signs of distress in the fabric of Building 3. The surfaces of the mosaic floors of rooms 1 (Fig. 12.1), 4 (Fig. 12.5), 6 (Fig. 12.6) and 8 (Fig. 12.8) were all pierced in one or more places by post holes. This is especially evident in the case of Room 6 where there is a linear arrangement of three post holes which suggest the positions of stout wooden props that are likely to have supported the sagging timbers of a roof that was sealed by the considerable combined weight of an arrangement of limestone pennant tiles capped by a ridge of Ham stone blocks. The presence of the props represents a homemade solution to an otherwise costly repair for which neither the materials nor the expertise was available. Since Building 3 continued to be the subject of extensions and refinements during the second part of the fourth century, it is unlikely that the roof was in a poor state of repair at that time. The need to support the roof with stout timber props implies that the problem set in during the fifth century and took some time to become critical, perhaps at a point in time beyond the first two decades of the fifth century. The extensive damage to the Room 11 floor might have been a contemporary event but for different reasons (see above).

Elsewhere, there were several instances of disturbance to the site including stone robbing, antiquarian digging, medieval ploughing and 20th century military activity (Chapter 1). Some of the medieval activity probably included field clearance but a 1976 Trial Trench (TT(S)4) in the extreme south corner of the Dewlish Park field, yielded fragments of imbrex and tegulae, a partial flue tile and a late coin of the House of Theodosius (SFN 490). This isolated group of finds possibly represents part of a fifth century dump of demolition rubble (Chapter 4).

The available evidence points to a continuation of occupation at Dewlish into the sub-Roman fifth century, though probably with a modified economic infrastructure and a revised social structure. Beyond this there is uncertainty, which leaves the door open for a continuation of field research at Dewlish, a suggested agenda for which is mapped out below.

THE LOOSE ENDS OF POST-EXCAVATION PROJECT 2 (PEP2)

Two remaining imperatives need to be addressed following the publication of Bill Putnam's excavations at Dewlish and these will remain within the remit of PEP2.

1   The electronic components of the site archives need to be expanded and made available via BORDaR (Bournemouth University Online Research Data Repository User Documentation). This resource will include site photographs, unpublished papers, context documentation, the Small Finds Register and a miscellany of other files of various formats. In association with this initiative, safe and permanent storage for the material archive needs to be negotiated and realised.

2   The corpus of painted plaster fragments from the villa site was the subject of a detailed draft report during the first decade of the present millennium (PEP1). An analysis of a limited number of samples is included in this publication as Chapter 11 (Morgan). The fragility of this assemblage is such that as a consequence of its removal from the stores at Bournemouth University at the start of PEP1 in 1999, the painted plaster is not available for study; what remains as accessible is the draft report and relevant photographic images that are stored within the Bill Putnam Collection of 35mm colour slides. These will be assessed with a view to publishing a stand-alone painted plaster report in due course.

FUTURE RESEARCH: A SUGGESTED AGENDA

In fulfilment of the stated objectives (see above and Chapter 3), a number of questions and issues for future consideration have been identified. It is not an exhaustive list but a response to the usual academic conundrum whereby the answer to any one question invariably gives rise to the formulation of new ones. The following sub-headings identify the key issues and provide a rationale for their relevance and importance. With regard to matters that appertain to specific buildings and/or features that comprise the villa complex, alpha-numeric site grid co-ordinates are given (e.g. B4). These co-ordinates should be used in conjunction with Figure 3.5.

Protection of the Dewlish villa heritage asset

Currently, the site of the Dewlish villa and its associated features are not protected by Scheduled Ancient Monument status. For the first time, this publication has provided a reasoned and evidence-based account of the complexity of the villa's pathway of development and identified an economic context within which its owners and dependants operated. The chapters of this report make the case for legal protection to be afforded to the villa buildings (excavated and unexcavated) and other associated archaeological features such as the pre-Romano British ridgeway enclosure to the north-west. The extent of such protection should be informed by geophysical surveys (e.g. Cheetham *et al* forthcoming).

The mosaic floors

During the 1973 excavation season, three of the fragmentary remains of the mosaic floors from Rooms 11 and 25 were lifted under the expert supervision of Rodney Alcock, then conservator at the Dorset County Museum (now Dorset Museum). Figure 21.13 depicts the lifting of the lower floor surface of Room 25. Two of the panels thus recovered are exhibits at the Museum, and at the time of writing, it is hoped that the third panel that features a leopard attack on a Dorcas gazelle will soon join them. A follow-up article in the Proceedings of the Dorset Natural History and Archaeological Society is planned as a post-publication project.

The excavated components of the villa complex

The Bill Putnam excavations explored around two thirds of the villa complex, specifically the north-west and south-west ranges. The use of the box grid excavation strategy required that 0.5m baulks be in place to separate each of the component boxes of the grid. These baulks were not routinely removed, and in many instances, they will remain as 'witness sections' for a future field archaeologist to exploit. Another consequence of the box grid system was that it did not necessarily follow that the component squares were excavated in a seemingly logical order. A good example of this can be found in Building 3 wherein squares D5 to D8 were examined in 1973 and Room numbers were allocated as appropriate (i.e. 23 and 24), whereas the adjoining squares, E6 and E7, remained unexplored until two years later (1975) when an additional Annexe room abutted to Room 24 was identified. By this time the room number '25' had been assigned to the Building 4 *apodyterium*. As a consequence, the newly discovered room had to be labelled '23A' (Fig. 3.4).

The spin-off problem was that the whole of the Annexe suite of rooms (10, 23, 23A and 24) was not seen as a single archaeological entity with even vaguely sequential context numbers, and this gave rise to a lack of recognition of a cache of late Roman coins, and a failure to appreciate the sequence of the construction of the component rooms of the Annexe suite. With this example in mind, listed below is a series of recommended 're-excavation' transects (trenches) each with a brief rationale of their desirability. They are labelled PET (Post-Excavation Trench) by numerical sequence from 01 onwards followed by the relevant alpha-numeric site grid co-ordinates.

PET 01: (M94, N94 and O94) to explore the relationships between the intercutting foundations of Buildings 1, 2 and 7 which have been excavated individually but not as an inter-related group. Importantly, this would enable each building to be relatively dated taking into consideration the observations made in Chapter 5. The characteristics of the proposed malting kiln in Room 39 (Building 2) could be mapped and their purpose verified.

PET 02: (N1, N2, O1, and O2) to ascertain the presence and characteristics of the conjectural Building 5 and the associated wall fragments WF6 to WF10 inclusive (Chapter 6). Relationship to Building 4 to be determined.

PET 03: (H2 to H5 inclusive) to confirm or ascertain the chronological relationships between Rooms 12, 14, 15, 16, 17 and 18. This trench needs to extend below floor level to test the depth and composition of the building platform that accommodates the foundations of Building 3 (Chapter 9).

PET 04: (D6 to D8 and E6 to 8 inclusive) to explore the structural relationships between Rooms 10, 23A and 24. The south-west portion of Room 24 has not been fully excavated, therefore this trench potentially offers the opportunity for collecting and analysing samples from its floor which has been interpreted as a food preparation zone (Chapter 9 and this chapter above).

PET 05: (A2, A3, B2, B3, C2 and C3) to determine the structural and relative chronological relationships between Rooms 2 and 3 and the north-west elevation of the unexcavated north-east range (Chapter 9).

The unexcavated components of the villa complex

Based upon current understanding, this sub-section relates only to the north-east range which comprises the ultimate 'witness section' and needs to be the subject of a research proposal informed by careful analysis of geophysical surveys. There is no reason to believe that this part of the site was the subject of antiquarian activity which seems to have been largely confined to Building 4 and, possibly, Room 4.

The nature of the north-east range is a matter of speculation. Like the rest of the villa site it is almost certainly multi-phase and therefore complex. Dewlish was a villa that overtly displayed wealth and substance, but there are some facilities that remain to be identified and this includes the latrines and possibly a second and private bath house if the Building 4 amenity was open to wider public participation (see above, this chapter). Positioned on the north-east side of the courtyard, this range would be potentially ideal for the siting of the latrines where the odours of effluence would be carried north-eastwards and away from the seat of affluence in the *domus* by the prevailing south-westerly winds.

The potential importance of the north-east range as an undisturbed store of confirmatory or contradictory evidence strengthens the case for protection of the site as a national heritage asset as argued above.

The courtyard and its potential

The 1969–79 Putnam excavations can be described as a 'find and follow' wall-chasing exercise. This approach left little scope or appetite for investigating the *c.* 720 square metres of the courtyard. Throughout the duration of the project, examination of the courtyard space was confined to seven grid squares that were adjacent to the south-east elevation of the Building 3 corridor. It was not until the final year of the Dewlish field schools series that a token investigation of 50% each of the combined courtyard grid squares G99 and F99 was archaeologically interrogated. Eventually the south-west half of G100 and *c.* 10% of G1 adjoining were also examined (Fig. 2.3). Observations in the site diary were scant, but a sketch plan reveals that the above-mentioned grid squares were situated immediately to the south-east of the porch *c.* 6% of the total courtyard area, 42.5 square metres.

A separate comment discloses that once de-turfed, the combined area of the courtyard grid trenches was found to consist of a gravel surface that in at least one place sealed a bright orange clay sub-layer which the excavator thought to have been 'dumped', but this is not the impression that is conveyed by the only site photograph of this feature (BU100DEW0007, 117, 125; Fig. 21.12). The gravelled surface presents as being hard packed, though possibly spread by medieval ploughing, but certainly deliberately placed, and its position next to the porch, Room 13, invites one to believe that it constituted a linear formal pathway from the *domus* onwards south-eastwards through the courtyard.

The importance of this seemingly uninspiring gravel surface is that it hints at the possibility of the existence of a paved approach to Building 3, that brought the visitor to the porch (Room 13) and, via the Room 12 corridor, to the portal of the grand hall, Room 11, as described in Chapter 9. The relevance of introducing the possible existence of a formal courtyard pathway here is that it potentially indicates the former presence of a designed garden space. 'Courtyard villa' is a term that is frequently used to describe villa types (see above), the paradox being that historically courtyards have been a neglected detail in the excavation of Romano-British villas and Dewlish was not an exception to this norm. This is an oversight

Figure 21.12   The courtyard trench (F99 and G99) showing the gravelled surface (1979). Photograph: R 4040.

that needs to be addressed because logic dictates that buildings with high status embellishments, such as mosaic floors, would have equally impressive well designed and executed gardens. Future field research at Dewlish needs to rectify the neglect of the courtyard space informed by appropriate geophysical surveys and by applying the excavation techniques of garden archaeology as elucidated by Currie (2005).

WATER SUPPLY AND DELIVERY, INCLUDING PLUMBING AND ORNAMENTAL FEATURES

To date, the Dewlish villa complex has produced no incontrovertible evidence of water supply from wells. The two known pit-shafts were initially considered to be well-shafts, but this interpretation was quickly revised as excavation proceeded (Chapters 7 and 8). Furthermore, without an effective pumping mechanism, a well water supply could not be expected to meet the requirements of a sophisticated and well-used suite of baths (Hodge 1991, 261–72).

In Chapter 1, and again in Chapter 8, it has been reasoned that at Dewlish the water supply was derived from a remote spring at nearby Cheselbourne via an aqueduct that connected with the north-west elevation of the bath house, Building 4. The existence of the aqueduct and details of its course remain to be verified and this has to be an important future research objective (Hodge 1991, 72–125). If, as proposed, an aqueduct did supply the baths, then it follows that it would have served ablution facilities including latrines in the unexcavated building(s) of the north-east range. This would entail the construction of a channel or piping system across the courtyard from south-west to north-east, potentially providing a water source for an ornamental water feature within the courtyard itself, such as the example at the reconstructed villa at Borg in the German Bundesland Saarland (Birkenhagen 2011, 329–8 and fig. 8). At Halstock, Dorset, a network of gullies was excavated within the villa's courtyard and although its workings are not fully understood, it did include a pond or tank that could have served a number of purposes both ornamental and functional (Lucas 1993, 135 and fig. 53).

When considering matters pertinent to water supply, it is important to take account of the demands

Figure 21.13 Dewlish 1974. Lifting of the Room 25 mosaic panel. Photograph: R3085.

on this resource made by small scale industrial processes within the villa estate. The evidence of metallurgical equipment from the fills of pit-shafts O100 and P4 confirms that such activities were taking place at Dewlish although their scale and frequency are matters of conjecture. The Romano-British settlement that was attached to the villa at Gatcombe, Somerset, included a number of buildings that were interpreted as having an industrial function including a smithy, iron and pewter working, and milling. These activities were supplied with water from a nearby stream that also served to demarcate the working area from the villa buildings and gardens (Branigan 1977, 182–92, Fig. 33).

Within the curtilage of the Dewlish villa, and within 200m to the north-west of Building 3, a cluster of rectangular parch marks could be seen during the drought summer of 1976. The Boyden air photograph that is included as Figure 4.1 shows that most of these rectangular features lie within the supposed Iron Age or earlier enclosure that is cut by the modern road to Druce Farm. The parch marks within the enclosure might represent the footprints of buildings, the remains of a small villa-dependent community. Further fieldwork is needed to clarify the situation, but if small scale industrial processes are identified, then unlike Gatcombe, there is no nearby stream to satiate any demand for water. However, the air photograph also shows traces of a linear feature that crosses the pre-Roman enclosure from the road and continues south-eastwards to cut the villa's twin curtilage ditches *en route* to the Building 4 bath house (see above). This, it seems, is the course of the aqueduct from its source at Cheselbourne. If so, then it is ideally placed so as to allow a spur from the aqueduct watercourse to provide for the needs of the satellite community described above.

The potential for villa courtyard studies is underlined by the examples given above. These spaces should not be seen as being irrelevant to the task of decoding the development and function of the associated complex of buildings. At Dewlish the courtyard zone is largely undisturbed and merits inclusion in any future field research project at the site.

OPPORTUNITIES FOR REGIONAL AND INTERREGIONAL STUDIES

Beyond site specific questions and issues, the 1969–79 Dewlish excavations highlight a number of opportunities for wider study. Three of the most obvious of these topics are numerically listed below but not in an order of importance.

1 ***Dewlish aisled barn, Building 2/2A*** In the discussion of the known villa buildings above, it has been noted that Building 2 might be regarded as unusual for two reasons. In its initial manifestation, it was probably an amalgam of residential accommodation Rooms 31, 32 and 32a, and an agricultural zone that consisted of Rooms 33, 35 and 39. As Building 2, it might have been first conceived as a form of long house thus explaining the absence of an aisle. When the aisle and Rooms 34 and 36 to 38 were added as Building 2A, the accommodation role seems to have ceased and this space was subsumed by the processes of food production.

There has not been sufficient scope within the remit of this report to allow for a wide-ranging comparative disquisition on the origin and development of aisled buildings, but it is recommended that this would be a fruitful area of investigation from which local and regional patterns might emerge.

2 ***Non-adult human remains*** During the eleven seasons of the Putnam excavations, three deposits of non-adult human remains were recovered. These discoveries attracted little comment in the interim reports, but initially they were all regarded as being solitary individual interments. Specialist examination during the current post-excavation project determined that the total number of individuals was eight (1 + 2 +5). Philpott (1991, 97–102) has identified the association of Romano-British 'infant' burials with buildings, pointing out that such interments are more commonly found sealed beneath floors, or outside the building within the foundation trenches of the exterior walls. This was the case with the remains that were studied by Rohnbogner (Chapter 19, Part A) in which all three deposits were found beneath floors.

Subsequently, non-adult remains were identified from within a corpus of animal bones from pit-shaft P4 during the summer of 2019 and these were examined by Schutkowski and Lebarre (Chapter 19, Part B). A further six individuals were represented, and it is clear that these remains were subject to informal discard with other miscellaneous categories of household refuse. There are no grounds for regarding these as ritual deposits.

Deposits of non-adult remains have been recovered at a number of villa sites, but numbers vary considerably and there is a real danger that deposits have been overlooked by inexperienced excavators working on Romano-British villa and other rural sites over the years. There is certainly scope for retrospective research here and a regional project is suggested as being a manageable starting point.

In the description and analysis of the Dewlish small finds (Putnam *et al*, Chapter 17) the authors have indicated that there is an urgent need to understand the typology and distribution of bone (hair) pins on a regional basis as an alternative to the commonly used Essex-based typology of Crummy (1979 and 1983). A similar need could also be expressed for other categories of small finds including glass (Allen, Chapter 14) and worked stone (Hayward, Chapter 10). Such regional and inter-regional studies/typologies would be of considerable benefit to the authors of future Romano-British villa reports.

Pit-shafts, as described in this report, require detailed study that takes account of the distribution (within individual sites, local, regional and national), geological context, and consideration of primary, secondary and subsequent uses. Above, it has been argued that at Dewlish, pit-shafts were an integral of the building construction process. Elsewhere other purposes have been postulated such as the preference of the authors of the 'roman' settlement at Amesbury (Wiltshire) who incline towards a ritual purpose for these pits which in this case did not provide evidence of deliberate backfilling, waterlogging or cess disposal (Cooke *et al* in prep.). In reality pit-shaft features might have had a number of primary and secondary purposes, thus providing scope for detailed investigation.

COMPARATIVE VILLA SITES

This chapter has identified a number of discussion points that relate to Dewlish villa specifically and to the study of Romano-British villas in general. Where appropriate, comparative sites have been drawn into the debate on an individual basis. Arguably, this is a narrow and somewhat limited approach that inhibits understanding of how the subject villa site fits in relation to a larger sample with regard to factors such as location determinants, layout, size, economy, building types, status, infrastructure and social interaction. In a north European context, valuable work has been published on villa economy, culture and lifestyles by Roymans and Derks (2011), but in the case of Dewlish, there is no thorough regional study

from within which intra-site comparisons can be made. A future phase of the Dewlish research agenda needs to include its relationship to a comparative regional grouping. If this need is accepted, then the next issue that arises concerns the identification of the component members of an appropriate group of villas within which Dewlish can sit with justification.

The Durotriges

To advance this process, it is logical to take account of the wider topographical, cultural and chronological complexion of the Romano-British south west. Papworth has published a thesis that focuses upon the Pre-Roman Iron Age communities that inhabited Dorset and the adjacent margins of neighbouring counties which, he argues, formed the territory of the tribal grouping known as the Durotriges. Papworth refers to this composite area as the 'Durotrigian Zone' (2008, 22–32) and set about mapping its core and limits with reference to artefact and site type distribution plans. For this exercise, four indicators of Durotrigian culture were used: pottery, farmsteads, burials and coinage. The results indicate a Durotrigian Zone centred upon the modern entity of Dorset and including south Somerset but merging with the cultural remains of other tribes in the liminal lands of neighbouring counties (Papworth 2011, 50–60 and citing the work of Brailsford 1957).

The villas of the Durotrigian Zone

Dewlish lies within the Durotrigian Zone, as defined by Papworth, along with the nearby villa at Druce Farm. The economy of both villas was founded upon the produce from a network of fields that had been established by, and possibly before, the Pre-Roman Iron Age (Chapters 1 and 4). This suggests that in the case of these two villas at least, there is a link between the native tribal land holdings and those of the succeeding Romano-British villa owners/tenants. For this reason, a 'Durotrigian villa' map has been created based upon the spread of cultural indicators referred to above and based upon the detailed work of Papworth. This is not a new initiative; Bill Putnam devised and published a similar distribution map in the first edition of his popular book on Roman Dorset (1984, forepaper).

For the second edition (Putnam 2007, 94–6), the map was reproduced but supplemented by a list of villa sites in Dorset and Somerset accompanied by four-figure map references derived from Scott (1993), but these location details lack critical accuracy. This is indicative of the unsatisfactory state of regional villa studies in the south-west.

Revised villa distribution map

Figure 21.14 has been created for the Durotrigian Zone of the modern counties of Dorset and south Somerset, but it should be noted that the map represents work in progress. In compiling the map, the initial challenge was to populate it with the locations of known villa sites from an up-to-date and credible source. For this purpose, Historic England's online facility was used because it claims to provide 'a list of Roman villas in England confirmed by archaeology' (PastScape.org. uk). Formerly, this site had the potential for *ad hoc* updates but it is now under the banner of Heritage Gateway. The available data includes site names, map references and monument numbers, but it became apparent that coverage was no longer comprehensive or up to date making it necessary to adjust the original PastScape list in three respects.

1   Updates. Recently identified sites have been added such as the Dorset examples at Poyntington (Randall 2020, 171–81), Shillingstone (Corney and Robinson 2007, 110–7) and Winterbourne Kingston (Russell *et al* 2017, 157–61).

2   Historical inaccuracies. Historic England lists Farnham, Dorset, as a villa site providing an indicative four-figure map reference for the location. The original source is Hutchins (1868, 547) but the description is vague. Given its close proximity, the entry probably refers to the excavated but largely unpublished villa site at Myncen Farm which is represented on Figure 21.14 and listed in Appendix 3A. See also Leach 1966, 104–7 re Thornford. Other aberrations almost certainly exist.

3   On occasion, villa sites have been excavated and published in local journals but have not enjoyed wide recognition. A Dorset example is that of Bradford Down, Pamphill (Field 1983, 71–92). The site is not included in the Historic England Pastscape list but it has been added to the table in Appendix 3A of this publication.

The above items are indicative of the size of the problem: the regional villa landscape is not well-mapped, recorded or understood. Figure 21.14 represents a starting point for ongoing data-gathering and research. Refreshing the data that underpins the map is set to be an ongoing challenge.

Interpreting the villa distribution map

The villa locations numbered 1 to 10 are those sites that are most frequently referred to in this chapter. The Romano-British tribal zone of the Durotriges had two *civitas* centres, Dorchester (*Durnovaria*) and Ilchester (*Lindinis*) (Papworth 2008, 27–8) and the location of these is identified by square-symbols. Bill Putnam (2007, 94–6) suggested that each of the Durotrigian *civitas* towns provided a fulcrum around which villa sites clustered. Reference to Figure 21.14 reinforces this impression with regard to Ilchester but known villa sites close to Dorchester are restricted to a five-strong east/west linear arrangement to the north of the town, one of these (Site 1) being Druce Farm on the River Piddle. The map shows that like Druce, villa sites tend to be close to rivers and their tributaries, predominantly at the point of interface between lowland and higher ground, suggesting that the *civitas* cluster hypothesis might be a fanciful notion. Although not apparent on the map, Dewlish also conforms to the watercourse/source association, the villa being sandwiched between two streams that are too diminutive to be conspicuous on a map of this scale. In Chapters 1 and 8 it has been argued that the Dewlish villa was also serviced by an aqueduct from a spring source at Cheselbourne. Undoubtedly, the presence of markets at the *civitas* centres of Dorchester and Ilchester were important locational factors, but access to prime agricultural land and a water supply would have been imperatives.

The archaeological evidence from Dewlish has its limitations, but even the imperfections play a part in identifying the categories of data that need to be added to the mix if Romano-British villas are to be better understood. There is a need for a database that would include as a working minimum:

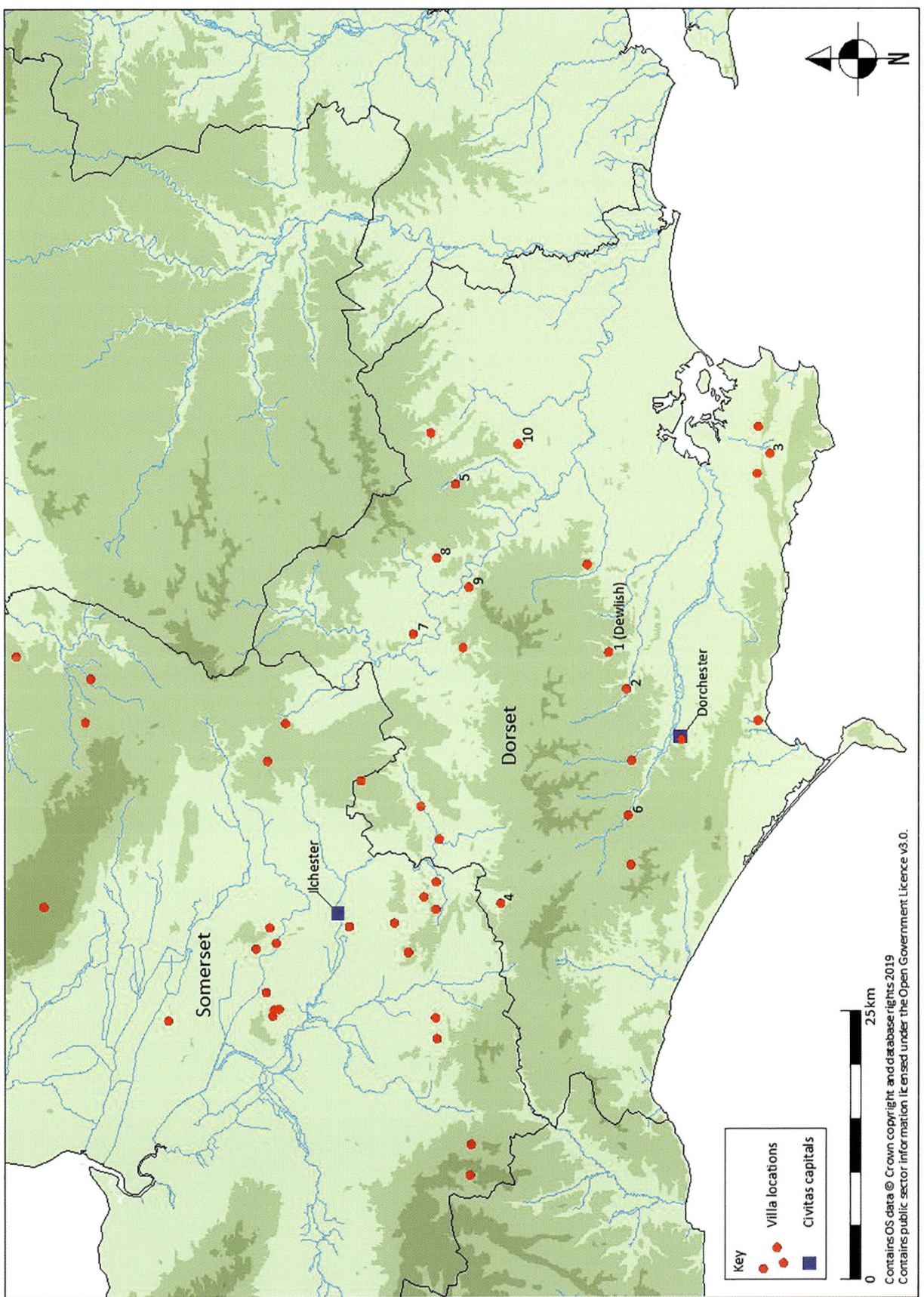

Figure 21.14   Villa distribution map for the Durotrigian Zone. See Appendix 3A for key to sites numbered 1 to 10. Drawing: Jonathan Milward.

1   The relationship between villas, Romano-Celtic field systems and other available economic resources. Sustainability is the key issue here.

2   Identification of associated route networks by water and overland roads/tracks. This could include Roman roads but not at the expense of traditional pathways through the villa landscape.

3   A classification system that coherently distinguishes other forms of Romano-British rural settlement from villas, and which maps progression from the embryonic forms of the class such as Park Farm/ Iwerne, through to the high status complexes of which Dewlish is an example.

End note

The task of resurrecting the Dewlish project for publication has revealed that the villa was more complex and thought-provoking than at first imagined. Some new insights into the origin and development of the site have been forthcoming, but it is certainly the case that the past fifty plus years of the Dewlish story is just the beginning. This volume represents the legacy of Bill Putnam. It is a bequest that should be regarded as a worthy inheritance by future researchers and archaeologists.

REFERENCES

Adams, A. E. and MacKenzie, W. E. 1998. *A Colour Atlas of Carbonate Sediments and Rocks under the Microscope*. London, Manson.

Albarella, U. 2005. 'Alternate fortunes? The role of domestic ducks and geese from Roman to Medieval times in Britain.' In G. Grupe and J. Peters (eds.), *Feathers, grit and symbolism: birds and humans in the ancient old and new worlds*. Verlag Marie Leidorf, Rahden, 249–258.

Allen, D.A. 2002. 'Roman Window Glass.' In M. Aldhouse-Green and P. Webster (eds.), *Artefacts and Archaeology, aspects of the Celtic and Roman World*. Cardiff, University of Wales, 102–111.

Allen, M., Blick, N., Brindle, T., Evans, T., Fulford, M., Holbrook, N., Lodwick, L., Richards, J.D. and Smith, A. 2018. *The rural settlement of Roman Britain: an online resource* [data-set]. York, Archaeology Data Service, https://doi.org/10.5284/1030449.

Allen, M., Lodwick, L., Brindle, T., Fulford, M. and Smith, A. 2017. *The Rural economy of Roman Britain: new visions of the countryside of Roman Britain Volume 2*. Oxford, Oxbow.

Allen, J.R.L. 2014. *Whetstones from Roman Silchester (Calleva Atrebatum), North Hampshire, character, manufacture, provenance and use; Putting an Edge on It*. British Archaeological Reports **597**. Oxford, Archaeopress.

ApSimon, A.M. 1965. 'The Roman Temple on Brean Down, Somerset.' *Proceedings of the University of Bristol Spelaeological Society* **10** (3), 195–258.

Arkell, W.J. 1947. 'The geology of the country around Weymouth, Swanage, Corfe and Lulworth.' *Memoir of the Geological Survey of Great Britain*. Sheets 341, 342, 343 and parts of 327, 328 and 329 (England and Wales). London, Her Majesty's Stationery Office.

Asouti, E. 2006. 'Factors affecting the formation of an archaeological wood charcoal assemblage.' http://pcwww.liv.ac.uk/~easouti/methodology_application.htm [Accessed 13 February 2015].

Austin, D. 1985. 'Dartmoor and the Upland Village of the South-West.' In D. Hooke *Medieval Villages: a review of current work*. Oxford University Committee for Archaeology Monograph **5**, 71–9.

Barnes, I. 1997. 'Fordington Bottom: Site Description.' In R.J.C. Smith, F. Healy, M.J. Allen, E.L. Morris, I. Barnes and P.J. Woodward, *Excavations Along the Route of the Dorchester By-pass, Dorset, 1986-8*. Salisbury, Wessex Archaeology, 203–23.

Barton, C.M., Woods, M.A., Bristow, C.R., Newell, A.J., Westhead, R.K., Evans, D.J., Kirby, G.A., Warrington, G., Riding, J.B., Freshney, E.C., Highley, D.E., Lott, G.K. and Gibson, A. 2011. 'Geology of south Dorset and south-east Devon and its World Heritage Coast.' *Special Memoir of the British Geological Survey*. Sheets 328, 341/342, 342/343 and parts of 326/340, 327, 329 and 330 (England and Wales).

Beavis, J. 1974. 'Interim report on excavations at Warren Hill, Dewlish, 1972.' *Proceedings of the Dorset Natural History and Archaeological Society* **95**, 88–9.

Beavis, J. and Hunt, A. (eds.) 1999. 'Bill Putnam: an appreciation.' In J. Beavis and A. Hunt, *Communicating Archaeology: papers presented to Bill Putnam at a conference held at Bournemouth University in September 1995*. Bournemouth University School of Conservation Sciences, Oxford, Oxbow Occasional Paper **4**, 1–10.

Bellamy, P. 1993. 'The Building Materials and Architectural Fragments'. In R.N. Lucas, *The Romano-British villa at Halstock, Dorset: Excavations 1967-1985*. Dorset Natural History and Archaeological Society Monograph **13**, 107–111.

Beresford, G. 1979. 'Three Deserted Medieval Settlements on Dartmoor: A report on the Late E. Marie Minter's Excavations.' *Medieval Archaeology* **23**, 98–159.

Beresford, G. 1988. 'The Deserted Medieval Settlements on Dartmoor. A Comment on David Austin's Re-interpretations.' *Medieval Archaeology* **32**, 175–83.

Bird, J. and Young, C. 1981. 'Migrant Potters – the Oxford Connection.' In A.C. Anderson and A.S. Anderson (eds.), *Roman Pottery research in Britain and North-West Europe. Papers presented to Graham Webster.* Oxford, British Archaeological Reports (International Series) **123**, 295–312.

Birkenhagen, B. 2011. 'The Roman Villa at Borg. Excavation and Reconstruction.' In N. Roymans and T. Derks (eds), *Villa Landscapes in the Roman North. Economy and Lifestyles.* Amsterdam Archaeological Studies **17**, Amsterdam, University Press, 317–330.

Blagg, T.F.C. 1976. 'Tools and techniques of the Roman stonemason in Britain.' *Britannia* **7**, 152–72.

Blagg, T.F.C. 1977. 'Schools of stonemasons in Roman Britain.' In J. Munby and M. Henig (eds.), *Roman Life and Art in Britain.* Oxford. British Archaeological Reports **41**, 51–70.

Blagg, T.F.C. 2002. *Roman Architectural Ornament in Britain.* Oxford, British Archaeological Reports (British Series) **329**.

Boardman, S. and Jones, G. 1990. 'Experiments on the Effect of Charring on Cereal plant Components.' *Journal of Archaeological Science* **17**, 1–11.

Bonsall L. 2013. 'Infanticide in Roman Britain: a critical review of the osteological evidence'. *Childhood in the Past* **6** (2), 73–88.

Boon, G.C. 1973. '*Serapsis* and *Tutela*. A Silchester co-incidence.' *Britannia* **4**, 107–114.

Boon, G.C. 1974. *Silchester: the Roman Town of Calleva.* Newton Abbott, David and Charles.

Bowden, W., Emery, G., Jackson, I., Keeley, R. and Pinner, M. 2020. 'New discoveries at the extra-mural temple at *Venta Icenorum*.' *Association for Roman Archaeology News* **44**, 24–27.

Bradley, T. and Butler, J. 2008. *From Temples to Thames Street 2000 years of Riverside Development: Archaeological Excavations at the Salvation Army Headquarters, 99-101 Queen Victoria Street, City of London.* London, Pre-Construct Archaeology Monograph **7**.

Brailsford, J. 1958. 'Early Iron Age C in Wessex.' *Proceedings of the Prehistoric Society* **24**, 101–119.

Branigan, K. 1977. *Gatcombe Roman villa.* Oxford. British Archaeological Reports (British Series) **44.**

Brickley, M. and Ives, R. 2006. 'Skeletal manifestations of infantile scurvy.' *American Journal of Physical Anthropology* **129**, 163–172.

Brickley, M. and McKinley, J. 2004. *Guidelines to the Standards for Recording Human Remains.* Institute of Field Archaeologists Paper **7**, Southampton, British Association for Biological Anthropology and Osteoarchaeology.

British Geological Survey, 1981. *Dorchester. England and Wales. Sheet 328. Drift Geology. 1:50 000.* Keyworth, British Geological Survey.

British Geological Survey, 2000. *Swanage. England and Wales Sheets 342 (east) and 343. Solid and Drift Geology. 1:50 000.* Keyworth, British Geological Survey.

British Geological Survey, 2000. *West Fleet and Weymouth. England and Wales Sheet 341 and part of 342. Solid and Drift Geology. 1:50 000.* Keyworth, British Geological Survey.

Brown, L. 1987. 'The late Prehistoric Pottery.' In B. Cunliffe, *Hengistbury Head, Dorset, Volume 1: the prehistoric and Roman settlement, 3500 BC – AD 500.* Oxford University Committee for Archaeology Monograph **13**, 207–266.

Brown, L. 1991. 'Later Prehistoric Pottery.' In N.M. Sharples, *Maiden Castle, excavations and field survey 1985-6.* English Heritage Archaeological Report **19**, 185–205.

Buckland-Wright, J.C. 1987. 'The animal bones.' In C.S. Green, *Excavations at Poundbury 1966-1982, volume I: the settlements.* Dorset Natural History and Archaeological Society Monograph **7**, 129–132.

Bull, G. and Payne, S. 1982. 'Tooth eruption and epiphysial fusion in pigs and wild boar.' In B. Wilson, C. Grigson, and S. Payne, (eds.), *Ageing and sexing animal bones from archaeological sites.* Oxford. British Archaeological Reports (British series) **109**, 55–72.

Bullock, A. and Allen, M. 1997. 'Animal bones.' In R. Smith, F. Healy, M. Allen, E. Morris, I. Barnes, and P. Woodward, *Excavations along the route of the Dorchester by-pass, Dorset, 1986-8.* Salisbury, Wessex Archaeology Monograph **11**, 191–193.

Calkin, J.B. 1954. 'Kimmeridge Coal Money', the Romano-British Shale Armlet Industry. *Proceedings of the Dorset Natural History and Archaeological Society* **75**, 45–7.

Campbell, G., Moffett, L. and Straker, V. 2011. *Environmental Archaeology. A Guide to the Theory and Practice of Methods, from Sampling and Recovery to Post-excavation (second edition).* Portsmouth, English Heritage.

Carruthers, W. 2011. 'Charred Plant Remains.' In R. Helm and W. Carruthers, 'Early Roman Evidence for Intensive Cultivation and Malting of Spelt Wheat at Nonington.' *Archaeologica Cantiana* **131**, 353 –372.

Charlier, P. 2012. 'Toilet hygiene in the classical era.' *British Medical Journal* **2012**, 345: e8287.

Clark, K. 1995. 'The later prehistoric and protohistoric dog: the emergence of canine diversity.' *Archaeozoologia* **7**, 9–32.

Collingwood, R.G. and Richmond, I. 1969. *The Archaeology of Roman Britain.* London, Methuen.

Committee on Higher Education 1963. *Higher Education Report.* London, Her Majesty's Stationery Office.

Cooke, N. 2007. 'A late Roman coin hoard from the County Hospital site, Dorchester.' *Proceedings of the Dorset Natural History and Archaeological Society* **128**, 17–52.

Cooke, N., McKinley, J.I., and Seager Smith, R.H. (in prep.) *A Roman Settlement to the South-east of Amesbury and its Cemeteries.* Unpublished, Wessex Archaeology.

Cool, H.E.M. 2006. *Eating and Drinking in Roman Britain.* Cambridge, University Press.

Corney, M. 2003a. *The Roman villa at Bradford on Avon. The Investigations of 2002.* Bradford on Avon, Ex Libris.

Corney, M. 2003b. *The Roman Villa at Bradford on Avon. The investigations of 2003.* Bradford on Avon, Ex Libris.

Corney, M. and Robinson, S. 2007. 'Shillingstone:

Roman Villa (ST 8295 1065). Summary account and interpretation.' *Proceedings of the Dorset Natural History and Archaeological Society* **128**, 110–117.

Corney, M. 2012. *The Romano- British Villa at Box, Wiltshire: a reappraisal and assessment 0f the archaeological evidence.* Box Archaeological and Natural History Society.

Cosh, S.R. 2000. 'A new look at the mosaic in Room 11, Dewlish, Dorset.' *Mosaic* **27**, 12–14.

Cosh, S.R. 2001. 'Seasonal dining-rooms in Romano-British houses', *Britannia* **32**, 219–42.

Cosh, S.R. and Neal, D.S. 2005. *Roman Mosaics of Britain, Vol II The South-West.* London, Society of Antiquaries.

Cosh, S.R. and Neal, D.S. 2010. *Roman Mosaics of Britain, Vol IV Western Britain.* London, Society of Antiquaries.

Crummy, N. 1979. 'A Chronology of Roman-British Bone Pins.' *Britannia* **10**, 157–63.

Crummy, N. 1983. 'The Roman Small Finds from Excavations in Colchester 1971–79'. *Colchester Archaeological Report* **2**. Colchester, Colchester Archaeological Trust.

Cunliffe, B.W. 1967. 'Excavations at Gatcombe, Somerset, in 1965 and 1966.' *Proceedings of the University of Bristol Spelaeological Society* **11** (2), 126–60.

Cunliffe, B.W. 1987. *Hengistbury Head, Dorset vol 1. The Prehistoric and Roman Settlement, 3500 BC–AD 500.* Oxford. Oxford University Committee for Archaeology Monograph **13**.

Cunliffe, B.W. and Fulford, M.G. 1982. *Corpus Signorum Imperii Romani, Great Britain 1. 2 Bath and the Rest of Wessex.* Oxford, Oxford University Press.

Currie, C. 2005. *Garden Archaeology.* Practical Handbook **17**, York Council for British Archaeology.

Darke, K. and Darke, P. 1997. *The Landscape of Roman Britain.* Stroud, Sutton.

Davey, N. and Ling, R. 1981. *Wall Painting in Roman Britain.* Britannia Monograph Series no. **3**.

Davies, S.M. and Hawkes, J.W. 1987. 'The Iron Age and Romano-British coarse pottery.' In C.J.S. Green, *Excavations at Poundbury Vol. I: The Settlements.* Dorset Natural History and Archaeological Society Monograph **7**, 123–127

Demirjian, A. Goldstein, H. and Tanner, J.M. 1972. 'A new system of dental age assessment.' *Human Biology* **45**(2), 211–227.

Dicks, J. 2007. 'Villas in East Hampshire and West Sussex: a study of their Roman pottery assemblages and settlement pattern.' *Hampshire Studies* **62**, 69–82.

Down, A. 1979. *The Roman Villas at Chilgrove and Upmarden.* Chichester Excavations vol. **4**, Chichester, Phillimore.

Draper, J. 2006. 'The Romano-British Pottery.' In A. Graham, *The Excavation of Five Beaker Burials, the Iron Age and Romano-British Settlements and the 4th Century Courtyard Villa at Barton Field, Tarrant Hinton, Dorset, 1968-1984.* Dorset Natural History and Archaeological Society Monograph **17**, 84–86.

Drew, C. and Collingwood Selby, K. 1937. 'Colliton Park, Roman Town House.' *Proceedings of the Dorset Natural History and Archaeological Society* **59**, 1–14.

Drew, C. and Collingwood Selby, K. 1938. 'Colliton Park, Roman Town House.' *Proceedings of the Dorset Natural History and Archaeological Society* **60**, 51–65.

von den Driesch, A. 1976. *A guide to the measurement of animal bones from archaeological sites.* Harvard, Peabody Museum Monograph **1**.

Dunham, R. J. 1962. 'Classification of carbonate rocks according to depositional texture.' In W.E. Ham, (ed.) 'Classification of carbonate rocks.' *American Association of Petroleum Geologists, Memoir* **1**, 108–121.

Ellis, S.P. 1995. 'Classical reception rooms in Romano-British houses.' *Britannia* **26**, 163–78.

English Heritage, 2011. *Environmental Archaeology: A Guide to the Theory and Practice of Methods, from Sampling and Recovery to Post-excavation.* Second edition, London, English Heritage.

Esmonde Cleary, A.S. 1989. *The Ending of Roman Britain.* London, Batsford.

Esmonde Cleary, A.S. 2000. 'Putting the dead in their place: burial location in Roman Britain.' In J. Pearce, M. Millett and M. Struck (eds.), *Burial, Society and Context in the Roman World.* Oxford, Oxbow, 127–129.

Everton, R.F. 1982. 'The human bone.' In R. Leech, *Excavations at Catsgore 1970-1973 – A Romano-British Village.* Taunton, Western Archaeological Trust Excavation Monograph **2**, 147–148.

Everton, R.F. and Leech, R.H. 1981 'The burials.' In R. Leech, E.M. Besly and R.F. Everton, 'The excavation of a Romano-British farmstead and cemetery on Bradley Hill, Somerton, Somerset.' *Britannia* **12**, 195–205.

Evin, A., Cucchi, T., Cardini, A., Vidardottir, U.S., Larson, G. and Dobney, K. 2014. 'The long and ham winding road: identifying pig domestication through molar size and shape.' *Journal of Archaeological Science* **40**, 735–743.

Faerman, M., Bar-Gal, G.K., Filon, D., Greenblatt, C.L., Stager, L., Oppenheim, A. and Smith, P. 1998. 'Determining the sex of infanticide victims from the Late Roman era through ancient DNA analysis.' *Journal of Archaeological Science* **25**, 861–865.

Farrah, R.A.H. 1953. 'Doles Hill Field System.' *Proceedings of the Dorset Natural History and Archaeological Society* **74**, 88–9.

Farwell, D.E. and Molleson, T.I. 1993. *Excavations at Poundbury, 1966-82. Volume II: The Cemeteries.* Dorset Natural History and Archaeological Society Monograph **11**.

Farrar, R.A.H. 1973. 'The techniques and sources of Romano-British Black Burnished Ware.' In A.P. Detsicas (ed.), *Current Research in Romano-British coarse pottery,* Council of British Archaeology Report **10**, 67–103.

Farrar, R.A.H. 1977. 'A Romano-British black-burnished ware industry at Ower in the Isle of Purbeck, Dorset.' In J. Dore and K. Greene (eds.), *Roman Pottery Studies in Britain and Beyond.* Oxford, British Archaeological Reports (Sub-Series) **30**, 199–228.

Fazekas, I.G. and Kosa, F. 1978. *Forensic Fetal Osteology.* Budapest. Akademiai Kiado.

Field, N.H. 1966. 'Romano-British Settlement at Studland, Dorset. Final Report on the Excavation, 1952–58.' *Proceedings of the Dorset Natural History and Archaeological Society* **87**, 142–207.

Field, N.H. 1983. 'The Iron Age and Romano-British Settlement on Bradford Down, Pamphill, Dorset.' *Proceedings of the Dorset Natural History and Archaeological Society* **104**, 71–92.

Finnegan, M. 1978. 'Nonmetric variation of the infracranial skeleton.' *Journal of Anatomy* **125**, 23–37.

Folk, R.L. 1959. 'Practical petrographic classification of limestones.' *American Association of Petroleum Geologists Bulletin*, **43**: 1–38.

Folk, R.L. 1962. 'Spectral subdivision of limestone types.' In W.E. Ham (ed.), 'Classification of carbonate rocks.' *American Association of Petroleum Geologists, Memoir* **1**, 62–84.

Fulford, M. 1975a. *New Forest Roman Pottery*, British Archaeological Reports (British Series) **17**.

Fulford, M. 1975b. 'The Pottery.' In B. Cunliffe, *Excavations at Porchester Castle, Volume 1*. Report of the Research Committee, Society of Antiquaries (London), **32**, 270–367.

Fulford, M.G. and Timby, J. 2001. 'Ritual Piercings? A consideration of deliberately 'holed' pots from Silchester and elsewhere.' *Britannia* **32**, 293–297.

Gale, A. 2013. 'The building stones and their sources.' In B. Cunliffe, *The Roman Villa at Brading, Isle of Wight: The Excavations of 2008-10*. Oxford University School of Archaeology Monograph **77**, 137–139.

Gerrard, J. 2010. 'Finding the Fifth Century: A Late Fourth- and Early Fifth-Century Pottery Fabric from South-east Dorset.' *Britannia* **41**, 293–312.

Gerrard, J. 2010. 'Cathedral or Granary? The Roman coins from Colchester House, City of London (PEP89)'. *Transactions of the London and Middlesex Archaeological Society* **61**, 81–8.

Gillam, J.P. 1976. 'Coarse fumed ware in northern Britain and beyond.' *Glasgow Archaeological Journal* **4**, 58–80.

von Gonzenbach, V. 1961. *Dei Römischen mosaiken der Schweiz*. Monographien zur Ur-und Frühge schichte der Schweiz vol. **13**, Basle.

Goodburn, R. (ed.) 1976. I: Sites Explored. *Britannia* **7**, 361.

Gowland, R.L. and Chamberlain, A.T. 2002. 'A Bayesian approach to ageing perinatal skeletal material from archaeological sites: implications for the evidence for infanticide in Roman Britain.' *Journal of Archaeological Science* **29**, 677–685.

Gowland, R., Chamberlain, A. and Redfern, R.C. 2014. 'On the brink of being: re-evaluating infanticide and infant burial in Roman Britain.' In M. Carroll and E. Graham (eds.), *Infant Health and Death in Roman Italy and Beyond*. Journal of Roman Archaeology Supplementary Series **96**, 69–88.

Graham, A. 2006. *Barton Field, Tarrant Hinton, Dorset. Excavations 1968-1984*. Dorset Natural History and Archaeological Society Monograph **17**.

Grant, A. 1982. 'The use of toothwear as a guide to the age of domestic ungulates.' In B. Wilson, C. Grigson, and S. Payne (eds.), *Ageing and sexing animal bones from archaeological sites*. Oxford, British Archaeological Reports (British series) **109**, 91–108.

Gray, H. St George, 1947. 'The Excavations at Iwerne, 1897.' In C.F.C. Hawkes with S. Piggott and H. St George Gray. 'Britons, Romans and Saxons round Salisbury and Cranborne Chase. Reviewing the Excavations of General Pitt-Rivers, 1881–1897.' *Archaeological Journal* **104**, 50–62.

Green, C. 2017. 'Querns and Millstones in Late Iron Age and Roman London and South-East England.' In D. Bird (ed.) *Agriculture and Industry in south-eastern Roman Britain*. Oxford, Oxbow, 156–179.

Greene, J.P. 1994. Excavations at Dorchester Hospital (Site C), Dorchester, Dorset. *Proceedings of the Dorset Natural History and Archaeological Society* **115**, 71–100.

Grimm, J. 2008. 'Animal bone. Additional specialist report.' In M. Trevarthen, *Suburban life in Roman Durnovaria: excavations in the former County Hospital site, Dorchester, 2000-2001*. Salisbury, Wessex Archaeology. http://www.wessexarch.co.uk/files/projects/dorchester_county_hospital/07_Animal_bone.pdf

Guido, M. 1978. *The Glass Beads of the Prehistoric and Roman periods in Britain and Ireland*. London. Society of Antiquaries and Thames and Hudson.

Hackman, G. 2014. *Stone to Build London: Portland's Legacy*. Folly Books, Monkton Farleigh.

Ham, W.E. (ed.) 1962. 'Classification of carbonate rocks.' *American Association of Petroleum Geologists, Memoir* **1**.

Hamilton-Dyer, S. 1993. 'The animal bones.' In R. Smith, *Excavations at County Hall, Colliton Park, Dorchester, Dorset, 1988 in the north-west quarter of Durnovaria*. Salisbury, Wessex Archaeology Report **4**, 77–82.

Hamilton-Dyer, S. 1999. 'Animal bones.' In C. Hearne and V. Birbeck, *A35 Tolpuddle to Puddletown bypass DBFO, Dorset, 1996-8*. Salisbury, Wessex Archaeological Report **15**, 188–202.

Hanf, M. 1983. *Weeds and their Seedlings*. Ipswich, BASF United Kingdom Limited.

Hammerson, M. 2014. 'Roman Coins'. In M. Papworth, 'The Romano-Celtic Temple at Badbury Rings, Dorset'. *Proceedings of the Dorset Natural History and Archaeological Society* **135,** 264–67.

Harcourt, R.A. 1974. 'The dog in prehistoric and early historic Britain.' *Journal of Archaeological Science* **1**, 151–175.

Harris, E. 1989 *Principles of archaeological stratigraphy*. Second Edition, London, Academic Press.

Harris, W. V. 1994. 'Child-exposure in the Roman Empire.' *The Journal of Roman Studies* **84**, 1–22.

Hayward, K.M.J. 2008. *Amesbury Sarcophagus: The Stone*. Unpublished, Wessex Archaeology stone report.

Hayward, K.M.J. 2009. *Roman Quarrying and Stone Supply on the periphery - southern England. A geological study of first century funerary monuments and monumental architecture.*

Oxford, British Archaeological Reports (British Series) **500**.

Hayward, K.M.J. 2010. *The worked stone. Shapwick.* Unpublished report for the National Trust.

Hayward, K.M.J. 2013. 'The Stone Roofing Material.' In B. Cunliffe, *The Roman Villa at Brading, Isle of Wight: The Excavations of 2008–10.* Oxford University School of Archaeology Monograph **77**, 139–143.

Hayward, K.M.J. 2015. 'Types and sources of stone.' In P.C. Coombe, F. Grew, K.M.J. Hayward and M. Henig, *Corpus Signorum Imperii Romani. Great Britain 1.10 Roman Sculpture from London and the South-East.* Oxford, University Press.

Hayward, K.M.J. 2016. *Assessment of the stone from Bridgewalk Villa.* Unpublished, Historic England.

Hayward, K.M.J. 2017. *Assessment of the stone from Teffont Evias.* Unpublished, Historic England.

Hayward, K.M.J. 2017. *Assessment of the stone from Tisbury Villa.* Unpublished, Historic England.

Hayward, K.M.J. 2018. *Assessment of the stone from Lufton Villa, Somerset.'* Unpublished, Pre-Construct Archaeology Ltd on behalf of Newcastle University.

Hayward, K.M.J. in prep. *Assessment of the stone from Dinnington Roman Villa.* Unpublished, Pre-Construct Archaeology Ltd for Winchester University.

Hebermehl, D. 2011. 'Exploring villa development in northern provinces of the Roman Empire.' In N. Roymans and T. Derks, *Villa landscapes in the Roman north, economy, culture and lifestyles.* Amsterdam, University Press.

Henig, M. 1984. 'James Engleheart's drawing of a mosaic at Frampton, 1794.' *Proceedings of the Dorset Natural History and Archaeological Society* **106**, 143–6.

Henig, M. 1993. *Corpus Signorum Imperii Romani. Great Britain 1. 7 Roman Sculpture from the Cotswold Region, with Devon and Cornwall.* Oxford, University Press.

Henig, M. 2006.'Neither Baths nor Baptisteries.' *Oxford Journal of Archaeology* **25**, 105–7.

Henig. M. 2013. 'The Mosaic Pavements and their Meaning and Social Context'. In Barry Cunliffe 2013. *The Roman villa at Brading, Isle of Wight: the Excavations of 2008–10.* Oxford University School of Archaeology, Monograph **77**.

Hewitt, I. 2014. 'Dewlish Roman villa: post-excavation report 2013.' *Proceedings of the Dorset Natural History and Archaeological Society* **135**, 203–4.

Hewitt, I. and Cammegh, T. 2015. 'Dewlish Roman Villa, Dorset.' *Association for Roman Archaeology News* **35**, 3–5.

Hillman, G. 1981. 'Reconstructing Crop Husbandry Practices from Charred Remains of Crops.' In R. Mercer (ed.), *Farming Practice in Prehistory.* Edinburgh University Press, Edinburgh, 123–192.

Hillman, G. 1982. 'Evidence for spelting malt,' In R. Leech (ed.), *Excavations at Catsgore 1970-73. A Romano-British Village.* Bristol, Western Archaeological Trust Excavation Monograph **2**, 137–41.

Historic England 2021, *PastScape.org.uk. A list of Roman villas in England confirmed by archaeology.* Available from: https://en.wikipedia.org/wiki/List_of_Roman_villas_in_England. NB. Now Heritage Gateway (19.1.2021).

Hodge, A.T. 1995. *Roman Aqueducts and Water Supply.* London, Duckworth.

Holbrook, N. and Bidwell, P.T. 1991. *Roman Finds from Exeter.* Exeter Archaeological Reports **4**.

Holmes, M. 2018. 'King of the birds! The changing role of white-tailed (*Haliaeetus albicilla*) and golden eagles (*Aquila chrysaetos*) in Britain's past.' *Archaeofauna* **27**, 173–194.

Hull, M.R. 1955. 'The south wing of the Roman forum at Colchester.' *Transactions of the Essex Archaeological Society* **25**, 24–61.

Hutchins, J. 1863. *The History and Antiquities of the County of Dorset*, Volume 2. London, Beyer Nichols.

Hunt, A. and Peers, R. 2010. 'Bill Putnam (1930–2008).' *Proceedings of the Dorset Natural History and Archaeological Society* **131**, 239–40.

Johnston, D.E. 1988. *Roman Villas.* Princes Risborough, Shire.

Johnston, D.E. 1994. 'Some possible North African influences in Romano-British mosaics.' In P. Johnson, R. Ling and D.J. Smith (eds), *Fifth International Colloquium on Ancient Mosaics* **1**, 295–306.

Johnston, D.E. 1995. 'Recreating Roman Buildings.' *Current Archaeology* **143**, 426–32.

Johnston, D.E. and Dicks, J. 2014. *Sparsholt Roman Villa, Hampshire, excavations by David E. Johnston.* Hampshire Field Club Monograph **11**.

Joint Standing Committee on the New Translation of the Bible, 1961. *The New English Bible.* Oxford and Cambridge, Oxford University Press and Cambridge University Press.

Jones, G. 1981. 'Crop Processing at Assiros Toumba- a Taphonomic Study.' *Zeitschift für Archäologie.* **15**, 105–111.

Jones, G. 1996. 'An ethnographical investigation of the effects of cereal grain sieving.' In *Circaea, The Journal of the Association for Environmental Archaeology* **12** (2), 177–182.

Jones, G. 2006. 'Tooth eruption and wear observed in live sheep from Butser Hill, the Cotswold Wildlife Park and five farms in the Pentland Hills, UK.' In D. Ruscillo, (ed.), *Recent advances in ageing and sexing animal bones.* Oxford, Oxbow, 155–178.

Jones, G. and Saddler. P. 2012. 'Age at death in cattle: methods, older cattle and known-age reference material.' *Environmental Archaeology* **17**, 11–28.

Jones, G.P. 2011. 'Romano-British Pottery.' In A.B. Powell, *An Iron Age Enclosure and Romano-British Features at High Post, near Salisbury.* Salisbury, Wessex Archaeology Monograph, 57–62.

Jones M. 1981. 'The Development of Crop husbandry.' In M. Jones, and G. Dimbleby, (eds), *The Environment of Man - From the Iron Age to the Anglo-Saxon Period.* British Archaeological Reports (British Series) **87**, 95–127.

Jope, E.M. 1964. 'The Saxon building-stone industry in Southern and Midland England.' *Medieval Archaeology* **8**, 91–118.

Keen, L. 1978. 'Dorset Archaeology in 1976. Dewlish.' *Proceedings of the Dorset Natural History and Archaeological Society* **98**, 54–5.

Keen, L. 1980a. 'Dorset Archaeology in 1977. Dewlish.' *Proceedings of the Dorset Natural History and Archaeological Society* **99**, 120.

Keen, L. 1980b. 'Dorset Archaeology in 1978. Dewlish.' *Proceedings of the Dorset Natural History and Archaeological Society* **100,** 113–14.

King, A. 1984. 'Animal bones and the dietary identity of military and civilian groups in Roman Britain, Germany and Gaul.' In T. Blagg and A. King, (eds.), *Military and civilian in Roman Britain: cultural relationships in a frontier province.* Oxford, British Archaeological Reports (British Series) **136**, 187–218.

King, A. 1999. 'Diet in the Roman world: a regional inter-site comparison of the animal bones.' *Journal of Roman studies* **12**, 168–202.

Kwon D.S., Spevak, M.R., Fletcher, K. and Kleinman, P.K. 2002. 'Physiologic subperiosteal new bone formation: prevalence, distribution, and thickness in neonates and infants.' *American Journal of Roentgenology* **179**, 985–988.

Ladle, L. 2012. *Excavations at Bestwall Quarry, Wareham 1992-2005 Volume 2: The Iron Age and Later Landscape.* Dorset Natural History and Archaeological Society Monograph **20**.

Ladle, L. and Morgan, A. 2017. 'Interim Report on Druce Farm Roman villa, Puddletown (SY 7330 9540).' *Proceedings of the Dorset Natural History and Archaeological Society* **138**, 146–8.

Leach, J. 1966. 'Interim report on excavations at Thornford, Dorset.' *Proceedings of the Dorset Natural History and Archaeological Society* **87**, 104–7.

Leary, E. 1989. *The Building Limestones of the British Isles.* Building Research Establishment Report. London, Her Majesty's Stationery Office.

Legg, R. 1990. *Literary Dorset.* Wincanton, Dorset Publishing.

Legg, R. 2002. *Dorset Families.* Tiverton, Dorset Books.

Levine, M. 1982. 'The use of crown height measurements and eruption-wear sequences to age horse teeth.' In B. Wilson, C. Grigson, and S. Payne, (eds.), *Ageing and sexing animal bones from archaeological sites.* Oxford, British Archaeological Reports (British Series) **109**, 223–250.

Lewis, M.E. 2007. *The Bioarchaeology of Children.* Cambridge, Cambridge University Press.

Lewis, M.E. and Gowland, R. 2007. 'Brief and precarious lives: infant mortality in contrasting sites from medieval and post-medieval England (AD 850-1859).' *American Journal of Physical Anthropology* **134** (1), 117–129.

Light, T. and Ellis P. 2009. *Bucknowle, a Romano-British villa and its antecedents: excavations 1976-1991.* Dorset Natural History and Archaeological Society Monograph **18**.

Light, T. 2009. 'The Pottery.' in T. Light and P. Ellis, *Bucknowle, A Romano-British Villa and its antecedents:*

Excavations 1976-1991, Dorset Natural History and Archaeological Society Monograph **18**, 127–8.

Ling, R. 1997. 'Mosaics in Roman Britain: discoveries and research since 1945.' *Britannia* **28**, 259–95.

Lucas, R.N. 1993. *The Romano-British villa at Halstock, Dorset. Excavations 1967-1985.* Dorset Natural History and Archaeological Society Monograph **13**.

Lyne, M.A.B. 2012. 'The Late Iron Age and Roman Black Burnished Ware Pottery.' In L. Ladle, *Excavations at Bestwall Quarry, Wareham, 1992-2005, Volume 2: The Iron Age and Later Landscape.* Dorset Natural History and Archaeological Society Monograph **20**, 201–242.

Lyne, M.A.B. and Jefferies, R.S. 1979. *The Alice Holt/Farnham Roman Pottery Industry.* London. Council for British Archaeology Research Report **30**.

Lysons, S. 1817. *Reliquiae Britannico-Romanae* II.

Macdonald, J. 1977. 'Pagan religions and burial practices in Roman Britain.' In R. Reece (ed), *Burial in the Roman World.* Council for British Archaeology Research Report Number 22, London, Council for British Archaeology, 35–38.

Mackintosh, M. 1986. 'The sources of the horseman and fallen enemy motif on tombstones of the Western Roman Empire.' *Journal of the British Archaeological Association* **139**, 1–21.

Maltby, M. 1990. *The animal bones from the Romano-British deposits at the Greyhound Yard and Methodist Chapel sites in Dorchester, Dorset.* London, Ancient Monument Laboratory Report 9/90. https://research.historicengland.org.uk/Report.aspx?i=4115&ru=%2FResults.aspx%3Fp%3D499

Maltby, M. 1993. 'Animal bones.' In P. Woodward, S. Davies, and A. Graham, *Excavations at the Old Methodist Chapel and Greyhound Yard, Dorchester 1981-1984.* Dorset Natural History and Archaeological Society Monograph **12**, 315–340.

Maltby, M. 2002. 'Animal bones.' In S. Davies, P. Bellamy, M. Heaton. and P. Woodward, *Excavations at Alington Avenue, Fordington, Dorset, 1984-87.* Dorset Natural History and Archaeological Society Monograph Series **15**, 53–55, 111–116, 168–170, 182–183.

Maltby, M. 2007. 'Chop and change: specialist cattle carcass processing in Roman Britain.' In B. Croxford, N. Ray, R. Roth, and N. White, (eds.), *TRAC 2006: Proceedings of the 16th Annual Theoretical Roman Archaeology Conference, Cambridge 2006.* Oxford, Oxbow, 59–76.

Maltby, M. 2009. 'Bones: mammals, birds and fish.' In S. Palmer, *Excavation of an enigmatic multi-period settlement on the Isle of Portland, Dorset.* Oxford, British Archaeological Reports (British Series) **499**, 27–43.

Maltby, M. 2010a. *Feeding a Roman town: environmental evidence from excavations in Winchester, 1972-1985.* Winchester, Winchester Museums Service.

Maltby, M. 2010b. 'Zooarchaeology and the interpretation of depositions in shafts.' In J. Morris and M. Maltby (eds.), *Integrating social and environmental archaeologies: reconsidering deposition.* Oxford, British Archaeological Reports (International Series) **S2077**, 24–32.

Maltby, M. 2013. *Animal bones from Marston Park, Marston Moretaine, Bedfordshire (Albion Archaeology project MP1571).* Unpublished, Bournemouth University.

Maltby, M. 2016. 'The exploitation of animals in Roman Britain.' In M. Millett, L. Revell and A. Moore, (eds.), *The Oxford handbook of Roman Britain.* Oxford, Oxford University Press, 791–806.

Maltby, M. 2017. 'The meat supply of Roman towns in southern England.' In D. Bird (ed.) *Agriculture and industry in southern Roman Britain.* Oxford, Oxbow, 180–209.

Maltby, M., Allen, M., Best, J., Fothergill, B.T. and Demarchi, B. 2018. 'Counting Roman chickens: multidisciplinary approaches to human-chicken interactions in Roman Britain.' *Journal of Archaeological Science* **19**, 1003–1015.

Manning, W.H. 1985. *Catalogue of Romano-British Iron Tools, Fittings and Weapons in the British Museum.* London, British Museum.

Margary, I.D. 1973 *Roman Roads in Britain.* Third Edition, London, Baker.

Mays, S, 1993. 'Infanticide in Roman Britain.' *Antiquity* **67**, 883–888.

Mays, S, 2003. 'Comment on, 'A Bayesian approach to ageing perinatal skeletal material from archaeological sites: implications for the evidence for infanticide in Roman Britain, by R. L. Gowland and A. T. Chamberlain.' *Journal of Archaeological Science* **30**, 1695–1700.

Mays, S. 2006. 'The Human Bone.' In T. Light and P. Ellis *Bucknowle, a Romano-British villa and its Antecedents: excavations 1976-1991.* Dorset Natural History and Archaeological Society. Monograph **18**, 155–8.

Mays, S. and Faerman, M, 2001. 'Sex identification in some putative infanticide victims from Roman Britain using ancient DNA.' *Journal of Archaeological Science* **28**(5), 555–559.

McCarthy, M. 2013. *The Romano-British Peasant.* Oxford, Windgather Press.

McGrail, S. 1983. *Ancient Boats.* Princes Risborough, Shire.

McParland, L.C., Hazell, Z., Campbell, G., Collinson, M.E. and Scott, A. 2009. 'How the Romans got themselves into hot water: temperatures and fuel types used in firing a hypocaust.' *Environmental Archaeology* **14** (2), 176–183.

Milek, K.B. 2012. 'Floor formation processes and the interpretation of site activity areas: An ethn-oarchaeological study of turf buildings at Thvera, north-east Iceland.' *Journal of Archaeological Anthropology* **31**, 119–37.

Millett, M. 1990. *The Romanization of Britain.* Cambridge, University Press.

Millett, M. and Gowland, R. 2015. 'Infant and child burial rites in Roman Britain: a study from East Yorkshire.' *Britannia* **46**, 171–89.

Mills, A.D. 1998. *Dorset Place-names: their origins and meanings.* Newbury, Countryside.

Milne, J.S. 1907. *Surgical Instruments in Greek and Roman Times.* Oxford, University Press.

Moore, A, 2009. 'Hearth and home: the burial of infants within Romano-British domestic contexts.' *Childhood in the Past* **2**, 33–54.

Moorhead, S. 2001. 'Roman coin finds from Wiltshire.' In P. Ellis (ed.), *Roman Wiltshire and After: Papers in Honour of Ken Annable.* Devizes, Wiltshire Archaeological and Natural History Society, 85–105.

Morgan, G.C. 1992. *Romano-British Mortar and Plaster.* University of Leicester doctoral thesis.

Morgan, M.H. (trans) 1969. *Vitruvius: The Ten Books on Architecture,* New York, Dover.

Morris, E.L. 1994. *The Analysis of Pottery.* Salisbury Wessex Archaeology Guideline No. **4**.

Morris, E.L. (ed.) 1997. 'Finds from the A37 Western Link Road.' In R.J.C. Smith, F. Healy, M.J. Allen, E.L. Morris, I. Barnes and P.J. Woodward, *Excavations Along the Route of the Dorchester By-pass, Dorset, 1986-8.* Salisbury, Wessex Archaeology, 224–57.

Morris, J. (ed.) 1983. *Domesday Book 7, Dorset.* Chichester, Phillimore.

Morris, J. 2011. *Investigating animal burials: ritual, mundane and beyond.* Oxford, British Archaeological Reports (British series) **535**.

Munsell Color Group 1975. *Munsell Soil Colour Charts.* Baltimore, Munsell Color Group.

Murphy, P., Albarella, U., Germany, M. and Locker, A. 2000. 'Production, imports and status: biological remains from a late Roman farm at Great Holts Farm, Boreham, Essex, UK.' *Environmental Archaeology* **5**, 35–48.

Nash-Williams, V.E. 1953. 'The Roman Villa at Llantwit Major in Glamorgan.' National Museum of Wales and Cambrian Archaeological Association **102**, 89–163.

Neal, D.S. and Cosh, S.R. 2002. *Roman Mosaics of Britain, Volume I Northern Britain incorporating the Midlands and East Anglia.* London, Society of Antiquaries.

Neal, D.S. and Cosh, S.R. 2004. *The Roman mosaics of Britain Volume III South-West Britain.* London, Society of Antiquaries.

Neal, D.S. and Cosh, S.R. 2009. *Roman Mosaics of Britain, Volume III, South-East Britain.* London, Society of Antiquaries.

O'Neil, H. 1971. *The Roman villa at Park Street near St Albans, Herts.* Hertfordshire Archaeological Society, HASPRINT **2**.

Papadopoulos, J.K. 2002. 'A Contextual Approach to Pessoi (Gaming Pieces, Counters or Convenient Wipes?).' *Hesperia* **71**, 423–7.

Papworth, M. 2008. *Deconstructing the Durotriges. A definition of Iron Age communities within the Dorset Environs.* Oxford. British Archaeological Reports (British Series) **462**.

Papworth, M. 2011. *The Search for the Durotriges. Dorset and the West Country in the Late Iron Age.* Stroud, History Press.

Papworth, M. 2014. 'The Romano-Celtic Temple at Badbury Rings, Dorset.' *Proceedings of the Dorset Natural History and Archaeological Society* **135**, 242–71.

Parlasca, K. 1959. *Die Römischen Mosaiken in Deutschland.* Berlin.

Paynter, S. and Dungworth, D. 2011. *Archaeological Evidence for Glassworking. Guidelines for Best Practice.* London, English Heritage.

Peacock, D.P.S. and Williams, D.F. 1986. *Amphorae and the Roman Economy.* London, Longman.

Peers, R.N.R. 1965. 'Dugout Canoe from Poole Harbour, Dorset.' *Proceedings of the Dorset Natural History and Archaeological Society* **86**, 131–4.

Pengelly, H. 2006. 'The Samian Ware.' In A. Graham, *Barton Field, Tarrant Hinton, Dorset. Excavations 1968-1984.* Dorset Natural History and Archaeological Society Monograph **17**, 75–83.

Penn, W.S. 1968. 'Springhead Temple VI/Gateway.' *Archaeologia Cantiana* **82**, 105–123.

Percival, J. 1976. *The Roman Villa.* London, Batsford.

Perring, D. 2002. *The Roman House in Britain.* London, Routledge.

Perring, D. 2003. 'Gnosticism' in Fourth-Century Britain: the Frampton Mosaics Reconsidered.' *Britannia* **34**, 97–127.

Philpott, R. 1991. *Burial Practices in Roma Britain. A Survey of Grave Treatment and Furnishing AD 43-410.* Oxford. British Archaeological Reports (British Series) **219**.

Poland, G. 2018. *A methodological approach to the identification of duck and goose remains from archaeological sites with an application to Roman.* University of Sheffield Ph.D. Thesis.

Poole, K. 2018.' Zooarchaeological evidence for falconry in England, up to AD 1500.' In K-H. Gersmann and O. Grimm (eds.), *Raptor and human: falconry and bird symbolism throughout the millennia on a global scale.* Kiel/Hamburg, Wachholtz Verlag, 1027–1053.

Popkin, P., Baker, P., Worley, F., Payne, S. and Hammon, A. 2012. 'The sheep project (1): determining skeletal growth, timing of epiphyseal fusion and morphometric variation in unimproved Shetland sheep of known age, sex, castration status and nutrition.' *Journal of Archaeological Science* **39**, 1775–1792.

Poulsen, J. and Draper, J. 1993. 'The Roman Pottery.' In R.N. Lucas, *The Romano-British Villa at Halstock, Dorset Excavations 1967-1985.* Dorset Natural History and Archaeological Society Monograph **13**, 120–124.

Price, J. and Cottam S. 1998. *Romano-British Glass Vessels: A Handbook.* York, Council for British Archaeology. Practical Handbook in Archaeology **14**.

Prudden, H. 2001. 'Somerset Building Stone – A guide.' *Proceedings of the Somerset Archaeological and Natural History Society* **146**, 27–36.

Pulman, R.B. 2007. *A Lithic Assemblage from the Roman villa at Dewlish, Dorset: an interpretative evaluation of prehistoric Dewlish based on macroscopic analysis.* Unpublished undergraduate dissertation, Bournemouth University.

Putnam, W.G. 1970a. 'Interim Report on the Excavations at Bowleaze Cove, Weymouth.' *Proceedings of the Dorset Natural History and Archaeological Society* **91**, 186.

Putnam, W.G. 1970b. 'The Dewlish Villa, Dorset; a Trial Excavation.' *Proceedings of the Dorset Natural History and Archaeological Society* **91**, 186–7.

Putnam, W.G. 1971. 'A section across the Roman Road from Badbury Rings to Dorchester.' *Proceedings of the Dorset Natural History and Archaeological Society* **92**, 147–8.

Putnam, W.G. 1971. 'Second Interim Report on Excavations at Dewlish Roman Villa, 1970.' *Proceedings of the Dorset Natural History and Archaeological Society* **92**, 146–7.

Putnam, W.G. 1972. 'Third Interim Report on Excavations at the Dewlish Roman Villa, 1971.' *Proceedings of the Dorset Natural History and Archaeological Society* **93**, 157–60.

Putnam, W.G. 1974. 'Fifth Interim Report on Excavations at the Dewlish Roman Villa 1973.' *Proceedings of the Dorset Natural History and Archaeological Society* **95**, 89–91.

Putnam, W.G. and Rainey, A. 1973. 'Fourth Interim Report on Excavations at Dewlish Roman Villa, 1972 and on the mosaic in Room 11.' *Proceedings of the Dorset Natural History and Archaeological Society* **94**, 81–6.

Putnam, W.G. and Rainey, A. 1975. 'Sixth Interim Report on Excavations at Dewlish Roman Villa, 1974.' *Proceedings of the Dorset Natural History and Archaeological Society* **96**, 59–62.

Putnam, W.G. and Rainey, A. 1976. 'Seventh Interim Report on Excavations at Dewlish Roman Villa, 1975.' *Proceedings of the Dorset Natural History and Archaeological Society* **97**, 54–7.

Putnam, W.G. 1984. *Roman Dorset.* Wimborne, Dovecote.

Putnam, W.G. 2002. 'Dewlish: the Roman villa.' *Dorset* **79**, 20–23.

Putnam, W.G. 2007. *Roman Dorset.* Stroud, Tempus.

Rainey, A. 1973. *Mosaics in Roman Britain.* Newton Abbot, David and Charles.

Rana, R.S., Wu, J.S. and Eisenberg R.L. 2009. 'Periosteal reaction.' *American Journal of Roentgenology* **193**, 259–272.

Randall, C. 2020. 'Later Prehistoric and Roman Occupation at Townsend Farm, Poyntington. Geophysical Survey and Evaluation 2010–11.' *Proceedings of the Dorset Natural History and Archaeological Society* **141**, 171–81.

Reece, R. 1990. *Roman Coins from 140 Sites.* Cirencester. Cotswolds Studies 4.

Reece, R. 1995. 'Site-finds in Roman Britain.' *Britannia* **26**, 179–206.

Reid, C. 1899. 'The geology of the country around Dorchester.' *Memoir of the Geological Survey of Great Britain.* Sheet 328 (England and Wales).

Reilly, K. 1997. 'Animal bone.' In R. Smith, F. Healy, M. Allen, E. Morris, I. Barnes and P. Woodward, *Excavations along the route of the Dorchester By-pass, Dorset, 1986-8.* Salisbury, Wessex Archaeology Report No. **11**, 270–3.

Reynolds, P.J. 1979. *Iron Age Farm. The Butser Experiment.* London, Colonnade.

Reynolds, P.J. and Langley, J.K. 1979. 'Romano-British Corn-drying Oven: an experiment.' *Archaeological Journal* **136**, 27–42.

Rizzetto, M., Crabtree, P. and Albarella, U. 2017. 'Livestock changes at the beginning and end of the Roman Period in Britain: issues of acculturation, adaptation, and 'improvement'.' *European Journal of Archaeology* **20** (3), 535–556.

Robb J. and Rogers J. M. 2009. 'Human Bones.' In T. Light and P. Ellis, *Bucknowle, A Romano-British Villa and its Antecedents: Excavations 1976-1991*. Dorset Natural History and Archaeological Society Monograph **18**, 155–158.

Ros, J., Evin, A., Bouby, L., Ruas. M-P. 2014. 'Geometric morphometric analysis of grain shape and the identification of two-rowed barley (*Hordeum vulgare* subsp. *distichum* L.) in southern France.' *Journal of Archaeological Science* **41**, 568–575.

Royal Commission on Historical Monuments, England (RCHME), 1970a. *An Inventory of the Historical Monuments in the County of Dorset. Vol. 2 South-east, Part 1*. London, Her Majesty's Stationery Office.

Royal Commission on Historical Monuments, England (RCHME), 1970a. *An Inventory of the Historical Monuments in the County of Dorset. Vol. 2 South-east, Part 2*. London, Her Majesty's Stationery Office.

Royal Commission on Historical Monuments, England (RCHME), 1970a. *An Inventory of the Historical Monuments in the County of Dorset. Vol. 2 South-east, Part 3*. London, Her Majesty's Stationery Office.

Royal Commission on Historical Monuments, England (RCHME), 1970b. *An Inventory of the Historical Monuments in the County of Dorset. Vol. 3 Central, Parts 1 and 2*. London. Her Majesty's Stationery Office.

Royal Commission on Historical Monuments (England), 1972. *An Inventory pf the Historical Monuments in the County of Dorset. Vol. 4 North*. London, Her Majesty's Stationery Office.

Roymans, N. and Derks, T. (eds) 2011. *Villa landscapes in the Roman North, Economy, Culture and Lifestyles*. Amsterdam. University Press. Amsterdam Archaeological Studies **17**.

Russell, M., Cheetham, P., Evans, D., Gerdau-Radonic, K., Hambleton, E., Hewitt, I., Manley, H. and Smith, M. 2015. 'The Durotriges Project, Phase Two: an interim statement.' *Proceedings of the Dorset Natural History and Archaeological Society* **136**, 157–61.

Schaefer, M., Black, S. and Scheuer, L. 2009. *Juvenile Osteology - A Laboratory and Field Manual*. London. Elsevier.

Scheuer, L. and Black, S. 2000. *Developmental Juvenile Osteology*. London, Academic Press. Elsevier.

Schofield, J. 2011. *Lime in Building. A practical guide*. Third edition, Crediton, Black Dog Press.

Schutkowski, H. 1993. 'Sex Determination of Infant and Juvenile Skeletons: I. Morphognostic Features.' *American Journal of Physical Anthropology* **90**, 199–205.

Scott, E. 1991. 'Animal and infant burials in Romano-British villas: a revitalization movement.' In P. Garwood (ed). *Sacred and Profane: Proceedings of a Conference on Archaeology, Ritual and Religion, Oxford*. Oxford, Oxford University Committee for Archaeology Monograph, 115–121.

Scott, E. 1993. *A Gazetteer of Roman Villas in Britain*. University of Leicester School of Archaeological Studies. University of Leicester Monograph **1**.

Scott, E. 1999. *The Archaeology of Infancy and Infant Death*. Oxford, British Archaeological Reports (International Series) **819**.

Seager Smith, R.H. 1997. 'Late Iron Age and Roman Pottery and Roman Pottery.' In R.J.C. Smith, F. Healy, M.J. Allen, E.L. Morris, I. Barnes and P.J. Woodward, *Excavations Along the Route of the Dorchester By-pass, Dorset, 1986-8*. Wessex Archaeology Monograph **11**, 102–118 and 225–35.

Seager Smith, R.H. 1999. 'Romano-British pottery.' In A.P. Fitzpatrick, C.A. Butterworth and J. Grove, *Prehistoric and Roman Sites in East Devon: the A30 Honiton to Exeter Improvement DBFO Scheme, 1996-9, volume2: Romano-British Sites*. Salisbury, Wessex Archaeological Report **16**, 286–327.

Seager Smith, R.H. 2002. 'Late Iron Age and Romano-British pottery.' In S.M. Davies, P.S. Bellamy, M.J. Heaton and P.J. Woodward, *Excavations at Alington Avenue, Fordington, Dorchester, Dorset, 1984-87*. Dorset Natural History and Archaeological Society Monograph **15**, 93–107.

Seager Smith, R.H. 2008. 'Pottery; additional specialist report.' In M Trevarthen, *Suburban life in Roman Durnovaria Excavations at the former County Hospital site, Dorchester, Dorset 2000-2001*. http://www.wessexarch.co.uk/files/projects/dorchester_county_hospital/09_Pottery.pdf

Seager Smith, R.H. 2011. 'Romano-British Pottery.' In K. Egging Dinwiddy and P. Bradley, *Prehistoric Activity and a Romano-British Settlement at Poundbury Farm. Dorchester, Dorset*. Salisbury, Wessex Archaeology Monograph, 97–101.

Seager Smith, R.H. and Corney, M. 1997. 'Samian.' In R.J.C. Smith, F. Healy, M.J. Allen, E.L. Morris and P.J. Woodward, *Excavations Along the Route of the Dorchester By-Pass, Dorset 1986-8*. Salisbury, Wessex Archaeology Report no. **11**.

Seager Smith, R.H. and Davies, S.M. 1993. 'Roman pottery.' In P.J. Woodward, A.H. Graham, and S.M. Davies, *Excavations at Greyhound Yard, Dorchester 1981-4*. Dorset Natural History and Archaeological Society Monograph **12**, 202–89.

Seager Smith, R.H. and Mills, J.M. 2015. 'Roman Finds.' In A.B. Powell, 'The Development of Properties inside the southern defences of Roman Durnovaria: an Excavation at Charles Street, Dorchester.' *Proceedings of the Dorset Natural History and Archaeological Society* **136**, 176–181.

Seager Smith, R., Marter Brown, K., and Mills, J.M. 2011. 'The pottery from Springhead.' In E. Biddulph, R. Seager Smith and J. Schuster, *Settling the Ebbsfleet Valley: High Speed 1 Excavations at Springhead and Northfleet, Kent, the Late Iron Age, Roman, Saxon and medieval landscape: Vol. 2, Late Iron Age to Roman Finds Reports*. Oxford, Wessex Archaeology, 1–134.

Sedgley, J.P. 1975. *The Roman Milestones of Britain: their Petrography and probable Origin.* Oxford. British Archaeological Reports (British Series) **18**.

Selkirk, R. 1983. *A Dramatic New View of Roman History: The Piercebridge Formula.* Cambridge. Patrick Stephens.

Shaffrey, R. 2006. 'The worked stone.' In M. Fulford, A. Clarke and H. Eckardt, *Life and Labour in Late Roman Silchester: Excavations in Insula IX since 1997.* Britannia Monograph **22**, 133–134.

Shaffrey, R. 2011. 'Whetstones and other worked stones.' In E. Biddulph, R. Seager-Smith and J. Schuster, *Settling the Ebbsfleet Valley. High Speed 1 Excavations at Springhead and Northfleet, Kent. The Late Iron Age, Roman, Saxon and Medieval. Landscapes.* Oxford, Wessex Archaeology, 368–371.

Shaffrey, R. and Roe, F. 2011. 'The widening use of Lodsworth Stone: Neolithic to Romano-British quern distribution.' In D. Williams and D. Peacock (eds.), *Bread for the People: the archaeology of mills and milling. Proceedings of a colloquium held in the British School at Rome 4th-7th November 2009.* Oxford, British Archaeological Reports (International Series) **2274**, 309–324.

Shopfner, C.F. 1966. 'Periosteal bone growth in normal infants – a preliminary report.' *American Journal of Roentgenology* **97(1)**, 154–163.

Siddell, J. 2008. Eggshell. 'Additional specialist report.' In M. Trevarthen, *Suburban life in Roman Durnovaria: excavations in the former County Hospital site, Dorchester, 2000-2001.* Salisbury, Wessex Archaeology. http://www.wessexarch.co.uk/files/projects/dorchester_county_hospital/04_ Eggshell.pdf.

Smith, D.J. 1969. 'The mosaic pavements.' In A.L.F. Rivet (ed.), *The Roman villa in Britain.* London, Routledge, 75–125.

Smith, D.J. 1984. 'Roman mosaics in Britain: a synthesis.' In R. Farioli Campanati (ed.), *Il Mosaic Antico* III. Colloquio internazionale sul mosaico antico, 357–80.

Smith, J.T. 1997. *Roman Villas.* London, Routledge.

Soffe, G. 2009. 'Bill Putnam (1930–2008).' *Association for Roman Archaeology News* **19**, 13–16.

Stacey, L. 1993. 'The Bone Pins and Pegs.' In P.J. Woodward, S.M. Davis and A.H. Graham. *Excavations at Greyhound Yard, Dorchester 1981-4.* Dorset Natural History and Archaeological Society Monograph **12**, 184–186.

Stanier, P. 2000. *Stone Quarry Landscapes: The Archaeology of Quarrying in England.* Stroud, Tempus.

Stern, H. 1957. *Recueil général des mosaïques de la Gaule I, Gaule - Belgique 1,* Paris (reprinted 1979).

Sunter, N. 1987. 'Excavations at Norden, Corfe Castle, Dorset, 1968-1969.' In N. Sunter and P.J. Woodward. *Romano-British Industries in Purbeck, Dorset.'* Dorset Natural History and Archaeological Society. Monograph Series **6**, 9–43.

Sutherland, D.S. 2003. *Northamptonshire Stone.* Wimborne, The Dovecote Press.

Sykes, N. and Curl, J. 2010. 'The rabbit.' In T. O'Connor and N. Sykes (eds.), *Extinctions and invasions: a social history of British fauna.* Oxford, Windgather Press, 116–126.

Sykes, N., Baker, K., Carden, R., Higham, T., Hoelzel, R. and Stevens, R. 2011. 'New evidence for the establishment and management of European fallow deer (*Dama dama dama*) in Roman Britain.' *Journal of Archaeological Science* **38** (1), 156–165.

Tasker, A., Wilkinson, I.P., Fulford, M.G. and Williams, M. 2011. 'Provenance of chalk tesserae from Brading Roman Villa, Isle of Wight, UK.' *Proceedings of the Geologists' Association,* **122** (5), 933–937.

Taylor, R. 2003. *Roman Builders. A Study in Archaeological Process.* Cambridge. University Press.

Thomas, J. 2008. *Dorset Stone.* Wimborne Minster, Dovecote.

Todd, M. 2005. 'Baths or Baptisteries? Holcombe, Lufton and their Analogues.' *Oxford Journal of Archaeology* **24** (3), 307–11.

Tomber, R. and Dore, J. 1998. *The National Roman Fabric Reference Collection; a handbook,* MoLAS Monograph **2**, London.

Trevarthen, M. 2008. *Suburban Life in Roman Durnovaria: excavations at the former County Hospital Site, Dorchester, Dorset 2000-2001.* Salisbury, Wessex Archaeology.

Ubelaker, D.H. 1989. *Human Skeletal Remains: Excavation, Analysis, Interpretation.* Second edition, Washington, Taraxacum.

Van Beek, C. 1983 *Dental Morphology. An Illustrated Guide.* Second edition, London, Elsevier.

van der Veen, M. 1989. 'Charred grain Assemblages from Roman-period Corn Driers in Britain.' *Archaeological Journal* **146**, 302–359.

Wacher, J. 1998. *Roman Britain.* Stroud, Sutton.

Wait, G.A. 1985. *Ritual and Religion in Iron Age* Britain. Part 1. Oxford, British Archaeological Reports British Series **149** (i).

Waldron, T., Taylor, G.M. and Rudling, D. 1999. 'Sexing of Romano-British baby burials from the Beddingham and Bignor villas.' *Sussex Archaeological Collections* **137**, 71–79.

Wallace, L.M. 2018. 'Community and the creation of the Romano-British Aisled Building at North Warnborough.' *Archaeological Journal* **175**, 231–254.

Walton, P. 2012. *Rethinking Roman Britain: Coinage and Archaeology.* Wettern, Moneta Monograph **137**.

Ward, J.S. 1912. *The Roman Era in Britain.* London, Methuen.

Watkinson, D. and Neal, V. 1998. *First Aid for Finds.* Hertford and London, RESCUE and the United Kingdom Institute for Conservation and the Museum of London.

Webster, P. 1996. *Roman Samian Pottery in Britain.* York, Council for British Archaeology, Practical Handbook **13**.

Welch, F.B.A. and Trotter, F.M. 1960. 'Geology of the Country around Monmouth and Chepstow.' *Memoir of the Geological Survey of Great Britain.* Sheet 233 and 250 (England and Wales). London, Her Majesty's Stationery Office.

Wessex Archaeology, 1989. *Excavations at Wessex Court,*

Charles Street, Dorchester, Dorset, 1989. Salisbury, Wessex Archaeology, unpublished client report W310a/32812,.

Wessex Archaeology, 2012. *MOD Headquarters, High Street, Durrington, Wiltshire: post-excavation assessment and updated project design.* Salisbury. Wessex Archaeology unpublished client report ref. 74414.02.

Williams, D. and Peacock, D. (eds.) 2011. Bread for the People: the archaeology of mills and milling. *Proceedings of a colloquium held in the British School at Rome 4th-7th November 2009.* Oxford, British Archaeological Reports (International Series) **2274**.

Williams, D. F. 1977. 'The Romano-British Black Burnished industry: an essay on characterisation by heavy mineral analysis.' In D.P.S. Peacock (ed.), *Pottery and Early Commerce.* Cambridge, University Press, 163–215.

Williams, J.H. 1971a. 'Roman Building Materials in South-East England.' *Britannia* **2**, 166–95.

Williams, J.H. 1971b. 'Roman building materials in the south-west.' *Transactions of the Bristol and Gloucester Archaeological Society* **90**, 95–119.

Willis, S. and Carne, P. 2013. *A Roman villa on the edge of Empire. Excavations at Ingleby Barwick, Stockton on Tees 2003-4.* Council for British Archaeology Research Report **170**.

Wilson, D. (ed.) 1973. 'I: Sites Explored.' *Britannia* **4**, 315.

Wilson, D. (ed.) 1974. 'I: Sites Explored.' *Britannia* **5**, 396–460.

Witts, P A. 2000. 'Mosaics and room function: the evidence from some fourth century Roman British villas.' *Britannia* **31**, 291–324.

Witts, P. 2016. *A Mosaic Managerie, Creatures of Land, Sea and Sky in Romano-British Mosaics.* Oxford, British Archaeological Reports Series **265**.

Witts, P. 2018. 'A New Angle on the Lufton Mosaics.' *Mosaic* **45**, 2–10.

Woodfield, C. 2005. 'Rare tazze, patera and a broad hint at a *Lararium* from *Lactodorum*.' *Journal of Roman Pottery Studies*, **12**, 209–212.

Woodward, A. 1992. *Shrines and Sacrifice.* London, Batsford.

Woodward, A.B. 1993. 'Discussion.' In D.E Farwell and T.I. Molleson, *Excavations at Poundbury 1966-80 volume 2: The Cemeteries.* Dorset Natural History and Archaeological Society Monograph **11**, 215–239.

Woodward, P.J. 1987. 'The excavation of a Late Iron Are settlement and Romano-British industrial site at Ower, Dorset.' In N. Sunter and P.J. Woodward, *Romano-British Industries in Purbeck.* Dorset Natural History and Archaeological Society Monograph **6**, 44–124.

Woodward, P., Davies, S.M. and Graham, A.H. 1993. *Excavations at Greyhound Yard, Dorchester 1981-4.* Dorset Natural History and Archaeological Society Monograph **12**.

Woodward, P. and Woodward, A. 2004. 'Dedicating the town: urban foundation deposits in Roman Britain.' *World Archaeology* **36**, 68–86.

Young, C. 1977. *Oxfordshire Roman Pottery*, British Archaeological Reports (British Series) **43**.

ARCHIVAL SOURCES

Bournemouth University

BU100DEW0002	Dewlish Roman villa phases		Typescript. Putnam, W.G.
BU100DEW0004	Dewlish Roman villa Trial Trenches 1969–1979.		Plan.
BU100DEW0005	Dewlish Roman villa Building sequences		Logbook. Putnam, W.G.
BU100DEW0006	Site diary 1971–1975		Putnam, W.G.
BU100DEW0007	Site Diary 1976–1979		Putnam, W.G.
BU100DEW0008	Site diary 1969–1970		Putnam, W.G.
BU100DEW0014	Grid trench record book	1971	D6 and E6 plus Extensions.
BU100DEW0015	Grid trench record book	1975	D7, E6, E7 and Room 24.
BU100DEW0016	Grid trench record book	1973	D8, E8 and Room 24.
BU100DEW0018	Grid trench record book	1972	E4, E5 and Rooms 7, 8, 9 and 11.
BU100DEW0034	Grid trench record book	1975	K2 (Room 12).
BU100DEW0036	Grid trench record book	1975	J2, J3 (room 12).
BU100DEW0042	Grid trench record book	1975	L3 (Room 12).
BU100DEW0052	Grid trench record book	1977	M94 (Rooms 44 and 49).
BU100DEW0053	Grid trench record book	1978	N99 (Rooms 40 and 31).
BU100DEW0054	Grid trench record book	1978	N98 (Room 40).
BU100DEW0055	Grid trench record book	1977	M95 (east to Room 42).
BU100DEW0057	Grid trench record book	1978	M98 (Rooms 40 and 41).
BU100DEW0075	Grid trench record book	1974	O5, O4 and P4.
BU100DEW0081	Grid trench record book	1978	O100.
BU100DEW0088	Grid trench record book	1976	P94 and P95 (Rooms 34 and 35).
BU100DEW0091	Grid trench record book	1976	Q94 and R91.
BU100DEW0092	Grid trench record book	1976	Q95, R95, S95 and T95.
BU100DEW0094	Grid trench record book	1978	Trial Trenches 1 to 9.
BU100DEW0095	Grid trench record book	1973–1974	Trial Trenches 1 to 9.
BU100DEW0130	Small Finds Records	1969–1979	Box 4: 2 x record books.
BU100DEW0156	Geophysical surveys	1973	Box 5. V. Williams, University of Southampton.
BU100DEW0180	PEP1 Plaster Project diary		Box 6.
BU100DEW0223	Ancient Monuments Laboratory report on crucible		Typescript and monochrome photographs.
BU100DEW0236	PEP1 correspondence		Leverhulme Trust.
BU100DEW0238	Chinchester field-name		Correspondence from A.D. Mills.
BU100DEW0319	Dewlish: local archaeology		Typescript.
BU100DEW0350	Dewlish Roman villa research questions		1999 (Putnam, W.G.); 2010 (Hewitt, I.).
BU100DEW0353	Post-excavation project notebook.		Hewitt, I.
BU100DEW0354	Introduction and summary to proposed report.		Putnam, W.G. (unpublished).
BU100DEW0358	Notes for trench supervisors (context records).		Weymouth College of Education.
BU100DEW0359	Dewlish Roman villa: environmental samples from Building 2/2A		Hewitt, I 2015. Unpublished briefing paper.
BU100DEW0360	Dewlish Roman villa: consolidated Context records		Access database.
BU100DEW0361	PEP2 correspondence		Word and pdf files.
BU100DEW	Sheet 627 (plan)		A2 format paper sheet.

Dorset Council Historic Environment Record

DC HER 1040 009A-MOD981
DC HER 1040 007A-MOF997
DC HER 1040 009A-MOD981
DC HER 1031 046 -MOD885
DC HER 1031 044 -MOD852
  DC HER 1031 044B-MOD853

Dorset History Centre

DHC/DEW   Tithe Map, Dewlish   1844

Dorset History Centre

DHC/DEW   Tithe Map, Dewlish   1844

APPENDICES

WEYMOUTH COLLEGE OF EDUCATION

TRAINING EXCAVATION

NOTES FOR TRENCH SUPERVISORS ON SITE BOOK RECORDING

A. (Before its excavation begins) Every distinct area of soil or other
    material recognized in plan or in section must be given a Layer Number
    and allocated adequate space in the site book.

B. To help in compiling the maximum amount of information about each layer
    and for the sake of uniformity, please make sure that the following
    questions are answered in the site book (in narrative form) whilst the
    layer is being dug.

    (a) What is the extent of the layer in plan? (Measured sketch plan on
         left hand page of site book showing relationship to grid and other
         layers)

    (b) Which layer(s) was resting immediately on top of this one? (At least
         one measured sketch section should be drawn on left hand page of site
         book showing this layer in relation to those above and below)

    Soil Based Layers

    (c) What is the surface appearance of the layer? (if recognized in plan)

              (i) Colour *
             (ii) Surface character: dry, friable, damp, sticky, smooth, rough
                  undulating, showing signs of wear, compacted, soft etc.
            (iii) Homogeneity*: note any surface concentrations of inclusions*
                  areas of unequal drying etc.

    (d) How, and by whom (initials), is the layer being dug? If in spits
         give depth and results of each spit (see (e)). If appropriate answer
         (a) and (c) for the new surface exposed on completion of each spit.

    (e) Whilst it is being dug away the layer must be described carefully and
         in detail under the following headings:-

              (i) Colour   )
             (ii) Texture   )
            (iii) Inclusions   )   *
             (iv) Homogeneity   )

    (f) Interpretation: How was the layer formed?
                          What does it mean?

         Discuss with Director, note in square brackets, any working
         hypotheses, with alternatives, however tentative, and possible
         similarities/relationships with features in other trenches.

Non-Soil Based Layers (i.e. Walls, tessellated floors, mortared surfaces etc)

(g) Make sure you have adequate descriptions/drawings of types of materials
     used (sample), details of dressing (retain), binding materials (sample)
     methods of construction, damage, wear, repairs, surfacing or decoration
     etc.

(h) Interpretation: What does it mean? Notes in square brackets as in (f)

     * See Sheet 4.

WEYMOUTH COLLEGE OF EDUCATION

DEPARTMENT OF HISTORY AND ARCHAEOLOGY

Sheet 4 of 4

Notes on Describing Layers

This is one of the most difficult and important tasks of the excavator. Despite this it must remain largely a matter of subjective judgement although scientific tests may be used to answer specific questions about occasional samples later. These notes are an attempt to reduce subjective variation between different workers on the same site, and to provide a uniform vocabulary.

COLOUR*

As the natural soil at Dewlish tends to be a "Brown Earth" type and the parent rock so often "clay with flints" soil colours will be basically brown due to oxidised iron compounds present. But the term "brown" is clearly too vague to be useful. In the absence of colour comparison charts (which would probably be the most objective way of measuring soil colour) attempt to describe the browns a little more precisely by considering their two major components:-
  (1) The basic colour component which will be:
       yellow, red/yellow, orange, yellow/red, red
  (2) An adulteration with grey: very light grey, light grey, medium grey,
       dark grey, very dark grey.

In combination the ranges of these two components give us a rough way of naming 30 shades of "brown", for example a light grey yellow/red (see colour example). Of course this is far too crude to yeild meaningful absolute colour values, but it should help to record variations between and with in layers without the worst ambiguities such as "browner".

TEXTURE*

This refers to the size of particles and their proportions in the soil. A rough idea of what these are may be obtained by rubbing a moist sample of soil between the fingers. If it feels:-
  (a) gritty, is incoherent, leaves the fingers clean, it is a SAND.
  (b) silky, is incoherent, stains the fingers, it is a SILT.
  (c) sticky, coherent, takes a polish when smoothed with the finger, it is
       a CLAY.
  (d) if neither of these applies (as is will not for most soils) the grades
       are fairly evenly mixed and it is a LOAM.

This terminology may be arranged in a scale of ascending coarseness:-
Clay
Clay loam
Silty loam
Loam
Sandy loam
Loamy sand
Sand

Gravel is parent rock particles larger than 2mm. diameter:-
  2 - 6mm.   FINE GRAVEL
  6 - 20mm.   MEDIUM GRAVEL
  20 - 60mm.   COARSE GRAVEL
  60 - 200mm.   COBBLES

* For further information on Colour and Texture, see Cornwall, 1.W., 1958
  Soils for the Archaelogist.

INCLUSIONS.
    We shall take this to mean anything present in the layer which is foreign
to the parent material. This may be classified as:-
    (a) Finds such as
                Pottery
                Animal bones
                Moluscs
                Metal artefacts
                Stone artefacts
                Slags etc.

    (b) charcoal (Special Find large pieces for identification)
         mortars
         fragments of "foreign" rocks
         flecks of brick, glass, shell, slag etc.

    (c) concentrations of rootlets.
         worm activity
         animal burrows etc.

    In the case of retained finds (group(a)) please list the kinds of objects
being recovered from each layer. Discuss with Finds Supervisor. E.G. "black
burnished , ware common, occasional sherds of colour coated ware, a few animal
bones, many fragments of combed flue tiles". If any Special Finds are recovered
please record their Special Finds numbers.
    Group (b): It is very important to note the nature and distribution of
objects under this heading as they will not usually be retained. Please record
the size of the flecks or fragments (rough range and mean), their state (e.g.
smooth, angular, burnt etc.), their concentration (e.g. how many in a 10cm.
square surface for instance.)
    Group (c): If there is evidence for an unusual degree of earthworm activity,
please note. Similarly it is useful to know whether there are many or few roots
or rootlets present. It is ofcourse essential that we record animal burrows; they
may get individual layer numbers.

HOMOGENEITY
    Few layers will be of constant composition throughout their horizontal or
vertical extent in terms of colour, texture or inclusions. For example an orange
layer might change from dark grey to light grey towards its edges, there maybe
a higher proportion of medium gravel towards its base, or rounded yellow mortar
fragments 1-2cm. diameter may be more concentrated 10-15in. 10cm. square near to the
West Wall of Room .... Deviations from homogeneity will ofcourse be small
(if they were not a separate layer would be called for), but please do not ignore
small variations. Please make verbal notes and support these with measured sketch
sections and plans if necessary. Final large scale sections should show clearly
variations in colour and texture within each layer.

JB/EB
1.5.74

WEYMOUTH COLLEGE OF EDUCATION

TRAINING EXCAVATION - RESPONSIBILITY STRUCTURE

DIRECTOR (W.G.P.)

(Archaeologist in Charge)

Responsible for success of excavation and publication or results. Particularly concerned with strategy, interpretation and photographic record.

Site Supervisor (J.B.)

Overall responsibility for detailed records: site books, plans, sections; surveying and sampling.

Trench Supervisors (usually experienced students)

Lead teams of excavators. Responsible for excavating and recording individual trenches.

Excavators

Responsible for observation, excavation and presentation of specific layers and features as directed by Trench Supervisors. Occasional duties as Finds Assistants.
P.R. Officers and coffee makers on rota basis.

Finds Supervisor (P.A.M)

Overall responsibility for treatment registration and packaging of all finds recovered by Excavators.

Finds Assistants

Responsible for cleaning, treatment, labelling and packing of all finds.

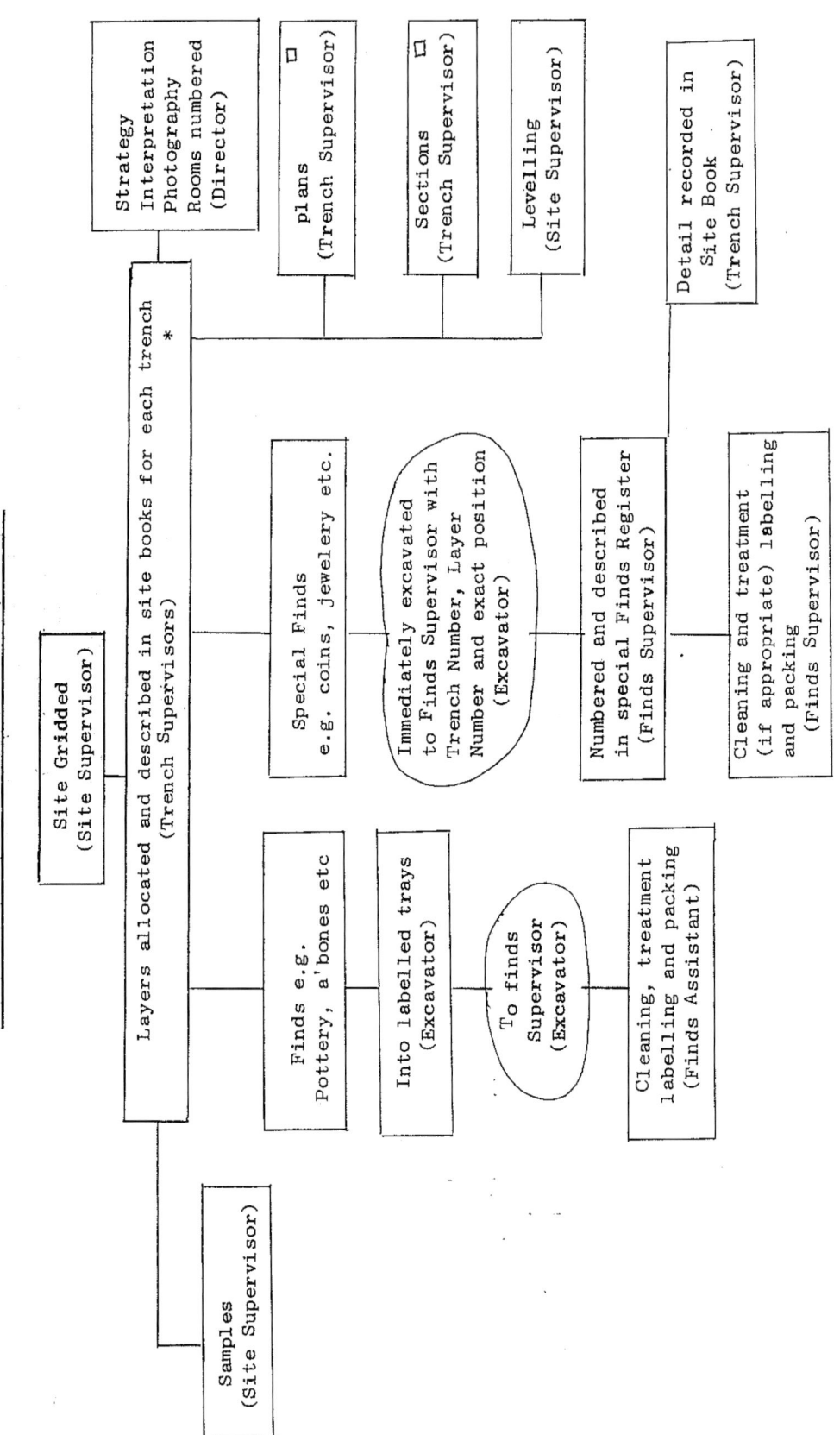

WEYMOUTH COLLEGE OF EDUCATION

TRAINING EXCAVATION - RECORDING PROCEDURES

Site Gridded
(Site Supervisor)

Samples
(Site Supervisor)

Layers allocated and described in site books for each trench *
(Trench Supervisors)

Strategy
Interpretation
Photography
Rooms numbered
(Director)

plans
(Trench Supervisor)

Sections
(Trench Supervisor)

Levelling
(Site Supervisor)

Detail recorded in
Site Book
(Trench Supervisor)

Special Finds
e.g. coins, jewelery etc.

Immediately excavated to Finds Supervisor with Trench Number, Layer Number and exact position
(Excavator)

Numbered and described in special Finds Register
(Finds Supervisor)

Cleaning and treatment (if appropriate) labelling and packing
(Finds Supervisor)

Finds e.g.
Pottery, a'bones etc

Into labelled trays
(Excavator)

To finds Supervisor
(Excavator)

Cleaning, treatment labelling and packing
(Finds Assistant)

* See Sheet 3
□ See chart of recommended symbols.

Beta Analytic
TESTING LABORATORY

Beta Analytic Inc
4985 SW 74 Court
Miami, Florida 33155
Tel: 305-667-5167
Fax: 305-663-0964
info@betalabservices.com

ISO/IEC 17025:2005-Accredited Testing Laboratory

November 26, 2019

Mr. Iain Hewitt
Bournemouth University
School of Applied Sciences
Deptartment of Archaeology and Anthropology
Christchurch House Fern Barrow
Poole, Dorset BH12 5BB
United Kingdom

RE: Radiocarbon Dating Results

Dear Mr. Hewitt,

Enclosed is the radiocarbon dating result for one sample recently sent to us. As usual, specifics of the analysis are listed on the report with the result and calibration data is provided where applicable. The Conventional Radiocarbon Age has been corrected for total fractionation effects and where applicable, calibration was performed using 2013 calibration databases (cited on the graph pages).

The web directory containing the table of results and PDF download also contains pictures, a cvs spreadsheet download option and a quality assurance report containing expected vs. measured values for 3-5 working standards analyzed simultaneously with your samples.

The reported result is accredited to ISO/IEC 17025:2005 Testing Accreditation PJLA #59423 standards and all pretreatments and chemistry were performed here in our laboratories and counted in our own accelerators here in Miami. Since Beta is not a teaching laboratory, only graduates trained to strict protocols of the ISO/IEC 17025:2005 Testing Accreditation PJLA #59423 program participated in the analysis.

As always Conventional Radiocarbon Ages and sigmas are rounded to the nearest 10 years per the conventions of the 1977 International Radiocarbon Conference. When counting statistics produce sigmas lower than +/- 30 years, a conservative +/- 30 BP is cited for the result. The reported d13C was measured separately in an IRMS (isotope ratio mass spectrometer). It is NOT the AMS d13C which would include fractionation effects from natural, chemistry and AMS induced sources.

When interpreting the result, please consider any communications you may have had with us regarding the sample. As always, your inquiries are most welcome. If you have any questions or would like further details of the analysis, please do not hesitate to contact us.

Our invoice will be emailed separately. Please forward it to the appropriate officer or send a credit card authorization. Thank you. As always, if you have any questions or would like to discuss the results, don't hesitate to contact us.

Sincerely,

Digital signature on file

Ronald E. Hatfield President

Beta Analytic Inc
4985 SW 74 Court
Miami, Florida 33155
Tel: 305-667-5167
Fax: 305-663-0964
info@betalabservices.com

ISO/IEC 17025:2005-Accredited Testing Laboratory

REPORT OF RADIOCARBON DATING ANALYSES

Iain Hewitt

Bournemouth University

Report Date: November 26, 2019

Material Received: November 07, 2019

Laboratory Number	Sample Code Number	Conventional Radiocarbon Age (BP) or Percent Modern Carbon (pMC) & Stable Isotopes Calendar Calibrated Results: 95.4 % Probability High Probability Density Range Method (HPD)	
Beta - 543096	**DH75 P4 23**	**1810 +/- 30 BP**	IRMS δ13C: -21.7 o/oo
			IRMS δ15N: +8.8 o/oo

(86.5%)	128 - 258 cal AD	(1822 - 1692 cal BP)	
(8.9%)	284 - 322 cal AD	(1666 - 1628 cal BP)	

Submitter Material: Bone (Non-heated)
Pretreatment: (bone collagen) collagen extraction; with alkali
Analyzed Material: Bone collagen
Analysis Service: AMS-Standard delivery
Percent Modern Carbon: 79.83 +/- 0.30 pMC
Fraction Modern Carbon: 0.7983 +/- 0.0030
D14C: -201.74 +/- 2.98 o/oo
Δ14C: -208.38 +/- 2.98 o/oo (1950:2019)
Measured Radiocarbon Age: (without d13C correction): 1760 +/- 30 BP
Calibration: BetaCal3.21: HPD method: INTCAL13
Carbon/Nitrogen: CN : 3.3 %C: 41.99 %N: 15.04

BetaCal 3.21

Calibration of Radiocarbon Age to Calendar Years

(High Probability Density Range Method (HPD): INTCAL13)

(Variables: d13C = -21.7 o/oo)

Laboratory number　　**Beta-543096**

Conventional radiocarbon age　　**1810 ± 30 BP**

95.4% probability

(86.5%)	128 - 258 cal AD	(1822 - 1692 cal BP)
(8.9%)	284 - 322 cal AD	(1666 - 1628 cal BP)

68.2% probability

(40.3%)	140 - 196 cal AD	(1810 - 1754 cal BP)
(27.9%)	208 - 242 cal AD	(1742 - 1708 cal BP)

DH75 P4 23

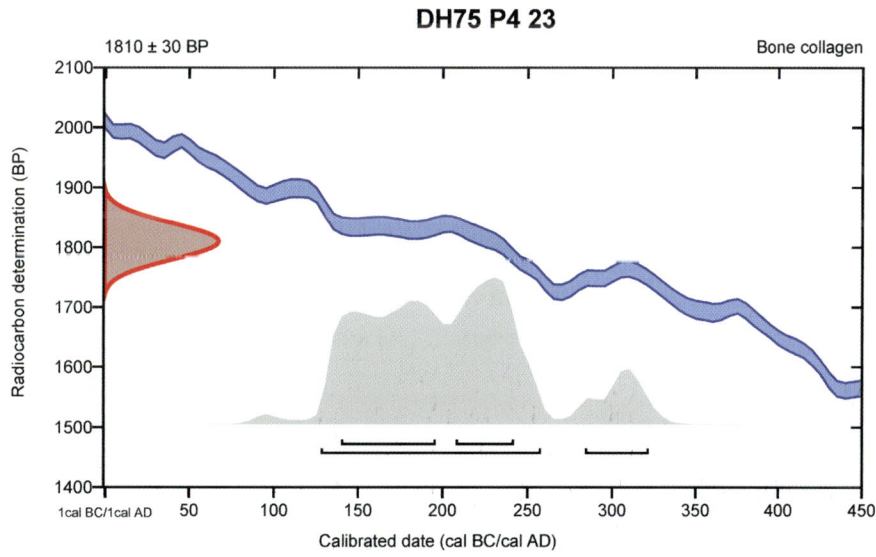

Database used
　INTCAL13

References
　References to Probability Method
　　Bronk Ramsey, C. (2009). Bayesian analysis of radiocarbon dates. Radiocarbon, 51(1), 337-360.
　References to Database INTCAL13
　　Reimer, et.al., 2013, Radiocarbon55(4).

Beta Analytic Radiocarbon Dating Laboratory

4985 S.W. 74th Court, Miami, Florida 33155 • Tel: (305)667-5167 • Fax: (305)663-0964 • Email: beta@radiocarbon.com

Beta Analytic Inc
4985 SW 74 Court
Miami, Florida 33155
Tel: 305-667-5167
Fax: 305-663-0964
info@betalabservices.com

ISO/IEC 17025:2005-Accredited Testing Laboratory

Quality Assurance Report

This report provides the results of reference materials used to validate radiocarbon analyses prior to reporting. Known-value reference materials were analyzed quasi-simultaneously with the unknowns. Results are reported as expected values vs measured values. Reported values are calculated relative to NIST SRM-4990B and corrected for isotopic fractionation. Results are reported using the direct analytical measure percent modern carbon (pMC) with one relative standard deviation. Agreement between expected and measured values is taken as being within 2 sigma agreement (error x 2) to account for total laboratory error.

Report Date: November 26, 2019
Submitter: Mr. Iain Hewitt

QA MEASUREMENTS

Reference 1

Expected Value: 0.40 +/- 0.04 pMC

Measured Value: 0.40 +/- 0.03 pMC

Agreement: Accepted

Reference 2

Expected Value: 129.41 +/- 0.06 pMC

Measured Value: 129.43 +/- 0.35 pMC

Agreement: Accepted

Reference 3

Expected Value: 96.69 +/- 0.50 pMC

Measured Value: 97.13 +/- 0.29 pMC

Agreement: Accepted

COMMENT: All measurements passed acceptance tests.

Validation: Date: November 26, 2019

Digital signature on file

APPENDIX 3A: ROMAN VILLAS IN DORSET CONFIRMED BY ARCHAEOLOGY

PEP2 site no.	Site name	BNG	Monument no.	Remarks
1	Dewlish	376834, 97222o	45440	Publication pending
2	Druce Farm	373400, 954490	No number	Publication pending
3	Bucknowle	395396, 814990	456872	Published
4	Halstock	353398, 107570	195721	Published
5	Tarrant Hinton	392593, 111933	210228	Published
6	Frampton (Nunnery Mead)	361595, 952950	453174	
7	Hinton St Mary	378543, 116017	202177	
8	Iwerne Minster	385666, 113741	206061	Published
9	Shillingstone	382942, 110656	No number	
10	Hemsworth	396290, 105881	209284	
11	Poyntington	364876, 121009	No number	Townsend Farm. Randall, C. 2020, 171–81
12	Preston	370417, 826570	454283	
13	Fifehead Neville	377291, 111224	202262	
14	Thornford	359394, 113535	196188	Leach 1966, 104–7
15	Brenscombe Farm	397900, 826470	456839	
16	Charminster, Walls Field	366720, 949250	453248	
17	Dorchester, Olga Road	368680, 901320	No number	
18	Myncen Farm	397366, 114288	912528	Minchington (Farnham?)
19	Wynford Eagle	356992, 950050	450700	
20	Sherborne	362460, 115290	199497	Lenthay Common
21	Winterborne Kingston	385035, 992270	No number	North Down
22	East Creech	393515, 827550	456920	RCHME 1970a, 395–6
23	Bradford Down, Pamphill	397840, 104270	No number	Witchampton? Field, N.R. 1983, 71–92

APPENDIX 3B: ROMAN VILLAS IN CENTRAL AND SOUTH SOMERSET CONFIRMED BY ARCHAEOLOGY

PEP2 site no.	Site name	BNG	Monument no.	Remarks
23	Dinnington	340742, 113767	193485	
24	East Coker	355411, 113813	156215	
25	Ham Hill	348827, 116495	193155	Hillfort
26	High Ham	342876, 129457	193634	
27	Hurcot	351127, 129707	196343	
28	Lopen	342697, 113901	1391028	
29	Low Ham	343480, 129280	193640	
30	Lufton	351558, 117840	196068	
31	Pitney 1	345104, 130074	194019	
32	Pitney 2	343548, 128837	No number	
33	Somerton	349694, 129085	193535	
34	West Coker	352848, 113821	196297	
35	Westland, Yeovil	353995, 115003	196095	
36	Banwell	339727, 158470	192470	
37	Wraxall, Birdcombe Farm	347878, 171579	192470	
38	Laverton, Blacklands	376493, 154105	203128	
39	Bratton Seymour	366690, 129903	199624	
40	Burnett	366497, 164541	201090	
41	Chew Magna	365197, 165209	198033	
42	Chew Park	357544, 160519	197267	Chew Valley Lake
43	Combe, Combe Down	376139, 162203	204067	
44	Compton Dundon	349160, 131053	194010	Same as Littleton
45	Iford, Farleigh Hungerford	379736, 158307	202980	
46	Ilchester	351222, 122132	196528	
47	Keynsham Cemetery	364494, 169261	201036	
48	Leigh-on-Mendip	370292, 147507	202840	Mells Park
49	Newton St Loe	371173, 165470	203682	
50	Paulton	367125, 156472	200482	
51	Priddy	353085, 151461	197734	
52	Shapwick	342461, 139483	1267212	
53	Somerdale, Keynsham	365727, 169383	200916 & 1480443	
54	Wadeford	330861, 110484	191803	
55	Wellow	372810, 157992	203043	
56	Wemberham, Yatton	340519, 165220	194992	
57	Whatley	374418, 146990	202781	
58	White Staunton	328017, 110579	190400	
59	Wincanton	370214, 128193	202365	

INDEX

Illustrations are denoted by page numbers in *italics* or by *illus* where figures are scattered throughout the text. Places are in Dorset unless indicated otherwise.